MW01687942

INSIDERS
MONEY TIPS

MAKING THE MOST OF WHAT YOU HAVE --- AND GETTING MORE

American Publishing Corporation

New Financial & Business Books Series

© American Publishing Corporation

© Copyright MCMXCIV
by American Publishing Corporation

All rights reserved under the laws of the United States and provisions of the Pan-American and International Copyright Conventions. This book may not be reproduced, in whole or in part, in any form or by any means, electronic or mechanical — including photocopying, recording or by any information storage and retrieval system now known or hereafter invented — without express written permission from the publisher. This report is for information purposes only and is not intended as an offer to sell nor a solicitation to buy securities.

This publication is designed to provide accurate and authoritative information in regard to the subject matter covered, but it is sold with the understanding that the publisher is not engaged in rendering legal, accounting or other professional service. If legal advice or other expert assistance is required, the services of a competent professional person should be sought. The publisher does not guarantee or warrant that readers who use the information provided in this report will achieve results similar to those discussed.

Additional copies of this book may be purchased directly from the publisher. To order, please enclose $26.95 plus $3 postage and handling. Send to:

American Publishing Corporation
Book Distribution Center
Post Box 15196
Montclair, CA 19763

Printed in the United States of America

0 9 8 7 6 5 4 3 2 1

INSDIERS MONEY TIPS

— Master Index —

INTRODUCTION

WHY YOU MUST MAKE THE MOST OF YOUR MONEY

In case you haven't noticed...

The American Dream has taken a battering of late. Fewer and fewer people seem to be grabbing the brass ring, while the rest of us go 'round and 'round on our daily whirl. Salaries remain static while credit card balances soar and bills seem to breed in the mail box. Laughable savings-account rates and CD yields lag behind inevitable rises in the cost of living. And, too often, our inadequate nest eggs get cracked open for emergencies anyway. Even lottery winners — when they match their installment-plan jackpots against inflation and soaring living costs — may find their El Dorados fading into a mirage.

Hope still springs eternal, of course, but the rewards for ambition, industry, perseverance — all the old-fashioned Horatio Alger virtues — seem smaller and smaller day by day.

What can a person do ... besides abandoning cherished dreams of wealth — or even financial well-being?

Just one thing: Never give up!

Keep searching for a way out of the puzzle, an alternate solution. Because it exists. It has to. Some people are indisputably rich — or at least financially secure. And, they have achieved their economic status not through inheritance or endless industry, but through applied smarts. In other words, there are things they know that most people don't — things you need to know!

This book will tell you some of those things. In fact, it will confide to you literally hundreds of their hard-won secrets — employment and retirement strategies, legal tactics, consumer and credit tips, money-management methods — all demonstrating that it is still possible to make and save a fortune. If you know how — and use what you know.

However, the most essential secret — a secret which the most successful people have always known — is that the only way to really get ahead is to put the money you do have to work for you.

Despite what that pompous old Smith Barney ad says, wealth today is rarely created "the old fashioned way" — earned through individual industry. We've all heard the dismal statistics of lowering expectations in the '90s: How personal-income growth, which averaged more than 8% during the 1960s and '70s, slowed to just 3% during the late '80s — and has nearly reached a standstill today. The 10% and 12% annual raises that were commonplace 10 and 20 years ago are almost unheard of now. Pay cuts, staff reductions, hiring freezes — these are the rules. Salary increases, when they come at all, are in the meager 3% to 4% range.

Yes, it's getting harder and harder to make money the "old-fashioned way" — and even more difficult to keep it. That's why you must make the most of your money. Put another way, the secret to building wealth today lies not in how much money you make — but in how you handle the money you do make.

And handling money better is what this book is all about. In fact, these money secrets - as they have for many other people - can make and save you $10,000 to $100,000 or more.

CHAPTER 1

AUTO SECRETS

A. Buying a New Car

BUY — OR FIX UP YOUR OLD CAR?

In most cases, it's actually cheaper to repair your present car. To decide if it's really cost effective for you, first find out the total cost of fixing your old car. Have a good mechanic list everything that's wrong and tell you what he'd charge to fix it. With that kind of thorough overhaul, the effective life of most cars can be prolonged by five years.

Value Note: Even if your old car needs a new engine, the cost will be far less than the depreciation loss you'll suffer the minute you drive the new car off the lot.

Gas Mileage Trap: Even if a new model gets twice the gas mileage of your old car, it may not be cheaper for you. Add up your annual costs by figuring the per-gallon price of gas, miles you drive per year and miles you get per gallon, then cut that number in half to get your savings. Chances are, it will take many years to recoup the added expense of the new car.

When NOT to Fix Up Your Old Car: When it's worth less than $1,000. When it has an advanced case of rust (which can't be fixed).

IS LEASING A BETTER DEAL FOR YOU?

In spite of all the ads in your newspaper's weekend Classified Section extolling the benefits of leasing rather than buying, the answer is most likely "no." Even though less cash is needed up front, the overall cost of leasing a car for three years is usually 15% to 20% higher than buying a vehicle and maintaining it for the same period yourself. Tax F law: Most ads cite the tax benefits of leasing, but there really are none — all business auto expenses are already deductible.

3 Times You Should Lease:

1. Your business needs a number of vehicles, but doesn't have the money for down payments.

2. You need to improve your balance sheet by reducing long-term liabilities (which is where car loans would fall).

3. A poor driving record has forced you into the costly assigned-risk insurance pool and the leasing company can offer cheaper coverage.

If You Do Lease: Don't buy a full-maintenance contract; they're overpriced. Beware of excessive surcharges for driving too many miles each year.

GET READY FOR SOME `STICKER SHOCK'

If it's been a while since you shopped for a new car, your wallet — and your psyche — may be in for a severe shock. Most new cars today sell for $12,000 to $15,000, plus sales taxes and fees — and many go for $25,000, $30,000 or more. That's more than some people can stomach — and, according to psychological experts, many even get moderately depressed (in the true medical sense) over how the current recessionary economy is affecting their life-styles.

However, according to Dr. Stanley Frager, psychologist and professor at the University of Louisville's Kent School of Social Work, there are several things you can do to prevent becoming a victim of real sticker shock — on both autos and other consumer items:

1. Recognize that things will get better. The economy runs in cycles and a period of prosperity always follows hard times.

2. Adjust your timing and bolster your buying power. Unless your car is totally dead, put off your purchase for a while.

Money $ecret: Go ahead and start making payments into your savings account. Then, when you do buy, you'll have a larger down payment, which will lower your monthly cost.

Emotional Trap: Don't get caught up in "depression hysteria" and quit buying entirely. If you really need something, go ahead and get it.

3. Be a good shopper. Visit showrooms and watch the ads closely so you'll be aware of sales, price reductions or rebates when they occur.

4. As a last resort, lower your sights. Remember, though glamour and status play a big part in auto marketing, what you're really buying is good, solid transportation — and a Chevy can provide that every bit as well as a Cadillac.

SAVE $500 OR MORE ON ANY NEW CAR

Everyone knows that the price of new cars is negotiable, but the $200 to $300 discount most buyers get is nothing compared to the typical $1,200 to $2,000 difference between the dealer's actual cost and the sticker price. That leaves plenty of room for you to negotiate double or even triple the normal discount on your next car — but only if you know what the dealer's actual cost was. To find out, you can take advantage of a special service offered by Consumer Reports magazine, one of the leading new-car evaluation and rating services in the country. For just $11 ($20 for 2 cars, $27 for 3 and $5 each for additional models), you can get a complete dealer-cost analysis for any of more than 1,300 new cars and trucks, both foreign and domestic. What you get:

1. A computer printout comparing the list price and dealer's cost for the car you're interested in and for every factory-installed option (dealer-added options are not included and options data is limited on some foreign models).

2. A listing of the optional equipment recommended for that model by CR's Auto Test Division.

3. A special CR report on how to deal with a car dealer. To order, specify the make (e.g., Ford), model (e.g., Taurus) and exact style (e.g., GL Sedan) for each car you want evaluated and send it with your name, address and appropriate payment (check or money order only) to Consumer Reports Auto Price Service, Box 80 05, Novi, MI 48376.

FORGO EXPENSIVE FACTORY OPTIONS

If you've spent much time reviewing price stickers, you've probably been amazed at how much options can drive up the total price of a new car — sometimes as much as $5,000 to $6,000. That's because mark-ups on options are much larger than the dealer's margin on the basic car — and some of the prices that result are outright rip-offs. For that reason, you should carefully consider what you really need before you begin shopping and eliminate models that are "over-equipped."

8 Auto Option Selection Tips:

1. Safety features — including steel-belted radial tires, anti-lock brakes and air bags — are worth the price in peace of mind, especially for your family car. Take all that are offered. Exception: Heavy-duty suspension systems don't do that much good unless you regularly carry heavy loads — or plan on driving like Mario Andretti (in which case, safety's probably not your prime concern anyway).

2. Air conditioning not only adds to your comfort, but adds to a car's resale value. Always get air.

3. Three speeding tickets will pay for cruise control — which also reduces stress on long drives. Worth your money.

4. Power windows are nice for commuters who have to pay tolls every day, but they also tend to malfunction and repair costs are high. They can also be a hazard to children, who like to play with the controls and could get hands or even head caught in a closing window. Don't get them unless there's a driver's-position lock that disables all other controls. Generally not worth the money. Exception: If you're buying a convertible, get power windows. You look like a geek driving with the top down and some windows raised, and it's a real pain having to climb around the car to manually open all windows.

5. Power seats can add to your comfort, but they're really not worth the money unless you take a lot of long trips. Also costly to repair. A manually adjustable seat back is worth the money if it's not standard equipment.

6. Electric door locks. Worthwhile for both convenience and safety — and they work much better than power windows and seats. Get them.

7. Decorative options — such as paint striping and wheel covers — don't affect the car's performance, but they do add to resale value. If you like them, get them.

8. Sunroofs are generally a costly disaster. Open, they're noisy and you get lashed by the wind; closed, they tend to leak. Also, if you have air conditioning, you won't use them nearly as often as you might think. Say no.

Costliest Option Mistake: Paying $700 or $800 for a top-of-the-line auto stereo system. You can do much better by taking the basic AM radio, which will provide the essential wiring, and then replacing it with components you buy yourself. You'll get better quality and save 25-30%. Exception: Ford's JBL Audio Systems are custom designed for the cars they're in and generally provide exceptional sound for the space. Unless your goal is to blast everyone else off the road with high-volume music, you're unlikely to get a better-quality system at any price.

Second-Thoughts Trap: If you think factory-installed extras are expensive, you'll be absolutely appalled at what a dealer-installed option will cost should you decide to get it later. If you think you might want something, go ahead and get the factory version.

BUY LIKE-NEW CARS FOR $3,000 TO $4,000 LESS

If you want a new car but can't muster up the money, consider buying a "demo," or salesman's sample. At any given time, large dealerships have five or six cars — usually their most popular models — that salespeople drive and use to give customers test rides. Because the dealers want to put their best foot forward on these demonstration drives, these cars are fully and regularly serviced to ensure top performance. They're also retired from demo service after 1,500 to 2, 000 miles and placed back on the sales lot. However, because of the mileage, they can't be sold as new, so the dealer will often knock as much as $4,000 off the sticker price (depending on the model). Demos are often advertised, but if they're not, simply ask if the dealer has one in the model you're looking for when you start shopping. Bonus: You get the full factory warranty, just as if you were buying a new car. Drawback: Selection is extremely limited; you can't pick and choose among many different cars to get the exact color or options you want.

PROS AND CONS OF DIESEL ENGINES

Several car manufacturers offer models with diesel engines, which can make sense if you spend a lot of time driving — and thus buying gas. Diesels get better mileage (6 to 8 miles per gallon), are easier and more economical to maintain and have a high resale value. On the negative side, they're noisier, tend to smell bad, give off exhaust smoke if out of tune and cost more to buy. Also, diesel fuel is difficult to find in many urban neighborhoods and rural areas away from major highways. Unless you drive more than 35,000 miles a year, making fuel costs a major consideration, the drawbacks probably outweigh the advantages.

BUY YOUR NEW CAR OVERSEAS AND SAVE

Taking delivery straight from the factory, can save you thousands of dollars on a European car (these programs aren't offered by Japanese automakers). Plus: You'll have free use of a car on your European vacation. Here are 6 things you need to know:

1. Biggest savings are for luxury cars — up to 15%, even after paying shipping and fees.

2. You can make arrangements through U.S. dealers for around a dozen European manufacturers. You order and pay for your car here, then go overseas to take delivery and arrange for shipment. Mercedes and BMW usually take care of all the red tape. Other companies may expect you to handle many of your own arrangements, such as shipping, but will recommend reputable transport firms. Your local dealer can advise you.

3. U.S. dealers generally need 2 to 3 months to process an order, so make arrangements well in advance of your planned overseas trip. To avoid disappointments, check with your dealer. Nail down all arrangements — including financing — before heading for Europe. You can also expect the U.S. dealer to ask for a deposit of up to $1,000 before placing your order.

4. Deal directly with European dealers and save even more — up to 35%. Problem: Cars sold through overseas dealerships may lack safety and pollution-control equipment required by U.S. law. Such cars can't be driven in this country without extensive — and expensive — modifications. For example, you may need to install a catalytic converter.

5. To cut shipping costs, start your European trip in the city where the factory is located and end it at the shipping port. If this doesn't work out, a modest fee will get the car delivered to you and later to the port. Shipping costs vary depending on distance. Customs levies will also run about 2.5% to 3% of the purchase price, payable when your car arrives at the U.S. port.

6. Don't forget to buy insurance for both your European vacation driving and for transshipment by freighter. You'll also need to register the car for European driving — and again once you get it back to the States.

Time Saver: Don't bother to comparison shop here for the best deal. European delivery prices are set by manufacturers — not individual dealers.

Bonus: A foreign-currency devaluation can save you hundreds of extra dollars if you watch exchange rates daily and move quickly.

NEW-CAR SAFETY TIP

Studies have shown that lighter-colored cars have higher visibility — and are thus safer — than dark-colored cars. A bright yellow is considered the most visible, which is why you're now seeing lemon-colored fire trucks in many cities rather than the traditional red.

B. Buy a Better Used Car for Less

SHOPPING TIPS FOR USED CAR BUYERS

Just as with a new car, you should make up your mind in advance what kind of used car you want — and how much you are willing to pay. Here are 5 pointers on making your selection:

1. What do you need the car for? Neighborhood commuting? A car up to 10 years old might be fine. For weekend driving? A 5- to 7-year-old car would fill the bill. For extensive daily driving or vacation use? Shop the 3- to 5-year-old range.

2. Avoid offbeat or exotic used cars. Parts may be hard to find and repairs may be costly. Stick with a standard or popular make and model.

3. If you're fairly knowledgeable about cars, skip the dealers and instead browse the private-party ads in the local newspaper. You should find prices 15% to 25% below those asked by dealers — and, if you're careful, well-maintained cars (especially on higher- priced or luxury models, whose owners cared for them better in order to protect their initial investments).

4. When shopping the private-party ads, avoid cars offered at prices well below the low Blue Book value or advertised average for that model. It's likely they haven't been well maintained or their owners would be asking more.

5. If buying from a private party makes you nervous — or you just don't like the idea of roaming all over the county to look at cars — you can also do well at a dealer. Just be sure to check out the Blue Book before you start shopping so you'll be able to make the best possible deal. There are several advantages in buying a used car from a dealer. For one , most states have laws requiring dealers to ensure the safety components of the car — e.g., brakes, lights, wipers and tires. Thus, if the car has a bald tire or marginal brakes, the dealer should replace them at no extra charge — even if you don't notice the problem until after you've taken possession of the car. Dealers may also offer limited warranties on their cars. Finally, since dealers have taken in most of their used cars in trade, it's likely they paid considerably less than Blue Book value — meaning you have a great deal of room for negotiation.

GET `GIVEAWAY' PRICES AT GOVERNMENT AUCTIONS

Buying a car at auctions conducted by the police, Sheriff's Department, Drug Enforcement Agency or other government entity can be a good deal, especially for people able to do their own repairs. Some of these vehicles have been abandoned, others are never-claimed towaways, others were impounded for evidence in connection with crimes. Here are 6 rules to follow when buying at auction:

1. Check the cars the day before the auction. Match the auction number on the windshield with the official list. Then check current prices for the same model and make in newspaper ads or

the Blue Book.

2. You probably won't be able to turn on the motor, but note tire tread wear, open the doors and windows, write down the mileage and generally inspect the interior. Then check under the hood. Look at the block, wiring, hoses and fluid levels.

3. Get an official bidding number from the auctioneers. And bring cash. You must pay full price, plus tax — and all sales are final.

4. Don't let competing bids take you beyond your self-imposed price limit. Stick to half the Blue Book value — and one-third is even safer. This way, you'll be okay even if major repairs are needed.

5. Get a bill of sale in order to register the vehicle with your state motor vehicles department. If you're from another state, check to see what documents are required to register the car in your state.

6. Even if the car runs or you can start it with jumper cables, you won't be able to drive it away without license or insurance. You'll have to have it towed home — and within a day or two of the auction.

Scam Alert: Don't respond to TV or newspaper ads or call "900" hotlines offering to tell you when and where auctions are and how to buy. The fees these people charge are outrageous, and you don't need them. Government sales in your area are always well advertised in your local paper, and some agencies even have mailing lists to notify past customers of upcoming auctions. Auctions are usually listed in the ""Legal Notices" section of the classifieds.

BIGGER COULD BE BETTER — AND CHEAPER

If you don't drive a lot (say 15,000 miles a year or less), you could save big by buying a 3- to 7-year-old full-sized car — even though the gas mileage isn't up to today's standards. The reason: Because of their higher gas usage, they generally sell for hundreds of dollars less than smaller cars of the same model year — and $7,000 to $10,000 less than comparable new cars. That initial cost savings will offset many years of higher gasoline bills. Added Bonuses: Big cars are safer, give a smoother ride, have more passenger and luggage space and have generally been well-maintained by more affluent original owners.

HOTLINE TELLS YOU WHAT IT'S WORTH

Whether you're buying, selling or trading, you'll be way ahead of the game if you know exactly what a used car is worth — and there's now a "900" number hotline that will tell you. The service, accessible from any Touch-Tone phone between 7 a.m. and 2 p.m. Eastern time daily, covers 1983 to 1992 model years and is regularly updated. Just dial 1-900-446-1120. When you call, be ready to key in your Zip Code (prices differ in various parts of the country), the model name and number, the number of cylinders, major options, mileage and condition of the vehicle. Calls cost $1.50 per minute, and the typical call lasts 5-6 minutes. The service is not available in Alaska, Hawaii and some other areas of the country.

C. Financing Your Purchase

SAVE UP TO $1,800 BY AVOIDING DEALER FINANCING

Believe it or not, many new-car dealers actually make more money financing new cars than selling them. That's why you should almost never get car loans through dealers. Their rates are typically 2 to 5 percentage points higher than on loans you can get through a credit union or bank. On a $15,000, 48-month auto loan, this can cost you $1,200 to $1,800 in extra finance charges. Exception: If you don't belong to a credit union and have truly bad credit or a bankruptcy on your record, a dealer may be the only one who will finance you. Try other sources first, but if they say no, you may just have to accept the higher dealer financing cost as the price you have to pay for your past bad credit habits.

SAVE $1,300 ON AN $11,000 NEW-CAR LOAN

As new car prices have spiraled higher and higher, financing terms have gotten longer and longer — with many now extending 60 months (or even 72 on some luxury or sports models). While this makes for lower monthly payments, it also dramatically increases your overall cost for a car. By shortening the term from 60 to 48 months on an $11,000 car loan, you can cut your cost by $900 to $1,300, depending on the interest rate, while raising your monthly payment a mere $44 to $56 a month. Even Better: Reduce the term to 36 months and save as much as $1,826, while increasing your monthly payment just $118 to $136.

Common Math Error: Many buyers reject a shorter term because they erroneously think that $44 extra a month for 48 months ($2,112) more than wipes out the $900 they'd save in interest. What they forget is that they'll be making 12 fewer payments of approximately $256, which totals $3,072 — meaning their actual savings will be around $1,860 ($3,072 + $900 - $2,112 = $1,860).

CONSIDER FINANCING WITH YOUR HOME EQUITY

Since Congress phased out the tax deductions for consumer interest, many advisors have recommended financing auto purchases with a home-equity line of credit, interest on which is still deductible. If you own a home and already have an equity credit line, you should definitely use this method for financing your car. Bonus: Not only will the interest be deductible (meaning Uncle Sam will reimburse you for up to 32% of your interest cost), but you'll also get a big break on the actual rates. Equity credit-line rates are currently 4 to 7 percentage points below those charged on a typical new car loan — and 7 to 10 points below used car loan rates.

When NOT to Use an Equity Line of Credit: When you don't already have one. Many lenders demand an application fee, some require a title search and nearly all will want an appraisal, all of which will cost you money. You may also have to pay points (an up-front loan fee). Result: It will take 12 or 15 years of interest and tax savings on car purchases to recover your initial cost — a bad deal any way you look at it. Hidden Danger: If you default on a car loan, all you lose is the car, but if you default on a home-equity loan, the lender could start foreclosure proceedings on your house.

For FREE Information: Send a stamped, self-addressed envelope to "Home Equity," CUNA Inc., Public Relations Dept., Box 431, Madison , WI 53701.

D. Winning the Auto Insurance War

CHECK INSURANCE RATES BEFORE YOU BUY

Your quest for the best deal in auto insurance rates should actually begin before you even buy your car. Insurance companies set initial rates using a 20-tier scale, with the rate levels rising along with a car's price. However, certain cars can be bumped one or two tiers above others that cost the same —

based on how costly it will be to repair or replace them, how statistically prone they are to accidents (i.e., racy sports models are more apt to be in accidents than family sedans) and how many fancy options they have. Thus, even though a car may cost only $12,000, if it's expensive to repair or has several high-risk options (fancy sound systems or deluxe wheel covers), it could cost as much to insure as a $15,000 model — meaning your premiums for comprehensive and collision coverage could be as much as 25% higher.

Special Cases: High-powered engines and 4- or 5-speed transmissions will bump rates up a tier from the normal level for standard engines and automatic transmissions, even if everything else on the car is exactly the same. Convertibles are always bumped up at least one tier above hard-top cars of the same price, reflecting the potential replacement cost of the cloth top and the easier access such tops offer to car or accessory thieves.

START BY PICKING THE RIGHT INSURANCE COMPANY

Auto insurance rates vary significantly from one insurance company to the next. Thus, one of the quickest and easiest ways to cut your auto insurance bill is to select an insurer that has lower rates to begin with. According to a recent survey of 49 large U.S. insurers, the following 7 companies offer rates substantially below the national average:

Company	Where Sold	How Sold	Limited To:
1. United Services Automobile +. (USAA)	Nationwide	Mail, phone	Military
2. Erie Insurance Exchange	Midwest, East	All methods	No restrictions
3. Nationwide Mutual	Nationwide	All methods	Farmers*
4. GEICO General Insurance	Nationwide	Mail, phone	Govt. employees
5. Liberty Mutual	Texas, N.C.	All methods	No restrictions
6. Allstate Insurance	Nationwide	All methods	No restrictions
7. Prudential Property & Casualty Insurance	Nationwide	All methods	No restrictions

*—Primary market, but not necessarily exclusive.

Look in the yellow pages under "Insurance" and call these companies or make sure your independent insurance agent gets rates from these companies.

The Other Side of the Coin: The same survey found these 3 companies to have rates substantially above the national average: State Farm Fire &

Casualty, Farmers Insurance Exchange and Allstate Indemnity (which insures mostly high-risk drivers).

LOW COST ISN'T EVERYTHING

Having given you the lowest-priced insurance companies, it now becomes necessary to note that cheapest isn't necessarily best. It's sometimes worth paying a bit extra to ensure quality of service — particularly with respect to claims processing — and prompt payment, as well as continuation of coverage. Following are the 7 top-rated companies, based on overall customer satisfaction, lack of claims problems, other service considerations (e.g., needs reviews and policy changes), speed of settlement and ease of renewal (or low cancellation rates):

Company	Where Sold	How Sold	Limited To:
1. Amica Mutual Insurance	Nationwide	Mail, phone	No restrictions
2. Cincinnati Insurance	Eastern U.S.	All methods	No restrictions
3. United Services Automobile +. (USAA)	Nationwide	Mail, phone	Military
4. PEMCO Mutual Exchange	Washington	All methods	School employees
5. USAA Casualty Insurance	Nationwide	Mail, phone	Military
6. National General	Nationwide	Mail, phone	Members*
7. Hartford Underwriters	Nationwide	All methods	AARP members*

*—Primary market, but not necessarily exclusive. The 3 Worst: Commerce Insurance (Massachusetts only), Hanover Insurance and Allstate Indemnity.

THE 8 LEADING TYPES OF AUTO COVERAGE

Before you can begin the process of insuring your vehicle, you need to know what kind of coverages are available. Following are the leading categories featured in most policies, with a brief description of each:

1. Bodily injury liability. Covers the other party's medical costs, plus the rehabilitation. Can be purchased with either a single limit (say $150,000 per accident) or a split limit ($150,000 per accident, but only $50,000 per person).

2. Property damage liability. Covers damage to another person's car or other property (such as a building, wall or other object you might run into). Sold with a single limit, usually $10,000 to $25,000.

3. Collision. Covers accident-related repairs or replacement of your car in the event you are at fault in an accident. Payments are limited to actual damages suffered. Coverage is optional in most states, but if you finance your car, you will be required by the lender to carry it in order to protect his interest in the vehicle.

4. Comprehensive. Covers damage to a car due to incidents other than auto accidents, including theft, vandalism, fire and bad weather. Payments limited to actual damages or replacement value. Optional in all states, but once again required by lenders if the vehicle is financed.

5. Uninsured motorist. Covers injuries to you or your passengers and, if desired, to your property as a result of being hit by either an uninsured motorist or a hit-and-run driver. Limits are discretionary and coverage is optional in some states, though you'll have to sign a waiver to reject it.

6. Underinsured motorist. Covers your expenses if they exceed the limits of the other party's liability coverage. Limits are again discretionary and coverage is optional in all but a few states.

7. Medical payments. Covers medical (and sometimes funeral) bills for you and your family, regardless of who was at fault. Usually sold without a deductible. Optional in nearly all states.

8. Personal injury protection (PIP). Broader medical coverage offered only in states with no-fault insurance laws.

HOW MUCH AUTO INSURANCE DO YOU NEED?

For starters, you will have to have both bodily injury and property damage liability. In most states, it's required by law. In addition, if you have a loan on your car — or if you merely want to protect your investment -- you will have to have collision and comprehensive coverage. The premiums for these four coverages account for as much as 90% of the total cost of your auto insurance, so we'll look at your probable needs for them first:

Bodily Injury Liability: Many states require you to carry at least $25,000 per person and $50,000 per accident. However, in these days of sue now and think later, that's probably not enough, particularly if you have a house or a lot of other personal assets that you need to protect. Though most bodily injury suits wind up being settled for the insurance maximum or less, there's nothing to prevent a jury from awarding the plaintiff in such a suit a judgment far in excess of those limits. If that happens, the person winning the judgment could claim all your liquid assets, your investment holdings, personal property (such as jewelry, furs, boats or recreational vehicles), the equity in your home (except in states with homestead laws) and even your estate if you were killed in the accident. In other words, they could take virtually everything you own, up to the amount of the jury's award. For that reason, you should immediately sit down and calculate your net worth — and then buy at least that amount of bodily injury liability coverage. For most home-owning families today, that means a minimum of $100,000 per person and $300,000 per accident.

Property Damage Liability: Many states also impose a minimum here — usually $10,000 — and, once again, that's probably not enough. Given the high cost of most cars today, you could easily be stuck for a $20,000 claim if you total another person's vehicle — and even more if it's a luxury model. For that reason, you should carry a minimum of $25,000 in property damage coverage — and $50 ,000 would be better. The odds of doing more than $50,000 in damage are slim unless you live in Beverly Hills, where Ferraris outnumber Toyotas two to one (that's a guess, not a factual statistic). Despite that, you'll no doubt be surprised at just how expensive it is to hit things. A 1988 survey by an Orange County, Calif., newspaper found that it could cost you $326 just for knocking down a stop sign (more and more cities are filing such claims). And, if the municipal crews have to put a metal streetlight standard back up as a result of your errant driving, you could get a bill for up to $2,750!

Collision & Comprehensive: If you have to carry these coverages because of an auto loan — or merely want to protect yourself against loss — you'll have no choice regarding premiums. They are set by the insurance company, based on the value and risk factors of each individual car model, and there's no way you can reduce the premiums other than increasing your deductible (the amount you have to pay out of your own pocket before the insurance kicks in), which we'll discuss later in a separate section.

The other four leading types of coverage are not major cost factors, but we'll take a quick look at them anyway:

Uninsured Motorist: If your state requires this coverage, it probably also requires a minimum of $25,000 per person and $50,000 per accident. That will typically cost you around $8 to $12 a year and is well worth the money, even if it's not required. In fact, you'd probably be smart to raise the limits to $100,000/$300,000, which will usually only cost you about $7 to $10 more.

Underinsured Motorist: Also a bargain whether your state requires it or not. Buy coverage to the same limits you set for your bodily injury liability policy; that way your personal wealth won't be wiped out by your own medical bills in the wake of a collision that's not your fault.

Medical Payments: A total waste of money — if you have health insurance. The hospitalization portion of your health policy should cover your medical costs and the liability coverage in your auto policy will cover any injuries to passengers. It's also expensive — as much as $50 per $5,000 of coverage.

Personal Injury Protection: Because of the widely varying provisions of the no-fault laws in the various states around the country that have adopted them, it's impossible to do a generally evaluation on this coverage. You'll have to look at the protections provided by your specific no-fault law and decide if you need extra coverage based on what you find.

Money $ecret: Regardless of the coverages you choose, you can save $35 to $75 a year on your auto insurance if you pay the annual premium all at once. That's how much most companies charge for letting you use a monthly payment plan.

A MORE COST-EFFECTIVE LIABILITY ALTERNATIVE

If the high prices of the high liability limits recommended above are too much for your pocketbook, or if you are wealthy and have substantial assets to protect, there's an alternative that can save you big money without reducing your overall protection. It's called an "umbrella" policy, meaning it covers you for all types of personal liability (except professional malpractice) when damages exceed the limits on your auto or homeowner's policies. You can get $1 million in umbrella coverage for as little as $98, though typical costs run $125 to $175, depending on the company. A $2 million umbrella policy (the maximum most companies will issue) will run about 60 % more. However, if you lower your regular bodily injury liability auto limits to $50,000/$150,000, you'll actually wind up saving money.

There Is a Catch: Most companies will issue you an umbrella policy only if they also provide both your auto and homeowner's (or renter's) policies.

SAVE THOUSANDS OF DOLLARS BY RAISING YOUR DEDUCTIBLES

Once you've pared your coverages down to the appropriate limits, the next best way to save money on car insurance is to increase the deductibles on your collision and comprehensive coverage. The collision coverage normally accounts for about one third of the cost of your auto insurance. However, you can cut those costs 20% to 30% by raising your deductible from $200 to $500. For example, the 45-year-old driver of a 2-year- old Ford Mustang in Los Angeles would pay about $647 a year for collision coverage with a $200 deductible, but only $498 with a $500 deductible — a yearly savings of $149. Assuming you have one auto accident every seven years — the recent national average — you'll pay $1,043 in extra premiums to keep from paying for $300 of extra damage. The exact same principle applies to comprehensive coverage, but the actual dollar amounts are a bit smaller since comprehensive usually accounts for only about 20% of your total policy cost.

Smartest Move: Increase your deductible to $1,000. In the Los Angeles example just described, that would knock another $176 off the annual premium, meaning you'd save an additional $1,232 while waiting to pay an extra $500 in damage. Ditto on your comprehensive , which really doesn't pay off unless you have major damage anyway. (Even if your car stereo is stolen — the most likely cause of a small claim — it's probably worth a maximum of only $700 to $800. That means you'd recover just $200 to $300 with a $500 deductible — hardly worth the extra premium.)

A NO-FEE CREDIT CARD CAN FILL THE GAP

Many people reject the potential cost savings of maintaining higher insurance deductibles because they're afraid they won't have the cash to cover them should an accident or other claim occur. However, there's a simple, no-cost solution to this dilemma, too. Just get a no-annual-fee credit card with a loan limit higher than your insurance deductible — and reserve it specifically for emergency use. (Several sources of such cards are detailed in both the Banking and Credit chapters of "Money Secrets.")

Strategy Tip: Use the credit card for one routine purchase every three or four months. Otherwise, the issuer may cancel the card for lack of use. However, always pay off the full balance on the first billing so your full credit limit will be available should an emergency arise.

STEER CLEAR OF `SPECIALTY' COVERAGES

As much as 10% of the premium of many auto insurance policies is the result of "specialty" coverages for things such as emergency towing or the rental of a replacement car while yours is being repaired. Insurance salesmen push these costly coverages because they offer high profit margins for the company — but you don't really need them. If you have an auto club membership, you've already got towing coverage, and the money you save on the premiums will more than offset the cost of renting a car should you need one. (Your no-fee credit card will also protect against not having cash for such a rental.)

Exception: If you have a high-priced cellular phone or a car-stereo system worth more than $1,000, the premium for specialty theft coverage on these items is a good investment.

CAR INSURANCE DISCOUNTS THAT CAN SAVE YOU UP TO 35%

Because some circumstances and practices either reduce your statistical level of risk or lower administrative costs for the insurance company, many insurers offer discounts when certain conditions exist. However, they sometimes won't tell you about them unless you ask — so always ask for all the discounts to which you're entitled, even if you don't specifically know what they might be.

8 Common Auto Insurance Discounts:

1. Multi-Car Policy — Multiple vehicles lower processing and administrative costs for the company, which can then afford to pass some of the savings on to you. Savings can range from 10% to 25% of the normal cost on liability, collision and medical-payments coverage.

2. Auto-Homeowner Combination — Companies offer a 5% to 15% discount as an incentive to get more of your business (it's cheaper than advertising).

3. Good Driver — Offered at renewal to policyholders who maintain a good driving record (no tickets, no claims); usually 5% to 10% .

4. Defensive-Driving Course — Take a state-approved course to improve your driving skills and get 5% to 10% off most of your coverages. Discounts are mandated by law in around 30 U.S. states, though the discounts may be restricted to drivers 55 and older.

5. Mature Driver — Usually starts at age 50, but may apply only to non-commuters. Reductions range from 5% to 15% on most coverages.

6. Student Discounts — Many companies offer discounts on youthful-driver premiums if your teen-ager has successfully completed a driver-training program, maintains good grades in school (usually requires a B average or better) or is away at college (usually must be at least 100 miles from home). These discounts can range from 5% to 40%, meaning they represent substantial savings since the addition of a teen-age driver to your policy can often triple your normal liability and collision premiums.

7. Safety Equipment — Air bags can earn you a 20% to 60% reduction in medical payments and personal injury coverage; automatic seatbelts get 10% to 30% off the same coverages. Anti-lock brakes are worth 5% to 10% off medical, liability and collision coverages. (Discounts for one or more of these items are mandated in some states.)

8. Anti-Theft Devices — From 5% to 50% off comprehensive premiums, depending on the device. (Discounts mandated in some states.)

ONE OTHER DISCOUNT (MAYBE)

Some auto insurance companies will also give you a substantial discount if you commute to work in a car pool where you drive only one or two days a week. The reasoning: Statistically speaking, the less time your car spends in snarled commuter traffic, the less likely its chances of being damaged in a collision. Opposing view: Other companies don't like their policyholders to carpool because of the increased number of individuals at risk in an accident — i.e., they could be liable for injuries to four or five people instead of just you.

NEVER PAY MORE THAN YOU CAN COLLECT

Collision and comprehensive coverages pay only up to the market value of a destroyed car — but the premiums don't decline nearly as fast as your car's value. As a result, after 5 or 6 years, you're laying out a huge annual premium relative to the potential amount you can recover after paying your deductible.

The Remedy: Cancel your collision and comprehensive coverages when the car is 5 years old, or when the combined premiums total 20% of the car's market value. (You can determine this by checking the Blue Book or reviewing dealer and private-party ads for your model car in the local newspaper.)

A Second Rule: Never pay for collision and comprehensive coverage on a car that's worth $2,500 or less.

Money $ecret: To give yourself some protection after you cancel your collision and comprehensive policies, take the money you would have paid in premiums and put it in your savings account (or other liquid investment). Then, if you suffer a loss, you will have some money available to offset it — and, if you don't, you will have increased your savings by several hundred dollars a year with no increase in income and no reduction in your standard of living.

INSURING SWIFT INSURANCE SERVICE

After filing a claim, there are at least 3 things you can do to boost chances of getting a quick and fair settlement:

1. Start a file folder in which you put all witness information, police reports, adjuster's forms, repair estimates, doctor and/or hospital bills, copies of submitted claims and any other letters to or from the insurance company. That way you'll have everything you need to support your claim if you need to dispute an underpayment or settlement refusal.

2. Take away the insurer's deniability. After any phone conversation or meeting with insurance company representatives, write a letter confirming what was said or agreed upon. List the date of the contact and the names of anyone with whom you spoke. Keep a copy for your file.

3. If your policy allows you to rent a car at the insurance company's expense during the settlement period, go ahead and rent one -- especially if they seem to be dragging their feet. Spending their money may get them to accelerate the processing of your claim.

INSURING YOUR TEEN-AGE DRIVERS

Among their many other problems, teen-agers — especially boys — are a nightmare to insure. On a typical family auto policy, the addition of a male teen-age driver can quadruple the collision and liability premiums, triple the comprehensive premium and double the medical premium. And, girls are only slightly better. If the teen-ager has his or her own car, with a separate insurance policy, the rates are even higher.

5 Ways to Cut Teen Insurance Costs:

1. Restrict driving time. If the teen uses a family car, make sure he or she drives it less than 25% of the time. This will allow you to classify the teen as an "occasional" driver, which will lower the coverage costs.

2. Put the teen's car on the family policy. If the teen has full-time use of a car, insurance rates for that car will be pretty much the same whether it has its own policy or is added to the family policy. However, if you put it on the family policy, you'll at least get the multi-car discount. (Even if you already have two cars on the family policy, you'll still get a 5% to 10% reduction on premiums for the teen's car.

Risk Factor: If the teen has a separate policy, the limits on it will apply in any liability claim and only the teen (who presumably has few assets) can be sued for excess damages. However, if the teen is on the family policy, you can be sued for any damages in excess of policy limits.

3. If the teen is going to have full-time use of a car on the family policy, make sure he or she is listed as primary driver on the oldest and cheapest vehicle. Since the insurer is going to triple or quadruple the comprehensive and collision premiums, it only makes since to have them start from the lowest base rate rather than the highest.

4. If you own your own business and have company cars, let the teen

drive one of those. Since most business policies are already rate-adjusted for a wide range of drivers, the rates probably won't go up because of the addition of one teen operator.

Risk Factor: If the teen is liable in an accident, the company can be sued for damages above the policy limit. (Note: Owners of business vehicles are already prime targets for lawsuits since plaintiffs figure the company will be capable of paying a bigger settlement.)

5. Try to convince your teenagers that walking is good for their health, and they shouldn't want to drive. (Just kidding, folks — besides, there's no chance of ever succeeding!)

E. More Economical Vehicle Operation

THE BEST THEFT-PROTECTION DEVICE YOU CAN BUY

The biggest trouble with most auto alarms is that people forget to set them. For that reason, you should get an auto alarm system that automatically turns on a minute or two after the key is removed from the ignition or door lock. The alarm should also trigger within a minute after the driver's side door is opened, unless the ignition key is inserted or the alarm turned off. These systems are fairly expensive, but most insurance companies will give a substantial discount (up to 50%) on your comprehensive coverage if you buy one — and that savings will pay for the device in a couple of years (as will the deductible you won' t have to pay if it prevents the theft of your stereo system).

Second Best: One or more of a variety of devices that disable the steering, ignition or fuel-injection system or lock the transmission if the car is started without the key. This, of course, won't prevent vandalism or the theft of wheels, radios, seats or items left in the car.

The Best Cheap Alternative: "The Club" — a tempered-steel bar with a tamper-proof lock that prevents the car from being steered. Available at most auto parts stores.

Other Helpful Protection Tips: Install a hood lock; disable the interior trunk-release mechanism if it works when the key's out of the ignition; install tapered door-lock buttons; turn your steering wheel until it locks whenever you park the car; don't give parking attendants anything but the ignition key; park only in well-lighted spots, and never park in the last space on the block (where a thief can easily hook up a tow truck and pull your car away). None of these tactics will stop a professional auto thief, but they will slow down joyriders and opportunists, who are responsible for about 75% of all car thefts.

Buyer Beware: Don't waste your money on factory-installed alarm systems. The manufacturer's official repair manual details exactly how they work — and those manuals are available to the literate auto thief at most good public libraries.

...AND ONE YOU CAN CREATE YOURSELF

If you regularly leave your car unattended for prolonged periods, remove the distributor rotor after you park. It's easy to do (so is replacing it), you won't damage your engine — and the car absolutely will not run without it.

SAVE 1 GALLON OF GAS FOR EVERY 10 YOU USE

Everyone wants to get better gas mileage, but most people don't want to change their driving habits to do it. Here are 6 simple things you can do that will improve your overall mileage by 8% to 10% without your having to slow down:

1. Start the car in neutral, not in park. Even though the car won't move in park, the transmission is engaged — putting more drag on the engine.

2. Never let the car sit and idle. One minute of idling uses more gas than restarting the engine — and five minutes uses as much as driving three miles.

3. Keep your windows closed. Open windows disrupt a car's aerodynamics, which can lower your fuel efficiency 7% to 8%.

4. Adjust your alignment and balance your tires. Wobbling tires increase road resistance and put added drag on the differential, transmission and engine — which can cut fuel efficiency by up to 5%.

5. Keep your tires properly inflated. Low tires also increase drag. Bonus: Tires will last longer, too.

6. Use a multi-grade oil, such as 10W-40. These oils, which are partially or totally synthetic, lubricate better than single-weight oils, reducing engine friction.

7. Park in a garage or protected area in winter. Oil thickens up when it gets cold, reducing engine efficiency and doubling fuel consumption during the first few minutes after you start the car.

11 CHECKS AGAINST ROADSIDE TROUBLE

Nothing can spoil your day faster than getting stranded on a busy freeway or deserted country road because of car troubles. These simple equipment checks and service tips can help you ensure that "ol' Betsy" won't let you down:

1. Check the water level regularly. Overheating is the biggest cause of roadside troubles.

2. Check the tires at least once a month. Improperly inflated tires are more likely to blow out or lose their seal with the rim. Rotate the tires at least once every 5,000 miles.

3. Check all hoses regularly. The rubber should be smooth and pliable, not hard or cracked.

4. Test all belts to make sure they aren't worn, cracked or loose. A worn or loose belt can slip, reducing fan and alternator efficiency, which can lead to overheating or a weak battery. A cracked belt is ready to break. To check belt tightness, press down on it with your thumb at a point about midway between pulleys or sprockets. The belt should go down about half an inch — no more, no less.

5. Check for leaks. Ask your friendly grocer or deli manager if you can buy a roll-end of the wide white paper the butcher uses (they'll probably give you one). Then, when you get home and park for the night, slide the clean strip under the engine and drive train of your car. Next morning, you'll know if there were leaks — and where they came from. Guide to Fluids: Clear spots probably aren't leaks, but rather drops of condensed moisture from the cooling engine or exhaust. Dark spots are likely to be engine oil. Pink or greenish-yellow spots are probably coolant. Oily, reddish spots should be transmission fluid. Dry, pink leaks are most likely gasoline.

6. Clean the battery terminals. Corrosion can prevent the starter from getting enough current to turn over the engine. Use steel wool, a wire brush or a knife blade to scrape the battery posts and cable clamps until you see a silver shine. Avoid getting the corrosive material on your skin as it is acid based and can sting or burn.

7. Check shock absorbers. Push down on the fender as far as you can and then let go. If the car bounces more than once, the shocks are getting weak. Replace shocks every 35,000 to 40,000 miles — or sooner if they start to leak.

8. Check wiper blades. They should bend back and forth and the rubber

should be soft to the touch. Replace hard or cracked blades. If the blade is soft, but the edge is glazed or hard, run some sandpaper over the edge to expose a more pliant surface.

9. Check your spare tire once a month. A blowout's doubly frustrating if your spare is also flat.

10. Check to make sure your jack is clean and working at least once a year and that your lug wrench is still in the trunk. A properly inflated spare does you no good if you can't lift the car or loosen the tire. Good Idea: Keep a can of WD-40 or other penetrating-type oil in the trunk, just in case the lug nuts are stuck or on too tightly for you to turn.

11. Find out when your regular service station gets its gas and fill up either before or well after. Why? When the tanker pumps gas into the station's tanks, it stirs up sediments — which can clog your fuel injectors, causing stalls or hard starting.

Safety Alert: Any time your car is up on a service station rack, check the exhaust system. A bad exhaust can leak carbon monoxide into the passenger compartment, causing the drive to get drowsy — or even pass out, leading to a crash.

IF YOUR ENGINE DOES OVERHEAT

You don't necessarily have to stop immediately, but you do need to take action. If the air conditioner is running, turn it off — nothing heats up an engine faster. Open your car window and turn on the heater full blast — that draws heat away from the engine. When you stop at a traffic light, put the car in neutral and rev the engine — that will make the fan turn faster and keep the coolant circulating. Pull into the first service station and, after letting the engine cool a bit, check the water level. If it's low, refill the radiator (with the engine running so the cool and hot water mix more quickly). If it's not, you've got another problem (probably the thermostat) and should head for a mechanic.

KEEPING YOUR CAR LOOKING GOOD

The best way to maintain a bright, glossy finish is to wash your car with cool or lukewarm water. Hot water can dull the finish. Avoid car washes that use brushes, which can scratch the paint. Never let a car wash apply hot wax, which can dull vinyls and convertible tops. Hand waxing and rubbing with a soft cloth is still the best method available.

Beware: Car manufacturers have not endorsed any of the new

"sealer/lusterizers" — which supposedly preserve or restore car finishes — claiming they may chemically alter the paint composition.

Rust Rejection: If you live in a northern climate where salt is used on the roads in winter, you should probably rustproof your new car — especially if you plan to keep it for more than three or four years.

15 WORDS TO GET OUT OF A SPEEDING TICKET

Actually, there are no magic words that are guaranteed to get you out of a speeding ticket. However, there are some words that will greatly improve your odds of getting off, starting with: "I'm sorry, Officer. I know I was going too fast, but..." At that point, if you hope to arouse any sympathy at all, you'd better have a reasonable and believable excuse — preferably something that demonstrates your concern for someone other than yourself (e.g., "my child is ill at school, and I need to pick him up and take him to the doctor.") Then close with these: "I promise I will be more careful in the future." Added Tip: Whatever you do, treat the police officer with the utmost respect — even if he or she is half your age. A belligerent attitude is the quickest way to ensure that you'll get written up, whereas a well-placed "Yes, sir" can go a long way toward keeping the ticket pad closed.

F. Quality Repairs Without Financial Ruin

GET FREE REPAIRS AFTER THE WARRANTY EXPIRES

Though automakers and car dealers don't advertise the fact, there are at least two cases in which you can get a problem with your car fixed free — even if the warranty has already expired:

1. Pre-existing conditions. Under most state consumer-protection laws, a dealer is required to repair a vehicle under the original warranty provisions if the problem was first reported before the warranty expired, but was not satisfactorily repaired. The same applies if a warranty repair was made before expiration, but one or more replacement parts failed within 90 days — after the warranty expired. If the dealer refuses to make the repairs, contact the automaker's regional manager and ask to have a factory representative review the case. If that fails, contact the local Better Business Bureau or the state Consumer Affairs office — or, as a last resort, take the dealer to court.

2. Informal warranties. Sometimes, a mechanical problem will arise with

significant numbers of a specific car model. Recognizing the pattern, the automaker will inform local dealers that it will cover the cost of repairs — even if the problem was not covered in the original warranty or the warranty period has expired. The Catch: Unlike safety recalls, where manufacturers are required to notify owners to bring their cars in for repair, neither the automaker nor the dealer has to announce the informal warranty to the public. If your car has a problem, you'll have to ask the dealer's service manager if it might be covered by an informal warranty. If he says no, you can double check by writing to the Center for Auto Safety, which monitors automaker bulletins and keeps files on models with problems that might fall under informal warranties. The address is 2001 S St. NW, Ste. 410, Washington, DC 20009. Enclose the specifics about your car make and model, details about the problem and include a stamped, self-addressed envelope. If you find your car is covered by an informal warranty, but the dealer refuses to make the repair, follow the same steps outlined above.

DON'T WASTE MONEY ON EXTENDED WARRANTIES

Most of them aren't worth the money. They can cost up to $1,000, yet they cover very little — you still have to pay for all tune-ups and normal maintenance items. Some put unreasonable or unrealistic limits on labor costs. Most require you to get approval from the warranty agency before you can begin repairs — and many insist that the selling dealer's service department perform the repairs. Some make you pay for the repairs yourself and then file for reimbursement. Most also have a deductible that you have to pay before the warranty kicks in. Finally, if you include the warranty premium in your original financing contract, you can wind up paying $300 to $400 in additional interest before the car's paid off.

INSIDERS' WAYS TO SAVE 50% ON CAR REPAIRS

If you've had your car worked on recently, you know that inflation definitely isn't dead at the repair shop. Auto repair costs have continued to rise at well above the overall inflation rate, and there are several reasons beyond the normal increases in wage rates and parts prices. One is increased demand for mechanics' services, reflecting the fact that, in recessionary times, more people fix up their old car rather than buying a new one. In addition, with new car sales down, dealers are forced to make more money from their service departments, which they do by raising prices and increasing margins. Finally, the complexity of many new models is driving prices up. Many shops can't fix computerized systems or complicated electronic parts, so they job the work out — and then add their own profit margin on top of the subcontractor's profit. Despite all the factors working against you, however, it is still possible to significantly reduce your auto-repair costs — sometimes by 50% or more.

9 Ways to Cut Auto-Repair Costs:

1. If you don't have to take your car to a dealer in order to fulfill warranty requirements, you'll generally be much better off using an independent mechanic or specialty repair shop. That's because labor charges make up half to two-thirds of the cost of any repair — and dealer service departments charge the highest labor rates around. In big cities such as Los Angeles and Chicago, dealer labor rates are running as high as $55 to $60 an hour, while dealers in smaller cities are now charging $30 to $45 an hour. By contrast, a recent auto club survey found the nationwide average for independent mechanics was just $22.38 per hour — almost 63% less than the highest big-city dealers.

2. Try to find a mechanic who will charge you for the actual time a repair takes, rather than using the "flat-rate manual," an industry guide that lists the amount of time given repairs are expected to take. Many shops will automatically charge you the listed flat rate — even when the job takes far less time (as most of them do, unless there are complications).

3. Even if you have a good mechanic that you like and trust, you can usually save money by shopping around for the best deal on specific jobs. Just because a shop has the lowest rates for one type of repair doesn't mean it will be cheapest on everything. For example, a recent Consumers Digest survey found that Chicago-area dealers had the highest prices on routine tune-ups (an average of $165), while specialty tune-up shops averaged just $100. However, when it came to cleaning fuel injectors, the average charge at tune-up shops was $70, while the dealers averaged just $65 — and, the typical local service station charged just $31. The survey also found that department store chains offered better prices than specialty shops on front disc-brake jobs, but were almost twice as high as specialty shops on mufflers and exhaust-system repairs. The biggest price difference uncovered in the survey was for replacing front suspension struts. Dealers averaged $486 for the job, while department store auto centers wanted just $220 — meaning you could save 54.7% just by choosing the right type of repair shop.

4. If the problem with the car isn't obvious, take it to a mechanic you trust. If you don't have a regular mechanic — or can't get the car to him — be careful what you say when you take the car in. Explain the symptoms, but don't try to make a diagnosis — the mechanic might take your word for it and fix the wrong thing. Refrain, too, from trying to show off your mechanical knowledge. You might wind up showing your ignorance instead, thereby setting yourself up to be taken by a dishonest repair shop.

5. Double up on repairs. For example, when you have the brakes redone, have an alignment done at the same time. Both repairs require many of the same procedures, so the labor time — and charge — could be reduced almost in half over what it would be if you had the two jobs done at separate

times.

6. Use rebuilt or used parts, which can cost 60% to 75% less than new ones. This is particularly good advice if your car is 7 or 8 years old or if you're planning on getting a new one soon. After all, why should you pay extra for parts that will last longer than the car — or that someone else will get most of the use from.

7. Take your car to a vocational school or mechanics' training center. Many of these take in public cars for repair, charging only for the parts in exchange for the practice the students get. The work is also generally as good or better than at other shops because you'll have four or five people — including the instructor — checking out the work. Drawback: They may want to keep your car several days even though a normal repair shop could handle the job in an afternoon.

8. Learn to do basic repairs yourself. You'll save both labor costs and the auto-shop mark-up on the parts. Warning: Restrict yourself to simple jobs — if you start messing around with the electronic fuel injection system or the computerized timing mechanisms, you could wind up costing yourself far, far more than you save.

9. Diligently practice preventive maintenance. The cheapest auto repair is one that doesn't have to be done.

HOW TO FIND A MECHANIC YOU CAN TRUST

When you're having car troubles, you already feel pretty miserable, so the last thing you need is added concern about having someone rip you off on your auto repairs. But, how do you find a mechanic you can trust — especially if you're new in town? Actually, as simple as it may seem, the very best way is to ask other people. More than almost any other type of business, independent auto repair shops live and die by word of mouth, getting about 75% of their new customers on referrals from satisfied existing customers. Thus, if several people suggest the same shop, it most likely gives good service — with reasonable prices. If you don't have an immediate problem, but are merely planning ahead, there are several other things you can do to check out a mechanic before giving him your business.

7 Ways to Find a Good Mechanic:

1. Start by visiting a few shops. You want personnel that are friendly, but not pushy — and, more importantly, people who will listen. If a shop owner takes the time to answer your questions and explain his operation to you, he'll most likely give the same attention to your car.

2. Find out if the shop has ASE certification. Issued by the National Institute for Automotive Service Excellence, an independent rating agency, these certificates attest to the shop's qualifications in up to 10 different areas of service, including engine repair, brakes, electrical systems, air conditioning, etc. Be aware, however, that a shop can post the ASE sign even if it employs only one certified mechanic. Thus, if you need a specific repair, you need to be sure both that the shop is certified in the area you need and that the certified mechanic is the one who will be working on your car. Note: The fact that a mechanic isn't ASE certified doesn't necessarily mean he's unqualified; many very good mechanics simply haven't tested for ASE certification, or they've been certified by other programs sponsored by automakers or oil companies.

3. Take note of the equipment in the shop, which should be up to date and well maintained. Look around the walls or workbenches to see if there is a good stock of service manuals and if they appear to have been used. You don't want a mechanic who "just wings it ." Also note whether the shop is clean — an orderly repair area is usually an indication of careful workmanship.

4. Ask if the shop guarantees its work and, if it does, find out what the terms of its standard warranty are.

5. Find out if the shop offers other services, such as a waiting room, a shuttle to take you to work or loan cars that you can drive while yours is undergoing major repair (insurance considerations sometimes prevent the latter).

6. Once you've narrowed your choice down to two or three shops, contact the local Better Business Bureau to see if complaints have been filed against any of them.

7. "Test drive" the shop. Take your car in for a minor job so you can rate the service before you need major repairs. Make sure you get a written estimate, then check it against the final bill to be sure all work was done. Ask for the old parts if you're concerned they might not have been replaced. Make sure no unauthorized repairs were performed. See if the mechanic advises you of any other needed repairs or potential problems.

Finally, if the job was done well and the price was right, thank the owner and/or mechanic — and tell them they can expect to see you again.

QUICK AUTO-REPAIR TIP

If possible, make an appointment to get your car fixed — and try to schedule the work during the middle of the week. Wednesday and Thursday are the slowest days for repair shops, meaning the mechanic may be able to take more time with your car, doing a better job.

LEMON LAST RESORT: SUING THE MANUFACTURER

Everyone has heard horror stories about people who have gotten stuck with "lemons" — cars plagued by persistent problems that defy repair, causing them to spend more time in the shop than on the road. What most people haven't heard about is the federal law that makes it possible to get relief if the dealer or automaker won't (or can't) repair a car in accordance with the warranty. Called the Magnuson-Moss Warranty Act, this law allows you to sue a car manufacturer for both actual damages — including the possible replacement of your vehicle — and attorney fees. Generally, a lawyer will take your case if you have made at least five attempts to have the dealer fix your car and have tried at least twice to work things out with the manufacturer's representative.

If you think your car may be a lemon, be sure to keep all paperwork relating to attempted repairs and all communications to and from the dealer and manufacturer. Such legal solutions can even be surprisingly quick since the suits are usually settled out of court. To find an attorney in your area who will take auto warranty cases, call the Center for Auto Safety in Washington, D.C. The number is 202-328-7700.

G. When You Have to Rent

GOOD TIMING CAN CUT YOUR RENTAL COSTS

Traveling business people account for the bulk of auto rentals, and most business people travel Monday through Friday. As a result, rental car companies usually have lots of available cars on Saturday and Sunday — and give substantial discounts to weekend renters. What most people don't know is that many rental companies will extend their weekend rates for up to three additional days, just to keep the car from sitting idle two days a week (after all, 5 days at $35 per day brings in more money than 3 days at $50). As a result, you can save 30% to 60%, depending on the car class, if you time your vacation trip to include one or more weekend days and ask for the special weekend rate.

Many companies also offer special rates for full-week rentals — rates that are actually cheaper than 3 to 4 days of regular-price rental. Thus, if you are taking a 5- or 6-day trip, you may save money by renting the car for a week and simply turning it in early.

4 Other Rental Savings Tips:

1. Many rental companies offer corporate discounts; if you're traveling on business, ask for one.

2. Many airlines have special fly/drive packages that can cut your rental cost if you book the car through the airline reservations system.

3. Reserve your car through the rental company's national reservation system and ask for the best rate available. Rental rates vary widely from city to city — even within the same company — and you could get stuck with a higher rate than expected if you go through the local agency.

4. Some people reserve a smaller car than they really want. It's likely one won't be available and the local clerk will give you a larger model at the same price.

LET UNCLE SAM HELP PAY YOUR WAY

As just explained, most rental companies offer package deals or full-week rates that are actually cheaper than 3 or 4 normal daily charges. By taking advantage of such deals on business trips, you can actually lower your business expense, which is fully deductible — and get a few free days of personal rental car use in the process. If you're on an expense account, you can use the same strategy to let your boss pay for your use of the car when you extend a business trip for a weekend of fun.

RENTAL INSURANCE IS A RIP-OFF

There's only one thing car-rental companies like better than renting cars — and that's selling insurance to the people who rent them. Of course, if you were pulling in more than $1 billion a year selling something that was virtually worthless, which is what the car rental companies are doing, you'd probably like it too. How can rental-car insurance bring in that much? It's easy when you consider that premiums for optional insurance on rental cars can add as much as $20 a day to the price of the rental. However, if you carry liability, collision and comprehensive coverage on your own car, you're most likely already covered — meaning you don't need rental-car insurance. To find out for sure, check your auto insurance policy, which will usually explain your rental coverage in a clause headed either "Coverage for the Use of Other Cars" or "Rental Car Deductible Expense Coverage." You may want to make a copy of this page of your policy and carry it with you when you travel, just so you can prove coverage if need be.

Alternate Strategy: Even if your own auto policy doesn't cover you when you rent, you can still avoid paying for rental insurance by charging the car rental on a credit card that provides this service automatically for its customers. American Express, Diners Club, MasterCard and Visa all offer this benefit — in varying amounts from $3,000 up to $50,000 — to preferred cardholders. Check your card's statement of benefits and services to see if you are covered — and, if you are, use that card to pay for the rental.

Warning: If you do charge a rental on your credit card and then have an accident, most rental companies will immediately put a hold on your credit card account for the amount of the deductible — even if you refuse to sign the charge slip. If that happens, immediately notify the credit card company of the situation, explain that your insurer will be making a direct settlement with the rental company and advise them that you will be disputing the charge. In most cases, the credit-card issuer will remove the hold, though you may have to talk to a supervisor to get approval.

...EXCEPT WHEN YOU'RE RENTING OVERSEAS

Regardless of how good your personal auto insurance coverage is, it probably won't cover you when you are driving a car (even your own) in a foreign country unless you get a special rider for your policy. Since such a rider will probably cost more than the rental-company insurance on a short-term basis, you are better off getting rental car insurance when you are driving overseas. In addition, the insurance offered by the overseas rental agency should take into account any peculiarities in local laws, perhaps even preventing your arrest following an accident — something your domestic policy can't do. Finally, you probably need the extra insurance overseas, simply because your lack of familiarity with local traffic laws, driving habits and road conditions will increase your chances of having an accident.

...OR WHEN YOU'RE RENTING A TRUCK

Unless you specifically request such coverage, most personal auto policies won't cover you in a vehicle you're normally not qualified to drive — and that includes rental trucks, particularly larger ones with a clutch, complex gears and a heavy-duty braking system. Trucks are also capable of causing far more damage than your regular car — damage your regular insurer doesn't want to be liable for. As a result, you should always take the rental insurance on trucks — even if you're only renting one for the day.

Additional Hazard: If you are renting the truck for a household move, you should also check your homeowner's or renter's policy to make sure your possessions are covered should they be damaged in an accident while you're moving. Most basic rental insurance policies don't cover cargo, though some companies do offer optional extra coverage — at a hefty premium.

NOTES

CHAPTER 2

BANKING SECRETS

A. Behind the Banker's Mystique

BASIC RULES OF THE BANKING GAME

All banks are not the same. Services and fees differ widely, and you sometimes need to expend a little extra effort to make sure you're getting the most for your banking dollar.

11 Ways to Beat the Bank:

1. Choose smaller banks. Larger banks don't like small depositors and, after deregulation, many dumped such accounts. Corporate accounts take less work and earn more. Small banks need — and serve — individual depositors.

2. Check the minimum-balance requirements on checking accounts. Beware of banks that base calculations on the lowest balance for the month. The average daily balance is a better formula for the account holder.

3. Make sure other account balances count toward the checking account minimum balance.

4. Check the holding period imposed on deposited checks. The longer the delay in clearing them, the more interest you lose — and the greater your chance of being charged for overdrafts.

5. Ask about overdraft charges. You may be in for a nasty surprise — fees can run as high as $20.

6. Savings account interest rates can be tricky. Depending on the computation method, 4.75% can earn more interest than 5%. Best is interest calculated from day of deposit to day of withdrawal and compounded daily. Compare only the "Total Yearly Yield."

7. The better you get to know your tellers and loan officers, the more likely they'll be responsive to your needs. Whenever possible, make deposits and withdrawals face to face, rather than through ATMs.

8. Split your CDs to maximize liquidity. Added together, smaller CDs will give the same yield — and you can cash in a smaller certificate without the heavy penalty you'd have to pay on a single large CD.

9. Watch out for insurance provisions that some banks add to the cost of your loan. These protect the bank, not you — paying the bank the balance of your loan if something happens to you. Any insurance agent can get you better coverage for less.

10. Front-end-loaded installment loans are another pitfall. These make you pay interest on the original balance throughout the term of the loan. Better is a single-payment note with simple interest and monthly payments. If you already have a front-end-loaded installment loan, don't make the mistake of paying it off early, which only adds to the cost of the loan.

11. Negotiate with loan officers. If you're a long-time customer with several accounts and a healthy balance, you should get a better deal on a loan than a brand-new depositor. But you won't get it if you don't ask.

THE RIGHT QUESTIONS TO ASK YOUR BANKER

Quite understandably, in light of the S&L bailout, most depositors are concerned about the safety of banks and thrifts. Here are steps you can take to protect yourself:

1. Ask to see the institution's semi-annual or annual financial statement.

2. Look first at the net worth, then the number of "workouts" (loan situations where officers are helping troubled companies), then the bank or thrift's real estate holdings. These will give you a feeling for the quality of the bank's investments. And, if it's a publicly held institution, it must file documents with the SEC (Securities and Exchange Commission).

3. Examine the institution's recent growth record. While growth should be a positive, it may represent a potential risk situation if it's been achieved by

putting out large amounts of money.

4. Another risk-related question: Are the institution's investments diversified — or concentrated in one specific area? The latter can be bad news.

5. Large depositors ($100,000 or more) are entitled to receive a thorough explanation of the institution's investment program.

6. Banks and thrifts also must publish an accountant's report. Check it out — especially any "exceptions" to the accountant's statement.

7. Inquire about any "at-risk" loans or loans that have been in default for 60 to 120 days ("scheduled items").

8. Lastly, make sure the institution is insured by the FDIC or FSLIC.

BECOMING A `PREFERRED CUSTOMER' AT YOUR BANK

Everyone likes to get special treatment, especially at the bank. And, surprisingly, you don't have to have a lot of money to become a "preferred customer" and enjoy such benefits as loans at rates below the going level, free protection against bounced checks, and waiver of service charges on such things as cashier's checks, traveler's checks and even your own checking account.

5 Ways to Make Your Bank Like You:

1. Do your banking in person so you get to know the tellers and officers. Using computerized home-banking services and ATMs may be convenient, but you wind up being little more than a number to the people at your bank.

2. Always make your loan payments on time and maintain your accounts in good order. Loan and account problems take time and money to work out, and banks don't like to waste either.

3. Be a loyal customer. Give one bank your checking, savings, safe-deposit and loan business if possible. (Obviously, this advice doesn't apply unless it makes good economic sense. If you have more than $100,000 in savings, you should split your account between two institutions. Likewise, if your bank's rate on a given loan is way out of line, you shouldn't pay the extra interest just to give the appearance of loyalty.)

4. Recommend the bank to your friends and relatives — and make sure they tell the bank that you referred them.

5. Be friendly and always thank bank personnel for good service or special attention. Note: Don't be afraid to request special treatment. Banks are

often willing to help you out — or even bend the rules a bit — but they won't offer extra services. You have to ask.

SAVE $120 A YEAR IN NEEDLESS BANKING FEES

Banks are in the money business, and that means they're always on the lookout for ways to take more of yours. For example, monthly checking account charges can cost up to $10 a month — or $120 a year — and you shouldn't have to pay them at all if you manage your money properly.

8 Ways to Reduce Bank Charges:

1. Review the bank's various checking account plans. Every bank has two or three that don't have monthly fees, based either on writing a minimum number of checks or maintaining a minimum account balance (or total balance in a combination of accounts). Then, pick the one that best suits your personal needs — and, if you have to, adjust your own banking habits to conform to the account rules.

2. Many banks also have a minimum-balance requirement on the use of ATM cards, or charge if you make too many ATM transactions in a month. Find out exactly what your bank's ATM rules are and either change your account classification to get a better deal or adjust your banking habits to conform to the rules. Sometimes banks will also waive ATM charges — but only if you ask.

3. Virtually all banks are linked to a nationwide ATM network. This can be a convenience for you when you're away from home, but it can cost you a bundle if you regularly use the network in your own hometown. Nearly every bank assesses a fee — sometimes as much as $3 — for using an ATM other than the bank's own, even if it is part of a network to which the bank belongs. Always use your own bank's ATM unless you're on the road.

4. Many banks also charge a fee if you use one of the new "Cash Machines" that are popping up in convenience stores around the country, or if you have a direct debit made from your account at the grocery store or gas station. If your bank charges fees for these convenience services, don't use them. Go to the bank ATM and get cash with which to buy gas and groceries.

5. Bounced-check charges can range from $6 to $20 (not counting the $15 to $20 fee the merchant you gave the check to will want). Keep good records so you don't bounce checks by accident, and definitely don't bounce a check on purpose — that's not only expensive, it's illegal.

6. Be careful who you take a check from. If you deposit a check in your account and it bounces, your bank will charge you a processing fee — from $5 to $15 in most cases.

7. Fees for stop-payment orders on checks can run from $6 to $16. If a check is lost or stolen, you don't have any choice — but if you stop payment because you've changed your mind about a purchase or decided you got poor service, you're being a bad shopper as well as a bad bank customer.

8. Many banks charge excessive prices for new checks. If your bank will honor them, order your blank checks from an independent check-printing firm. You can save up to 50%.

BE WARY OF DECEPTIVE BANK ADS

Bank ads for certificates of deposit don't always tell the truth, the whole truth and nothing but the truth. For instance, one bank advertises its effective annual yield for a 3-month CD. What's wrong with that? A couple of things. First, the annual yield is meaningless on a 3-month CD — and, "effective annual yield" is not the same as compounded annual yield. Many banks advertise CDs that are just simple-interest securities — i.e., there's really no compounding.

Conclusion: If you're dealing with a bank, don't buy CDs. Instead, buy shares in money market mutual funds. Managers of such funds have far more resources than you do, enabling them to shop for the best CDs anywhere in the country.

FIND OUT IF YOUR BANK IS SAFE

The Federal Deposit Insurance Corp. (FDIC) maintains a system to measure the safety rating of all federally insured banks in the United States. Unfortunately, the FDIC won't release its lists to the public because, an agency spokesperson says, "we don't want to get involved in publishing the ratings of individual banks." There are, however, private tracking agencies that monitor the FDIC reviews and will, for a small fee (usually $10 to $20), send you a list of the estimated capital rankings for all banks in a given state. Two of the leading ones are Veribanc, Inc., 800-442-2657, and Bauer Financial Reports, 800 -388-6686. Bauer will tell you over the phone, with no charge, if it considers your bank financially sound.

WHAT TO DO WHEN YOUR BANK'S IN TROUBLE

The banking business showed some signs of a recovery in 1992, but a lot of individual banks — as many as 300 if you believe the FDIC — still have more than their share of problems. As a result, you could wind up with your own financial troubles should your bank be one of the ones that goes under.

Fortunately, there are several things you can do to protect yourself:

1. Never keep more than $100,000 in any single institution — even if it's in different accounts or at different branches. While you may eventually get some or all of your excess money back, it probably won't happen until the bank's assets are sold or liquidated — and you won't receive interest on the money in the meantime. (Note: It could take as much as a week to 10 days to get your insured funds back from the FDIC after the government closes your bank, so it's not a bad idea to have at least a small reserve account in another bank, credit union or savings and loan.)

2. If you are in the process of applying for a bank loan, make sure you have an alternate source. Keep the application process going at two different institutions until one of them actually puts the money in your hand. (Note: Once you have a loan, you don't have to worry about it being called if the lending bank fails. The FDIC will sell the loan and the new holder is prohibited by law from calling it in so long as you keep up your payments.)

3. Don't contract for on-going work that you plan to pay for piecemeal using a personal or equity-based bank line of credit. If the bank fails, your line of credit will probably be canceled — meaning you could wind up with a half-finished swimming pool or room addition. It's better to get a loan for the full amount of the project and then use the credit line to subsidize your payments if you find it necessary.

4. Make sure you have credit cards issued by more than one bank. If you have a bank-issued card and the bank fails, your account will likely be canceled (though it could be sold to the institution buying your bank's assets if that institution also has a credit card program).

8 MAJOR BANKS WITH SAFETY CONCERNS

Though the FDIC won't reveal the names of banks it considers to be in trouble, a private survey conducted early in 1992 found a number of large banks that appear to be undercapitalized. The 8 biggest are First National Bank of Boston, Midlantic National Bank (New Jersey), Connecticut National Bank, Fleet Bank of Massachusetts, Hibernia National Bank (Louisiana), Apple Bank for Savings (New York), Howard Savings Bank (New Jersey) and First City Texas (Houston).

HOW TO CORRECT YOUR BANK'S MISTAKES

Outside of the game of "Monopoly," it's extremely rare to find a "bank error in your favor." Most of them go against you — and, even if they don't, the bank will quickly rescind your good fortune when it finds the error. Unfortunately, they're not so quick to correct the ones in their favor. So, what do you do when the bank makes a mistake?

5 Steps to Correcting Bank Errors:

1. Talk to the appropriate bank officer and see if it can be resolved. Take in as much documentation as you can find to support your position, including canceled checks, deposit receipts, ATM receipts, account statements or loan papers and payment books.

2. If you don't get satisfaction there, go a step higher and talk to the branch manager (or, if it's a local bank, the president). That person should have the authority to solve most problems.

3. If that doesn't work, write a letter explaining the problem to the bank's consumer affairs department or corporate headquarters. Include copies of your documentation, as well as any written explanations from bank personnel as to why they can't — or won't — correct the problem. (You'll probably have to ask for these latter items since most bank officers and branch managers will try to get by with a verbal response to your complaint.)

4. If you still can't get satisfaction, send another letter — along with copies of everything you've amassed so far — to the appropriate regulatory agency. (A list of who regulates each type of financial institution follows this section.)

5. If all this fails — and you're still convinced you're right — take the bank to small claims court. If you can convince the judge the bank did make an error, you can win a judgment for damages and costs up to $10,000. (Some states have lower limits — $1,500 to $3,000 — on small-claims awards, but that should still be enough to cover most routine banking disputes.) If the amount is larger — or you think there might be fraud involved — you can also contact a regular lawyer or the media. They can apply much more pressure than can you as an individual.

Note: Whatever you do, keep your cool. Explain your case in a reasoned, business-like manner and you'll get a better response at all levels. Go in ranting and screaming, and you'll likely be written off as a crank — or escorted out of the bank by a security officer.

WHO TO CONTACT FOR BANKING HELP

Having problems with your bank? Regardless of the type of institution, you should be able to find government help of some kind since all financial institutions in the United States are regulated by at least one supervisory agency. The following guide defines the type of institution and lists the specific regulatory body or type of state agency that provides oversight. Check your phone directory for the applicable agency or closest federal office in your state:

Who Regulates What: National Banks — These are chartered by the federal government, are members of the Federal Reserve System and are insured by the Federal Deposit Insurance Corp. (FDIC). Look for the word "National" or the initials "NA" (for National Association) in the bank's name. Regulated by U.S. Comptroller of the Currency, which has offices in major cities throughout the country.

State Banks — These are chartered by the states, are members of the Federal Reserve System and are insured by the FDIC. The word " National" or the letters "NA" will not appear in the bank's name. Call either the Federal Reserve Bank office for your district or the state banking or commerce department for your state.

State Non-Member Banks — Chartered by the state, insured by the FDIC, but not members of the Federal Reserve System. The word "National" or the letters "NA" will not appear in the bank's name. Call either the Federal Deposit Insurance Corp. office for your district or your state's banking or commerce department.

Savings & Loans — All federally chartered and most state-chartered S&Ls and all federally chartered savings banks are insured by the FDIC. Call either the FDIC office for your district or your state's department of thrift supervision.

Federal Credit Unions — These are federally chartered and insured by the National Credit Union Share Insurance Fund (NCUSIF). Look for the word "Federal" in the credit union's name. Call the National Credit Union Administration, 300 Park Blvd., Suite 155, Nasca, IL 60143; phone, 708-250-6000.

State Credit Unions — These are state chartered, but may be insured by the NCUSIF. The word "Federal" will not appear in the name. Regulated by the state commerce department or state department of thrift supervision.

Non-Depository Institutions — These include mortgage companies, retailers, department stores, consumer finance companies and all other creditors who are non-bank credit card issuers. Call the Federal Trade Commission office listed in your local phone directory .

B. Getting Better Banking Services

KEY QUESTIONS TO ASK ABOUT CHECKING ACCOUNTS

It's important to know exactly what your rights and obligations are when you open a checking account — and even more important to understand how much it may cost you.

10 Questions to Ask:

1. Does the account pay interest? (If it does, it's really a NOW account; see the next section.)

2. Is there a monthly fee?

3. If not, is a minimum account balance required to avoid having a fee assessed?

4. If so, what is that minimum — and how is it calculated? (A figure based on average daily balance is better for you than one based on the lowest level the account reaches during the month.)

5. Do the balances in my other accounts count toward the minimum?

6. How long before my deposited checks are credited to the account? (A period of 3 to 4 days is best; some banks hold checks up to 14 days.)

7. What are the fees if one of my checks bounces? ($6 is about the best you will find; some banks charge $20 or morc.)

8. Can I get an ATM card with which to access my funds?

9. If so, are there any charges associated with ATM usage — and how can I avoid them?

10. Can I expect any other fees or restrictions associated with my checking account?

GETTING THE RIGHT NOW ACCOUNT RIGHT NOW

A NOW account is simply an interest-bearing checking account — and, even as low as interest rates are right now, it's still best to get something for the money you have on deposit in a checking account. However, not all NOW accounts are alike, so you want to be sure you get the best one for your style of life.

6 Things to Look For:

1. An account with no minimum-balance requirement. Most NOW accounts demand a minimum balance of at least $750 — and some want as much as $3,000. Usually, the lower the minimum balance, the lower the interest rate paid.

2. If a minimum balance is required, it should be based on the average daily balance in the account — not the lowest account balance of the month.

3. Balances in other accounts at the same bank should count toward your NOW account minimum.

4. If the balance falls below the minimum, there should be no penalty other than the forfeiture of that month's interest payment. Some bank's not only take away your interest, but assess either a flat fee or a per-check charge on all checks written until the account balance is restored to the minimum level.

5. Interest should be paid based on the average daily balance, not the lowest balance of the month.

6. Interest should be compounded daily, not quarterly. Note: If you don't write very many checks each month and those you do write are generally for large amounts, you might earn a better return by forgetting a NOW account and instead putting your cash in a money market mutual fund that offers check-writing privileges.

8 THINGS YOU NEED TO KNOW ABOUT CHECKS

There are a number of common misconceptions about checks and how they work — misconceptions that could cost you money or even get you in trouble.

8 Myths About Checks:

1. A post-dated check can't be cashed. In fact, in these days of machine processing, post-dated checks often get cashed because the ECR (electronic character reader) is programmed to verify only the account number and the amount of the check, not the date. If this happens, you could have problems — either because the post-dated check bounces or because it clears, leaving insufficient funds to cover your other checks.

2. It's illegal to write a bad check. Actually, the law doesn't care about an occasional bad check due to poor bookkeeping. For a bad check to be illegal, it must have been written with intent to defraud.

3. The bank will always bounce a check if you don't have enough money

in your account to cover it. Actually, if you've been a good customer for a long time and don't have a history of kiting checks, the bank will probably go ahead and pay. Then, they'll send you a notice to alert you of the problem.

4. Only an official bank check is valid. Actually, over the course of banking history, checks have been written (and honored) on virtually every surface on which you can write — including the proverbial "shirt off one's back" (the IRS has received more than a few of these). As long as a document — be it a letter (most common) or an ink-covered shirt — contains proper instructions to the bank, including the payee, the account number and a legible amount, it will usually be honored.

5. Checks marked "payment in full" may not be. If someone has a claim against you for more than the amount of a check you've sent in marked "payment in full," they can go ahead and cash the check without forfeiting the right to collect the rest of their money.

6. Unsigned checks can't be cashed. Actually, you can usually cash a check without a signature, so long as you endorse it with your signature and a promise to take it back if the check writer's bank refuses to honor it.

7. A check with two different amounts written on it can't be cashed. The check is still valid. The official payment amount Is always the one written in words — and that's the sum the bank will pay.

8. Checks are good forever. As a general rule (there are some exceptions, as in the case of U.S. government checks), the bank won't cash a check more than 6 months old even if there's sufficient money in the account to cover it.

SAVING CHOICES IN SAFE DEPOSIT BOXES

Safe-deposit boxes can be rented from banks or from private companies. Check out both before making your decision. Here are some things you'll find in your comparison:

Cost: Bank boxes are generally less expensive than private safe-deposit boxes. Sealing: Private-company boxes can be sealed, but a court order, usually from the IRS, is required. And, since your private box is not labeled with your bank account number, it is harder to trace.

Security Rating: Banks are often rated less secure than private companies by the Insurance Institute.

Confidentiality: Confidentiality is higher with a private safe-deposit box since they're not referenced to your bank account number . Instead, your access is by numbered code. Insurance: Banks offer a minimum amount of insurance on their safe-deposit boxes, although the depositor can supplement that with his own insurance policy. Private corporations automatically insure the contents of your box for $10,000, with more available.

Business Hours: Some private safe-deposit corporations are open 365 days a year. Of course, many banks have dramatically increased their hours — but private concerns will even let you into your box after business hours if you make an appointment.

STRATEGIES TO BETTER TODAY'S LOW YIELDS

In 1993, interest rates fell to their lowest levels since 1963. In early January , 6-month certificates of deposit were paying an average yield of just 3.55% at banks and thrift institutions around the United States. That has created big problems for many people, particularly retires, who depend on the return from their savings for their everyday living expenses. Fortunately, there are several strategies even the most conservative individuals can follow to increase the return on their savings without substantially increasing their risk.

General rule: Most economists feel that interest rates have bottomed and will be heading up during the next few years. For that reason, your efforts to increase current low yields should involve investments that don't lock up your money for more than 6 months. That way, you'll have the flexibility to move your money back into CDs or other guaranteed-safe investments as rates move back up.

5 Choices for Increasing Yields:

1. Though money market mutual funds are also yielding historically low rates of return, the best funds still offer rates nearly a full point above 6-month CDs — with the added benefit of full liquidity and almost total safety (to date, only one money market fund has ever produced a loss of principal for its shareholders).

2. U.S. government securities funds invest in portfolios of short- to medium-term U.S. Treasury issues. Since these funds, which are currently yielding from 4.25% to 4.75%, are also exempt from state taxes, their equivalent taxable yield can rise well above 5% if you live in a high-tax state.

3. Tax-exempt money funds, which invest in municipal bonds and other obligations of cities, counties and special districts, are currently yielding an average of about 2.75%. However, because they are exempt from federal taxes, the equivalent taxable yield can be as high as 5% for an individual in the top (31%) U.S. tax bracket.

4. If you're sure you won't need your money for at least 6 months, consider buying 6-month U.S. Treasury bills. As of Nov. 2, 1992, they were yielding 3.20% — but, once again, because they are exempt from state and local taxes, the equivalent taxable yield rises to around 4%. In addition, they are absolutely safe and you can buy them direct from your local Federal Reserve Bank (call 202- 452-3000 to find out how), thus saving brokers' commissions of around $40 to $50. Catch: To purchase a T-bill from the government, you'll have to put up a minimum of $10,000.

5. If you can accept a small amount of risk (probably no more than 2% of the principal over the next year), short-term corporate bond funds are currently yielding 5% to 8%. However, that's a before-tax yield, so if you are in the top federal tax bracket, you might do better with a short-term tax-exempt bond fund, some of which are currently offering equivalent taxable yields of slightly more than 8%.

2 ABSOLUTELY SAFE WAYS TO BEAT LOW CD RATES

There are two strategies for increasing the earning power of your money that are exceedingly simple, yet most people tend to overlook them:

1. Buy U.S. Savings Bonds. Available at your local bank or through payroll purchase plans at most companies, these bonds are exempt from state and local taxes and currently yield 4.16% if held for 6 months. However, if you hold them for 5 years, the government guarantees a yield of at least 6%. In addition, they can be purchased in amounts as small as $25, with no commission.

2. Instead of saving your money, use it to pay off debts. If you put $1,000 in a 3.6% CD, you'll earn about $39 over the next year. However, if you use that $1,000 to pay off a credit card account on which you're paying only 12%, your taxable equivalent yield on that money will be a risk-free 17.4% — which is impossible to match anywhere today.

TRY `LADDERING' AS AN ALTERNATIVE

If you feel you absolutely have to have the safety offered by CDs, you can still give yourself some added flexibility and increase your chances of locking in higher rates when they do come. The strategy is called "laddering," and it works like this: The next time one of your large CDs (at least $10,000) matures, don't roll the money over into another long-term CD at the current low rates. Instead, break the money into fourths and buy a 3-month, 6-month, 9-month and 1-year CD in equal amounts. Then, as each of those CDs matures, roll the money into a 1-year CD. That way, you'll have access to some of your money every three months, and you'll be able to capture consistently higher yields as rates rise. Then, when media reports and economic conditions indicate rates may be topping out, you can once again move to longer terms, locking in the higher yields.

CASH IN YOUR CDs EARLY

Most banks assess a substantial penalty and make you forfeit some of your interest if you need to cash in your CD before it matures. However, bank CDs don't necessarily have to be bought from banks. Many stock brokerage firms maintain pools of bank CDs that they will pass on to their own clients. Buy your CDs through such a broker and you can usually sell them back early with no penalty. The brokerage firm merely credits you with the interest earned to date, then holds the CD until maturity — collecting the remaining interest for its own account.

LOW RATES MAY BE HIGHER THAN YOU THINK

Before you give in to excess worry about today's low interest rates and jump into much higher-risk vehicles in search of relief, recognize one thing: Today's low rates are actually higher than you think — in real terms , at least. According to Prudential Securities Inc., tax-free municipal bonds were yielding 12% in 1982, but inflation was running at 10% — meaning the real rate of return was just 2%. In 1992, the average tax-free municipal bond yield was 6.5%, but inflation was just 2.5% — meaning the real rate of return was 4%. Thus, though your savings are bringing in fewer dollars, those dollars are holding their buying power about twice as well as the dollars you earned in 1982.

C. The Best Deals in Bank Plastics

PROS & CONS OF BANK DEBIT CARDS

Many people confuse bank "debit cards" with credit cards because, in many cases, they are issued for the bank by Visa or MasterCard. However, when you use a debit card, you don't actually get a loan for the amount of your purchase. Rather, the purchase amount is automatically withdrawn from an underlying bank or money market account linked to the card. Despite this, these cards do have certain advantages.

For one, they are available to people whose credit rating is such that they could not qualify for a regular credit card. As a result, these people can partake in many of the conveniences most of us take for granted — things such as access to ATM cash withdrawals, check cashing, even the ability to rent a car — that they might otherwise be denied. For another, they provide an easy way to ensure you don't fall into severe credit-card debt since you're not actually getting credit — you're spending your own money, much as you would if you wrote a check.

There's also one advantage to a debit card even if you don't have credit or debt problems — if it is linked to an interest-bearing account, it can let you continue earning interest on money you've already spent. The reason: Like checks, there is a "float" involved with debit cards. In many cases, it can take from 3 to 15 days from the time you make a purchase until the money is actually withdrawn from your account. Thus, whereas a regular credit card just gives you an interest-free loan for the duration of the float period, debit cards may actually let money you've spent keep earning interest for you.

PROTECTIVE STRATEGIES FOR ATM CARDS

The automated teller machine has led to a major change in the American style of life, making it possible to get cash 24 hours a day, 7 days a week. However, it has also given con men and outright thieves a new way to take your money. While a lost or stolen ATM card doesn't pose as big a threat as a missing credit card, it could still cost you several hundred dollars in the hands of a clever thief — unless you notify the bank of the loss quickly. Here are some hints for protecting yourself from ATM-card losses:

1. Withdraw cash from an ATM only during daylight hours or when other people are around. It doesn't take an electronic genius to rob you of your money <u>after</u> you've withdrawn it from the ATM.

2. If you must use an ATM during off hours, use only one located in a well-lighted area — and park as close to the machine as possible.

3. If you do get accosted during or after an ATM transaction, don't resist. Give up the money and do what the bandit says — it's better than being injured, or even killed.

4. When using an ATM, try to position your body so it blocks the view of the keypad while you're pushing in your code number. Lest you think the possibility of someone stealing your code is minimal, check with Burbank, Calif., police, who recently arrested two men sitting in a car near an ATM videotaping people as they punched in their numbers.

5. Never throw away your receipt in the ATM's trash bin or a nearby container. In the Burbank case, the men immediately retrieved any discarded

receipts, which listed the account number the customer had used. With both the account number and the access code, it's easy to encode a blank plastic card so it will work in the machine (many electronics stores sell card-encoding equipment over the counter and blank cards are widely available).

6. If you do lose your card, notify the bank immediately. That will limit your liability to $50.

7. Keep careful records of your ATM transactions and immediately check them against your bank statement when it comes. If you spot any discrepancies, call the bank immediately.

THE 5 BEST NO-FEE CREDIT CARDS

The best credit cards are so-called "gold" cards, which are usually restricted to higher-income individuals with proven credit records. They offer substantial advantages over regular credit cards, including: Higher credit limits ($10,000 or more), lower interest rates and extra services such as purchase protection and extended warranties. Unfortunately, the extra benefits often carry a high annual fee — as much as $75 in some cases. However, there are some banks that do offer nation wide gold cards with both competitive interest rates and no annual fee — but only to qualifying individuals who meet minimum income standards.

5 Best Deals* on Gold Cards:

1. Amalgamated Bank of Chicago, 1-800-365-6464, 11.00%, $40,000 income required.

2. AFBA Industrial Bank, 1-800-776-2265, 12.50%, $40,000 income required.

3. Oak Brook Bank, 1-800-666-1011, 12.90%, $35,000 income required.

4. Union Planters National Bank, 1-800-628-8946, 13.50%, $35,000 income required.

5. Security Bank & Trust, 1-800-443-5465, 13.50%, $50,000 income required. *For current rates for the best cards, refer to latest issue of Money Magazine or Barrons Weekly available at any public library.

WHERE TO FIND THE LOWEST BANK-CARD RATES /SAVE $500 A YEAR

As valuable as it may be to have a credit card with no annual fee, if you're one of the people who doesn't pay off your bill in full every month, you're probably better off with a card that charges a low interest rate — even if you have to pay an annual fee. Fortunately, there are a number of banks around the country with low-rate credit cards — some as low as 8% at the time this was written. Of course, those rates are subject to change with shifts in the overall credit market, but there's one very simple way to find the lowest rates at any given time. Money magazine, in its monthly Banking Scorecard section, always lists the 7 banks offering the lowest credit-card rates (MasterCard or Visa) available at the time of publication. Following is a sample of Money's listing from the November 1992 issue:

1. Arkansas Federal Credit Card Service — Rate, 8.00% (variable); annual fee, $35, grace period, none; phone number, 1-800-477-334 8 (501-224-7283 in Arkansas).

2. Wachovia Bank Card Services (Delaware) — Rate, 8.90% (variable); annual fee, $39; grace period, 25 days; phone number, 1-800-842-3262.

3. Oak Brook Bank (Illinois) — Rate, 10.40% (variable); annual fee, $20; grace period, 25 days; phone number, 1-800-666-1011.

4. People's Bank (Connecticut) — Rate, 11.50% (fixed); annual fee, $25; grace period, 25 days; phone number, 1-800-423-3273.

5. Bank of Montana — Rate, 11.75% (variable); annual fee, $19; grace period, 25 days; phone number, 1-800-735-5536.

6. Bank of New York (Delaware) — Rate, 11.90% (variable); annual fee, none; grace period, none; phone number, 1-800-942-1977.

7. Bank One Cleveland — Rate, 12.10% (variable); annual fee, $20; grace period, 25 days; phone number, 1-800-395-0010.

WHEN LOWER BANK-CARD RATES ARE NO BARGAIN

When the card lacks the usual 25-day grace period before interest charges are applied. With no grace period, you begin paying interest the day you make a purchase — meaning you will have an automatic interest charge each time you use the card. As a result, you could wind up paying more in finance charges than with a card that had a high rate, but also offered a grace period (meaning you could pay your balance in full without incurring any interest charge at all). Protect yourself by reading credit-card offers thoroughly, checking not only the interest rate and annual fee, but whether or not the card features a grace period.

D. Beat the Bank on Loans

HOW TO PROFIT FROM CURRENT LOW LOAN RATES

Obviously, the best way to take advantage of today's low loan rates is to borrow money — but only if you can significantly lower the payments on your current debt, or if you can use the money to make investments that will produce capital growth as well as providing a good yield on your money.

The best area of opportunity involves mortgages, which are currently going for rates unseen since the late 1960s. Throughout the fall of 1992, fixed-rate mortgages averaged right around 8.0%, while some variable-rate mortgages were starting at as low as 4.0%. As a result, more than 60% of the new mortgages approved in the first 10 months of 1992 involved the refinancing of old loans. If you haven't refinanced yet, here are some guidelines:

* If you can get a new fixed-rate mortgage at a rate more than 2 percentage points lower than your current rate, you should definitely refinance.

* If you can get an adjustable-rate mortgage 2 percentage points below the best fixed rate — and, if the adjustment terms are to your advantage (see Chapter 11, Real Estate Secrets, for more details on evaluating adjustable-rate mortgages) — get a new ARM rather than a fixed-rate loan.

* If you plan on moving within the next 3 to 5 years, get an adjustable-rate mortgage, even if the starting rate is not more than 2 percentage points lower than the best fixed rate. You'll reap big savings now — and be gone before the rate adjustments carry payments to a higher level than the current fixed-rate mortgage would demand.

The savings in refinancing can be substantial. For example, if you have a 30-year, $100,000 loan at 10.5%, and you refinance to get an 8.0% loan, your payments will drop about $180 a month, which should cover your closing costs in under 2 years. Go to a 5.5% ARM, and your savings would be closer to $300 — which would offset the refinancing costs in only 10 to 14 months.

An even better strategy would be to refinance from a 30-year, 10.5% loan to a 15-year, 8.0% loan. Your monthly payments would go up slightly (under $20 a month), but your long-term interest savings would be in the thousands of dollars — and your equity buildup would be twice as fast.

Home-equity loans and equity lines of credit, most of which carry variable rates, are at an all-time low — with the national average running at about 7.8% and some banks charging just 6.5%. With these rates, it's a smart strategy to use loans of this type to refinance other, higher-rate loans, such as those for cars, home remodeling and, especially, credit card debt.

Catch: If you don't already have an equity credit line, it may not pay to get one just to refinance small debts. Some banks charge points on home equity loans and, even if they don't, fees can sometimes run to $700 or $800. Thus, you'd be better off to simply pay off the debt as quickly as possible out of regular funds as any savings on the interest rate would be wiped out by the fees.

Auto loans are also at a 25-year low, averaging around 9.4% at major credit unions. If you have a car that's a couple of years old and you're carrying a 48- or 60-month loan at 12% or more, it's probably worthwhile to refinance the car loan. The goal here, however, should not be to lower monthly payments, but rather to shorten the term of the loan. At the lower interest rate, you can shorten the remaining 36 months on a 60-month loan to 24 months for the same payment and save $1,200 or so in interest payments on a $ 10,000 original loan. (Note: Some banks and credit unions won't refinance a car at new-car rates, insisting instead on charging used-car rates, which could be high enough to negate the potential benefit.)

Though they've come down, credit-card rates are still averaging more than 18% nationwide — which, everyone should agree is outrageous. However you come up with the cash — even if you take it from savings — your best strategy is still to pay off any outstanding balances, and then pay your bill in full each month.

THE KEYS TO NEGOTIATING BETTER LOANS

Whether you're shopping for a new mortgage, an equity line of credit or a new car loan, there are some tricks you can use to get a better deal. In spite of what the banks may say, nearly all loan rates are negotiable, even if you don't have a long-standing account with the institution. The key is to push for the best rate possible, rather than taking what the bank offers. One way to do this is to shop around, comparing rates and terms at three or four different banks — and letting each of them know what you are doing. See if they will waive certain fees or offer a better rate in order to match or beat a competitor. Most will.

Another good trick is to skip the loan department and go straight to the branch manager (or president if it's a small bank). Introduce yourself and explain that you are looking to open an account (or already have one) and will also be interested in borrowing some money in the near future. Ask the manager to introduce you to the chief loan officer. With this kind of beginning, the loan officer will be much more accommodating since he or she will know you can always go back to the top if you don't like the deal.

Finally, be reasonable, but be firm in asking for the best deal. Remember, it's always more profitable for the bank to waive a fee or lower the loan rate a half percent than it is to let you take your business to the competition.

BORROWING AT RATES BARELY ABOVE PRIME

The United States is such an economy-conscious country that it's big news when a major bank raises or lowers its prime rate (the rate at which it lends money to its best customers) — especially since most other banks usually follow suit. Because of this fuss, many people think loan rates based on the prime are the same throughout the country. However, that's not the case. Banks differ widely in the way they calculate their lending rates. Even if the rate is based on the prime set by the major money-center banks, individual institutions use their own arbitrary formulas to calculate and apply their rates.

Thus, you can often get a loan rate much closer to the prime than you might think possible. Simply check out the interest-rate adjustment formulas on any loan you apply for — then check to see if other banks use a different formula that could give you a lower rate.

WHERE TO GET THE BEST LOAN RATES

The following tables list the 5 banks or mortgage companies in the United States with the best loan rates and lowest fees on 30-year, fixed-rate mortgages; 30-year, adjustable-rate mortgages; equity lines of credit and new-car loans, as of Oct. 1, 1992. All rates are, of course, subject to change, and most are available only to residents in the institutions' normal service areas:

30-Year, Fixed-Rate Mortgages

1. United Savings Bank (Los Angeles, Calif.) — 7.625%; 5% down; 1.75 points; phone: 818-543-3939.

2. First American Mortgage (Connecticut) — 7.625%; 10% down; 2.375 points; phone: 203-629-8164.

3. Holland Mortgage (Cleveland, Ohio) — 7.625%; 5% down; 2.50 points; phone: 216-524-8374.

4. Detroit Savings Bank (Michigan) — 7.625%; 5% down; 2.50 points; phone: 313-961-7600.

5. Holland Mortgage (Houston, Texas) — 7.625%; 5% down; 2.50

points; phone: 713-630-1300.

30-Year, Adjustable-Rate Mortgages

1. Detroit Savings Bank (Michigan) — 3.88%; 10% down; 2.125 points; 11.80% lifetime cap; phone: 313-961-7600.

2. National City Mortgage (Atlanta, Ga.) — 3.88%; 10% down; 3.375 points; 9.0% lifetime cap; phone: 404-396-1445.

3. Arbor National Mortgage (New York/New Jersey/Washington, D.C.) — 3.95%; 10% down; 3.00 points; 9.90% lifetime cap; phone: check directory in area served.

4. First Advantage Mortgage (Baltimore, Md.) — 4.00%; 10% down; 2.50 points; 10.00% lifetime cap; phone: 410-995-0710.

5. Hart Mortgage (Philadelphia, Pa.) — 4.00%; 10% down; 3.00 points; 10.00% lifetime cap; phone: 215-628-3131.

Equity Lines of Credit

1. Boulevard Bank (Chicago, Ill.) — Prime + 1.00%; no points; 12.00% maximum; phone: 312-836-6500.

2. Union Bank (San Francisco, Calif.) — Prime + 1.00%; no points; 12.00% maximum; phone: 415-550-9311.

3. Peninsula Bank (San Diego, Calif.) — Prime + 1.00%; no points; 13.00% maximum; phone: 619-226-5431.

4. Fairfax Savings (Baltimore, Md.) — Prime + 1.00%; no points; 16.00% maximum; phone: 301-659-0800.

5. Crestar Bank (Washington, D.C.) — Prime + 1.00%; no points; 24.00% maximum; phone: 1-800-451-2435.

New-Car Loans

1. Nations Bank (Atlanta, Ga.) — 7.75%; 10% down; 36-month term; phone: 404-581-3221.

2. Pulaski Bank (St. Louis, Mo.) — 7.75%; 10% down; 36-month term; phone: 314-878-2210.

3. Cole Taylor Bank (Chicago, Ill.) — 7.75%; 20% down; 48-month term; phone: 708-857-3369.

4. Bank of America (So. California) — 7.75%; 20% down; 48-month term; phone: 1-800-553-7762

5. Union Savings Bank (Connecticut) — 7.75%; 20% down; 60-month term; phone: 203-792-2200.

NOTES

CHAPTER 3

CREDIT SECRETS

A. Rating Your Credit Rating

RECOGNIZING THE DEBT DANGER SIGNALS

If your debt problems are really, really bad, you won't have any trouble recognizing the fact; your creditors will tell you — constantly. But, if you aren't yet completely over the edge, you may still be practicing "debt denial" — refusing to admit your crisis in the hope (probably false) that things will work themselves out over time. Here are some of the behavioral signs that indicate you're probably approaching truly dangerous personal debt levels:

* You don't really know for sure how much consumer debt you owe — and you're afraid to add it up.

* You hide bills from your spouse so he or she won't see how big the balances are and how many new charges you've made.

* You're late paying some of your bills and have already been assessed late charges on one or more of your accounts.

* You're running your checking account balance so close to zero that you've already bounced a couple of checks.

* You rush to the bank on payday so the money you deposit will cover checks you've already written.

* You postdate checks in hopes they won't bounce.

* Your savings account balance is shrinking — and you no longer make

regular deposits.

* Your savings account balance is too small to cover your short-term debt, and you no longer have an emergency fund.

* You borrow to buy items you once purchased for cash.

* You use credit cards for groceries or other regular household expenses.

* You're making only the minimum payment on your credit-card accounts — if you make a payment at all.

* Your credit-card balances increase each month — and several of your cards are at or over their limits.

* You've taken out cash on one credit-card account to make the payment on another.

* You've applied for additional cards so you can get more room to maneuver.

* You've received a disconnect warning on one or more of your utilities.

* You've received calls from credit-card companies or other creditors urging you to make your payments or reduce your balance.

* You think you'll be okay if you can just hold on until you get a raise.

* You find yourself thinking more and more about money, becoming depressed and short tempered. Obviously, you probably won't have all of these symptoms — but if you have even a few, you're headed for trouble and need to take action to halt your personal debt spiral.

THE VERY BEST DEBT-REDUCTION STRATEGY

If you've reached the point where there's consistently more month at the end of the money, you definitely need to take steps to get your financial situation under control — before it's too late. Most people try to ease their way out of a bad debt situation, but that very seldom works. Really drastic financial problems generally require dramatic solutions — and that means a concentrated debt-reduction strategy. According to most experts, the best plan involves 3 steps.

Step 1 — Stop Spending: That's what got you in trouble in the first place, and you can never expect to dig your way out if you continue the same patterns. Go into a strictly maintenance mode, repairing things rather than replacing them — or doing without if the items aren't really necessary to your day to day existence. (For example, if the electric can opener breaks, use an old-fashioned manual one for a while; they cost about $1.39.) Delay all major purchases, and eliminate all discretionary spending. Stay away from stores and shopping malls — particularly if you're prone to impulse buying. Your lifestyle may suffer for a while — but not nearly as much as it will if you keep spending yourself right into bankruptcy.

Step 2 — Stop Borrowing: Unless you're in trouble because of a job loss or family illness, it's likely that credit cards and other consumer loans are the major culprits behind your financial problems. If you keep using them — even if you're still able to make your payments — you'll never dig yourself out, simply because of the steady addition of excessive interest charges. The best rule is simply this: If you can't pay cash for something, don't buy it. And, whatever you do, don't use credit cards for day-to-day expenses such as groceries and household items. If you can't exercise this kind of self-discipline, the easiest course may be to simply cut up your cards. You don't have to close your accounts (which could trigger a demand for payment in full of the outstanding balance), but cutting them up will at least remove the temptation until the bank mails out new ones at renewal time.

Step 3 — Tap All Cash Sources to Pay Off Bills: Once you've gotten a handle on your spending and borrowing, it's time to start paying down your debts. Obviously, the reduced spending will generate some extra money you can apply to payments, but to really make significant inroads on your debt, you need to increase your short-term cash flow. Here are some potential sources of additional cash:

* If you're already so far behind you're being hit with late-payment or overdraft fees, try to get a short-term loan from relatives to bring your accounts current and prevent further charges or bounced checks. This will give you some time for other cash-generating strategies to kick in.

* Review all your insurance policies. You may be able to substantially cut your monthly payments and free up more cash by increasing deductibles, eliminating some coverages (see the insurance Section in Chapter 1, Auto Secrets, and Chapter 7, Insurance Secrets, for strategies) and lowering the coverage amounts.

* Check all family life-insurance policies to see if any have cash values you can borrow or cash in. Cash-value policies are generally a bad deal anyway, so you can save money by terminating them and switching to term insurance. If, for some reason, you feel you must keep a cash-value policy, the interest rate for borrowing is only about 5% — much less than even the best credit card rate. Warning: If you do borrow against a policy, use all of the proceeds to pay down higher-interest debts. If you take money out for other purposes, you'll just be compounding your problems.

* Increase the allowances claimed on your W-4 form to temporarily reduce the withholding tax bite and raise your take-home pay.

* Get a temporary loan from your 401(k) or other retirement plan. In most plans, you can do this without incurring penalties — and some even allow interest-free loans. If you qualify under the plan's hardship definitions, you may also be able to make a permanent, penalty-free withdrawal.

* Ask your employer to let you work as much paid overtime as possible.

* Take a second job for a few months until you're back on your feet.

* Hold a garage or yard sale and sell off some of the stuff you bought but didn't really need.

Payment Strategy: As you generate extra cash from these sources, don't just add a little bit to each of your monthly debt payments. Instead, continue to make minimum payments on accounts with low interest rates, and use the extra money to pay down the principal on debts with the highest interest charges. That way you'll reduce your overall interest burden and slow your non-spending-related debt growth.

A LESS PAINFUL ALTERNATIVE

If you own a home and haven't already put too many black marks on your credit rating with late payments and such, you could consider either a home equity loan, an equity line of credit or a total refinance. The equity line of credit is probably the best choice, because the application fees and upfront charges tend to be the lowest. Interest rates on equity credit lines are currently 10 to 14 percentage points below the average credit-card rate, so you can significantly lower your monthly interest charges by switching your debt from plastic to an equity line. Home equity loans (second mortgages) and full refinancings usually involve substantial upfront charges — including application, documentation and appraisal fees and lender's points — so they aren't as practical since it could take a year or more of lower payments just to offset the initial costs. However, if that is the only way you can pay off high credit-card balances and lower your monthly payment burden, it's worth a shot.

Bonus: If you do manage to qualify for an equity-based loan and keep it current, you can quickly improve your credit rating, as good performance on these types of loans is always ranked high by credit evaluators.

USE CONSOLIDATION LOANS ONLY AS A LAST RESORT

If you don't own a home and can't generate enough cash from other sources to get you out of trouble, one other alternative is a commercial bill-consolidation loan. With these loans, you total up all your existing loans — except for your mortgage and, in most cases, your car payment — and borrow enough money to pay them off. You then make just one monthly payment to the loan company — a payment that, because of the longer term of the consolidation loan, is considerably lower than the total payments you were making before. These deals sound appealing — but, as a general rule, they should be avoided unless you have no other way out. Why? For one thing, they carry fairly high interest rates — a reflection of the increased risk involved in loaning money to someone who's already in financial trouble. For another, since they lower your monthly payments by stretching your debt out over a much longer period of time, you wind up paying substantially more in interest than you would have had you merely paid off your old debts on time. Finally, if you have several debts with only a few payments remaining, you may not really need a bill-consolidation loan. You would be better off to adjust your payments, paying the minimum on your longer-term debts and sending in extra on the short-term ones, until you get the shorter ones paid off. Once you're rid of the short-term loans , your monthly payment total will drop — even without benefit of a consolidation loan — and you can begin paying more on the longer-term debts.

Beware: If you owe only a few more payments on your car, many lenders will try to get you to include the auto loan in the consolidation package because it gives them more security. However, this is a bad deal for you because it stretches your car payments out several more years, costing you additional interest, and also gives the lender a repossession claim against the car should you default.

Rule of Thumb: Any time you have fewer than a year's worth of payments left on a loan, don't include it in any bill-consolidation package.

PROS & CONS OF CREDIT COUNSELORS

If one or more of the debt-reduction plans we've just outlined sounds appealing, but you don't think you have the discipline to pull it off alone, you may want to enlist the services of a consumer credit counselor. Credit counselors provide one-on-one assistance, working with both you and your creditors to come up with a plan that will keep them off your back while you work your way out of trouble. Often, these plans involve having you make payments into a trust account, which then distributes payments to the creditors. The best credit counselors work for non-profit organizations and will charge only a minimal fee — if they charge a fee at all. To find one in your area, write the National Foundation for Consumer Credit, 8611 Second Ave ., Ste. 100, Silver Spring, MD 20910, or call the organization at 1-800-388-2227.

Warning: Having told you about legitimate debt-counseling services, we must also warn you that the credit-repair business is fraught with rip-off artists. We see TV, radio and print ads almost every day promising that you can get creditors off your back and restore your credit rating easily — if you will just call a certain "900" number. Of course, there's a charge of $3 to $5 per minute for that call, which means you'll pay $30 to $50 (or more) just to get the initial information. And, that's just the beginning. Most of these outfits will want anywhere from $250 to more than $1,000 to enroll you in their programs, which won't tell you anything more than you've just learned here. Avoid these credit-repair scammers at all costs.

PAY THESE BILLS FIRST TO PRESERVE YOUR CREDIT

Should it ever reach the point where you can only afford to pay some of your bills, it's important to choose the right ones to pay. You can miss a payment or two on a credit card without damaging your credit rating. They'll add on some more interest and a late charge, but they probably won't report you to the credit bureau. The same is true of most department-store accounts and loans you've taken out for furniture or household appliances. You can even skip a utility payment if you're willing to risk having your electricity or gas shut off. However, you don't want to skip either your mortgage payment or your car payment.

Reason: Mortgage companies and auto dealers have a virtual open line to the credit bureaus because they deal with them on an almost daily basis. And, because they are generally dealing with much larger sums than other lenders, they are much more conscientious about bad credit risks. As a result, both your mortgage lender and the holder of your auto loan will report a missed payment to the credit bureau within days after the grace period ends. Both will also be fairly quick to take action against you. Miss two car payments and you're likely to face at least a threat of repossession, if not the action itself. And, miss three mortgage payments and you can count on the lender starting foreclosure proceedings.

HOW TO GET A COPY OF YOUR OWN CREDIT REPORT - Free

Whether you have current credit problems or not, it's a good idea to know exactly where you stand with the major credit reporting agencies — just to be on the safe side. Fortunately, it's fairly easy — and inexpensive (or even free) — to get a copy of your credit file:

* TRW, the leading credit bureau, now offers one free copy of your credit report each year, but only on request. Write to TRW Consumer Assistance, P.O. Box 2350, Chatsworth, CA 91313-2350. Be sure to include your full name (with middle initial), your spouse's full name, your Social Security numbers and

birthdates, current address, any previous addresses during the past five years and a copy of your driver's license or a recent bill as proof of your current address.

* Equifax, the No. 2 credit agency, charges $8 for a copy of your report. Call 1-800-685-1111, and be prepared to provide the same information listed for the TRW requests.

* Trans Union, the last of the 3 majors, charges $15 for its reports except in those states that mandate lower fees. The company has no national customer service number, so check your local phone directory for the office nearest you.

Note: If you are turned down for a loan, you are automatically entitled to a free copy of your report from all three agencies — but you must request it within 60 days of the rejection. Otherwise, the fees go back into effect at those agencies that have them.

IF YOU FIND A MISTAKE

Once you get a copy of your credit report, review it carefully. If you find a mistake, contact the credit agency immediately and request a review. The credit bureau will then go back to the business that reported the information and ask for a clarification. If the erroneous entry isn't confirmed, it must be removed from your file within 60 days.

Look for Omissions: In addition to reviewing what is in your credit file, you should also note anything that might be missing — at least if the missing data reflects positively on your borrowing habits. As much information as most credit files contain, there are also a surprising number of gaps — and it is your right to request that any positive information be added. You will have to supply details of the missing material to the credit bureau, complete with the name of the creditor and when the loans were paid or if the accounts are still open and current. By law, the credit agency must verify the information you've supplied and update your file within 20 days.

Check Inquiries Too: Your credit report will also contain a list of every business or lender that has requested a copy of your file in recent months — or, in some cases, recent years. That can also be a problem since too many inquiries will make it seem you are either on a buying spree or intent on getting as much credit as possible — both of which can cause a potential lender to reject your credit application. If you didn't authorize the inquiries — or if you feel they are out of date — you have the right to request their removal. And, even if you did authorize an inquiry, you have the right to add a note to the file explaining why (perhaps a potential lender changed terms on you at the last minute, forcing you to seek an alternate loan source).

Preventive Measure: If you have a number of inquiries on your file and don't want to go to the trouble of having them removed, simply note on any new credit applications that you have also applied for other recent loans, explain the reasons why and note whether you got the credit or not.

ASK FOR — AND GET — A RATING UPGRADE

If you find something you don't like on your credit report, don't run off yelling and screaming to the credit agency. Remember, credit bureaus don't set credit ratings — they merely report the information provided to them by your creditors. Thus, if you want a black mark removed from your file, you're going to have to impress the creditor — not the credit agency. Let's assume, for the sake of example, that you had some problems with payments on a new refrigerator a few months back and, as a result, the appliance store has rated you "I-2, pays 30 to 60 days late." If you have since gotten back on schedule with your payments, you should make a trip to the appliance store and ask to see the credit manager. Introduce yourself, and then explain that you could use some help. Tell him that, though you had some payment problems in the past, your more recent payments have been on time. Outline why you had the earlier problems — and why those same problems won't recur. Then tell the credit manager it would be a great help to you and your family if he or she could update the store's credit report on you, upgrading your rating from I-2 to I-1. Perhaps surprisingly given the bad reputation of most credit officers, your request will be granted most of the time. And, once your rating is upgraded, other potential creditors who check your file will have no way of knowing that it was ever anything but I-1 — meaning you regularly make your payments as agreed.

USE THE BANK'S MONEY TO MEND YOUR CREDIT

As long as we're on the subject of asking for help, we'll outline one other credit-repair strategy. If you need to build some positive payment records, go to your own bank and ask to speak to a loan officer. Once you've been introduced, explain to the officer that you want to borrow, say, $2,500. Normally, the officer would ask you to fill out an application and then make you wait while the bank requests a copy of your credit file. However, you want to beat the bank to the punch, so you tell the loan officer that you have had some past loan problems and need the bank's help in rebuilding your credit rating. Explain that you would like the bank to put the borrowed money into a savings account — with a "hold" on it so it can't be withdrawn. The savings account will thus serve as security for the loan. By doing this, you note, the bank has no risk since it has the money. Meanwhile, however, you get a chance to make payments on the loan, thereby restoring your credit rating. If you're both pleasant and insistent in requesting the bank's help, you'll get it more often than not. This strategy will, of course, cost you the interest charges on the loan — but you'll recover some of that in the form of interest payments on the savings account. And, in any event, it's a small price to pay to repair your damaged credit rating.

HOW TO DEVELOP AN A+ CREDIT RATING

If you were a loan officer, what would you look for in a borrower? Most people don't really know what's important and what isn't when it comes to their credit ratings. However, there are certain key factors that lenders always look for — factors that identify the potential borrower as an A-1 candidate for new credit.

The 8 Keys to Great Credit:

1. A positive and fully current credit report.
2. Home ownership (with an up-to-date mortgage).
3. An American Express or Diners Club card.
4. More than a year at your current job.
5. At least one fully paid or current bank loan.
6. A Visa or MasterCard.
7. Current department store accounts.
8. A telephone in your name.

Work diligently to meet as many of these criteria as possible — and, before you know it, your credit rating will be top rate.

B. Cashing in on Credit Cards

BEWARE THESE CREDIT CARD GIMMICKS

All credit cards aren't alike — and the differences extend well beyond the interest rates. In today's highly competitive market, many card issuers are coming up with ways to offer lower rates, while still squeezing extra money out of your pockets. Some of the favorite gimmicks include:

* High Annual Fees: These can run as high as $75 a year, which will

offset a substantial reduction in interest rates — especially if you generally pay off your balance in full each month. And, there's no reason to stay with a card that has a high fee — there are now plenty around with no fee, and even more with fees of $25 or less. Some of the best no-fee cards are listed in Chapter 2, Banking Secrets, and more are included later in this section.

* No Grace Period: Most cards offer a 25-day grace period, meaning you incur no interest charges if you pay your bill in full within a few days after you are billed. However, some low-rate, no-fee cards have eliminated or shortened the grace period so you begin incurring interest charges as soon as your purchase is posted. This means you wind up paying interest charges every time you use the card — even if you pay the bill in full.

* Cash Advance Fees: Many cards heavily promote the fact that you can get cash on your credit card at ATM machines around the country. What they don't say is that these cash advances often come with high fees — as much as 2% of the amount withdrawn or a flat fee of up to $15. Many cards that offer grace periods on regular purchases also withdraw this privilege on cash advances, beginning to assess interest charges as soon as the money is in your hand.

* Payment-in-Full Fees: This is a sneaky way some card issuers use to make money off people who don't maintain ongoing credit balances. Since they don't collect any interest charges, they simply tack on a flat fee of $2 or $3 every time you pay your monthly bill in full.

* Short Billing Cycles: Some banks have started billing every 24 days instead of every 30 days. This means you have a shorter grace period — and also means you could receive up to 15 bills a year, which can really mess up your budgeting and bookkeeping.

* Dubious Benefits: Many cards also promote added features, such as purchase rebates, rental car discounts, travel discounts, etc. These cost you nothing, but the card issuers still make money since they get promotional fees from the companies offering the discounts. However, in most cases, the discounts have severe restrictions or apply only to full-price purchases. You can generally do better by just shopping around.

* Credit Insurance: Makes your credit card payments if you die or become disabled. This is the worst deal in the credit game. For details on why, read "The Great Credit-Card Insurance Rip-Off" later in this Section.

* Unneeded Upgrades: If you've been a good customer for a couple of years, your card issuer may offer you an upgrade to a "gold" or "platinum" card. These premium cards usually offer some additional benefits — and a higher credit limit — but they also have higher annual fees. However, you really don't need these upgrades. The benefits aren't worth the added fee, and your credit

limit will automatically rise over time if you're a good customer. Besides, if you really want a higher limit, they'll usually give you one if you just ask.

* Home-Equity Credit Cards: These cards, secured by the equity in your house or condominium, offer low interest rates and high credit limits — as much as $100,000 in some cases. They also offer high risk — if you don't make your payments, they can take your house.

DEALING WITH HIGH CREDIT-CARD COSTS

Thanks to both public outcry and the threat of governmental restrictions, interest rates have come down on many credit cards in recent years. However, despite these reductions, the average annual interest rate on U.S. cards is still more than 18% — meaning the actual cost for people who usually carry a credit balance is over 20%. There are, however, several ways to lower your interest expenses and other credit-card costs:

1. Look for cards with the lowest combination of rates, annual fees and other charges. (Several cards with low rates and/or no annual fees are listed later in this Section, as well as in Chapter 2, Banking Secrets.)

2. Avoid cards that don't offer a grace period. By charging interest from the day of purchase, card issuers can raise the effective interest rate several percentage points. You also lose the right to avoid interest charges by paying off your monthly bill in full.

3. Look for cards that calculate their interest charges based on your average daily balance excluding any new charges. Note: These cards are fairly rare; most include new purchases in figuring the average balance.

4. Make more than the minimum payment (usually 2.0% to 3.0% of the balance, down from an average of 5.0% in 1985). If you pay only what's required, it will take you years to pay off your balance — and the card company will be able to charge maximum rates on a high average balance the entire time. For example, if you owe $1,000 on an 18.5% card and pay only a minimum of 2.0% each month, it will take you just over 8 years to pay off the bill, and cost you nearly $950 in interest — even if you never make another purchase. By contrast, if you pay 5.0% of the balance each month, you'll clear your debt in just over 4 years, paying under $400 in interest.

5. Pay your bill on time. Late charges run $7 to $15 a month, depending on the balance.

6. Don't exceed your credit limit. Many cards charge fees of $10 to $15 for exceeding the limit.

7. Do not purchase card-related services such as credit life insurance or card-registration services. (The first is a bad deal, and we'll show you how to get the second for free later in this Section). These will invariably be charged to the card, meaning you'll pay not only the fees, but interest on them as well.

8. Don't use the cash-advance privilege on your card unless it's an emergency. Fees typically run about 2.5% of the amount withdrawn, but some cards charge flat fees of up to $20 per transaction.

GET A CREDIT CARD EVEN IF YOU HAVE BAD CREDIT

In America, cash is no longer king. In fact, if you don't have a credit card, you' re almost an economic invalid — unable to cash checks, rent a car, shop over the phone, buy theater tickets, etc. Some businesses (many Federal Express offices, for example) won't even accept cash if you offer. So, what do you do if your credit rating is so bad you can't get a normal card? The answer is what is known as a secured credit card. These cards, issued by banks or other financial institutions, require you to open an account and make a deposit of from $500 to $5,000. The money is then put in a restricted savings account or certificate of deposit, and you are given a credit card (Visa or MasterCard) with a limit equal to or slightly less than the amount of your deposit. Thus, the card is "secured" by your own cash. If you demonstrate responsibility over 6 months to a year, spending sensibly and making payments on time, the bank will lift the cash requirement, returning your deposit if you so desire. The bank will also provide a positive report to the credit-rating agencies. If you can't get a card any other way, these are good deals, though fees and interest rates are fairly high.

5 Banks That Offer Secured Cards:

1. American National Bank, 890 Palmer Ave., Ste. 403, Larchmont, NY 10538, 1-800-533-3295. Fee: $69.

2. American Pacific Bank, P.O. Box 193605, Portland, OR 97280, 1-800-879-8745. Fee: $30.

3. Star Bank, P.O. Box 956, Cincinnati, OH 45273, 1-800-999-0619. Fee: $20.

4. Suburban National Bank, 34 Read's Way, New Castle, DE 19720. 302-322-4305. Fee: $35.

5. Community Bank of Parker, 19590 East Main, Parker, CO 80134, 1-

800-779-8472. Fee: $20.

For information about other secured credit card programs, you can also call 1-800-326-3311 and request a free promotional packet.

HIDDEN COSTS BEHIND SOME LOW CARD RATES

As mentioned in the Banking Secrets Chapter, low interest rates on credit cards aren't always the best deal. Sometimes, low-rate cards won't have grace periods — meaning you begin paying interest as soon as you make a purchase, with no opportunity to wipe out the charges by paying off your monthly balance in full. That can often result in higher overall interest charges than had you used a card with higher rates. In addition, many low-rate cards also have much higher annual fees — sometimes $75 or more. Broken down, that can amount to an extra charge of $3 to $4 a month — which will more than offset several percentage points worth of lower interest rates unless you maintain a very high balance. As a result of these potential hidden costs, be very sure you look at more than just the promised low interest rate whenever you're offered a new credit card.

MORE CREDIT CARDS WITH NO ANNUAL FEES

In Chapter 2 on "Banking Secrets," we listed the five best no-fee credit cards available today. However, each of those was a so-called "gold card" — limited to higher-income individuals with proven credit records. If you can't qualify for a gold card, but still like the idea of skirting the annual fee, here are 7 more card issuers that offer that feature:

1. Bank of New York (Delaware), 1-800-942-1977, 11.90% (variable), no grace period.

2. USAA Federal Savings Bank (Texas), 1-800-922-9092, 12.50% (variable), 25-day grace period.

3. Wachovia Bank (Delaware), 1-800-842-3262, 15.90% (variable), 25-day grace period.

4. The Abbott Bank (Nebraska), 1-800-999-6977, 16.30% (variable), 25-day grace period.

5. Fidelity National Bank (Georgia), 1-800-753-2900, 17.90%, 25-day grace period.

6. Riggs National Bank (Washington, D.C.), 1-800-368-5800, 17.90%, 25-day grace period.

7. Security Bank & Trust (Michigan), 1-800-443-5465, 18.00%, 25-day grace period.

If you'd like a complete list of current no-fee cards, you can write to Bankcard Holders of America, 333 Pennsylvania Ave. SE, Washington, DC 20003. There's a small handling fee for the list, but it was less than $5 the last time we checked. If you don't feel like calling all over the country in search of a no-fee credit card, there's also one place you can check right in your own hometown. Sears charges no annual fee for its Discover card, gives you a 25-day grace period and you can apply at any Sears store. You also get up to a 5% rebate on all purchases made with the card. However, if you don't pay your bill in full each month, you'll more than pay for both the rebate and the lack of an annual fee because of the card's high 19.80% fixed interest rate.

NO FEE — AND FREE TRAVELER'S CHECKS, TOO

The American Automobile Association (AAA) offers its members a no-fee Gold MasterCard that also features a variety of extras — including free American Express Travelers Cheques. The card offers a 25-day grace period, has a variable interest rate that's currently pegged at 14.9% and each purchase earns bonus points that you can redeem for Auto Club products and services. In addition, the card offers purchase protection, free auto rental collision damage waiver coverage, checking and instant-cash privileges and full protection against liability if your card is lost or stolen (with most cards, you're at risk for the first $50).

YOUR RIGHTS REGARDING CREDIT CARDS

Credit cards offer considerable convenience, but using them can also subject you to certain abuses if you don't know your rights. Here are 4 potential problem areas:

1. Surcharges for credit-card use. If a merchant posts a price, he cannot add on an extra fee if you want to pay with a credit card . Such surcharges are specifically prohibited by both Visa and MasterCard, as well as by American Express in most states. (Note: Many stores build credit-card processing charges into their prices, meaning they can give you a discount for not using a credit card.)

2. Purchase minimums. Despite posted signs at many firms — particularly restaurants — requiring that you purchase at least $5 or $10 before using your credit card, such practices are prohibited by Visa, MasterCard and American Express (in most states).

3. I.D. demands. Though many stores ask for your driver's license number, phone number or address when you charge something with a major credit card, you are not obligated to provide the information. In fact, California, Delaware, Georgia, Maryland, Minnesota, Nevada, New Jersey and New York have specific laws prohibiting merchants from requiring such information.

4. Credit-card requirements when cashing checks. Many stores demand that you have a credit card before they will allow you to cash a personal check. However, while they may legally ask to see a card, they cannot force you to give them the card number — and you should never allow them to write it on the check. For one thing, it opens the door for fraudulent use of your credit card account . For another, the card number does the merchant no good since Visa, MasterCard and American Express all bar member stores from assessing a charge against your credit card to cover a bounced check. They also refuse to go into their billing files to help a merchant locate you in order to collect on a bounced check. Each of the states mentioned in No. 3 have laws prohibiting this practice, as do Florida, Iowa, Kansas, North Dakota, Ohio, Virginia and Washington.

If you'd like more information about credit-card rights, write Bankcard Holders of America, 333 Pennsylvania Ave. SE, Washington, D C 20003, or call 1-800-553-8025.

WHEN TO WITHHOLD CREDIT CARD PAYMENTS

When you use a credit card to buy goods or services that prove substandard, you may be able to legally withhold your payments to the card issuer for those items. That's because the Fair Credit Billing Act permits credit-card companies to reclaim such disputed amounts from merchants, even after credit-card slips are signed — but only when certain conditions of purchase are satisfied.

The 4 Conditions for Withholding Payment:

1. The purchase must have been made within your home state — or within a 100-mile radius of your residence.

2. The amount of the disputed charge must be in excess of $50.

3. You must have tried to settle the matter first with the merchant.

4. You must notify the card-issuing institution that you have already tried and failed to settle the dispute and that you will be withholding payment. After getting your notice, the card issuer will credit your account in the amount of the charge, then bill the amount back to the merchant.

Exceptions: The amount and distance limitations are waived if defective goods were purchased from the same company that issued the credit card (e.g., if you purchased a defective tire at a Texaco station using a Texaco credit card), or from one of its corporate affiliates (e.g., you buy a defective power drill from Sears using a Discover card).

Warning: You must dispute the charge before you pay your credit-card bill. Once you send in the check, you're stuck with the merchandise.

THE GREAT CREDIT-CARD INSURANCE RIP-OFF / SAVE $200 OR MORE

Of all the bad types of insurance marketed today, the absolute biggest waste of your money is credit-card coverage — designed to make payments on your plastic debt should you lose your job or become disabled.

Why it's so bad:

First, though the marketing brochures do a good job of obscuring the fact, it is outrageously expensive. The premiums run between 50 and 75 cents per $100, which sounds reasonable. However, when you apply that to the total outstanding balance, the actual costs can mount up quite quickly. For example, if you have an average outstanding balance of just $3,000, your annual insurance premium at a rate of 60 cents per $100 would be a whopping $216!

Second, most credit-card insurance provides really poor coverage. For example, it usually pays only the minimum monthly payment — meaning the interest only, or the interest plus a small percentage of the principal — not the full balance. And, it usually does that only after a waiting period of 30 to 45 days — which is longer than most disabilities last.

Finally, since the premiums are billed to your credit-card account, you wind up paying extra interest, raising the total cost still further.

GET CREDIT CARD REGISTRATION FREE

In these days of high crime, it's a virtual certainty that, at some time or another, you're going to have a wallet or purse stolen — and, if you're like most Americans, it's going to be full of credit cards. That's what makes credit-card registration services so valuable. These services, which maintain lists of all your card numbers and the issuing institutions, will handle all the notification chores for you if your cards are lost or stolen, meaning you have to make just one call — to them. Many also cover you against excess liability due to unauthorized card use. Of course, these services usually come with a price — normally around $15 a year, but sometimes as much as $35 or $40 annually. However, because the credit-card business is so lucrative, many small specialty card issuers — such as department stores and oil companies — are offering additional free services in an effort to entice consumers to use their cards rather than the "big 4" (Visa, MasterCard, American Express and Discover). And, one of these services is FREE credit card registration.

A Prime Choice: For example, BP — the big international oil company (BP stands for British Petroleum) — offers holders of its BP Horizon card free registration services for both credit cards and important documents (driver's license, Social Security card, passport, etc.). In addition, the BP card provides:

* Travel discounts and services — including emergency cash, ticket replacement, free $100,000 travel accident insurance and free $ 25,000 rental car collision damage waiver reimbursement.

* A special optometry buying program through which you can get savings of up to 50% on eyeglass frames and lenses, and up to 20% off on contacts and eyecare accessories.

* A prescription fulfillment program that can save you up to 60% on the cost of most common medications.

* Valuable bonus points that you accumulate when you use the card to buy gasoline or auto services at more than 15,000 stations across the United States and Canada.

To get an application for a BP Horizon card, call BP Customer Service at 1-800-321-9555.

C. Getting Credit Where Credit Is Due

5 STEPS IN REVERSING A CREDIT REJECTION

When you are turned down for a loan, it's not unusual to feel confused, hurt or helpless — especially if you really need the money. However, a rejection doesn't have to be the final word. There are a number of steps you can take to reverse the rejection, or improve your chances of getting approved elsewhere:

1. Find out why you were turned down. Any time you are turned down for a loan, the lender is required by law to inform you of the reason — but you must file a written request for the explanation within 10 days of being denied credit. Do so — and, when you receive the reply, decide if you can provide additional data or references that will counter the lender's rejection. Even if you

can' t redeem yourself with that lender, you may find out something that will let you fill out a better application with another potential lender. For example, if the first lender said you didn't have enough income to qualify, you may be able to come up with additional income sources to list on your next application. (Note: If you're single, but live with someone, you may be able to count their income toward your loan qualification since the Equal Credit Opportunity Act bars discrimination based on marital status.)

2. Check out your credit report. If the lender says you were turned down because of detrimental information in your credit report, immediately apply for a copy of your report (as explained in Section A of this Chapter). Each of the major credit-reporting agencies will provide you with a free copy of your file if you request one within 60 days of your loan rejection. If you find mistakes, missing information or other negative data, have it corrected — or, if applicable, add an explanation to the file — and resubmit your application to the lender once the changes have been made.

3. Use a co-signer. If you can't counter the lender's concerns or spruce up your credit report, find out if the lender will accept a co-signer. Then try to get a family member or friend to put their name on the dotted line with yours. (Note: Though you shouldn't hesitate to ask someone to co-sign a loan for you if necessary, we advise against ever co-signing a loan for someone else.)

4. Ask the lender what you would have to do to qualify. Some lenders will adjust their requirements if you offer to move an account to their institution, abide by a special payment plan or make some other concession. However, you will have to ask — they will never volunteer their flexibility in such matters.

5. Keep trying. Each lender has different qualification standards, so you should never give up. If one, two or even three lenders say no, try one, two or even three more. If your credit rating is merely marginal — and not truly dreadful — you'll probably find a willing lender eventually. (Note: As mentioned earlier, however, each inquiry will show up on your credit report, so you may need to go back later and file a request for their removal or add an explanation of the circumstances.)

Application Trap: Never try to counter a loan rejection by leaving out information or lying on the application. You will almost always be found out — and a false or incomplete application will result in an automatic rejection.

DO YOU HAVE TOO MUCH INSTALLMENT DEBT?

One of the most common reasons lenders cite for rejecting a loan applicant is an excessive level of existing installment debt (loans other than a mortgage that require monthly payments). So, how much is too much? As a general rule, lenders will have reservations about giving you a loan if payments on your current installment debt exceed 10% of your take-home pay. And, if they exceed 20%, it's a guaranteed rejection.

KEEP CREDITORS FROM HOUNDING YOU — LEGALLY

One reason credit costs have remained so high in recent years even though overall interest-rate levels have fallen is that creditors face significant losses from debtors who file for bankruptcy. Since passage of the Federal Bankruptcy Act of 1978, more and more Americans have chosen this route to escape heavy debt burdens. In fact, many lawyers now limit their practices solely to personal bankruptcy filings — flooding the airways and newspapers with ads for their services. Obviously, then, if you are being hounded by your creditors, you can legally get them off your back by filing for bankruptcy (discussed in more detail in Chapter 9, Legal Secrets). However, you will have to pay a lawyer — and the bankruptcy will go on your credit record for 10 full years.

A better course of action — and one that often works just as well — is to contact your creditors and explain that, because of their pressure, you are in danger of having to file for bankruptcy. Say you would prefer not to do this because it would both damage your credit rating and cost them money. Explain that you would like to set up an extended-payment plan, similar to that mandated in a Chapter 13 bankruptcy filing, under which you would make regular, but smaller payments until your debt is cleared. In exchange, they would stop bothering you. In most cases — faced with the threat of losses should you go ahead and file for bankruptcy — your creditors will agree to such a plan. (Note: If you do not feel you can manage such a strategy on your own, you may want to contact a credit-counseling agency, as explained earlier in this Chapter.)

5 TRAPS IN LOAN AGREEMENTS

Any time you make an installment purchase or take out a loan, you will be asked to sign a credit contract. If you want the loan, you won't have any choice in the matter. However, that doesn't mean you should ignore these 5 dangerous clauses that appear in many loan agreements:

1. Lien provisions. These give the lender the right to seize your home (except in homestead states), car or other items of personal property if needed to pay off an overdue debt.

2. Wage garnishment clause. This gives the lender the right to attach a portion of your salary in order to satisfy a delinquent loan.

3. Acceleration clause. This allows the lender to call the entire note if you miss a single payment.

4. Confession of judgment. This clause waives your right to defend yourself against foreclosures, repossessions or seizures by the lender.

5. Assumption of legal fees. This provision states that you agree to pay any attorneys' fees the lender may incur in collecting an overdue loan.

If you spot any of these provisions in the fine print of your loan document, attempt to have them stricken — or at least modified — before signing on the dotted line.

SAVE THOUSANDS BY PAYING EXTRA PRINCIPAL

As we've mentioned a couple of times, lenders and credit-card companies love people who make the minimum payment each month. Why? Because that ensures the loan term is stretched out for as long as possible, enabling the creditor to collect the maximum amount of interest. For example, assume you have a $3,000 balance on a credit card with a 15% interest rate. The minimum payment might be calculated based on interest (0.0125% per month x the balance), plus 1/60th of the principal (a 5-year payoff term). Thus, your initial payment would be $87.50 — or $37.50 in interest (0.0125% x $3,000 = $37.50), plus $50 in principal ($3,000/60 = $50). In case the obvious eludes you, that means almost 43% of your monthly payment was interest and only 57% went to retiring your debt. No wonder you can't seem to get ahead of your bills!

If you make the minimum payment, the same circumstances will prevail the following month, with the balance dropping to just $2,950 and the minimum payment falling to only $86.05 — $36.88 in interest and $49.17 in principal. If, however, you make a payment in excess of the minimum, every penny of the additional money goes toward principal, which quickly shortens the payoff time — saving you hundreds (or even thousands) in extra interest charges. For example, if you take the above situation and pay just $50 more than the minimum each month, you will cut your payoff term almost in half and save about $1,100 in total interest payments.

Payoff Strategy: Don't try to divide your money so that you can make extra principal payments on all of your debts. Instead, concentrate your extra payments on those loans or bills that carry the highest interest rates. This will save you more in interest charges than if you spread your money around.

SHORTER TERMS MEAN LOWER CREDIT COSTS

If you don't have the discipline to make extra principal payments on your own, you can force the issue on installment debts by taking the shortest loan term possible. In other words, rather than financing a new car for 60 months, finance it only for 36 months. The monthly payment will be only slightly more, but the interest savings from cutting the loan term by 24 months will run into the thousands. As a general rule, you should never finance anything for more than 36 months. If the loan amount is under $3,000, cut the term to 24 months — and, if it is under $1,000, finance for only 1 year. This strategy will cost you a little more in the short term, but your total borrowing cost will fall dramatically over the full life of your loans — freeing up money that can be used for savings, investments or merely an improved quality of life.

BUSINESS OWNER'S STRATEGY FOR GETTING CREDIT

Lenders have a natural aversion to small business owners, simply because they often lack a steady cash flow and a proven income stream. Many also have most of their assets tied up in their companies, meaning there is little security available for new loans. However, there are a couple of strategies you can adopt if you own a small business and need to improve your creditworthiness:

* List yourself as an employee of the business rather than the owner, and have an accountant verify your income for the lender.

* Incorporate your business and pay yourself a salary, verifiable by W-2 forms instead of your business tax returns. Arrange for a contact person whom the lender can call to confirm your employment with the company (your bookkeeper or accountant will often do this for you).

As ridiculous as it may seem, this will make you much more appealing to lenders, even though your actual financial status is absolutely the same.

CHAPTER 4

DAY-TO-DAY LIVING SECRETS

A. Better Utilizing Your Utilities

CUTTING THE HIGH COST OF ENERGY

Other than the mortgage, heating and electricity are the biggest household expenses for most people. However, you don't have to give up comfort to cut down on these costs. Here are 10 ways to trim your heating and electric bills:

1. Storm windows are a worthwhile investment, reducing energy costs by 30% or more. However, if you can't afford custom storm windows, even homemade versions — plastic sheets held in place by tape — can significantly cut heat loss.

2. Air conditioners bring cool air in the summer, but let lots of heat escape in the winter. Cover your air conditioner — both the outside unit and the interior vents. Good covers, made from plastic or foam, not only block drafts, but increase the life of the air conditioner.

3. Windows and doors are another major source of lost heat (and cool

air in the summer). Minimize indoor/outdoor traffic and install draft guards around all doors and windows. Caution: Don't overdo this. If you make the house too tight, it can become stuffy and also lead to mildew and moisture buildup in the walls.

4. Use flow deflectors and heat reflectors to direct air away from exterior walls and out into the room.

5. Close the damper on your fireplace when it's not in use, and employ heat-induction tubes to increase warming power when it is.

6. Change your furnace filter monthly, and clean the furnace regularly. It will operate more efficiently and use less fuel.

7. Close off heating and air-conditioning vents in rooms that aren't used regularly.

8. Lower the heat setting on your water heater. Most are set at 160 degrees, but you really don't need water much hotter than 140 degrees (though you may want to insulate the water line if it's a long way from the water heater to the clothes washer or dishwasher.

9. Install light dimmers, which can cut lighting costs up to 50% a year when used regularly.

10. Take advantage of free utility company home-energy audits — then follow their suggestions to reduce energy costs.

SMART APPLIANCES CAN PAY FOR THEMSELVES

Most people don't replace appliances unless the old ones break down or are left behind in a move. However, that may be a costly strategy. There have been great strides in energy-saving technology over the past decade, and many of the new "smart" appliances can pay for themselves in energy savings within 3 to 5 years. This is particularly true of dishwashers, clothes driers and refrigerators, which now use 50% to 60% less energy than models manufactured just 10 years ago. If your major appliances are getting a bit long in the tooth, go shopping and check the energy-saving data posted on most new appliances. You may find it's cheaper to buy a new model than keep the old one running.

KEEPING YOUR SUMMERTIME COOL

Summer used to mean lower electric bills, but the age of air conditioning has changed that. However, it's still possible to keep your house cool — and your utility bills low — if you know what you're doing. Here's how:

* Buy an air conditioner with an EER (Energy Efficiency Rating) of at least 9 (out of a possible 12). The unit may cost more, but it will save as much as 10 cents an hour in energy costs, which will recoup the added expense in just 2 to 3 years.

* Get the right air conditioner for the space you want to cool. A unit that's too small will run itself to death and still not get the cooling job done, while a unit that's too large will cool too quickly and then shut down without removing all the humidity, which will leave the room feeling damp and clammy.

* Use a timer. That way, you can have the air conditioner switch on an hour before you get home, rather than leaving it on all day.

* Close outside vents when trying to cool a room, but open them when it's cooler outside than in.

* Keep the unit's temperature control at the highest comfortable setting. If you can live with 78 degrees instead of 72, you'll save about 40% on your cooling costs.

* Use airflow deflectors to aim cooled air toward the ceiling. It will then fall and improve circulation.

* Turn off lights when trying to cool a room; the bulbs give off heat.

* Raise the temperature setting at bedtime. Your body throws off less heat while you sleep, so you should be comfortable even if the room warms up a bit after you doze off.

* Take advantage of natural ventilation when possible. Open windows at night to let in cool air rather than running the air conditioner.

* Change filters regularly, and clean the outside intake vents at least once a month.

* Weather strip doors and windows, and close your fireplace damper.

* If the room being cooled has an outside wall that gets direct sunlight, close the drapes or blinds to reduce solar heating. Also consider installing awnings to help deflect the sun.

* Upgrade your attic insulation.

DON'T FORGET THE LOWLY FAN

Fans are much less expensive to operate than air conditioners — and will often cool a room just as well during normal summer weather conditioners. Here are some tips on getting the most cooling from your fans:

* Use windows to bring in cool air from the shady side of the house. All other windows should be closed — and shaded from sunlight with blinds and drapes.

* If a room has windows on two sides, face box fans outward on the hottest side and let them blow hot air out while simultaneously sucking in cooler air from open windows on the other side of the room.

* Attic fans can cool a whole house — but a doorway or other opening must allow the fan to pull air directly up from the rest of the house.

* Some attic fans turn off and on automatically when attic temperatures reach a certain level.

* Window fans are less powerful, but work fine for limited spaces.

* Portable box fans are effective for smaller areas, especially if you tilt them so they blow the cooler air toward the ceiling, where it will sink and recirculate.

NEW HIGH-TECH BULBS — SAME LIGHT, LESS MONEY

If you can bring yourself to pay as much as $20 for a single light bulb, new ones have recently been introduced that use a third the energy of standard bulbs and last 10 years or longer. At that rate, you'll offset the extra cost in about 2 years of standard use — and roll up big savings over the remaining life of the bulb. The new bulbs aren't available everywhere, so ask about them at your lighting store.

FLUORESCENT TUBES CAN ALSO LIGHTEN YOUR ELECTRIC BILL

Fluorescent lights won't last as long as the new long-life bulbs (only 3 to 4 years), but they can still produce substantial savings. Convert just 2 fixtures that use incandescent bulbs to fluorescent lighting, and you can save around $50 a year in electric costs (assuming you pay the national average of 14 cents per kilowatt hour) — which will quickly recoup the $20 cost of a typical tube. Fluorescent lights are best suited for high-use areas such as kitchens or dens, where they will be turned on at least 4 hours a day. Buying Tip: Fluorescent bulbs can often be purchased more cheaply and in a wider selection of sizes from mail-order companies. One firm that specializes in lighting accessories is B&B Ventures. For a catalog, call 516-822-2852.

BEWARE OF COSTLY PHONE-SERVICE CONTRACTS

Now that Ma Bell has been broken up and no longer keeps our phone system running smoothly at no cost, many of us have been conned into taking out so-called enhanced-service contracts — which purportedly pay for service calls for both phone lines and the phone itself. However, these contracts — which cost from $2 to $5 a month — aren't worth the money. Why? Well, if your phone problem is the result of a fault in the outside wiring — as about 40% of them are — the phone company is obligated to fix it anyway. And, if you own your own phone, all the service technician will do is identify it as the source of your problem — as is the case about 50% of the time. You'll have to pay to get it repaired or replaced yourself. Thus, you are really paying from $24 to $60 a year to protect yourself against the 10% possibility that your problem will be with the inside wiring. A better course of action is to use the money you'd spend on a service contract to buy a cheap phone with a modular jack that you can use as a "tester unit." Then, if you have trouble with your regular phone, you can merely unplug it and plug in the test phone. If it works, you'll know the problem is with the phone, not the wiring.

There's also a fairly simple device you can buy to protect against unneeded service calls (which can cost $50 to $75) related to wiring problems. It's called a "network interface" and it will tell you whether the wiring problem is internal or external. You merely plug a phone into the interface and listen — if you hear a dial tone, the problem is internal; if you don't, it's external. You can buy a network interface and installation materials at any phone-supply store or at Radio Shack. Added Advantage: If you find you have an internal wiring problem, you don't necessarily have to call the phone company technician. A private repairman can often do the job for half the cost.

PICKING THE BEST LONG-DISTANCE COMPANY

Despite all the advertisements on television, no single lost-distance company is best for everyone. Here are some tips on picking the one that's most economical for you:

* Review your old phone bills and find out your calling patterns — when you call most, where you call and how long you tend to talk. Then pick the company with a discount calling plan that best matches your pattern.

* If you don't make many long-distance calls, beware of carriers with a high minimum monthly charge or minimum usage requirements.

* If you make lots of calls, look for a company that offers volume discounts.

* Ask how the company calculates its billing times. Some companies

round off to the nearest whole minute, while others bill based on 6- or 10-second segments. If you make a lot of shorter calls, you can save as much as 10% by using a carrier that rounds off bills to the nearest 6-second time segment.

* Find out whether a company charges by distance or by service convenience. If you make a lot of calls to faraway places with limited phone access, a company that tacks on connection charges could be more expensive even if its base rate is lower than other companies.

* Make sure you get quality service for your money, even if you're paying less. Despite the ad claims, the various long-distance carriers still differ substantially in speed of connection, voice quality and line stability (important for data of fax transmissions).

* If you find problems, don't hesitate to switch again. Most carriers will pay the cost of having you switch your service to them, so it doesn't pay to stick with a company you don't like.

Our Choice as the Best: After studying and comparing the overall rates and various discount plans offered by the leading long-distance carriers, our research staff has determined that MCI provides the most economical service for the typical residential phone customer. Our research showed that, when making maximum use of the "Friends & Family" calling plan and limiting calls to off-peak hours, MCI customers could save 6% to 8% over the best Sprint rates and 10% to 12% over typical AT&T residential service prices.

WATER-SAVING TIPS THAT AREN'T ALL WET

Even if you're very thirsty, there a still lots of ways to save water and thereby trim your monthly bill. Here are 7 of the best ideas:

1. Put a weighted plastic container in the toilet tank to cut the amount of water used in flushing. (Note: Don't use a brick; it can damage the tank.)

2. Wash only full loads in your dishwasher and clothes washer.

3. Install low-flow showerheads, then take shorter showers.

4. Turn off the water while shaving, brushing teeth and washing hands; then turn it back on briefly to rinse.

5. Install new washers or replace faucets and connections that leak. A faucet that drips once every 10 seconds can waste up to 200 gallons of water a month.

6. Use buckets of water instead of a hose to wash the car.

7. When cleaning up the patio or driveway, don't use a hose in place of a broom.

B. Yard & Garden Yardsticks

BOOST YOUR HOME'S VALUE 10% WITH QUALITY LANDSCAPING

Few home improvements add to the resale value of a property more than landscaping — and even the smallest project can produce big dividends. A recent Gallup survey found that attractive landscaping adds 7 % to 14% to a home's value, so take a look at your yard and see where you can begin. Here are 7 guides to help you get the best return from sprucing up the exterior appearance of your place:

1. Don't try to do everything at once. Start by developing a master plan that you can implement over a period of several years. (Note: Don't feel like a plan locks you in; any strategy can be adjusted if your tastes or financial resources change.)

2. Remember that appearance isn't the only consideration. When choosing improvements, take into account the amount of time you will have to spend on maintenance. A typical 75- by 100-foot landscaped lot can require 20 to 40 hours of upkeep a month during the growing season. If you can't handle that, you'll have to use a gardener, most of whom charge $15 to $35 an hour. With major garden projects, water requirements are also an important factor, from both a cost and an availability standpoint.

3. Take advantage of low-cost help. Many garden centers offer free planning kits, complete with charts and a grid adaptable to your yards dimensions. You simply fill it out, and they suggest a plan for your budget. Many also have staff designers who will sketch an overview of your plan for under $100, or do a detailed schematic showing plants, pool and patio with exact measurements for under $500. Usually, the nursery will give you a rebate on later purchases to offset the design fees.

4. If you want a more professional job, garden designers and landscape architects usually charge from $50 to $120 an hour, though some will accept a percentage of the total project cost (usually 15% to 18%). For major jobs, get a couple of bids and compare costs. To find the best people in your area, write the American Society of Landscape Architects, 4401 Connecticut Ave. NW, Washington, D.C. 20008.

5. Use a home-equity credit line for financing. Interest rates on these have been running from 6.0% to 8.5% recently, and the interest is deductible. Since the value you're creating will go into the house equity, it only makes sense to use it to finance the job rather than draining your savings.

6. Consider a gazebo, waterfall or other permanent element. These types of improvements provide a much bigger payback than plants or trees, which could vanish with a stretch of drought, cold weather or poor maintenance.

7. Don't "out-landscape" your home's value. A $200,000 house in a neighborhood of $200,000 houses can't support a $50,000 garden. About the most you can hope to raise the value of your house with landscaping is 15%, so it's a good idea not to spend more than about 10% of its value on any project if you want to come out ahead.

CATALOG SHOPPING CAN HOE DOWN GARDEN COSTS

The cheapest landscaping is that done with plants. However, many homeowners are deter red by the high cost and limited selection of plants and seeds. Fortunately, a full range of flowers, vegetables, trees and shrubs — as well as most gardening and landscaping supplies — can be purchased more inexpensively by mail. Here are 12 of the best mail-order catalogs that you can get for free:

* Breck's, Peoria, IL 61632. Dutch tulip, crocus and other bulbs.

* W. Atlee Burpee Co., 2103 Burpee Building, Warminster, PA 19874. Many varieties of vegetables and flowers.

* Henry Field's Seed & Nursery, 1008 Oak St., Shenandoah, IA 51602. 100 pages of fruits and vegetables.

* Jackson & Perkins Co., Medford, OR 97501. Bulbs, trees and a wide variety of roses.

* J.W. Jung Seed Co., Randolf, WI 53956. Trees, flowers and vegetables.

* Earl May Seed Co., Shenandoah, IA 51603. Tomatoes, midget vegetables.

* J.E. Miller Nurseries, 510 West Lake Rd., Canandaigua, NY 14424. Fruit trees, vines and berries.

* Musser, Box 53N-A, Indiana, PA 15701. Fine-quality tree seedlings.

* Olds Seed Co., Box 7790, Madison, WI 53707. Flowers from A to Z.

* George W. Park Seed Co., 410 Cokesbury Rd., Greenwood, SC 29647. Complete garden supplies.

* Stokes' Seed Catalog, 1733 Stokes Building, Buffalo, NY 14240. Everything.

* Vermont Bean Seed Co., Garden Lane, Bomoseen, VT 05732. Vegetables. If you want something more exotic — such as antique roses or heirloom plants, which are the latest rage in garden planning — a couple of good low-cost catalogs are available from:

* Antique Rose Emporium, Box 143, Route 5, Brenham, TX 77833; $5.00.

* Seeds Blum, Idaho City Stage, Boise, ID 83706; $3.00. You may also want some reference guides, such as:

* "Gardening by Mail," by Barbara J. Barton (Houghton Mifflin), $16.95 at your local bookstore, provides a wide-ranging review of mail-order landscaping materials, from antique applies to wildflower seeds.

* "Get Ready, Get Set, Grow," a gardening video aimed at both parents and kids, is available by mail for $33.70. Call the Brooklyn Botanic Garden at 718-941-4044 to order.

HOLDING A SUCCESSFUL YARD (OR GARAGE) SALE

If you've lived in the same place for more than a year or two, you have probably accumulated a lot of things you don't need or use. And, a good way to dispose of it — and make a little cash to boot — is with a yard or garage sale. After all, one man's trash is another man's treasure. However, if you want your sale to be a success, there are several key rules to follow:

* Prepare. Set up tables or create shelves by stretching boards across boxes so that everything can be neatly displayed. Stacks and piles make the merchandise look like it was poorly maintained, discouraging buyers.

* Wash all clothes and dishes and dust (or even polish) larger items and furniture pieces. Clean items look better cared for and bring higher prices.

* Put price tags on everything. People are less likely to bid for an item or buy on impulse if they have to guess about the price you'll take.

* Make your prices reasonable. Remember, though something may have been special to you, it's just another piece of used merchandise to someone else. Even new items still in the original packaging must be marked down substantially or you'll wind up still having them after the sale is over.

* Be willing to bargain. This is part of the garage-sale game and, if you don't play, you'll wind up hauling a lot of stuff back to the basement.

* Play any radios or televisions that work well, and have an extension cord hooked up and run to the sale area so people can test thermostat electrical items to make sure they work. It's also a good idea to have a tape measure handy and, if you have lots of large items, a hand-truck to help people get furniture or boxes to their cars.

* If an appliance doesn't work, don't expect to get more than a dollar or two for it — regardless of how much it cost new.

* Start your sale early. If most sales in your area start at 8, open yours at 7. You want to catch people while they still have money and haven't had time to comparison shop. Veteran garage-sale shoppers get up early to find the best merchandise, so you won't have to worry about a lack of customers.

* Have lots of change — both bills and coins — on hand. You may also want to buy a bundle of paper bags so people will have something in which to carry their purchases.

* Consider closing early. Experts say 90% of all sales are made by noon, so you may be wasting your time by staying open till 5 or 6.

Liability Tip: Your homeowner's policy will usually protect you against injury claims by shoppers at an occasional garage sale. However, if you hold sales often, you may need a special liability rider. If you have any doubts about your coverage, read your policy or check with your insurance agent before you hold the sale.

...AND FINDING BARGAINS AT SOMEBODY ELSE'S

Most people who go to garage sales do so for the social contact and entertainment value as much as for the potential bargains. As a result, they often wind up with closets, attics or basements full of lava lamps, rusty tools and almost-new items with no apparent function at all. However, if you really are interested in getting bargain merchandise, a yard or garage sale can be a good source — if you're careful.

7 Rules for Yard-Sale Buyers:

1. Arrive early. If the ad or sign says the sale starts at 9 a.m., get there at 8:30. If you don't make it until 9:30, most of the good stuff will have been snapped up by antique dealers, second-hand store owners and more-experienced garage-sale shoppers.

2. Don't even look at things you don't need. Keep a list of tools, appliances, sporting equipment and other household goods you can really use — and buy only things on your list.

3. If you are shopping for appliances or electronics equipment, make sure you know enough about retail pricing and product performance to determine if something really is a good buy.

4. Don't buy items that don't work unless you know you can fix them yourself. It's usually cheaper to buy new than fix the old — which is probably why the item is being sold rather than repaired in the first place.

5. Even if you can do minor repairs, an item might not be a good buy — simply because you are far less likely to get around to fixing them than you might think you are.

6. Always bargain. A good rule of thumb is to offer 50% of the asking price (assuming it's reasonable) and try to reach a consensus from there.

7. Carry a wad of $1 bills and a pocketful of change. Getting someone to sell you a $10 power drill for $4 is a lot harder when you 're flashing a roll of $20 bills.

LOW-COST DIRECTORY OF HOUSEHOLD HINTS

Having problems figuring out the best way to build, maintain, repair, clean or plant something around your house, garage, yard or garden? Chances are the answer you're seeking is among the nearly 700 helpful tips featured in a recently published, low-cost household hints book. To order a copy, send $6.95 to The Sure Shopper Guide, Inc., Box 26, Beech Grove, IN 46107.

C. This Ol' House Needs Repairs

HOME IMPROVEMENTS THAT PAY FOR THEMSELVES

It's always nice to make your home a more comfortable or more attractive place to live, but you should do most home remodeling or upgrading because you want those benefits — not because you hope to make money on them when you sell. Only a few popular home improvements actually return more in increased resale value than it costs to make them. Here are 15 popular improvements, with an estimate of how much of the expense you can expect to recover when you sell (figures are based on return per $100 of cost):

1. Central air conditioning — $115.

2. Exterior landscaping, including a gazebo or other permanent improvements as well as flowers and shrubs — $112.

3. An interior facelift, including carpets, paint and wallpaper — $109.

4. Bathroom remodeling, including new toilet, tub (or shower tile), vanity, flooring and faucets — $95.

5. Fireplace — $94.

6. Addition of a two car garage — $90.

7. Finishing the basement — $86.

8. Kitchen remodel, including new appliances — $86.

9. Exterior paint and trim — $82.

10. A new furnace — $81.

11. Addition of an outside deck — $75.

12. Attic conversion to add two rooms with closets and addition of double-hung windows — $55

13. Room addition, including finishing, decorating and carpet — $53.

14. An in-ground swimming pool — $35.

15. Vinyl siding and/or awnings — $31.

5 WAYS TO SAVE UP TO 60% ON HOME REMODELING

Even though many home-improvement costs are totally or partially recoverable on resale, the cost of making those improvements can still be a strain on your budget. However, there are several ways to reduce the price shock and still get the results you want:

1. Do some of the work yourself. By either handling preparatory work or finishing work on a major project, you can often save up to 60% of the total cost of having a contractor do all the work for you. Caution: If you opt to do the preparation, make sure you consult with the contractor first and do the work to his specifications. If he comes in and has to redo something you have messed

up, your costs could go up rather than down.

2. Arrange to buy all materials for the job yourself. Many contractors have arrangements with building-supply companies to use their materials on jobs. They get a discount on the supplies, but charge you the full retail price. By shopping for your own lumber, concrete and other supplies, you can usually find discounts of up to 20% to 25% over full retail price.

3. Combine improvements with insurance repair work. If you have storm or fire damage that is going to be paid for by your insurance company, you can often get a discount on additional jobs performed by the same contractor at the same time. He saves because his crews and equipment will already be on site — and also because he has no sales or marketing costs. Thus, he can afford to pass savings on to you.

4. Make sure your remodeling costs are deductible — i.e., that they can be added to the cost basis of your house, so that your taxable gain will be reduced when you eventually sell the property. This can return up to 43% of the improvement cost, depending on the state in which you live.

5. Get written bids from at least 3 contractors. Prices can vary by 25% or more.

HOME IMPROVEMENT COSTS YOU CAN DEDUCT

Almost any type of home improvement can be deductible (when you eventually sell the house) so long as it meets one simple requirement: It must add to the value of the house, not just maintain its existing condition. However, the IRS can sometimes be pretty picky about improvement claims, so it's a good idea to understand the distinction between improvement and simple repair. Here are some examples:

* Planting new trees as part of a landscaping project is deductible; replacing a dead tree is not.

* Putting up a new fence is deductible; replacing boards in the old fence is not.

* Adding a new fireplace is deductible; rebricking or stuccoing an old one is not.

* Carpeting an uncarpeted room is deductible; cleaning or replacing an old carpet is not.

* Adding a room is deductible; painting an old room is not. (However, if you add built-ins or paneling to an existing room, it is deductible.)

* Paving a dirt or gravel drive is deductible; patching an existing concrete or asphalt drive is not.

Exception: If you can show that normal repairs and maintenance items were done specifically to ready a house for sale, they can be deducted. However, the house must be sold within 90 days of the repairs for them to count, which can be a problem in today's slow real estate market.

Conversion Trick: It's possible to convert normal maintenance items into deductible items by upgrading. For example, if you have a leaky roof, you can replace the existing asphalt shingles with more expensive and desirable wooden shakes, thus turning your non-deductible repair into a deductible improvement. Likewise, if you texture coat or add siding instead of just painting, you turn a maintenance item into a deductible expense. Even some appliance repairs can be converted. For example, if your 40-gallon water heater breaks down, you can replace it with a 100-gallon model and deduct the difference in cost.

8 RULES FOR DEALING WITH REMODELERS

Since home remodeling is not something you do everyday, you probably don't have an established relationship with a contractor you can trust. However, there are a number of ways to protect yourself, even if you're forced to deal with someone you don't know:

1. Make sure the remodeler is licensed if your state or city requires it. (A check with the local building department will confirm if licenses are needed for different types of jobs.)

2. Show any complex contracts to a lawyer.

3. Write void across any blank spaces in the contract.

4. Make sure the contractor has liability insurance. Many jobs, especially exterior painting, require ladders or scaffolds, which can be dangerous to both workers and curious children or passersby.

5. Before signing any work completion certificate, make sure the contractor has paid off all subcontractors and material suppliers.

6. The contract should include a payment schedule. Usually, 10% of the fee is payable upon signing of the contract, with partial payments due on completion of specific stages of the job. For your protection, the contractor should not have earned his profit until all work is finished.

7. Don't pay in full until completely satisfied — and all work has been approved by building inspectors.

8. Don't pay cash.

7 TRICKS CONTRACTORS USE TO RIP YOU OFF

In spite of the above-listed precautions, many people still get taken by less-than-honest remodelers. Here are a few of the ways a contractor can rip you off — and what you should do to protect yourself:

1. Making verbal promises, then putting something different in the contract on the assumption you won't read it closely or recognize the switch if you do. Protect yourself by demanding all conditions be put in writing, and then read the contract carefully, making any corrections before putting out any money.

2. Using substandard or lower-grade materials. Make sure all material grades are detailed in the contract, and specify brand names where applicable (paints, blinds, appliances, etc.)

3. Stretching out your job in order to take on other work. Specify a completion date, not just a time schedule. If your job must be done by a given date, demand a financial penalty clause for any late work.

4. False guarantees. Some contracts will say the work is guaranteed, but will specify in the contract that only manufacturers' guarantees apply and that his work is not covered. Again, read the contract closely and make sure that exact remedies are spelled out should you be dissatisfied or if materials or workmanship prove defective.

5. Blaming problems or delays on subcontractors. Make sure the contract has a clause making the lead contractor responsible for all work and scheduling, even if it includes services provided by subcontractors. He should also be responsible for any negligence by subcontractors or liability arising out of their actions. You don't want a subcontractor or one of his creditors coming back to you for payment or damages, rather than going to the lead contractor. (You may need a lawyer to help write some of these clauses if the contractor's standard form doesn't include them.)

6. Failure to clean up after the job. This can add several hundred dollars to your cost if you have to have it done by someone else, so make sure the contract ensures that the remodeler will handle it.

7. Attaching a lien on your home in the event of a dispute. Many contractors will use the threat of a lien to force you into paying for cost overruns or other problems. However, you can protect yourself by making sure the original contract has an arbitration clause, which requires a third-party ruling in any dispute, and bars imposition of a lien without one.

ADDITIONAL NOTES ON REMODELING CONTRACTS

Here are a few more protective tips regarding home-improvement contracts:

* You don't need a lawyer to amend or modify the contract. Simply take a separate piece of paper and write: "Notwithstanding anything else in this contract to the contrary, we agree as follows..." Then spell out the contract changes. Of course, both you and the contractor must sign the modification.

* The contract should spell out how changes in terms or specifications will be made. It's best to require that all changes over $100 be agreed to in writing by both parties.

* For large jobs, you might want a clause saying what damages you'll pay if you cancel a job before work begins. However, don't break off a project once work begins; courts usually favor contractors in such cases.

When to Renegotiate: Don't try to hold a contractor to unreasonable terms. If he doesn't walk off the job, he'll probably cut corners or stall. If unforeseen problems run his costs beyond his estimate, be willing to renegotiate.

FURNACE REPLACEMENT GUIDELINES

Your furnace is one of the biggest energy users in your home — but it's also one of the most expensive items to replace. Here's a 3-step formula to help you decide whether it will be worthwhile for you to buy a new furnace:

1. Estimate your annual fuel bills.

2. Divide the efficiency rating of your furnace by the rating of a new model.

3. Multiply this by your annual fuel bill to figure savings. A new furnace should recoup its costs in 5 to 7 years.

DOES YOUR HOUSE NEED A SECURITY SYSTEM?

Alarm equipment and installation is expensive — and you may not even need a security system if you take some basic precautions. The insurance industry has just issued a FREE brochure that tells you how to "case" your home the same way a burglar would — and provides tips on how to make it harder for thieves to get in and out. For a copy, send a stamped, self-addressed, business-sized envelope to the Insurance Information Institute, Publication Service

Center, 110 William St ., New York, NY 10038.

D. Giving So It Doesn't Hurt

THE RIGHT WAY TO MAKE CHARITABLE DONATIONS

One of the things that makes our country great is the willingness of Americans to help those less fortunate than themselves. Unfortunately, America is also populated by a great number of people who are merely interested in helping themselves — at your expense. And, charity scams are among their most popular tools. So, with nearly half a million organizations clamoring for your donations, how do you pick the ones most deserving of your dollars? Here are some tips:

* The large, well-known organizations tend to be the safest bet — the recent United Way administrative pay scandal notwithstanding . In fact, agencies that monitor charities say United Way has fully cleaned up its act and is now a worthy recipient for your donations.

* Older, more established charities tend to get more of your money where you want it to go. New organizations have higher start-up, administrative and fund-raising costs, which leaves less money available for the cause the charity is set up to support.

* Check a charity's financial statement before giving, or request a copy of the group's IRS Form 990, which all tax-exempt organizations are required to file. What you want to know is how the money raised is allocated. The best charities spend at least 75% of the money raised on "program services" (the cause), and 25% or less on fund raising and administration — the other two legitimate expenses incurred by charitable groups. Newer charities, or those with hard-to-administer causes, may spend as little as 50% on services, which is alright. However, if a charity spends less than 50% of your money on program services, you probably shouldn't give them your cash in the first place.

* Check administrative salaries. Even when a charity spends most of its money on the stated cause, you could still be supporting fairly lavish life-styles on the part of those running the organization. A recent survey found that 1 in 5 top executives of leading U.S. charities makes more than $200,000 a year. Some of these people are obviously worth it, based on the amount of money they raise each year. However, others aren't. A good benchmark: The charity's

top executive should make no more than 0.25% of the total funds raised each year.

* Beware of word games. For example, some charities try to pass "public education" off as a program service, when it should actually be a fund-raising expense. Make sure you look at the programs you're funding, not just at the words in the solicitation.

* If a solicitor comes to your door, ask for a copy of his local permit. Legitimate door-to-door charities have copies printed for your use in checking them out.

* Never make donations over the phone if you have to give out your credit card number. Instead, make a pledge and have the solicitor send you a bill for the pledge amount, along with supportive materials documenting the legitimacy of the charity.

4 WAYS TO SPOT A CHARITY SCAM

There's no perfect way to spot a bogus solicitation, but there are several things to watch out for :

1. Charities that use high-pressure sales tactics. One popular trick is offering to send a messenger to your home to pick up the donation, or asking you to send your contribution by overnight or priority mail. If a charity is legitimate, it will be willing to wait for your money. The only ones who need it right now are the ones planning to split with it.

2. Charities that refuse to provide annual reports or financial statements. Getting such a report is no guarantee that a charity is legitimate, but having your request for one refused is almost certainly a guarantee that the charity is bogus.

3. Charities that disguise their appeal as a bill or invoice, making it appear that you have already committed to give. This practice is illegal — but it's still used frequently by scam artists, especially on elderly people, who may not remember whether or not they made a commitment.

4. Charities that send out products, such as Christmas cards, with their solicitations. While this is not illegal, it is a blatant attempt to shame you into making a donation — and it is also frequently used by scam artists, who think (rightly so) that you're more likely to assume their cause is legitimate if you get something from them.

A Legal Rip-Off: Many legitimate charities have formed affiliations with credit-card issuers for so-called "affinity" cards. These deals give the charity a percentage of the purchase value every time you use the credit card to buy something. However, they are a bad deal for you, because:

* The cards usually have very high interest rates and annual fees, which more than offset the amount donated to the charity.

* The sponsoring charity usually gets only half a percent (0.5%) of the purchase value, which means very little of your money is going to the cause.

* The IRS considers these rebate deals, rather than contributions — and doesn't allow deductions for them. (For more information about the tax deductibility of charitable donations, see Chapter 15, Tax Secrets & Traps.)

FIND OUT MORE ABOUT YOUR CHARITY

If you have questions about any charity, there are three good sources for detailed information on legitimate organizations and early warnings about potential scams:

1. IRS Publication 78, "Cumulative List of Organizations," is an annual listing of thousands of tax-exempt groups to which donations are deductible. To request a copy, call 1-800-829-3676.

2. The National Charities Information Bureau publishes an annual "Wise Giving Guide," which rates 400 leading U.S. organizations. For a copy, write to NCIB, 10 Union Square West, Dept. 145, New York, NY 10003.

3. The Philanthropic Advisory Service is an arm of the Council of Better Business Bureaus that publishes an annual report called "Give but Give Wisely," which reviews 300 U.S. charities. To get a copy, send a check for $2 to Council of Better Business Bureaus, 4200 Wilson Blvd., Arlington, VA 22203. PAS also publishes free reports on individual charities that you can request by calling 70 3-276-0100.

HELPING YOUR CAUSE — AND YOUR HEIRS

As many people get older, they find they would like to make substantial donations to favorite charities. Unfortunately, they usually feel they can't do so without depriving their heirs of their rightful inheritances. However, there is a way to make a substantial donation to charity — and actually increase the potential benefits to your surviving family members. Here's how it works:

Assume you are 65 years old and live in California, which subjects you to a maximum combined (state and federal) income tax of 41.2 5%. You have a portfolio of tax-exempt bonds and growth stocks worth approximately $200,000.

You would like to give your holdings to a special charity, but you are afraid you will need at least some income from your portfolio and you also want to leave an ample inheritance for your two grown children. Given this situation, your first step is to have an attorney establish what is known as a charitable remainder trust, funded with the $200,000 in securities — which will go to the charity upon your death. (Note: If you are married, the trust can be set up to last until the death of both you and your spouse.) Prior to your death, however, the income from the trust will be used to finance an annuity that will give you a guaranteed annual income. The attorney will determine the actual payout arrangement, based on your age and life expectancy — but, for the sake of our example, we'll say it would amount to 6.0%, or $12,000 a year, a quite reasonable performance expectation for the portfolio.

This arrangement will give you a charitable tax deduction of approximately $85,620 (depending on the federal discount rate at the time the trust is established), which will produce a cash tax savings of roughly $35,320. However, rather than taking this tax savings, you use it to fund a second trust, with your children as beneficiaries. This trust uses the funds to purchase a single-payment insurance policy on your life (or a "universal survivorship policy" on the lives of you and your spouse), which will provide a tax-free death benefit to your children of around $286,735.

By taking these steps, you have accomplished three things:

* You have made a $200,000 gift to your favorite charity.

* You have ensured an annual income flow of $12,000 for the remainder of your life.

* You have guaranteed an inheritance for your children totaling $286,735 — which, by the way, is more than triple the after-estate -tax sum (roughly $90,000) they would have received had you done nothing but leave them the $200,000 in securities.

Who says you can't beat the system!

E. Fun & Leisure With Limited Funds

33 LOW-COST WAYS TO HAVE FUN

Okay, so maybe the best things in life aren't really free — but fun certainly doesn't have to be expensive. Here are some cheap — and wholesome — "thrills" you or your family might enjoy:

1. Play tourist in your own city.
2. Serve yourself breakfast in bed.
3. Study a foreign language.
4. Try a gourmet recipe.
5. Join a choir or drama club.
6. Investigate your local public library.
7. Explore your county's back roads.
8. Visit friends across town or in a neighboring city.
9. Eat in, but have dessert and coffee out.
10. Go to a discount movie matinee.
11. Attend free or low-priced public lectures.
12. Go for an afternoon stroll.
13. Row a low-priced rental boat on the local lake.
14. Pull out some favorite board games.
15. Walk on the beach and collect seashells.
16. Go to free public concerts.
17. Have a pot-luck dinner.
18. Start a do-it-yourself project.
19. Join a debating society or political club.
20. Play poker for pennies or toothpicks.
21. Go on a picnic.
22. Go window shopping.
23. Check out early-bird restaurant dinner specials.
24. Dress up for a formal, candle-lit dinner at home.
25. Go backpacking or camping.
26. Check out the local art galleries.
27. Start a window-box herb garden.

28. Watch airport takeoffs and landings.

29. Stroll through a low-admission amusement park.

30. Go to the racetrack without betting — or bet $2.

31. Go to a local school athletic event.

32. Play tennis at public courts.

33. Rummage through a used-book store.

DEDUCTING THE COST OF YOUR HOBBY

One of things that increases the enjoyment of life for many people is a hobby, be it gardening, model railroading, collecting or some other activity. Unfortunately, many hobbies tend to be a major drain on your budget. However, with a little planning, you can turn your hobby into a business — at least for tax purposes — and get Uncle Sam to help pay for your leisure-time pleasure. Here are some tips on qualifying your hobby as a business, with tax-deductible expenses.

* The key test for a business is whether your motive is to make a profit. Thus, if can you structure your hobby so that you can show a profit in 3 out of any 5 consecutive years, the IRS will generally not question any expenses you deduct. If you don't show a profit in 3 out of 5 years, you may still be able to deduct expenses — but, if the IRS challenges them, you will have to prove your intent was to make a profit, even though you failed.

* One way to provide this proof is to run your hobby in a business-like manner. Register your business by filing a "dba (doing business as) statement" with your county clerk's office, keep accurate books and records, set up a business bank account, get a separate business phone line and a listing in the Yellow Pages, have cards and stationery printed, and place an occasional ad in a local newspaper.

* It's important to show some income, even if you don't make a profit. Thus, you need to either sell some of your hobby items occasionally — or arrange to speak or serve as a consultant in order to generate some fee income related to your specialty.

* Associate yourself with other professionals in the same field. Join a professional association. Maintain a client and prospect list of contacts you have made in your business. Keep records to show that you have consulted with experts about your business — and taken their advice.

* Revise your business procedures or adopt some new ones every few

years to demonstrate that your are trying to correct problems that led to your past losses.

Bonus for Collectors: If your hobby involves collecting items of value or restoring collectibles, you can show a loss in more than 2 out of 5 years and still qualify as a business if you can demonstrate that your holdings (the assets of your business) are expected to appreciate in value.

COLLECTING ANTIQUES ON A BARGAIN BUDGET

Most people interested in antiques shy away from one of the best ways of shopping for them — auctions. With this survival guide you'll be able to buy quality items for much less than dealer prices:

1. Inspect the items at the pre-sale exhibition. Bring a flashlight and tape measure.

2. Check out wooden furniture carefully, looking for patches and repairs with different kinds of wood.

3. If you're interested in something, ask the attendant how much it's likely to go for.

4. You don't actually have to attend the auction. You can just decide on your maximum bid and submit it in advance. If a piece isn't' t bid up to your price, your bid will prevail.

5. You should know: "Antique" means that an object is 100 years old or older. "Style" means "influenced" or "in the manner of." It doesn't mean an object is from a particular period.

6. You'll do better during slow months at auction houses — June, July, August and December.

7. All sales are final, and bidders are responsible for any errors they make. Don't be over-eager.

...AND INCREASING THEIR VALUE WITH RESTORATION

More and more folks are trying their hand at antique restoration. It's not only an enjoyable hobby, but can be a very profitable one. Here are a few books — available from libraries and book stores — to help get you started on the road to fine craftsmanship:

* A. Lucas, "Antiques, Their Restoration and Preservation," London, 1932.

* John Fitzmaurice Mills, "The Care of Antiques," New York, Hastings House, 1964.

* Thomas H. Ormsbee, "Care and Repair of Antiques," New York, Medill McBride Co., 1949.

* George Savage, "The Art and Antique Restorer's Handbook," New York, Praeger, 1967.

* Frederick Taubes, "Restoring and Preserving Antiques," New York, Watson-Guptill, 1963.

THE INS & OUTS OF RARE (AND COMMON) COINS

Coin collecting is one of the world's most popular hobbies — and it's also big business. In recent years, speculators have turned what was once a steady coin market into a highly volatile one. However, despite the risk, the investment rewards can be huge — U.S. gold coins outperformed all other investments, including stocks, in the 1980s. That's why some of the big brokerage firms — Merrill-Lynch, Kidder Peabody and others — have started coin portfolios (shares are sold to individual investors much as with a mutual fund). Thus, if you are a casual collector, you might do well to convert your hobby into a more serious interest. Here are some guidelines to ensure you do it right:

1. The more you learn, the less your chances of buying junk.

2. Read coin collectors' newsletters for the latest prices.

3. Get to know coin dealers; ask questions and listen.

4. Gradually wean yourself away from their advice by attending coin shows and auctions and reading up on the subject in professional journals.

5. Sell some of your coins every year. If you get more than you paid, you're a good investor. If not, change your methods.

6. As you become more knowledgeable, you'll probably find one area that particularly interests you. Take advantage of this by specializing in that area, and gradually sell off your lesser-quality coins and those from areas you're no longer collecting.

7. Protect your collection. Copper coins, for instance, can turn green over time, simply from being kept in plastic holders. If you're interested in finding out more about coin collecting — particularly from an investment standpoint, Winvest Inc., one of the West Coast's most respected dealers in investment-grade coins, offers a free consumer's guide to the rare coin market. To request a

copy, call 1-800-346-8378.

GUN COLLECTING ISN'T JUST FOR BIG SHOTS

Firearms have been around for 700 years — and people have been collecting them for just as long. Here are 8 pointers for modern gun collectors:

1. Pick a period and region, then specialize — even down to a single gun series.

2. Learn the finer points; workmanship can be of museum quality.

3. Study the history of your period, and then the background of the gun-makers.

4. Paired firearms are worth more than singles.

5. Miniature guns are a worthwhile specialty, with their own collector societies.

6. Take good care of your collection — especially taking precautions against rust.

7. Black powder is still available for shooting antique weapons, but don't do it! Firing corrodes metal and scars wood.

8. You don't need a license to own firearms made before 1898.

THE WHOLE STORY ABOUT BOOK COLLECTING

Few things can provide more pleasure than a good book — and, if you're willing to concentrate on rare titles or first editions instead of paperbacks, collecting books can prove both a rewarding and profitable hobby. However, few collectibles are more fragile than books when it comes to preserving value. Here are 4 tips to make sure you don't damage your valuable books:

* A faded cover can cut a book's value by one-third, so keep your collection away from direct sunlight.

* Excess heat and dry air can cause book pages to curl or become brittle. Keep your valuable volumes in a cool room and monitor humidity levels.

* Dust particles can scratch covers and discolor pages. Keep your books clean by storing them in an enclosed case.

* Books are meant to be read — but valuable books should always be

handled with care. Don't use colored bookmarks that might bleed onto the pages, and never lay a book face-down — it cracks the binding, which can instantly cut a volume's value in as much as half.

ART'S NOT ART IF YOU DON'T LIKE IT

You don't have to be a wealthy investor to collect art. There are plenty of affordable pieces out there — from prints and etchings to lithographs and antique oils. However, you should never buy any piece of art just because you think it's a good investment. Collect only what appeals to you — and then take the time to learn all you can about the style and the artists that dominate that particular field. If you'd like to collect art the right way, here's how to get started:

1. Visit museums, shows and galleries, looking for artists and styles you like.

2. Talk to the museum curators or gallery owners, asking about various artists and recent prices. If you find a gallery that specializes in something or someone you like, get to know the owner so you'll be able to trust his or her advice.

3. Make an inexpensive first purchase. Paintings and prints are more popular, but you'll probably find better buys in drawings and sculpture. An artist's early works are often cheaper.

4. Avoid the styles that are currently in vogue — their prices will be higher because of the interest. Instead, try to anticipate the next trend.

5. Whenever you travel, visit galleries in other cities and find out what's hot there that might be due to catch on in your area.

6. Attend auctions and make bids. Dealers do — then they double the prices to their customers. Why not avoid the middleman?

7. If an artist you like is still hard at work, try making contact. The work of most popular artists is consigned to galleries before it's even finished — but if it's not, you'll get the best price buying direct from the source.

8. Don't buy prints from mail-order offerings. Investment potential is minimal.

9. If you're collecting for profit, don't get married to your artwork. Put a piece up for sale every so often, especially if you feel the artist or style is about to lose popularity. On the other hand, if you're collecting for love, don't feel like you must sell something just to justify the investment value of your collection.

BASEBALL CARDS ARE MORE THAN KID STUFF

In the 1950s, when most baby boomers were in their pre-teen years, baseball cards were just fun items that came along with some rather good bubble gum. No more! In recent sales, single cards have gone for as much as $12 ,000 (Honus Wagner, 1910), and the line-up of cards selling for more than $2,000 is growing every year. In other words, baseball-card collecting is now big business — which also makes it prime territory for rip-off artists. As with any specialized hobby, however, you can protect yourself with a few simple steps:

* Know your subject. Card shops also carry books that both picture and describe the most valuable cards in detail, with tips on judging condition and potential availability. The major dealers also have comprehensive catalogs you can use as pricing guides.

* Deal only with reputable card shops or, if you're at the higher end of the market, established auction houses. Beware of special deals you find at card shows, flea markets and other uncontrolled public sales. Counterfeiters love working these events.

* Start off on a limited basis with lower-priced cards. Then, as you become more knowledgeable, you can begin trading up, specialize in a given era or develop some other plan to make your collection special (such as going for complete teams from notable years).

* Remember that your cards are worth only what someone is willing to pay for them. If the hobby wanes in popularity, your collection could go down dramatically in value. For that reason, collect because you enjoy it and the tradition surrounding the sport of baseball, not because you're looking to make a killing.

SIGNING UP FOR THE AUTOGRAPH MARKET

Autograph collecting is another hobby that has become big business in recent years, with some better specimens going for $100,000 and more, particularly when attached to special documents, letters or photographs. Stores have even sprung up in several upscale malls around the country dealing in beautifully displayed and framed packages containing historical documents with notable signatures and photos or drawings. Key collecting categories include historical figures (signers of the Declaration of Independence are most valuable), presidents, movie stars from the 1920s and '30s, sports figures (mostly baseball players and boxers) and even noted criminals. As with baseball cards, knowledge of your subject area and association with reputable dealers or collecting associations are your best protections. Two good collector support groups are:

* The Manuscript Society, 429 Daisy Ave., Pasadena, CA 91107.

* The Universal Autograph Collectors Club, Box 467, Rockville Centre, NY 11571. Some leading dealers include:

* Archives & Historical Autographs, 119 Chestnut Hill, Wilton, CT 06897.

* Cambridge-Essex Stamp Co., 500 Eighth Ave., New York, NY 10018.

* Edmunds Book Shop, 6658 Hollywood Blvd., Hollywood, CA 90028.

* Charles Hamilton & Co., 25 E. 77th St., New York, NY 10021.

* Lion Hoart Autographs, 12 W. 37th St., New York, NY 10018.

* James Lowe Autographs, 30 E. 60th St., New York, NY 10022.

* Kenneth W. Rendell Inc., 154 Wells Ave., Newton, MA 02159.

* The Scriptorium, 427 N. Canon Drive, Beverly Hills, CA 90210.

THROWING DARTS FOR FUN — AND PROFIT

Dart games, once found almost exclusively in British pubs, have become extremely popular in bars and taverns throughout America — and for good reason. The games are easy to learn, no special physical skills are required to play and anyone can be a winner with a little practice. In addition, though most state laws prohibit such activity, throwing darts has become almost as popular for casual wagering as pool. Here are 10 pointers to help you enjoy this fast-growing activity:

1. Start with brass darts with a one-piece plastic shaft and flight. They're big, but light and easy to handle. As your skill improves, move up to tungsten darts, which are heavier, narrower and slightly harder to control.

2. Pressed bristle board targets are best. Cork and wood are cheaper, but don't wear as well.

3. To improve hand/eye coordination, keep your head still as your eyes fix on the target.

4. Throw with your forearm, not your entire body.

5. Keep the follow-through fluid after the dart leaves your hand. Don't jerk your arm back.

6. If you tend to throw left — like most beginners — you can aim right or move right on the toe line.

7. Where to aim: the triple 20 and the outer double ring.

8. Shake your opponent's hand before and after play.

9. Remove your darts from the board promptly.

10. Be silent when others are shooting.

HOW WINNERS CASH IN ON CONTESTS

Many people make a hobby out of entering contests — and, if you do it right, it can be a very profitable pastime. After all, there are nearly 1,000 national or regional contests every year in the United States, giving away an estimated $150 million in cash and merchandise prizes. How do you get your share of this bounty? Here are some tips from the pros who edit the Contest Newsletter (Fern Beach, FL), the nation's largest circulation publication devoted strictly to contests:

* Enter early and often. Monitor newspapers, magazines, junk mail and store displays for announcements of new contests. Then send in 2 or 3 entries per day for short contests and a couple a week for longer ones. The more you enter, the better your chances of winning. In addition, by spreading your entries out, you improve your chances if the contest is one where a few finalists are drawn from each day's mail receipts.

* Follow the rules precisely. Since you won't be able to use an official entry form every time, you'll have to make your own — and you want to make them right. If the rules say a 3x5 card, make it exactly 3x5. If the rules say "print" your name, don't write it out or type it. The smallest mistake can be grounds for disqualification.

* Don't bother with contests that have prizes you don't want or will have trouble selling, unless you can opt for taking the cash equivalent. Remember, you will have to pay taxes on the value of your prize, and you don't want to have to deplete your savings to pay for something you don't want and can't sell.

* If you do win, check with your accountant about how to determine the taxable value of your prize, which can vary depending on whether you keep it, sell it or give it away. Remember, too, that you can deduct all your contest entry expenses for the year in which you won against the value of the prize.

* If you have special talents — such as writing, drawing, cooking, etc. — focus your efforts on contests that require those skills. Fewer people enter skill-based contests, so your chances of winning are better.

* Keep up with what's going on by subscribing to contest newsletters or joining a local contest club. Both will help you with strategies, warn you about problems or trick contests and alert you to new opportunities.

STRATEGIES FOR SWEEPSTAKES SUCCESS

A sweepstakes is a special kind of contest, based strictly on the luck of the draw. However, you can improve your odds of having an entry drawn if you use these 3 simple tricks:

* If entries are drawn from a bag, carton or drum, make yours easier to grab hold of by folding it diagonally or in accordion style . This creates more edges and exposes more surface area to a groping hand.

* If entries are drawn in their sealed envelopes, mail yours in oversized packages. Again, this will make them easier to grasp in a blind drawing.

* Spread multiple entries out over the length of the sweepstakes. If the contest is a large, nationwide affair, the judging agency will usually open each bag of entries that comes in and select a few envelopes for the final drawing — and the more bags your entries are in, the better your chances of having one of them selected.

FIND THE THINGS YOU NEED FOR FUN

The sun's shining, the temperature's fine and it would be a great day for some backyard fun with the kids. But where did you put the croquet set? Or the volleyball net? If your house and garage are like many these days, it's hard to find whatever you need — whether for work or play. Fortunately, low-cost help is available. Organizing Solutions, Inc., Box AC, Katonah, NY 10536, has just published a new brochure offering more than 100 hints for better organizing your household. To receive the booklet, which also features four comprehensive organizational checklists, send in $3.00 and a stamped, self-addressed, business-sized envelope.

F. For the Gamblers Among Us

DON'T GET TAKEN FOR A RIDE AT THE RACES

Betting on horse races is one of the most popular and widespread forms of gambling in the United States, and the reasons are simple: You get to be outdoors, there is considerable ceremony, the races are exciting and — unlike slots or lotteries — horse-race betting is a game of skill as well as chance. Here are a few tips on playing the ponies:

* Betting only the favorites is a sure way to lose over the long run. At best, the favored horse race wins only 1 of every 3 races — and statistics at some tracks show a winning record as poor as 1 in 7. In addition, when you do win, the payoff is so low you have little chance of making up your losses on other races.

* The most successful bettors look for good horses that are likely to pay 5- or 6-to-1. Horses that go off in this range are usually strong contenders with a good chance of beating the favorite — and, if they do, the payoff is large enough to justify the risk.

* If you like to play long shots — generally, horses that go off at odds of 9-to-1 or higher — the best times are early in the racing season, before the handicappers have had a chance to become familiar with all the new horses at the meet, and when the weather is bad (you can throw out past records on a muddy track).

* A good way to pick a winner is to look for a horse that has finished second or third in a slightly longer race. The place or show finish could be a sign that the horse ran out of gas at the end of the longer run, but will still be in front at the wire in the current shorter race.

If you think you'd enjoy this popular American pastime and want to improve your handicapping and betting skills, there's a new book out that details dozens of techniques the professionals use to put the odds on their side and help them pick more winners. To get a copy, just send $10 to Discovery Publishers, 11160 Veirs Mill Road, L-15, Dept. 240-X, Wheaton, MD 10902. Includes a money-back guarantee.

LOTTERY LUCK /INCREASE YOUR CHANCE OF WINNING 40% WITHOUT SPENDING MORE

In a number lottery, such as those being adopted in most states these days, all eligible numbers have an equal probability of being selected in any given drawing. Does this mean that your expected payoff is independent of which numbers you select — that you might as well pick numbers at random? Interestingly enough, the answer is no! The payoff on any given lottery drawing reflects not just the numbers that are drawn, but also how many participants selected those winning numbers. Thus, if you select unpopular numbers and they wind up being drawn, you will receive a proportionally larger payoff than you would had you selected popular numbers. (Remember, they all have an equal probability of being drawn.)

Actuaries call these unpopular choices "ugly" and "non-focal" numbers. The theory is that "ugly" numbers are the prime numbers (those that can be divided only by themselves and by 1), and that "non-focal" numbers are those that aren't associated with specific events, such as birthdays or anniversaries. Combining the two categories would suggest you can improve your potential lottery payoff by selecting prime numbers above 31. In a 53-number lottery, the combined "ugly" and "non-focal" numbers are 37, 41, 43, 47 and 53.

Improve Your Winning Chances 400% With No Extra Cost: If you spend $10 a week on the lottery and know 4 other people who do the same, you can increase your chances of winning 400% by forming a pool with those other players. Sign a contract (this is important as most states won't split payoffs without one) agreeing to split all winnings equally among the 5 of you, then go ahead with your normal playing. You'll each have 50 chances a week to win rather than just 10 — and you won't be spending any more money.

`B1' BIG WINNER AT BINGO

Believe it or not, bingo is not a game of chance. You can improve your odds dramatically by correctly choosing the cards you play. This method not only generates consistent profits with "straight" bingo and "cover-all" bingo, but with any other variation of the game. Here's how it works: Every bingo card has 24 squares (the 25th, or center, square is a "free space"). You want to get as many of the 75 numbers as possible on your cards. So, if permitted to choose your cards before the session, try to find sets of three cards with no duplicates — 72 different numbers. This gives you a 25% better chance to win a given game than a player with a random set.

Forget "Lucky" Cards: Some players look for cards with "lucky" numbers — 7 or 11, for example — especially at the corners. This is a bad strategy — any given number, whether "lucky" or not, will be called on average in only 1 of 5 games.

Picking Your Parlor: Most games hold back at least 50% of the amount paid for cards to cover overhead and revenue for whatever cause or charity benefits from the game. However, a few operators return as much as 75%. Look for the posted percentage somewhere in the hall, and play the games that give back more of your money.

TIPS FROM THE PROS AT POKER

More Americans play poker than any other card game. Here are a dozen tactical tips for becoming a winner at the game:

1. When you join a new game be friendly, but unpredictable. Confusion is your ally.

2. In a low-stakes game, your competition will usually be weak, meaning you can

profit from your opponents' mistakes — such as calling with marginal hands.

3. You, on the other hand, should be both cautious and aggressive. Don't end a hand by simply calling. Either raise — or, if you can't, throw your hand away. Don't be a victim of vulnerable hands, like two pair; if someone else has shown strength by raising, fold.

4. Don't bluff in a low-limit game. When there's not a lot of money involved, your deception may be lost on the other players.

5. Discipline is the most critical element in a low-stakes game. You can't afford to go all out on one losing hand, because it takes too many pots to recover your losses.

6. Never play a hand on a hunch. Adopt a basic strategy — and stick to it.

7. When you win a hand, don't gloat.

8. Admit your mistakes, and put them behind you. Don't let one bad play derail you.

9. Don't try for revenge when you lose a big pot. If you focus on one player who has beaten you, you're apt to get careless about others in the game and wind up getting burned again by someone else.

10. Luck tends to run in streaks (actually, it's less a matter of luck than it is your relative strength versus other players in the game). Thus, if you're losing, it's best to leave early — but, if you're winning, you should stick around.

11. To read your opponents' mannerisms, adopt a contrarian strategy — i.e., when players feign weakness, they usually have strong hands, and when they act strong, their hands are typically weak.

12. Keep a balanced outlook with respect to both your hands and your opponents. In other words, look for reasons to fold as well as reasons to call or raise.

HOW NOT TO GET CLIPPED ON FOOTBALL BETS

Football is the most popular sport among American bettors — from those who plunk a dollar down in an office pool to those who wager thousands at the Nevada sports books. And, because of the massive publicity surrounding both the sport and the betting lines, it's also one of the most difficult in which to gain an edge. The oddsmakers, both legal and illegal, monitor events constantly and regularly adjust the lines to reflect changes in personnel, weather conditions, etc. As a result, you may do better playing some of the specialty bets — such as the over/under (whether the total points scored will be over or under a certain level) — rather than trying to pick the winner versus the spread, simply because these bets aren't adjusted as quickly as the main line. If it's announced, for example, that a key player has been hurt in practice, the overall line will shift instantly. However, you may still have time to place a bet on the "unders" before the betting level is lowered to reflect the player's loss.

Tip for Pool Players: Most pools involve buying spaces on a board divided into 100 squares, which covers all the possible scoring combinations for two teams (only the last digit of the score counts). However, since players are usually anxious to know their numbers as soon as possible, pool operators often draw the numbers before the board is completely filled. If that's the case, you can improve your odds by waiting and picking your squares after the drawing, when you know the numbers. Best Numbers: 0, 3 and 7. Second Best: 4, 6, 9 and 1. Hardest to Hit: 2, 5 and 8. Best Combinations: 3-0, 7-0 and 7-3.

BEATING THE ONE-ARMED BANDITS

Longer-term returns (over at least six hours of steady play) for Las Vegas slot machines are about 88 to 98 cents per dollar. The latter figure compares favorably with the best percentages at craps, roulette or blackjack. However, returns on short-term play vary much more widely. For instance, machines go through pay cycles and down cycles. During a pay cycle, the machine can pump out far more than you put in — and stay hot for a hundred pulls or more. Unfortunately, cold cycles can last just as long — and empty your wallet.

How to Find Hot Machines:

* Watch before you play. If you see a machine gulp $100 or more (even with a few small payouts) and the player walks away empty, give it a try. It may be time for its pay cycle.

* If you walk up to machine "blind," feel the coins after your first payoff. Warm coins have been sitting inside a while, indicating a pay cycle may be due. If coins are cool, try another machine.

* Ask a change clerk to recommend a hot slot. Casinos don't mind, and you are likely to get a good tip. If so, tip the clerk back - - 10% of your winnings off that machine.

* Try machines near casino entrances and exits. They're often programmed for jackpots — to draw people inside. One-armed bandits near gaming tables also tend to be good payers, used to lure wives watching their husbands play. Machines in less conspicuous spots have less advertising potential and, thus, pay fewer jackpots.

* Look for three-reel machines with a cherry in the middle. This can be a sign that a pay cycle is coming.

* Single-line dollar slots have the best odds. You get more jackpots with multiple-line slots, but the payoffs are smaller. Play the maximum number of coins on each wager.

* "Progressive" slots with jackpots growing to $1 million usually only pay off when the jackpot is within a programmed range. Unfortunately, it's not easy to discover just what that range is.

* New machines are programmed to pay generously for the first couple of days in order to draw more business later. If you see one being uncrated and being set up, grab it.

THE BEST BLACKJACK BETTING STRATEGY

More than any other casino game, blackjack (21) is a game of skill as well as chance. According to Doug D'Elia, a professional player from Las Vegas, knowing the right way to play can reduce the house advantage to 1.2%, depending on the circumstances. Here are his guidelines:

* When the dealer has a 2, 3 or 4 up, hit if you have 12 or less, and stand with 13 or more.

* When the dealer has a 5 or 6 up, hit if you have 11 or less, and stand with 12 or more.

* When the dealer has a 7, 8, 9, 10 (face cards) or ace up, hit if you have 16 or less, and stand with 17 or more. Splitting pairs to make two hands — and doubling your bet in the process — can also reduce the house advantage. Here are some basic rules:

* Never split 4's, 5's, 6's or 10's.

* Always split aces, even though most casinos allow you take only one additional card on each ace.

* Split 2's and 3's only when the dealer is showing a 2, 3, 4, 5, 6 or 7.

* Split 7's only when the dealer's up card is 4, 5, 6 or 7.

* Always split 8's unless the dealer has a 9, 10 or ace up.

* Always split 9's unless the dealer has a 10 or an ace up.

D'Elia notes, however, that playing well isn't enough to guarantee a win at the blackjack table. Even more important is good money management. Wins and losses tend to come in bunches, so you need to maximize your winnings when the deck is hot and minimize your losses when it's cold. A good way to do this is to use what is known as a "winning progression," increasing your bet steadily as long as you keep winning. You'll never be a winner betting the same amount each time (the house odds will eventually wear you down) or betting $10 one hand and $100 the next, based on hunches or whatever. And, a "losing progression" — where you double your bet each time you lose — is a sure road to ruin (you'll either run out of money or hit the table limit). Here are some suggested winning progressions for 4 popular starting bets:

$2 bettor — $2, $4, $4, $6, $10, $10, $15, $25, $40, $40, $60, $100.

$5 bettor — $5, $10, $10, $15, $25, $40, $40, $60, $100, $150, $150.

$10 bettor — $10, $20, $20, $30, $40, $60, $60, $100, $150, $200, $200.

$25 bettor — $25, $50, $50, $75, $100, $150, $150, $250, $400, $400.

Note that, in each case, you bet the same amount on the third hand in a progression. This returns your original bet, plus a one bet profit, and means you are playing on the house's money throughout the rest of a given progression. Remembering this can often keep you from getting nervous when you — a normal $2 bettor — suddenly hit a hot streak and wind up with a $100 wager on the table. When you lose a hand, at whatever point you happen to be in a progression, go back to your starting bet and keep betting that amount until you begin winning again. (Note: Ignore pushes, or ties, continuing with the same bet on the next hand.) This makes it very difficult for you to give back your winnings. For example, if a $10 better wins 6 hands in a row before losing, his profit on that run will be $120 (excluding any extra winnings due to splits, doubles or blackjacks — which, by the way, should not alter your progression). That means he will have to lose 12 times to give back what he won in 6 hands, which shouldn't happen if you know...

When to Quit: A good rule of thumb is to get up any time you lose 50% of the chips you have on the table — until you double your original stake. At that point, you should quit any time you lose an amount equal to 50% of your starting stake, regardless of how high your winnings rise. For example, if you sit down with $100 and run your total to $160, you should quit if you give back $80. However, if you run your total to $250, you should quit if you fall back to $200. That way, you guarantee you'll quit a winner.

WINNING WAYS OF CASINO WAGERING

Regardless of how well you play a casino game, the house always has an edge — otherwise, it wouldn't be in business. However, with sensible wagering and money-management strategies, you can cut that house advantage to around 2% — or even less. Here's how:

* When you head for Las Vegas or Atlantic City, take along a gambling stake equal to about 40 times your usual minimum bet for each day of your stay. You can't play wisely or comfortably with anything less. Divide your stake into two parts, but not less than $100 per gambling session, which is the bare minimum for survival at a $5 table. (If you go mid-week, most casinos have $3 or even $ 2 tables, meaning you can live with a smaller stake.)

* When you're losing, don't borrow from the next session's stake. If you go through the entire $100, walk away from the table — and the casino. You can gamble another time. If you're losing, or barely holding your own, set a time limit for the session — say, 30 minutes — and quit if nothing happens in the period.

* If your budget is limited, work harder to preserve your stake. When you lose half, stop playing.

* If you're winning, secure your original stake as soon as you double your money. Take the chips off the table and put them in your pocket — and don't remove them until you're ready to cash out. You'll then be playing with the casino's money. Continue removing money each time you hit another plateau — say $50 in winnings — so that you always have only $100 to $150 on the table (assuming you started with $100). If your luck turns, quit when you've lost 50%

of the money on the table.

* Most people find it difficult to quit while they're winning — and it is hard. However, you should try it at least once — it just might get to be habit-forming!

G. When It's Time to Move

8 WAYS TO CUT YOUR MOVING COSTS

Moving can be expensive, particularly if you don't have any financial help from an employer. However, if you're moving because you want to, rather than because you have to, the added flexibility can open the door to substantial savings. Here are some tips on reducing moving expenses:

1. Move between October and May — and, if possible, pick the middle of the month. These are slack times for moving companies, and they're often willing to give discounts of 10% to 15% to keep their trucks and crews working. In addition, you're also likely to get faster service, which can save you money on peripheral expenses such as temporary housing and outside meals.

2. Sell, give away or donate (to charity) unneeded possessions. Movers charge by both weight and distance — and the less weight you move, the less it will cost.

3. If you have large, heavy items that are getting old — such as sofas or refrigerators — ask for a specific estimate on how much moving them will add to the cost. You may save money by selling them and buying new ones at your new location.

4. Do the packing yourself. This can save as much as 40% to 50% over the cost of a full-service move.

5. If you have things you won't need right away, you might consider shipping them rather than having them moved. This can often be 30% to 40% cheaper if you choose the slowest shipping method.

6. Don't make the van wait for you at your new location. Time is money in the moving business, and you don't want to waste either.

7. Be prepared to pay the moving company's estimate, plus 10%. Personal checks may not be accepted, so make sure you can cover the cost with traveler's checks or a certified bank check. Get a receipt for your payment, as well as an itemized invoice of all expenses involved.

8. For more useful tips, check these Interstate Commerce Commission publications:

* Household Guides to Accurate Weights

* Arranging for Transportation of Small Shipments

* People on the Move

* Lost or Damaged Household Goods

THE MERITS OF MOVING YOURSELF

Many people attempt to move themselves in an effort to save money. However, in a lot of cases, the savings may not be that great — especially on big or long-distance jobs — so it's best to do some calculations before making a final decision. Be sure to include costs for packing materials, a hand cart for heavy items, shipping pads, truck rental and insurance on both your property and the truck. You should also put a reasonable valuation on the time you'll spend both loading up and driving across country, which will also entail motel bills, meals and gasoline charges. You may also want to consider the potential ill will created when you beg friends or neighbors for help with the heavy stuff. Realize, too, that you won't have anyone to help on the other end — unless you hire someone. If the difference is only a few hundred dollars, you'll probably be better off letting the pros handle your move — especially if you can reduce their cost by using some of the tips listed in the item above.

BEWARE OF THIS TRUCK-RENTAL TRAP

Most personal auto insurance policies cover you when you rent a car — and, if you charge the rental on a credit card that offers collision damage deductible waiver coverage, you'll be protected on that, too. However, both your personal auto policy and your credit card may have exclusions for trucks or other types of vehicles that you don't normally drive. If you do decide to move yourself, check your auto policy to see if you're covered for truck rentals — and, if you're not, take the insurance offered by the rental company. It's fairly expensive, but a truck can cause a lot of damage — and you don't want to get stuck with a big liability claim just because you misunderstood your coverage.

ASKING FOR HELP FROM YOUR NEW EMPLOYER

Many companies underwrite both moving and housing-exchange expenses when they ask new or existing employees to relocate. Among the items you can often request are:

* Full reimbursement for packing and moving performed by a professional van company.

* Payment of any costs involved in storing your furnishings while you find a new home.

* Reimbursement for temporary housing costs incurred while looking for a new permanent resident.

* Reimbursement for losses suffered as a result of trading an old, low-rate mortgage for a new one with a higher interest rate.

* Assistance with financing. Some companies offer their key employees loans at below-market interest rates, while others are willing to pay such miscellaneous expense items as points and appraisal fees. Many companies will also provide loan guarantees or arrange for preferred treatment if you seek a loan through the firm's regular bank.

* A down-payment subsidy, perhaps in conjunction with a co-purchase agreement wherein the company shares in any profits from future appreciation in exchange for helping with upfront costs.

NOTES

CHAPTER 5

EDUCATION SECRETS

A. Planning Ahead for College Costs

HOW MUCH YOU NEED TO SAVE FOR COLLEGE

Everybody knows education costs — and specifically college costs — are growing higher every year. Confronting this money-gobbling giant can be pretty frightening. Politicians make encouraging promises, but prudent parents can't wait around for empty pledges to be fulfilled. They know it's up to them to begin investing for their children's college costs as early as possible. To draw up your own plan, estimate how much you'll need — for tuition, fees, room, board and peripheral expenses. The next step is to estimate how much to invest for how long to come up with that yield. Here's a worksheet to get you started (it assumes a 7.0% annual increase in college costs, a 7.0% after-tax yield on your investments, that your child starts college at 18 and that you keep saving through college):

Line 1: ______________Enter current annual college costs. $5,488 is about average for public schools, $14,403 for private. Or use a specific school's tuition costs.

Line 2: ______________Compute the future cost of first year of college. Multiply Line 1 times the applicable factor from Column A below.

Line 3: ______________Compute the future cost of 4 years of college. Mult iply Line 2 times 4.44.

Line 4: ______________Compute the annual amount you need to invest. Multiply

Line 3 times the applicable factor from Column B below

CHILD'S AGE	COL. A	COL. B
Newborn	3.380	0.0246
1	3.159	0.0269
2	2.952	0.0295
3	2.759	0.0325
4	2.579	0.0358
5	2.410	0.0396
6	2.252	0.0439
7	2.105	0.0489
8	1.967	0.0548
9	1.838	0.0617
10	1.718	0.0699
11	1.606	0.0799
12	1.501	0.0921
13	1.403	0.1076
14	1.311	0.1275
15	1.225	0.1543
16	1.145	0.1919
17	1.070	0.2486

What If It's Too Late to Save? — Okay, so you left things till the last minute. It's never too late to apply for financial aid. Here's how it works:

Applying for Financial Aid — Fill out a financial aid application. Be prepared to reveal your finances in detail — annual earnings, investment income, home mortgage, car payments, outstanding debts, how many children you will be sending to college, etc., etc., etc.

How Do You Qualify? — You don't have to claim outright poverty. For instance, a family of 4 with a yearly income of $40,000 and assets of $10,000 might qualify, but be required to contribute about $4,000 a year toward costs. Or a family might be turned down for aid on a first child starting college, but qualify on a second child. Financial aid programs don't rule out high-priced colleges . Prestige schools may offer heftier grants than lesser colleges. Harvard, for example, gives an average annual grant of $7,500. And whether a child goes to Harvard or a local state college, families qualifying for financial aid have to pay the same contribution.

Where Else Can You Turn? — If you don't qualify for a financial-aid package, don't give up the academic ship. There are other life preservers out there in the sea of red ink — student loans, college grants, work-study programs, academic or athletic scholarships or military service. You can also tell your freshman-to-be to tug a bit on his or her own bootstraps. Here are some ideas:

1. Tell the student to find a part-time, after-school job and a full-time summer job to help.

2. Summer courses taken at a local college can save bucks — if credits are transferrable.

3. Advanced-placement high school courses permit students to skip similar courses in college. Catch: They must, of course, pass the courses!

4. Gifted students who graduate in three years via accelerated degree programs obviously save a year's tuition.

5. Students can live at home the first 2 years while attending a local community or junior college. Accumulated credits are then transferred to a 4-year university.

6. Work part time, attend classes part time.

7. ROTC programs take care of all tuition and books, plus providing a living allowance in exchange for a commitment to military service.

8. Merit and specialized scholarships — "Peterson's College Money Handbook" lists institutions that offer non-need-based scholarships for first-generation college students, children of veterans and union members. Football and basketball scholarships are well known — but athletic scholarships are also offered in lesser sports. There are scholarship search services offering to help parents. ProPlan, for instance, will investigate scholarship and financial-aid options on the basis of a 4-page description of your child's grades, interests, activities and a family profile. The charge is $69, refundable if they don't come up with 6 to 25 options. Phone: 718-446-0238. (Note: Other specialized scholarships are based on such factors as ethnic origin, hobbies and state of residence.)

Probably a better way to shop for colleges and scholarships is to talk with your high school's college counselor, then consult some of these excellent reference books:

* "The Scholarship Book," Daniel Cassidy (Prentice Hall, Englewood Cliffs, NJ).

* "Free Money for College," Laurie Blum.

* "Peterson's Guide to Four-Year Colleges," (Peterson's Guides Inc., Princeton, NJ). * "Comparative Guide to American Colleges," Case and Birnbaum.

* "College Financial Aid Annual," John Schwartz, editor (Arco Publications, New York, NY).

* "Government Assistance Almanac," J. Robert Dumouchel (Omnigraphics, Inc., Detroit, MI).

* "Catalog of Federal Domestic Assistance," U.S. General Services Administration (Washington, D.C. 20405).

COLLEGE SAVINGS PLANS THAT WORK

Every time you blink, the cost of a college education has ticked higher. Adding in tuition, room and board, books and other expenses, the bottom line is now around $80,000 for 4 years at a private school and $36,000 at a public university. Naturally, parents have to figure those costs are going to keep right on growing along with their offspring. So, if you're a parent looking down that golden brick road toward future ivy-covered walls, how and where should you invest for the highest growth and least risk?

Flexible Strategies — Rule 1 is "start now" — but right after that is, "alter your investment strategy as your children grow." Conservatism makes the least sense when your child is in infancy, the most the closer you get to tuition time.

Sesame Street Years — Parents of toddlers can afford to invest in growth stocks or top-performing mutual funds that will make the stock selections for them. Here's a sampling:

* Monetta. Minimum investment: $100. Phone: 1-800-666-3882.

* Janus Fund and Janus Twenty. $1,000 minimum initial investment is waived if you sign up to have money automatically transferred from your checking account. Phone: 1-800-525-8983.

* Gabelli Growth also waives its investment minimum for automatic

savers. Phone: 1-800-422-3554.

* 20th Century Growth has no minimum. Phone: 1-800-345-2021. Plotting the Teen-Age Curve — By the time your future collegian hits 11 or so, you should think of trading out of your stocks and growth funds and into bond funds for safety and security. An alternative would be funds that invest in both stocks and bonds. Dodge & Cox Balanced is one such (415-434-0311); another is Pax World (1-800-767-1729).

When your child is 14 or 15, further investment safety precautions are in order. The usual recommendation is to move your assets from growth-stock or bond funds into money-market funds — then, in the final teen-age years, into CDs or other fixed-income investments. Here is a short list:

* EE savings bonds — The rate adjusts twice a year, but a 6% floor applies if held 5 years or longer. And some or all of the earnings on EE bonds bought in your name and used for your children's college tuition may be tax-free (depending on your adjusted gross income).

* Short-term bond funds — Bond funds stretching their maturity up to 5 years nearly double the yield of money-market funds. Check the short-term funds of Fidelity (1-800-544-8888) or Scudder (1-800-225-2470).

In Your Name or the Kid's? — A custodial account to save in a child's name can be arranged at banks, brokerage houses or with mutual funds. However, any funds so deposited are legally the children's and control passes to them at the age of majority (usually 18 or 21) — meaning they are legally free to spend the money anyway they please. With that caveat stated, you should also be aware of potential tax advantages. The first $600 of annual investment income generated in a child's account is tax-free. The next $600 is taxed at the child's rate, currently 15%. This obviously amounts to a sizable tax savings over what you would pay on that $1,200 in your own tax bracket. Investment income over $1,200 is taxed at the parents' top rate — the "kiddie tax" (which, however, no longer applies after the youngster reaches 14). The federal gift tax does not apply as long as you don't give any child more than $10,0 00 a year. And both spouses can join in a $20,000 gift without incurring the tax.

To Save or Not to Save — There are those who fear their thriftiness will backfire. What if their college savings plan falls short of what's needed, but still disqualifies them from receiving financial aid? Answer: Go ahead and save. You'll be sorry if you don't. And, even if you deliberately keep your assets low, any financial-aid program is going to look at your income to decide on your contribution to your child's education.

LAST-MINUTE COLLEGE SAVINGS STRATEGIES

The best-laid college-savings plans — as too many parents find out — can go awry. Often the funds intended for educational investment get eaten up by other child-rearing expenses. And what of well-intentioned parents who somehow never got around to making any college savings plans — and suddenly find themselves only a year or two away from monstrous tuition costs?

Panic is one option. After that passes, however, you can also check out these 11th-hour, emergency-funding schemes:

* Home-equity loans — One of the most frequently tapped sources of college expense money.

* 401(k) plans — These and other corporate retirement accounts allow large sums to be borrowed — up to a maximum of $50,000. However, unless you agree to repay the loan within 5 years, you won't qualify for low interest rates and will incur large tax penalties. Some people declare a hardship and simply remove the money — permissible if the funds are expressly for college bills. Of course, the withdrawn 401(k) money is still taxable at your current bracket rate, defeating the original purpose of the retirement plan .

* Life-insurance policies — This doesn't work with term insurance, only with whole life — and you must have contributed for 10 years. Interest rates on these loans are lower than with 401(k) accounts, and the 5 year payback doesn't apply; in fact, if you don't mind diminishing your death benefit, don't pay it back at all. However, new parents shouldn't buy whole-life policies as investments for their children's future college education. Much better yields are obtainable through mutual funds.

A Few Riskier Strategies — If these alternatives won't pay the college freight for your son or daughter, you might consider one of the following cash-raising strategies:

* Buy your grandparents' home for a monthly annuity payment to be spread over the course of their lifetimes. If they're agreeable (and want to relocate anyway to smaller quarters), for a manageable, long-term financial obligation to them, you'll be able to raise tuition money quickly by selling or mortgaging the house.

* Convince any generous and well-off relations to make out a check directly to your child's college toward tuition. Such a gift is totally deductible. (If given to your child instead, anything over $10,000 incurs a gift tax.)

* Cry poverty — and qualify for financial aid. There are actually ways to lower your financial standing while still protecting assets. For instance, you can apply for a large home-equity credit line (to increase your debts) and use it to pay off credit-card accounts (which don't count against your assets for college-

assistance programs). Any long-term savings in IRAs, 401(k)s or other retirement accounts are similarly not figured into your assets, while CDs and savings accounts are. However, don't make the mistake of shifting assets to a child. Financial-aid programs take a much bigger bite out of the qualifying student's income and assets than they do the parents.

BEWARE THE TAX MAN'S SAVINGS BITE

Several IRS-prepared pitfalls lie in wait for parents cashing in investments to send their kids off to college. Here are a couple of particularly nasty ones to watch out for:

1. Capital-gains taxes come due when you start cashing in taxable investments to pay for college costs — and this can reduce the amount of money available for school expenses by 30% or more.

2. 401(k)s, profit-sharing plans and other corporate retirement accounts are convenient sources for borrowing college money. You can withdraw up to 50% of vested interests, up to a $50,000 maximum. But if you don't commit to paying back the loan in 5 years, you'll get clobbered by the IRS for tax penalties and overdue-interest charges. The IRS will let you withdraw the money outright if you declare hardship and use the funds exclusively for college expenses — but you'll be taxed on the full amount.

3. Gift taxes — If your rich Uncle Jack hands a generous cash gift to Junior for college, he's also making a generous and unnecessary present to the IRS — for every penny over $10,000. The way around this is for Uncle Jack to make out his check to the college of Junior's choice, earmarked for tuition. The entire gift amount is then free of taxation.

GO TO COLLEGE FREE — KEY GRANT SOURCES

It's possible to go to college free, thanks to educational grants issued by private foundations, corporations and even some government agencies. Unlike loans, which have to be paid back, and scholarships, which have to be earned, grants are available to almost anyone whose income doesn't exceed specific limits. Grant sizes range from around $2,000 per year to more than $30,000. Here are some of the leading sources of grants:

Pell Grants — Sponsored by the U.S. government, these grants are available to students from families with incomes of less than $35,000 (rising to $42,000 in 1993-94). The grants range from $2,400 to $3,700 per year. For a copy of the government booklet explaining the program, write to Pell Grant Formula Book, Dept. M-11, Pueblo, CO 81009.

Supplemental Educational Opportunity Grants — Also sponsored by the U.S. government, these grants are for undergraduates with extreme financial need. The maximum grant amount is $4,000 per year and priority goes to students who have already qualified for Pell Grants. For information, write the Federal Student Aid Information Center, P.O. Box 84, Washington, D.C. 20044, or call 1-800-433- 3243.

College Work-Study Grants — This federal program provides jobs for students who need help paying educational expenses. The program is open to both undergraduate and graduate students. Pay is usually calculated on an hourly basis, up to the maximum covered by the grant. Information on this program is also available from the Federal Student Aid Information Center.

For information on other private and corporate grant sources, you can send a stamped, self-addressed envelope to the Grant Information Service, P.O. Box 5100, Vero Beach, FL 32961.

OTHER HELPFUL COLLEGE-FINANCING SOURCES

If parents or other family members can't foot the bill and you can't find a grant, there are still many other government sources that can help with college funding, either making direct loans or providing guarantees so banks will come across with the needed cash. Here are some of the most popular loan programs sponsored by the U.S. Department of Education:

Stafford loans — These low-interest loans are made by commercial lenders and insured by state agencies and reinsured by the federal government. Annual loan limits are $2,625 for freshmen and sophomores, $4,000 for juniors or seniors and $7,500 for grad students. Family income cannot exceed $30,000.

Parent Loans for Undergraduate Students (PLUS) — Parents who want to borrow for their child's education can take out a variable-interest PLUS loan up to $4,000 a year per child from commercial lenders. In contrast to Staffords, PLUS loans are easier to get the higher the family income. Dependent students must be enrolled at least half-time.

Supplemental Loans for Students (SLS) — SLS loans are made to students rather than parents, but otherwise work the same, with the same $4,000 limit. High school guidance counselors or financial aid offices have applications and further information. Unlike most federal student aid, PLUS and SLS loans are not based on need. Borrowers must begin repayment within 60 days after the last payment — or until the end of any deferment for being in school.

Perkins Loans — Colleges make these low-interest loans in exchange for a promissory note. Students have up to 10 years to pay them back, and 9 months after graduation (or quitting) to begin repayment. To qualify, students must be U.S. citizens, have high school diplomas or general-equivalency diplomas and maintain a C average (from the end of the second year on). They must also attend school at least half time and sign an anti-drug-abuse certificate. For further information on any of these programs, contact the Federal Student Aid Information Center, Box 84, Washington, D.C. 20044, or call 1-800-433-3243.

Sources for Commercial College Loans — These remain the best and easiest sources for college financing. Here are some of the most popular types:

* Nellie Mae — Interest rate is prime plus 2 to 4 points; offered by the New England Marketing Corp. Can be secured as home-equity loans, providing tax deductions on interest. Phone 1-800-634-9308.

* Sallie Mae — The Student Loan Marketing Association offers several kinds of Sallie Maes. One, from Bank of America and First American, provides up to $10,000 a year (or more, if tuition is higher) at the T-bill rate plus 4 points, adjusted monthly. Phone 1-800-831-5626.

* PLATO — Guaranteed by University Support Services. Parents or students can borrow up to $25,000 a year and take up to 15 years to repay. Interest rates are adjusted monthly to a level 3.85% above the commercial paper rate. Phone 1-800-767-5626.

* TERI — A commercial lender, The Education Resources Institute loans up to $20,000 a year per student, with up to 20 years to repay. A guarantee fee of 4% is required. The interest rate is prime plus 1% to 2%, adjusted monthly. Phone 1-800-255-8374.

State Guarantee Agencies for PLUS and SLS loans — These state agencies can provide the latest information on loan availability, repayment and deferment conditions, as well as put you in touch with lenders in your home state:

Alabama Commission on Higher Education, One Court Square, Ste. 221, Montgomery, AL 36197.

Alaska Commission on Postsecondary Education, 400 Willoughby Ave., Box FP, Juneau, AK 99811.

Arizona Educational Loan Program, 2600 North Central Ave., Ste. 621, Phoenix, AZ 85004.

Student Loan Guarantee Foundation of Arkansas, 219 South Victory, Little Rock, AR 72201.

California Student Aid Commission, Box 945625, Sacramento, CA 94245.

Colorado Guaranteed Student Loan Program, 11990 Grant, Ste. 500, North Glen, CO 80233.

Connecticut Student Loan Foundation, 25 Pratt St., Hartford, CT 06103.

Delaware Higher Education Loan Program, Carvel State Office Building, 830 North French St., 4th Floor, Wilmington, DE 19801.

Higher Education Loan Program of Washington, D.C., 1023 15th Street NW, 10th Floor, Ste. 1000, Washington, DC 20005.

(Florida) Office of Student Financial Assistance, Department of Education, Knott Building, Tallahassee, FL 32399.

Georgia Student Finance Commission, 2082 East Exchange Place, Ste. 200, Tucker, GA 30084.

Hawaii Education Loan Program, Box 22187, Honolulu, HI 96822.

Student Loan Fund of Idaho, Inc., Processing Center, Box 730, Fruitland, ID 83619.

Illinois State Scholarship Commission, 106 Wilmot Road, Deerfield, IL 60015.

State Student Assistance Commission of Indiana, 964 North Pennsylvania St., Indianapolis, IN 46204.

Iowa College Aid Commission, 201 Jewett Building, 9th & Grand Ave., Des Moines, IA 50309.

(Kansas) Higher Education Assistance Foundation, 6800 College Blvd., Ste. 600, Overland Park, KS 66211.

Kentucky Higher Education Assistance Authority, 1050 U.S. 127 South, Frankfort, KY 40601.

(Louisiana) Governor's Special Commission on Education Services, Box 44127, Capitol Station, Baton Rouge, LA 70804.

Maine Department of Educational and Cultural Services, Division of Higher Education Services, State House Station 119, Augusta, ME 04333.

Maryland Higher Education Loan Corp., 2100 Guilford Ave., Room 305, Baltimore, MD 21218.

Massachusetts Higher Education Assistance Corp., Berkeley Place, 330

Stuart Place, Boston, MA 02116.

Michigan Department of Education Guaranteed Student Loan Program, Box 30047, Lansing, MI 48909.

(Minnesota) Higher Education Assistance Foundation, 85 East 7th St., Ste. 500, St. Paul, MN 55101.

Mississippi Guarantee Student Loan Agency, Box 342, Jackson, MS 39205.

Missouri Coordinating Board for Higher Education, Box 1438, Jefferson City, MO 65102.

Montana University System, 33 South Last Chance Gulch, Helena, MT 59620. (Nebraska) Higher Education Assistance Foundation, Cornhusker Bank Building, 11th and Cornhusker Highway, Ste. 304, Lincoln, NE 685 21.

Nevada Guaranteed Student Loan Program, Nevada State Department of Education, 400 West King St., Capitol Complex, Carson City, NV 8 9710.

New Hampshire Higher Education Assistance Foundation, Box 877, Concord, NH 03302.

New Jersey Higher Education Assistance Authority, C.N. 543, Trenton, NJ 08625.

New Mexico Educational Assistance Foundation, Box 27020, Albuquerque, NM 87125.

New York State Higher Education Services Corp., 99 Washington Ave., Albany, NY 12255.

North Carolina State Education Assistance Authority, Box 2688, Chapel Hill, NC 27515.

Bank of North Dakota, Student Loan Department, Box 5509, Bismarck, ND 58502.

Ohio Student Loan Commission, Box 16610, Columbus, OH 43266.

Oklahoma State Regents for Higher Education, 500 Education Building, State Capitol Complex, Oklahoma City, OK 73105.

Oregon State Scholarship Commission, 1445 Willamette, Eugene, OR 97401. Pennsylvania Higher Education Assistance Agency, 660 Boas St., Harrisburg, PA 17102.

Rhode Island Higher Education Assistance Authority, 560 Jefferson Blvd.,

Warwick, RI 02886.

South Carolina Student Loan Corp., Interstate Center, Ste. 210, Box 21487, Columbia, SC 29221.

South Dakota Education Assistance Corp., 115 First Ave., SW, Aberdeen, SD 57401.

Tennessee Student Assistance Corp., 400 James Robertson Parkway, Ste. 1950, Parkway Tower, Nashville, TN 37219.

Texas Guaranteed Student Loan Corp., Box 15996, Austin, TX 78761.

Loan Servicing Corp. of Utah, Box 30803, Salt Lake City, UT 84130.

Vermont Student Assistance Corp., Champlain Mill, Box 2000, Winooski, VT 05404.

Virginia State Education Assistance Authority, Six North Sixth St., Ste. 300, Richmond, VA 23219.

Washington Student Loan Guaranty Association, 500 Colman Building, 811 First Ave., Seattle, WA 98104.

Higher Education Loan Program of West Virginia, Inc., Box 591, Charleston, WV 25322.

Wisconsin Higher Education Corp., 2401 International Lane, Madison, WI 53704.

(Wyoming) Higher Education Assistance Foundation, American National Bank Building, 1912 Capitol Ave., Ste. 320, Cheyenne, WY 82001.

Puerto Rico Higher Education Assistance Corp., Box 42001, Minillas Station, San Juan, PR 00940.

CHANGES IN FEDERAL LAW HELP THE COLLEGE BOUND

The 1992 session of Congress may have seemed fairly uneventful, but it did pass some amendments to federal higher-education laws that will help parents and students pay for their college educations. Among the changes:

* Simplified Application Process — Families now need to fill out only a single form to apply for federal aid. Most families that earn under $50,000 a year will also need to supply only basic income information, rather than a complete family financial profile. (Note: Private-aid sources may still require more detailed information.)

* More Borrowing Power — Loan limits for virtually all U.S. college aid programs have been increased. Parents, regardless of income, will be free to borrow up to the full year's tuition plus expenses for their child, minus any scholarship aid or grants from other sources. However, loans may have to be repaid while students are still in school.

* Penalties Dropped for Home and Farm Equity — Liquid residential real estate assets, including farms, will no longer be counted in calculating eligibility for federal college aid programs. This will allow approximately 1.1 million additional moderate-income students a year to qualify for loan and grant programs.

* Direct-Loan Experiment — This law authorizes a temporary test program that will provide up to $500 million in direct loans to students, bypassing banks and other loan agencies in an effort to save on paperwork and administrative costs.

LITTLE-KNOWN SCHOLARSHIPS YOUR KID CAN GET

With a little effort, almost anyone can find some type of scholarship to help with college expenses. A good place to start is your public library — most maintain collections of college catalogs, many of which have sections on financial aid. Libraries also frequently maintain files containing funding brochures and notices of scholarship programs, as well as books on how to find college financial aid. If you don't have any luck there, here are a number of other ideas regarding sources of college scholarships:

* Children of federal employees and postal workers are eligible for scholarships from the Federal Employee Education and Assistance Fund. For applications or additional information, send a stamped, self-addressed envelope to FEEAF, 8441 W. Bowles Ave., Ste. 200 , Littleton, CO 80123, or call 1-800-323-4140.

* Many local fraternal organizations and civic clubs maintain scholarship funds to provide aid to children of members or to worthy students in the community at large. Check on availability with the larger groups in your area.

* Churches often provide scholarships for children of members, particularly if the religion has an affiliated university. Check with your pastor or church administrator.

* At least 4 aid sources are available to needy or deserving children of current, former or deceased members of the military. They are: Army Emergency Relief Assistance Program, Department of the Army, 200 Stovall St., Alexandria, VA 22332; Air Force Aid Society, General Arnold Student Loan Program, 1735, N. Lynn, Room 202, Arlington, VA 22209; Navy Relief Society, 801 N. Randolph

St., St e. 1228, Arlington, VA 22203; and Retired Officers Association, 201 N. Washington St., Alexandria, VA 22314.

* Many corporations sponsor scholarships for children of employees — both on an independent basis and through national testing systems, such as the National Merit Scholarship Program. Check with your company benefits officer, or have your child's school request a list of corporate sponsors for scholarship programs administered through the school.

* Students with special talents in music, dance, theater or the arts can often qualify for scholarships to special schools operated by artistic groups or arts foundations.

* Students with advanced skills in science or mathematics can often get scholarships from corporations or research foundations that need to develop promising new intellectual resources.

Virtually every college and university also has a supply of scholarships that can be made available to incoming or current students . When you apply for admission (or before, to be on the safe side), include a letter requesting information on scholarship availability. If you need to know about the possibility of getting a scholarship before you decide on a school, a good source is the book , "The A's & B's of Academic Scholarships," available from Octameron Press, Alexandria, VA 22326.

If all else fails, you may want to try one of several scholarship search services. For a fee of $25 to $50, these agencies will review your abilities and finances and then attempt to match you with an appropriate scholarship or aid source. The best organizations are:

* College Scholarship Search Service, 45 Columbus Ave., New York, NY 10023.

* College Student Financial Aid Services, 16220 S. Frederick Road, Ste. 208, Gaithersburg, MD 20877.

* National Scholarship Research Service, 122 Alto St., San Rafael, CA 94901.

* Peterson's College Selection Service, Box 2123, Princeton, NJ 08540.

B. Choosing the Right College

THE BEST INEXPENSIVE COLLEGES

The search for the best college can become a real challenge when cash is in short supply. However, there are some general guidelines to help you find the most education for your money:

* As a general rule, state-operated colleges and universities in your home state will offer the most economical education. The combination of state subsidies to the school and tuition reductions for in-state residents is hard to beat. State universities usually offer a wider range of course selections and have more prestige than state colleges, but they are slightly more expensive. If you opt for a state college, be sure to choose one that has a reputation for top-flight instruction as academic quality levels vary widely at these institutions. Make sure, too, that the college you pick offers a field of study in which you are interested. Many state colleges were created to concentrate on a particular area of education and thus don't offer a full range of studies. (Note: This can also be an advantage if you are looking for the best program in a specialized field as many state colleges have one particular program for which they are noted and in which their instruction excels.

* Private colleges are more expensive than state institutions, but they generally offer more scholarships and other types of financial aid. As a result, if you can qualify for this kind of help, you may do better at a private school than at a public institution .

* The region of the country is also an important consideration. Tuition and fees for both private and public colleges are highest in the Northeast. The lowest costs for public schools are in the West and Southwest, and the least expensive private schools can be found in the South and Southwest.

* If cost considerations are critical, the cheapest way to get a higher education is to live at home and attend a 2-year community college, then transfer to a state college or university for the final two years.

* Good value for your higher-education dollar can also often be found in foreign countries, particularly Canada and throughout the Caribbean. Check with your high school financial aid expert.

ALWAYS CONSIDER THE RESIDENCY RULES

State colleges and universities — and even some private schools — give tuition breaks to residents of their home states. Lest you think this is not a major consideration, we'll simply cite the 1992 fees for state colleges in California, which charged state residents $1,200 per year and non-residents almost $8,000. As such, if you want to go to a university or college in a state other than your own, you should give some advance thought to establishing residency in the state where your educational choice is located. Though requirements vary, most states require that you maintain a permanent residence within the state for at least a year prior to your application for admission (a few states require only 6 months). Under court order, all states must give consideration to allowing non-resident students to qualify for in-state tuition by virtue of their time spent in residence while attending the college. However, many states require students to maintain year-round residency (no summers off), demonstrate financial independence from parents in another state and show intent to later establish permanent residence in the state. As a result, the burden of residency proof usually falls on the student. Here are some things you can do to establish yourself as a resident of a particular state:

* Apply for a driver's license and register your car in the state.

* Get a job within the state.

* Buy property within the state. (Be careful, however, as property ownership could impact your ability to qualify for scholarships, loans or grants.)

* Register to vote and participate in local elections.

* File a state income-tax return or, if the state has no income tax, a federal return listing the state as your official tax home.

PRIVATE SCHOOLS AT BARGAIN PRICES

If the idea of being just another face in the crowd at a large state university seems less than appealing, there are some small private schools around the United States that offer that small-college feel without the high prices normally associated with such institutions. Most are liberal arts colleges originally set up by religious groups but now operating independent of church control. All rank high in academic standings, and also have substantial student-aid resources: Here are 20 of the best:

1. Albright College, Reading, PA 19603. Operated by United Methodist Ministries; requires 3 courses in religion and philosophy.

2. Allegheny College, Meadville, PA 16335. Affiliated with United Methodist

Ministries, but has no religious course requirements.

3. Coe College, Cedar Rapids, IA 52402. Founded by the United Presbyterian Church, but now independent.

4. Cornell College, Mount Vernon, IA 52314. Affiliated with United Methodist Ministries, but has no religious course requirements.

5. University of Dallas, Irving, TX 75061. Operated by the Catholic diocese of Dallas/Fort Worth, but has no religious course requirements.

6. Fordham University, Bronx, NY 10458. Founded by Jesuits, but now independent; requires 2 courses in religious studies.

7. Furman University, Greenville, SC 29613. Run by the Southern Baptist Council of Churches, but only 1 religion course is required.

8. Gustavus Adolphus College, St. Peter, MN 56032. Lutheran, but requires only 1 course in religion.

9. Hamline University, St. Paul, MN. Methodist, but no religious requirements.

10. Hofstra University, Hempstead, NY 11550. No religious affiliation.

11. Holy Cross, Worcester, MA 01610. Jesuit, but no religious requirements.

12. Illinois Wesleyan University, Bloomington, IL 61701. Founded by Methodists, but now independent; requires 1 course in religion.

13. Kalamazoo College, Kalamazoo, MI 49007. Founded by American Baptists, but now independent; requires 2 courses in religion and/or philosophy.

14. Luther College, Decorah, IA 52101. Lutheran; requires 2 courses in religion.

15. Ripon College, Ripon, WI 54971. Independent.

16. Rose-Hulman Institute of Technology, Terre Haute, IN 47803. Independent college of science and technology.

17. University of Santa Clara, Santa Clara, CA 95053. Jesuit; requires 3 religion courses.

18. Southwestern at Memphis, Memphis, TN 38112. Presbyterian; requires 2 courses in religion and/or humanities.

19. Stetson University, DeLand, FL 32720. Southern Baptist; requires 1 course in religion and 1 in philosophy.

20. Whitman College, Walla Walla, WA 99362. Independent.

C. Innovative College-Financing Methods

USING YOUR HOME EQUITY TO PAY FOR COLLEGE

Prior to the 1992 tax year, at least some of the interest on student loans was deductible. However, beginning in 1993, that deduction has been entirely eliminated. If you own your own home, however, you can still get a tax break on your children's college costs by using a second mortgage or equity credit line instead of a student loan. Interest on equity loans up to a maximum of $100,000 is fully deductible when used to pay for educational expenses.

MAKING COLLEGE COSTS DEDUCTIBLE

The cost of higher education itself can be fully deductible if the studies are directly related to improving your skills in your current career or job. If you attend classes away from home, you can also deduct all travel expenses, including food, lodging and mileage. (As a rule, however, the school must be at least 50 miles away from your home before travel expenses can be deducted.) The key test for deductibility is a direct link to your current line of work; expenses are not deductible if the studies are designed to lead to a career change (e.g., if you are a teacher, you can't deduct expenses for courses leading to a degree in engineering — unless, of course, you need it to qualify to teach engineering).

SHOULD YOUR STUDENT BE A DEPENDENT?

In most cases, you will want to continue claiming your college-age children as dependents until they finish their degree work. However, there are times — particularly if your family is well off — when it could prove advantageous to declare a child independent of parental support. The reason is simple: When a dependent child applies for a scholarship or student aid, the income and assets of the parents are considered in determining eligibility. However, when a young person has independent financial status, only his or her income and assets can be considered. Administrators of federal and state student-aid programs are, of course, aware of this tactic, so some advance planning is necessary to ensure your child will be recognized as independent. As a general rule, there are three tests for independence:

* Was the student claimed as a dependent on the parents' tax return in the year prior to the aid application?

* Did the student live with his or her parents for more than 6 weeks during the past year?

* Did the student receive more than $750 in financial support from the parents during the past year?

Married students are generally considered to be independent, though some states impose the same 3 tests even if you're married. Some private aid programs also refuse to consider student independence, taking into account total family income in all cases. Thus, you should check the requirements for the aid you're planning to seek early on — just to ensure that you don't go to a lot of trouble establishing independence, only to find out it doesn't count.

CONSIDER GOING INTO THE DORMITORY BUSINESS

Even if parental educational investments are not prematurely tapped, their ultimate cash value may still be woefully inadequate to meet the spiralling costs of a 4-year college education. Student loans and scholarships may or may not fill in the huge gap, but here is a nifty 5-step strategy that could bail out a distraught parent willing to try something a bit different — becoming a "dormlord:"

Step 1 — A few months before your child enters college, buy a condo, duplex or multi-bedroom home close to the campus. Get as big a mortgage as you can. Furnish it from your garage or a thrift store (your cost is tax deductible), then rent it to several students with 1-year leases — co-signed by their parents (for your protection). Students can furnish their own linens and kitchen utensils. If you buy right, the combined rent could pay for your mortgage, taxes and maintenance, plus give you extra dough for college expenses.

Step 2 — Apply at the college financial aid office for a PLUS loan (Parent Loan for Undergraduate Students). A couple of other commercial loans might be needed to finance your child's education. (The loans can be paid off when you sell the property after graduation — probably for a lot more than you paid for it; see Step 5.)

Step 3 — Hire your son or daughter as property manager and pay him or her a tax-deductible salary (say, $100 a month, which they'll have no problem spending). This should be a real job, not just a title — with your child renting rooms and collecting rents, contracting for repair work and periodically inspecting the premises.

Step 4 — Each year, your mini-dorm will provide substantial depreciation deductions — more dollars for college expenses.

Step 5 — After your child finally snags a diploma, sell the property — maybe to another parent facing the same financial dilemma you had 4 years earlier — and use the money to pay off any loans taken out in the interim.

D. Other Educational Opportunities

GET A DEGREE THROUGH THE MAIL

Advertisements for colleges that grant degrees by mail abound these days — and, though many are little more than "diploma mills," shipping out sheepskins in exchange for a hefty cash payment, there are also a number of legitimate mail-order education organizations. The National University Continuing Education Association publishes an independent-study catalog listing nearly 10,000 accredited courses offered through the mail, many of them leading to degrees. Call 202-659-3130 to request a copy. The Council on Postsecondary Accreditation also publishes a directory of all accredited institutions that offer home-study courses. The book should be available at your local library, but if it's not you can call 202-452-1433 and request information about a specific institution you may be considering. Many major universities also offer advanced-degree programs — particularly in business administration (MBA's) — through the mail. Problem: Most of the universities require you to spend a few days on campus at the beginning of each semester or trimester for orientation, which can disrupt your work and add to your cost. Still, if you can't afford the time or money for full-time course work, a degree by mail is a very viable way to upgrade your education and improve your career prospects. To get a feel for the exact type of offerings available, you may want to contact an actual program for information. One source is California's Columbia Pacific University, which boasts 5,000 students and 400 faculty members and offers home study for Bachelor's, Master's and Ph.D. degrees. Write to: Richard Crews, President, Columbia Pacific University, Dept. 3K3D, 1415 Third St., San Rafael, CA 94901, or call 1-800-227-0119 or 1-800-552- 5522 in California.

EARN COLLEGE CREDITS WITHOUT CLASSES

If going back to school is out because of either time or money constraints, and even home study would put too big a dent in your busy schedule, there are a couple of ways to earn college credits without classes — and without paying tuition:

* Life-Experience Credits — Many universities offer programs in which you can receive recognized college credits based on the things you have done in your life or the progress you have made in your chosen career field. Most of these programs are restricted to students who already have had an association with a university or college, but who failed to get a degree for one reason or another or who took a degree, but wound up going into a career unrelated to their educational background. If you fall into either of these categories, contact the Registrar's Office or the Department of Continuing Education at your school and ask about the availability of such a program. You won't be able to get a degree based on life experiences (other than an honorary one if you're famous), but you could earn enough credits to greatly reduce both the time and cost involved in eventually getting one.

Credits by Examination — More than 2,000 colleges and universities in the United States offer students the opportunity to earn credits by taking exams to demonstrate proficiency in a given subject area. If you pass the test, you get credit for a course without actually having to sit through it. Some of the best programs of this type include:

* The College-Level Examination Program (CLEP), operated by the Educational Testing Service, administers more than 50 exams in fields ranging from the humanities to science and business. For information, write CLEP, College Boards, Box 1822, Princeton, NJ 08540 , or call 609-921-9000.

* The Proficiency Examination Program (PEP), run by the American College Testing Program, specializes in business administration subjects. For information, write ACT PEP Study Guides, Box 18, Iowa City, IA 52240.

* The Advanced Placement Program (AP) gives examinations to students now in high school. Passage earns them credits when they enter college without having to take the associated courses. For more information, write AP Exams, Box 977-IS, Princeton, NJ 08540, or check with your high school's college placement counselor.

Warning: Some colleges want you to pay the same tuition for exam credits as you would for course credits. Pass them by.

INTERNSHIPS AND STUDY PROGRAMS

One way to both advance your educational goals and earn some extra cash for school is through internships and summer study programs. Many individual companies maintain their own internship programs, and many corporations and government bodies also sponsor job programs for youth. However, if you can't find an entree to such programs at the local level, here are some national and regional sources to check out:

* State government information offices usually maintain lists of summer jobs and internships available with state agencies and departments. Check the state government section in your local phone directory.

* Career-placement offices at most major universities maintain lists of summer-internship programs in both government and the private sector.

* The National Society for Internships and Experiential Education, 124 St. Mary's St., Raleigh, NC 27605, provides information on programs in specific business fields.

* The Office of Personnel Management, 1900 E Street NW, Washington, DC 20415, administers the U.S. government's summer-jobs program, coordinating applications for both paying and non-paying positions.

* The Council on International Educational Exchange, 205 E. 42nd St., New York, NY 10017, coordinates foreign work and study programs, for both summer and year-round students.

* The Institute of International Education, 809 U.N. Plaza, New York, NY 10017, provides information on more than 1,000 summer study programs sponsored by U.S. and overseas organizations.

* Writer's Digest Books, 9933 Alliance Road, Cincinnati, OH 45242, publishes "Internships: 16,000 On-the-Job Training Opportunities ," a comprehensive listing of student positions offering salaries and/or academic credits.

TRAINING AT HOME FOR A BETTER JOB

Correspondence schools provide opportunities for at-home study for credit at nearly all educational levels. Whether you want to get a high school degree, learn a new trade or earn credits toward 2- or 4-year college degrees, you should be able to find a correspondence school that offers accredited programs tailored to your needs. One of the largest and most respected organizations in this field is International Correspondence Schools, 925 Oak St., Scranton, PA 18515. In business for more than 100 years, ICS offers Associate's Degree (2-year) programs in a variety of business and technical fields, as well as more than 50 specialty careers, from computer programming or repair through medical and dental work to police sciences and private security. For more information, call 1-800-234-9070, Ext. 478, or write to Dept. WATS22S at the above address.

YOUR EMPLOYER MAY HELP YOU LEARN

Many corporations offer outstanding management-training programs, open to both liberal arts graduates and to more specialized degree holders. Interested and qualified young people should query specific companies in the industries that interest them, or ask corporate industry associations. A few examples:

* Many New York advertising firms conduct flexible training programs, providing dialogue between trainees and supervisors.

* Carter, Hawley Hale is one of many giant retailers combining classroom sessions and department store assignments.

* Procter & Gamble's 4-year course in brand management has been praised as more valuable than an MBA in advertising and marketing.

* SmithKline Beckman provides a fast track to managing in the modern, high-tech health-care industry.

* Morgan Guaranty and First National Bank of Chicago, among other financial firms, administer intensive instruction in accounting, international and corporate finance.

TAKE ADVANTAGE OF FREE SEMINARS

If your educational goal is merely learning for learning's sake, don't overlook the wide variety of free educational seminars offered in almost every major city. These programs range from purely educational events put on by public libraries, schools, hospitals and government agencies to promotional seminars put on by such businesses as garden centers, home-improvement stores, travel agencies, Realtors, financial brokers and even law firms (obviously, the goal is to increase sales, but you can attend without buying anything). If all you are really interested in is self improvement — and, in some cases, free entertainment — don't overlook these great free information opportunities.

CHAPTER 6

MONEY SECRETS FOR YOUR HEALTH & FAMILY

A. Family Help With Family Finances

HOW TO AFFORD A BABY

Let's face it. The last thing a couple wants to think about when planning to have a baby is money. After all, the mystery of new life, the thrill of counting those 10 tiny fingers and 10 tiny toes for the first time and the joy of hearing the soft coos of your own little newborn are the only thing that really matter once you've made the decision. However, without meaning to burst that magical bubble and ruin the moment, it should be pointed out that a little planning can go a long way toward coping with the ultimate reality — babies are expensive! You've probably heard by now that prenatal care and hospital expenses for the first year alone will normally average $6,200 — and that, according to U.S. Department of Agriculture estimates, raising the baby to the age of 18 (with no frills, such as private school, and no major health problems) will cost upwards of $120,000. If you want your child to attend college, think about spending at least $77,000 — and probably much more. And, don't forget to average in lost income due to mother's time off work to deliver the baby and spend a few precious weeks with her newborn.

How do couples provide for these facts of life? A little planning goes a long way. Here are some tips to help keep that big event financially manageable:

1. Draw up a will. Take time — before the baby is born — to designate an appointed guardian for the child, and at least two alternates. (A lot can happen in a short period of time to alter your first and best plan.) List your assets and how

you want them managed in order to provide for the child's future — just in case.

2. Prepare your living space. Do you have room for a child in your present home? Babies are tiny, but they take up more space in your home than you'll ever imagine. You need space for a crib, diapers, toys, strollers, infant seats, rockers and a multitude of cumbersome equipment that no modern baby can do without. If you can't create room by making a few rearrangements and holding a garage sale to dispose of excess belongings, consider adding on to your present home or begin planning for a larger one. It's better to begin this process before the baby comes than later, when the cost may be prohibitive after paying off the hospital bill.

3. What kind of car do you drive? If your main transportation is a sporty 2-seater, you won't even be able to take the baby home from the hospital — except in a taxi. Hospitals inform new parents that the baby must be strapped into a protective infant seat — no ifs, ands or buts! Even if you do have room in your car for the infant seat, you are also going to need room for packing a stroller, diaper bag, porta-crib or playpen (for trips to Grandma's house) and extra bags of groceries for that tiny extra mouth to eat . You'll need at least a mid-sized car with a large trunk.

4. Check your medical insurance policies. What costs does your insurance cover? Does your policy include well-baby care? (For example, many parents are surprised to learn that, once a healthy baby is born, its stay in the hospital is not covered. Unless the infant is jaundiced or has some other complication "justifying" a hospital stay, the baby's hospital expenses are not provided for by insurance. There's also the question of circumcision if you have a boy. Carriers consider that an elective surgery, and many will not pay for it. Find out how much the hospital charges for the procedure if you should choose to have your son to undergo it, and compare it to the cost of an out-patient procedure at your pediatrician's office.)

5. Call several pediatricians and make arrangements to interview them before the baby comes. Find the one that will best serve the needs of your baby and you. Inquire about the costs of check-ups and immunizations.

6. Check your life and disability insurance policies. Do they provide for family needs in case something should happen to you? Would your monthly mortgage be covered?

7. Do you have relatives and/or friends with children and who might share hand-me-downs with you? If so, you'll save lots of money on clothes, toys, equipment and accessories for that fast-growing newborn. Otherwise, plan for another large expense.

8. Don't waste a moment in starting a college savings account for your new addition. College costs are rising, and such long-term planning can only be a

benefit.

9. Make a plan for meeting expenses for the time the mother must take off work. Even after she resumes her career, mother will earn less money due to her inability to work overtime and lost time when the baby or babysitter is sick.

10. Plan for the cost of child care. If a couple can afford the luxury of having the mother stay home to raise the child — which will greatly affect family income — there will still be a need for child care. Every mother needs time out for errands — or just to do a little shopping or have lunch with a friend. Even a few hours away from home each week can add up fast at $2.50 to $5 per hour for an infant. That cost will double if you happen to have twins or a second child comes along.

TEACHING KIDS THE VALUE OF MONEY

Every kid knows that money doesn't grow on trees — you get it from your parents. That attitude on the part of children can greatly increase the financial strain of raising a family — and, if you hope to survive, you will have to begin teaching your kids the value of both money and good money management at an early age.

5 General Guidelines on Kids and Money:

1. Too much money can make a kid wasteful. Too little creates envy and resentment. Try to scale the amount to what other neighborhood children get.

2. Once an allowance figure is agreed upon, stick to it. Any exceptions should be clearly identified as such.

3. Don't use money as a punishment — withholding or cutting their allowance — unless your child is specifically misusing money.

4. Money can be used as a reward, if done on a careful basis. A better report card, for example, might be worth the same amount your child could get from after-school earnings.

5. Teaching children money-management takes time. Mistakes will be made. Praise and criticism should both be low-key. Patience and understanding will be rewarded.

Setting an Allowance: Most kids get their first exposure to money as a result of an allowance — but how much should your children get? Here are some guidelines, broken down by age:

Under 5 — An allowance is usually a waste of both time and money at this level since the best most kids will be able to do is either feed a piggy bank or lose whatever change you give them.

5 to 9 — A fair starting point, even in these expensive times, is 50 cents a week, with a 25- to 50-cent raise each year as the child becomes more aware of how to handle the money and what he can buy. Once the child starts school, you should also provide extra money for expenses, such as bus fare or school lunches, and you may also want to provide a small amount for supplies, letting the child actually select some of the more basic items.

10-12 — By this time, your kids will probably need at least $3 to $5 a week, and more if you expect them to pay for some of their own entertainment or clothing expenses. This is also a good time to start pressing the notion of budgeting and saving, explaining that they'll have to plan ahead and put some of their allowance aside to make special purchases in the future.

Age 13 — By this time, your child should definitely be budgeting his or her own money — however much you choose to provide. One good way to facilitate this process is to shift to a monthly allowance and then help your child construct a spending plan so that the money will last. There will obviously be some difficult moments when the budget goes awry and the month lasts longer than the money, but you should stick to your guns and not provide extra cash unless there's a true emergency. Most adults have to suffer through money problems fairly regularly, and this is a good age for kids to begin learning that fact.

Age 15 — At this age, you should begin including your children in regular family budget discussions (though its not a good idea to bring them into talks about severe financial dilemmas). Exactly how much the child gets will depend on your personal financial situation and the demands of the area in which you live (city kids need more than those in small towns). Whatever the amount, however, the children should learn to view their money as part of the overall family budget and recognize their responsibility to live within their means — though you may offer to "finance" certain big-ticket items (bikes, stereos, etc.) with loans. Be sure, though, that you don't make the payments so steep the teen is left with no pocket money.

Age 17 — This is a good point to have your teen-ager start a relationship with a bank (over and above any savings account they may have had). Most teens will be making some money on their own at this age, and nearly all will be looking ahead to college or independence. As such, they need to learn the mechanics and responsibilities of checking accounts, ATM cards and other bank services, which they will have to deal with once they leave for school or new jobs. This is also the time to explain the nature of credit and credit cards, as well as discussing other adult financial issues.

A CLEVER WAY TO EASE PARENTAL MONEY PROBLEMS

Here's one way to help your parents fight inflation, rising property taxes and growing home-maintenance bills without forcing them to sell their house or accept an outright gift:

Using a bank with which you have an established relationship or one where you keep a hefty minimum balance, take out a non-amortized loan for your parents using their house as collateral. The bank will usually agree to such an interest-only payment arrangement if the loan documents contain a specific provision providing that the loan will be repaid in full after they die and the house is sold. With the proceeds of the loan, buy an annuity that will not only cover the interest payments, but supplement the parents' pension or other retirement income.

Here's how it might work for a couple in their late 60s with a mortgage-free home worth $150,000. Based on his income and the value of the house, the couple's son gets a loan from his bank for 80% of the home's value ($120,000) at 8% interest. The son then uses the $120,000 to purchase a 20-year annuity providing a return sufficient to both cover the parents' interest payments and generate some additional monthly income (you should be able to net $500 a month or more, even in today's low-interest-rate environment). This lets the parents keep the house and increase their income, while also providing a tax break on the interest payments and allowing the family to continue benefiting from any appreciation in the value of the house.

WHEN GROWN CHILDREN NEED FINANCIAL HELP

Our children remain our children, regardless of how old they get. And, when they have money problems, we hate to say no to their requests for help. However, loaning (or giving) money to adult children can be fraught with danger if not handled correctly. Here are some guidelines:

1. Make sure the need is legitimate. Sometimes children view parents as an easy way out — or, even worse, use a request for money as a substitute means of satisfying other, more emotional needs (e.g., "if you really love me, you'll give me the money").

2. Keep the arrangement business-like. This is vitally important in the case of loans, which should be structured with a set rate of interest and firm repayment terms (in order to qualify under IRS rules as a loan rather than a taxable gift or income). It is also smart to keep gifts on a non-emotional basis. In other words, don't attach hidden or unreasonable conditions — such as demanding a more active role in your child's life in exchange for the money. However, you do want to make sure the money is being used properly. For example, if you've been asked for money to help start a business, you should

ask to review the business plan and reserve the right to withhold the gift if you feel the plan isn't viable.

3. Other than reviewing the suitability of a business or property for which the loan or gift is to be used, refrain from offering advice unless you are asked. Once you've made the initial decision to supply the money, step aside and let the child make his or her own decisions — and live with the consequences.

4. Don't provide the requested money unless you have it. If you have to sacrifice your own needs or reduce your standard of living, you could wind up resenting the child or playing the martyr — and the child could wind up feeling guilty or pressured, putting a strain on your relationship.

5. Don't use the fact that you provided money as a weapon against the child in any future disputes on other subjects. This will definitely create resentment and strained relationships.

6. If you have other children, it's important to be fair to them as well. At the very least, this means explaining what you've done and why, letting them know that no favoritism was involved. If necessary to keep from fostering ill feelings, you may want to adjust your will to reflect the loan or gift, reducing your legacy to the child who received the money. However, this should be done openly — and the child receiving the money should be aware of this provision up front.

SURVIVING THE FAMILY FINANCIAL `TRIPLE WHAMMY'

A warning to all baby-boomer couples: A 3-horned financial dilemma could be bearing down on you — and, without some advance preparation, you may wind up in big trouble, trying to simultaneously cope with:

1. Your children's escalating college expenses.
2. Your own neglected retirement needs.
3. The financial needs of elderly parents.

How do you decide whom to help first — or whom to neglect? Obviously, tough choices have to be made. There is no magical formula for spreading too often inadequate resources in 3 directions — but, if you're not already in too deep, there are some steps you can take to make the job easier:

1. Carefully assess your current situation from a time standpoint. How long before your children enter (or finish) college? How long until your own retirement? How old are your parents, what is their expected lifespan and how is their present health?

2. Review your current financial situation. What are your current assets? Your current liabilities? How heavy is your debt load? What's your current

income, and what are your prospects for increasing it? How well off are your parents, and what is the likelihood that they will need your help?

3. Assess your potential needs. How much will your children's education cost? How much will you need for your retirement? If your parents should need help, what form is it likely to take and how much will it likely be?

4. Get your current financial house in order, cutting down on unnecessary expenses, reducing high-cost credit-card debt burdens, restructuring savings for higher yields and shifting investments to improve returns and growth potential.

5. Establish priorities based on time available to achieve goals. Usually, this will mean moving fastest on college financing, setting a medium-term plan for assisting parents and adopting a longer-term plan for your own retirement. In each case, look for alternatives to standard savings plans — such as a search for grants and scholarships for your children, insurance to cover potential medical and nursing-home needs for your parents and a more aggressive investment plan, with an emphasis on growth, for your own retirement. You may also want to protect your own earning power and current assets with increased disability and liability insurance coverage. Important: Try to balance your efforts so that some preparation is devoted to all 3 needs. In other words, don't totally neglect your own retirement plans in order to fund your children's college costs or your parents' medical needs.

6. Maximize tax-free and tax-deferred investments. In any hurry-up financial plan, the tax bite is a major factor in reducing returns. Make full use of IRAs, 401(k) plans (if they are available), municipal bond funds, etc., so that every penny you can afford to invest works fully for you.

7. Don't sacrifice current liquidity for future needs. An unexpected emergency can force you to abandon your longer-term plans anyway, so you might as well plan for such a contingency by maintaining an adequate emergency fund in more liquid investments. If you wind up not needing it, the money will always be there for other purposes.

Obviously, given your individual financial situation, you may not be able to do everything you would like to fully prepare for all 3 of these potential needs. However, you should make your best effort — and you should start now. As you get your financial house in order, the total challenge will seem less and less daunting, and you will find additional ways to refine and improve your plans. However, you cannot delay a minute longer — your absolute worst choice for dealing with this triple family financial whammy is to do nothing.

MONITOR YOUR PARENTS' FINANCIAL NEEDS

One way to avoid surprises with respect to caring for aging parents is to stay informed about their financial situation. It's important to explain that you are not attempting to pry, but that you need to know where they stand so you can evaluate how much help you may be called on to provide. Discuss options such as special savings accounts to cover housing needs and possible nursing-home care costs. If your parents are already showing signs of deteriorating health — either physical or financial — you may want to consider asking for at least a limited power of attorney so you can help in managing their affairs.

YOUR SPOUSE AND YOUR BUSINESS

Many of the biggest family financial traumas occur when a self-employed person dies or encounters health problems. The normal emotional pressures associated with death or illness are compounded by the fact that no one knows enough to keep the business operating and generating income for the family during the time of crisis. Solution: If you operate a business, have your spouse work for you at least four weeks a year. This way, the spouse will have a basic understanding of how the business functions and how to handle specific situations. The spouse should also be introduced to all key people in the company, as well as major suppliers and key outside advisors such as attorneys, accountants, bankers and consultants. And, these key people should be made aware of what powers the spouse will have in the event of your death or disability. Additional safeguard: Prepare a transition plan, outlining who has responsibility for what, what business functions must be continued and what can be put on hold until you either recover or your estate is settled.

PUT THE FAMILY ON THE PAYROLL & CUT YOUR TAXES

One way to both provide continuity and cut both taxes and expenses is to put family members on the payroll of your business. Here are some potential benefits — and some things to watch out for:

1. The arrangement cannot be strictly a paper affair. Family members who receive company pay must provide services to the company, even if only on a part-time basis. The IRS looks very closely to see that family members do not receive compensation in excess of the actual worth of services performed. If the amounts seem suspicious, the IRS can reclassify the payments as either income taxable to you or gifts taxable to the children or other relatives.

2. The biggest benefit of such arrangements is the opportunity to "split" family income from the business, shifting it out of your high tax bracket and into the lower brackets of children or other family members. Catch: If your company is incorporated, your family members may incur Social Security, unemployment or self-employment taxes. However, these cost will probably be less than the tax savings from income splitting.

3. If a joint return is filed, putting a spouse on the payroll may not result in

any net reduction in income taxes for the family.

4. Part-time or summer earnings from the parental business can be used by a student to fund college expenses with pre-tax dollars.

5. By shifting a share in the business to a family member — through a family partnership, say, or corporation — income can be split among family members who do not actually perform services for the business. Legal Tip: Check with a tax lawyer to avoid running afoul of exceptions.

HOW TO DEDUCT YOUR CHILD'S ALLOWANCE /SAVE $1,200 IN TAXES

In addition to helping provide funds for college, putting a child to work in your business is also a good way to make his allowance deductible. The child can earn up to $3,000 a year without having to pay income taxes, but you still get to deduct the payments as a legitimate business expense. In addition, if your company is not incorporated, wages paid to children are not subject to Social Security or unemployment taxes until they reach 18 years of age. Be sure to keep records of the actual work performed and make sure that the compensation rate is fairly set. While there is nothing illegal about this arrangement, the IRS may demand detailed explanations in the event you are audited. Note: Your children's earnings won't impact their dependent status on your tax return, so long as you continue to provide more than 50% of their total support. If you pay your child $2,900 a year and are in a 41% combined federal and state tax bracket, you will save $1,200 a year on your taxes.

COULD YOUR KID BE A STAR?

When it comes to helping out with the family finances, kids aren't limited just to working for your company — they are also capable of making substantial sums of money in their own right. One of the best ways for kids to cash in on just being kids is to appear in TV commercials — especially if you live in New York, Los Angeles, Chicago or any of the other big cities where commercial advertisements are regularly produced. A child could conceivably make $30,000 a year appearing in commercials — and $100,000 is possible for kids who become stars. Each year, about 50,000 roles are open to children, but qualifying takes a bit of effort and planning. Here are some hints:

1. Infants are always in demand, but most commercials go to children from ages 7 to 12.

2. Appearance is the most important factor in being chosen, so you need close-up pictures of your child to send to commercial agents. These photos should not be posed or in costume, and you should enclose a data sheet with

your child's vital statistics, including height, weight, clothes size, hair and eye color.

3. The child should have a good personality, and also demonstrate intelligence, poise and self-confidence.

4. Both child and parent must be emotionally stable. Competing with 40 to 50 other kids at auditions can generate pressure, jealousy and feelings of rejection, so children need both encouragement and reassurance that your love does not depend on their getting a part.

5. You must have both flexibility and endurance. Commercial agents have zero tolerance for parental excuses, so you must be able to drop everything to get to auditions — and, if your kid lands a part, you must then be prepared to spend long hours (or even days) on the "shoot."

For more information, look in your yellow pages under "Modeling Agencies" or "Talent Agencies."

HOW ABOUT YOUR PET?

If you don't have children — or don't want to subject yours to the rigors of the TV game — that doesn't mean you're automatically eliminated from the race for big media bucks. Pets are also in demand — and, with some luck, yours could wind up being a star. Here are 8 things you need to know about getting your pet into the ad game:

1. Like any model or actor, your pet will need an agent. Larger cities have animal talent agencies; elsewhere, animal trainers can often put you in touch with commercial producers.

2. Your pet must not only be photogenic, but be trained. Dogs should obey basic obedience commands — sit, down and stay.

3. Commercial sets are noisy places, so agents will expect your pet to be able to respond in spite of distractions. Give your pet this test in advance.

4. Teach your pet other useful skills, like "speaking" on command, fetching and carrying things gently in his mouth.

5. Pets can't have finicky appetites if they're going to work in pet-food commercials. Retakes often require them to eat several times.

6. Trained cats are rare, so a cat that does tricks has a definite edge.

7. When you bring your pet to an audition or interview, take along color snapshots that show your animal close-up at eye level. Also leave a resume with

your phone number, the pet's vital statistics, its training and any special tricks.

8. Fees for pets vary widely since there are no animal unions. TV work tops the scale; ads are generally lower.

B. Better Family Health for Less

PAY 40% LESS AND GET THE BEST HEALTH INSURANCE

The only thing these days that's going up faster than medical costs is the price of health insurance. However, there are some ways to cut your health insurance costs by as much as 40% — and still get the best medical care available:

1. Stop smoking. According to insurance industry statistics, smoking is not only the biggest risk factor in life insurance, but also has a major impact on health care costs. Most independent health insurers give non-smoker discounts, and many will cut premiums for smokers once they've been off the weed for at least a year.

2. Shop around. As with life insurance, there are big differences in premiums for health coverage. Get quotes from at least two independent insurance agents, who can give you quotes from several different companies.

3. Call one of the services that monitor insurance company rates, such as SelectQuote (1-800-643-5115) or InsuranceQuote (1-800-972-1104).

4. Raise your annual or per-claim deductibles. Even a modest increase in deductibles can result in a substantial reduction in your annual premiums. This is a particularly good option if your basic health is good and you maintain a healthy lifestyle.

5. Consider a health maintenance organization (HMO) or preferred provider organization (PPO). These groups limit your choices a bit , but generally provide excellent overall medical care for substantially less money than you would pay for regular health insurance. If you do choose an HMO or PPO — or are already a member — you may be able to cut costs by practicing preventative health care. Some organizations give discounts if you stop smoking, lose weight, take nutrition classes or do other things to increase your own health awareness and thereby lower your risk levels.

GIVE YOUR HEALTH INSURER A CHECK-UP

These days, it's not enough just to have health insurance. You also have to make sure that your health insurer is healthy. According to Standard & Poor's, 121 life and health insurance companies went broke from 1988 through 1991, and at least 131 health maintenance organizations failed between 1986 and 1990. And, it's not just small or little-known companies that are having problems — Blue Cross and Blue Shield of Charleston, W. Va., collapsed in 1990, leaving some $41 million in unpaid claims. So, how can you check up on the health of your health insurance company? The obvious answer is to use one of the professional insurance rating services, such as A.M. Best or Standard & Poor's. Best's ratings are cited by most insurance companies, or you can check them on your own by going to the public library, which will usually carry a complete list of Best ratings. You can also contact Best directly by calling 1-900-420-0400 — a call that will cost you about $5 to $7 for each company you want rated.

Some important notes on evaluating your health insurer:

* Best changed its rating system effective June 1992, adding several new categories, so make sure the rating you look at is the current one — for example, A+ used to be Best's top rating, but it's now second best.

* You may also want to check more than one rating service as Best's track record has a few blemishes — several of the companies it had rated as high as "A" were among those that failed in recent years.

* There is no rating service for HMOs or Blue Cross or Blue Shield companies, though S&P does rate some of them. To get the current financial statement of the Blue Cross or Blue Shield plan that applies in your area, contact the company's public information office or your state insurance commissioner.

* Learn the danger signs that indicate an insurance company may be in trouble. These include a low (or falling) level of loss reserves, cuts in shareholder dividends, a falling stock price, insider stock sales (as reported in the financial press) or a poor financial performance ranking in the annual study published by the National Association of Insurance Commissioners (available at your local library).

* The state insurance commission is also a good source of information on Multiple-Employer Welfare Arrangements (MEWAs), cooperative plans that sign up small companies that can't afford coverage from major insurers. A number of these plans have failed — several due to fraud — and most states now require that they be licensed, as well as maintaining files of complaints.

* Check to see if your insurer offers you a "hold-harmless" clause. These are valuable safety nets since they prevent doctors and hospitals from billing you for charges that the health insurer was obligated to pay.

* Check to see if you are covered by your state's insurance guaranty fund. All 50 states now have such funds to cover individuals whose insurance companies go bust, paying medical expenses up to $100,000 (insurance

companies pay into these funds as part of their state licensing requirement). However, only a few states extend guaranty fund coverage to group policies, and almost none cover MEWAs.

* Check to see if your insurance agent has a liability policy. If so, you may be able to collect from the agent's insurer if he or she sold you a policy from a company that failed or wasn't properly licensed.

* Here is a list of the 7 safest U.S. health insurers in October 1992, as rated by Weiss Research, Inc., of West Palm Beach, FL (1- 800-29-9222):

1. Physicians Mutual Insurance — A+
2. Country Life & Health Insurance — A+
3. United Insurance Company of America — A+
4. Guardian Life & Health — A
5. United American Insurance — A
6. Time Insurance — A-
7. Globe Life & Accident Insurance Company — A-

HOW HEALTH INSURERS CAN CHEAT YOU — As medical costs get higher and higher, more and more health insurers are looking for ways to save money — and one way many are choosing is to delay payments, or even deny your claims. If you have to wait more than six weeks for reimbursement of a claim — or if you feel you have had a claim wrongly denied — you should fight back. About half the states require reimbursement within 45 days or less — and if you don't get it, you should call your company and demand payment. If that still does not produce results, file a complaint with your state insurance commission.

The same applies with claims that have been denied — with a couple of extra steps. If the company refuses payment, you will have to ask first for an explanation, then for a formal review. At this stage, you will have to contest the company's decision — bringing statements from your doctor about the necessity and validity of the treatment and, if possible, citing other insurers who pay such claims. The company will take your arguments into consideration, but it may still refuse to act. If it does, once again file a complaint with the state insurance commissioner. If all else fails, you have the option to file a bad-faith lawsuit — particularly if you can show that the company has established a pattern of non-payment of claims or policy cancellations. A number of such suits have been filed in recent years, and several have resulted in multi-million-dollar verdicts in favor of insurance company customers.

SAVE UP TO 50% ON ALL YOUR PRESCRIPTIONS

Medicine accounts for a large percentage of the health budget for many families — more so even than doctor or hospital bills. However, there are a number of ways to save 50% or more on your prescription bills:

1. Buy generic drugs. These are identical in strength and composition to major brand-name drugs, but are much cheaper because the makers don't have to recover the heavy development and marketing costs incurred by the major drug companies.

2. Take advantage of senior discounts or volume buying plans. Many major drug-store chains offer such discounts as a way of getting you to bring your business exclusively to them.

3. Buy from major mail-order pharmaceutical houses. These companies maintain a full line of drug products and many will fill your prescriptions on an overnight basis, charging prices substantially lower than drug stores because of elimination of the middle man.

4. A number of health-insurance companies maintain preferred-provider arrangements with specific pharmaceutical firms, offering substantial discounts to insured patients who direct their business to them. Check your insurance policy or call your agent.

5. Look for innovative alternate sources. Some auto clubs, consumer clubs and shopping services have special prescription divisions that give members discounts of 50% or more. For example, British Petroleum's Horizon Club gives its members a prescription fulfillment program that can save you up to 60% on the cost of most common medications. (For information about the Horizon program, call BP Customer Service at 1-800-321-9555.)

GETTING DOCTORS AND SURGEONS TO CUT THEIR FEES

Many people hold doctors in such awe they would never dream of asking for a discount on medical treatment — particularly if it involves surgical work. However, despite their years of education and training, doctors and surgeons are, in essence, still service personnel — and, as is the case with all service people, their fees are negotiable. In fact, if you are paying your own way rather than billing an insurance company, many doctors are quite willing to reduce charges to a level you can afford rather than either withholding treatment (a violation of their Hippocratic oath) or providing it and risking total non-payment. Likewise, if you have limited insurance, many doctors will agree to accept what coverage you do have as payment in full. In most cases, all you have to do is discuss your situation with the doctor and request his or her help. Even if you are not in dire financial straits, there are several other ways you can get lower medical or surgical fees:

1. Agree to schedule your surgery or medical treatment during a slack

period or off-peak time in exchange for a reduced fee. Doctors — and particularly surgeons — have slow periods (such as right before holidays) and may be willing to charge less rather than sitting idle.

2. Be on call for the doctor. Rather than calling your physician for an appointment, offer to make yourself available whenever he or she has an opening and can give you 30 minutes notice to show up. The same can apply with elective surgery, though you'll obviously need more notice.

3. Use a younger or newer doctor. Many beginning practitioners charge much less than established physicians who have built up a reputation in their field. Young surgeons are particularly eager for experience and charge lower fees in order to get it. (In most cases, the treatment will be every bit as good, if not better, because the newer doctor will be freshly trained and up to date on the latest procedures.)

4. Bunch your appointments. For routine check-ups or preventative care, many doctors will charge substantially less if you bring the entire family in at once rather than scheduling a whole series of individual appointments.

PROTECT YOURSELF AGAINST HOSPITAL BILLING ERRORS - EVEN GET FREE MONEY

Insurance company auditors routinely turn up billions of dollars in unwarranted hospital charges every year. They also miss far, far more overbillings than they find, since fewer than 5% of the 300 million claims processed annually ever come under their microscope. Some auditors estimate 9 out of 10 hospital bills contain errors — and (surprise!) very few of those are in the patient's favor. Most billing errors are due to simple mistakes — along with a lack of auditing checks. A data-entry clerk may add a zero to a lab charge, turning $75 to $750, or use a wrong charge code, billing you for a more expensive procedure than was actually used. Tests originally called for by the doctor, then later canceled, may still show up on your bill. Other procedures may be double billed by two people in the same department. Expensive equipment ordered for the patient in the next bed might mysteriously appear among your charges. As mentioned, these and countless other mistakes are mainly attributable to bureaucratic bungling. But, in a few instances, outrageous overcharges have been traced to fraudulont billing practices.

Whatever the cause, the effect on you, and on your medical insurance costs, remains the same: You're being bled dry. In 1991, the a average family's medical insurance costs rose by nearly 20% — much of it due to overcharges.

How You Can Protest: First, make sure you get an itemized accounting, not just a summary. Then ask the hospital billing department to explain anything you don't understand — line by line if necessary. Even better, keep a log of your hospital stay, recording admission and checkout dates, doctor visits, medications, services and procedures. Then compare your notes with the itemized bill, looking for discrepancies such as:

* Do dates and times match? Hospitals have been known to charge for extra hours, or even an extra day — at luxury hotel prices.

* Are any procedures or tests listed that don't apply to you? You may need a translation to be sure — i.e., "hydration kit" means water pitcher.

* Are you being charged for medicine or other services you never got? Or more than you actually used? Such glitches are common. Hospital pharmacies don't seem to be very good about issuing credits for unused medicine.

If You Find a Mistake: A. Call your insurance company and ask if they will give you part of the overcharges you find or a credit towards your insurance and, if so, how you should proceed. This could mean free money for you. B. Don't wait to complain — call the hospital billing department right away. You may get an immediate reversal of some charges. However, if you're not satisfied, don't stop there. Write a follow-up letter, detailing the errors, and send a copy to your insurance company. If the billing department is not responsive (within two weeks), contact the hospital's patient representative or the administrator. Other possible sources of appeal are your insurer's complaint department or your employer's benefits department. If you feel you have been the victim of outright fraud, contact your state's consumer affairs department or any agency that regulates hospital finances. Two national organizations will also help you decipher your bill and file complaints:

1. The American Association of Retired Persons (AARP), 601 E St. NW, Washington, DC 20049; Attention: Medicare/Medical Assistance Program.

2. People's Medical Society, 462 Walnut Street, Allentown, PA 18102 ($15 annual membership required).

THE BASICS OF DISABILITY INSURANCE

In some cases — particularly for self-employed people — disability insurance is even more important than health or life insurance. But, what kind of disability coverage is best? Here are some guidelines:

* Make sure the policy cannot be cancelled.

* Look for a policy that has a guaranteed premium rate through your 65th birthday. Not as good: A policy with guaranteed renewal. Premiums on such policies can be increased substantially as you age, making them too expensive

to keep.

* Deal only with an insurer that has a good reputation for paying claims.

* Buy only a policy that pays benefits over a long period. A lifetime policy is best; one with coverage until age 65 is second choice. Any policy that pays for a shorter period is a bad deal.

* Make sure benefits are pegged to the cost of living. Even if you have to pay a slightly higher premium to get such an indexing clause, it's worth the money.

* The policy should pay benefits as long as you cannot practice your "own occupation" — the work you did full time before the disability. With such a policy, you can "double dip" — i.e., collect full benefits while working at another, less-demanding job. Second choice: A policy that guarantees you will receive the full amount you earned before your disability (plus inflation adjustments), reducing your benefits if you work only by the amount you earn. Avoid policies that suspend benefits entirely if you are able to work at any job, even if it pays less than you formerly earned.

* You also want a policy that won't reduce your benefits if you also collect Social Security disability benefits. Social Security has 2 disability programs:

1. Supplemental Security Income, which provides payments to people of any age who are unemployable because of physical or mental health problems.

2. Old Age and Survivors Disability Insurance, which is the basic federal insurance program you pay for with your Social Security payroll deductions or your self-employment tax.

Benefits for both programs are based on the amount you have paid into the Social Security system, and you do not have to prove financial need to qualify. For more details, check with your local Social Security office.

FREE MEDICAL TESTS YOU CAN GET

It's possible to keep a pretty good handle on your health without ever visiting a doctor — and without paying bills for expensive medical tests. Most local medical associations regularly offer free health screenings where volunteers do such things as take blood pressure readings, check your pulse and ask about any other symptoms you may be experiencing, providing referrals if it appears you may have problems. Similar services are provided by many specialty medical groups, such as podiatrists (who offer free foot exams) and ear, nose and throat specialists (who provide free hearing tests). Your county health department may also have a mobile clinic that visits malls, schools or libraries on a regular basis, and the local Red Cross chapter sometimes offers similar tests at its facilities. In fact, if you want to get a basic health check and perform a public service at the same time, try donating blood. You will get your temperature taken, your pulse and blood pressure checked, receive a basic blood test and get juice and cookies — and all it will cost you is one pint of blood. (Note: Blood banks also do routine AIDS testing on donated blood, but you will have to request specific notification if you want to be advised of the results.)

GET A PROFESSIONAL WEIGHT-LOSS PROGRAM FOR FREE

If you have a weight problem, you know that diet programs can be quite expensive — whether you go through your doctor or through one of the professional weight-loss centers. However, if you live in a city with a medical school or a major research hospital, you can often participate in a doctor-supervised weight loss study at no cost (in fact, some hospitals will even pay you to take part in their programs, particularly if they are conducting tests to obtain Food & Drug Administration approval for a new therapy or drug). Many of these hospitals also offer similar test programs for sufferers of other maladies, ranging from hypertension to Alzheimer's disease. If you'd rather not play the part of a guinea pig, there's also one other approach you can try. Go to NutriSystem, the Diet Center or one of the other commercial weight-loss centers in your area and offer to stick to their program and appear in their advertisements in exchange for a waiver of their service fees. This is a highly competitive business, so all of the program operators are constantly on the lookout for success stories they can fully document and use for promotional purposes.

SOME HEALTH-CLUB CONTRACT CAUTIONS

One of the best ways to get and stay in shape is through regular visits to a health club. However, most clubs operate first as businesses and second as health centers — meaning they want you to sign a membership contract when you join. Most of these contracts — especially those with the larger national chains — are fair and reasonable, but you should still be fully aware of what you're agreeing to before you sign. Here's a brief list of things to do and look for:

* Visit the club during the hours you'd like to attend. Is the pool crowded? What about exercise equipment? Are the aerobics classes jammed? If you can't work out when you want to, then you most likely won't work out — meaning you won't get your money's worth from the club.

* Are all the facilities listed by the sales staff working and available?

* Avoid long-term contracts, and don't be pushed into signing on the spot by

a low-price special.

* If you are pressured into signing, you have three days to change your mind without penalty. If you decide to terminate later than that, you can usually still avoid liability by notifying the club of your intentions by registered mail, then paying for services rendered, plus a small cancellation fee.

PAYING FOR WHAT MEDICARE DOESN'T COVER

Retirees on Medicare today are reimbursed on average for only half their medical expenses . And, many so-called "medigap" policies — designed to cover what Medicare doesn't — fall far short of fulfilling their promise. To protect yourself, you need to know how Medicare works — and what to look for in a Medicare supplement policy.

For starters, Medicare has 2 parts:

* Part A, which covers hospital expenses, is free and the coverage is pretty good.

* Part B, which covers doctor bills and other medical costs, is optional — and is mostly inadequate. As for medigap policies, there are some key questions to ask before you buy, including:

* Is there a maximum per dime that the policy will pay? Does it pay the hospital's semi-private rate?

* How does the policy define "new benefit period"? If it only follows Medicare's guidelines, you won't be eligible for full coverage on a new illness unless you've been out of the hospital 60 days.

* Will the policy pick up the difference between Medicare's "reasonable" costs and the amount you actually paid? "Reasonable" means what Medicare has decided is the usual doctor's bill in your area. Unfortunately, its estimation of reasonable may be well below what you actually paid.

* Can you upgrade the policy's benefit scale (i.e., its definition of "reasonable costs") by paying a higher premium? If so — and you want to provide for the best medical care — the extra price is probably worth it. To find such a policy in your state, contact the American Association of Retired Persons, 919 Third Avenue, New York NY 10022.

* Does the medigap policy have a sliding scale depending on age? If you are still fairly young, you can probably get a lower price by choosing a sliding scale. However, those over age 75 should look for a policy with a standard price, regardless of age.

* Many state insurance departments offer booklets comparing the benefits of policies offered in the state. If your state has one, write for it.

* When you retire, don't automatically allow your existing health coverage to lapse. Your current policy may cover Medicare gaps better than anything you can buy after 65, so find out if you can keep it after retirement as a Medicare supplement. If not, consider buying another major medical policy a couple of years before you retire — even though you don't plan to use it until after retirement. To keep the price low, choose the highest deductible. You can increase your premium and lower the deductible after retirement. This may give you better protection than any medigap policy.

* Don't neglect your spouse's coverage. Too often the husband retires and drops his company policy, assuming he'll be covered by Medicare, forgetting that his wife is not yet old enough to be covered by Medicare.

THE MEDICARE FLAW THAT CAN WIPE YOU OUT

Most people don't realize that Medicare covers only "normal" health costs for the elderly. There is no provision for long-term care for the chronically ill, nor does the government pay custodial care or non-skilled care, whether at home or in a nursing home.

What To Do: Plan ahead for the possibility of a long-term illness that may require extended care. This involves protecting family assets so they won't be wiped out by a family illness, either through specific insurance coverage or through the use of trusts and careful estate planning. If you have any doubts about your potential risks, consult an attorney who specializes in asset protection and financial planning for the elderly.

FREE GUIDE TO LONG-TERM CARE INSURANCE

The Health Insurance Association of America offers a free consumer brochure explaining what at to look for when shopping for insurance providing coverage for long-term medical care. For a copy, send a stamped, self-addressed envelope to the association at P.O. Box 4145, Washington, DC 20018.

HOW TO CHOOSE THE BEST NURSING HOME

Sending a loved one to a nursing home is always a heart-wrenching step. How can you know if it's really time? Age isn't always the critical factor, but "yes" answers to a few key questions about the person may help you make the tough decision:

* Is there is a loss of control of body functions?

* Is there severe memory loss?

* Has the person lost the ability to perform basic activities like shopping, personal hygiene and dressing?

Once you've carefully examined the situation, reach a family consensus — and then discuss the matter with the dependent person. Try to avoid coercion whenever possible. Helpful Hint: If the dependent person shows extreme resistance, suggest that he or she part participate in selecting the best home.

Non-Profit vs. For-Profit Homes: Nursing homes run by churches, fraternal orders and charities have the best reputations, the highest staff-to-patient ratios and the longest waiting lists. Unfortunately, only about 25% of all homes are non-profit; the rest are proprietary, or for profit.

Other Important Differences:

* Patients with serious mental and physical disabilities need to be in skilled nursing facilities. Most of these are proprietary.

* Non-profit facilities usually charge a flat, high monthly fee with no extras for added services. For-profit homes have lower monthly fees, but charge extra for services. Be certain you understand all rates and service charges.

* Many proprietary homes won't take Medicaid patients since the amounts paid by the state and federal health plans may not be enough to cover their costs. Patients without money should be placed in non-profit nursing homes.

How to Select a Home: Start with advice from the patient's doctor. Then ask for recommendations from any friends and relatives who've gone through a search of their own. Don't overlook state departments of health or social services. Because it can be such a wrenching decision, many families put off the search for a nursing home until it becomes critical. This is a mistake since it can increase the emotional stress on the elderly person, who is left in limbo and deprived of needed care. Helpful Hint: Because this is such an emotional decision, take a close friend along when you inspect nursing homes. He or she may see things you miss.

Checklist in Looking for a Home:

* Location. Is it close enough for frequent visits? Is the neighborhood clean and pleasant? Are there nearby gardens and benches?

* Environment. Is it well-lit, pleasing? Do residents have privacy (no windows in room doors, lockable drawers)? A nursing home shouldn't look like a

hospital.

* Affiliations. How many patients are on Medicaid? If more than 50%, the home is less likely to provide good care.

* Staff. Is there a full-time doctor, or one who visits regularly? Does he or she specialize in geriatrics? Is the number of registered nurses, licensed practical nurses and nurses' aides equal to at least 40% of the number of beds? Do staff members treat residents with respect?

* Residents. Ask residents for comments or complaints. Watch for residents remaining in bed or in bedclothes all day and patients catheterized to avoid linen changing. If the proportion of such patients is high, something is wrong.

* Safety equipment. Handrails should be in all hallways and bathrooms, all public areas and each individual room should have smoke alarms and the fire and health-inspection logs should be up to date.

* Dining areas should be clean and attractive. Check to see if special diets are being followed.

* Residents' rooms should be comfortable. Look for personal objects and intimate touches such as pictures, plants, collectibles.

* Activities. Are newspapers and large-print books available? Does the home show movies, bring in entertainers, provide outings? What about gardening, workshops, education courses? Do residents have worship services? Provisions for voting?

* Special services. Ask about a licensed physical therapist and therapy equipment. Are there speech therapists for stroke victims? Audiologists, dentists, podiatrists, psychiatrists, optometrists?

* General ambience. Could you imagine yourself living there? One visit may not be sufficient for this.

5 NURSING HOME WARNING SIGNS

Here are 5 things that could indicate potential problems with a nursing facility:

1. Many of the patients appear sedated.

2. The home demands a large sum of money prior to admission.

3. The visiting doctor sees 40 to 50 patients during each call at the home.

4. The home administrator refuses to let you inspect the kitchen or laundry

facilities.

5. The home doesn't prominently display the Patient's Bill of Rights.

4 WAYS TO SPOT NURSING-HOME ABUSES — If you're worried about practices at a nursing home where a relative is living, here are 4 quick ways to check for abuses:

1. Arrive unannounced at mealtime or any busy time — 11 a.m., say, or 7 p.m. — to see if things are operating in an orderly fashion.

2. Make a small pen mark on the patient's body or bandages to check frequency of bathing and bandage changes.

3. Make weekly weight checks of your relative to verify the adequacy of his or her diet.

4. Get on a first-name basis with nurses and aides on all shifts, so you will know exactly who's responsible for your loved one's care — and then ask them about any problems or concerns you may have, rather than relying on the canned responses of administrators.

WHEN A NURSING HOME'S NOT THE RIGHT PLACE

Here are three alternatives to nursing homes. All offer the advantage of keeping older patients functioning in their own homes as long as possible:

1. Adult day-care centers. These provide one meal a day, transportation to and from medical appointments and other activities to keep seniors healthy and alert. More information is available from your state's department of social services.

2. Congregate homes. These are apartment buildings or detached homes that offer low-cost rental housing and essential services for elderly people who require minimal day-to-day help. Eligibility is based on income. Contact the nearest office of the U.S. Department of Housing and Urban Development.

3. Home care. Available services include nursing, convalescent care, household maintenance and Meals-on-Wheels. Most programs are administered through the state or a local community-services agency.

CHAPTER 7

INSURANCE SECRETS

A. Life Insurance You Can Live With

CALCULATING HOW MUCH COVERAGE YOU NEED

When the primary income producer dies, the surviving family needs about 75% of its former after-tax income to maintain its prior standard of living — and at least 60% just to get by. The amount of life insurance needed to provide this replacement income varies according to the current age of the insured. However, the following table can assist you in making a rough estimate. To use the table, find your current age in the column at left, decide whether you want to replace 75% or 60% or current income and then multiply your current income by the appropriate number in the table. For example, if you are 35 years old, want to replace 75% of current income and now earn $40,000 a year, you would multiply $40,000 by 8.0 and discover you need approximately $320,000 in coverage. (Note: The multipliers assume your family will get Social Security benefits and that the insurance proceeds will be invested for an after-inflation return of 5% a year, with the principal consumed over the survivor's life expectancy.)EARNINGS MULTIPLE NEEDED GIVEN CURRENT

While stressing insurance needs, the chart really shows capital requirements. These requirements can be met by life insurance — or through savings and investments employee benefits or inheritance. As independent capital resources are increased, insurance needs diminish.

LIFE INSURANCE ISN'T AN INVESTMENT

Despite the claims of insurance sales people, who would like nothing better than to sell you a lucrative (for them) whole-life policy, life insurance should not be considered an investment or a savings plan. Life insurance should be viewed strictly as a means to protect your family's income in the event of your death (or the death of another family member whose earnings contribute to the family's financial health). If you want both insurance coverage and an investment, you are much better off to forgo costly whole-life insurance with its cash-value buildup, instead buying cheaper term-life insurance and using the premium savings to begin an investment or savings program. Exception: If you are absolutely convinced that you lack the discipline to save any other way, a whole-life policy can be used as a forced-savings tool. However, you would still be better off to use some other savings method — even if it's just payroll deductions for the purchase of U.S. Savings Bonds — simply because sales commissions take such a big bite out of your whole-life savings.

SHOP AROUND AND BOOST YOUR SAVINGS

Life insurance rates have dropped sharply in recent years. You may be able to cash in your current life insurance policy and buy a comparable — or even better — one at a much lower cost. Example: A non-smoking male, 45 or younger, able to pass a simple physical, can buy $1 million in coverage now for an annual premium one-fourth the price charged 10 years ago. Rates for women are even lower. In fact, some individual life insurance policies can now be purchased for less than your company's group rate. If you want to get the best value on your life insurance, here are some key shopping tips:

* Policies with coverages of $1 million or more are good bargains. Some offer a 25% discount for people who can pay the annual premium up front.

* It sometimes pays executives to overinsure since companies can only provide up to $50,000 in coverage for single individuals under current tax laws. Premiums for coverage over $50,000 are treated as taxable income.

* Shop for preferential rates to non-smokers and the physically fit.

* Many insurers have dropped requirements for physicals, even for substantial policies.

* Shop for back-end loads. Insurance companies typically take the sales charges out of premiums paid during the first 5 years of the policy. Such front-end loads cut the amount the buyer actually puts in the savings portion of whole-life insurance, annuities and even universal-life policies. Back-end load products put the premiums directly into the purchase of insurance and interest-generating savings until the policy is terminated.

* Alternative: A so-called "low-load" policy, which is sold directly to consumers without benefit of an agent. These policies build cash value much

more quickly than regular whole-life or universal-life policies because the insurer doesn't have to pay high commissions to sales people. For example, a $200,000 low-load universal-life policy for a 45-year-old non-smoking male would cost about $3,500 a year. If he canceled after one year, he would get back about $3,400 in cash value. However, a full-load policy for the same man would return only about $100 if cancelled at the end of the first year. Two of the leading companies in the low-load insurance field are Ameritas Life Insurance Corp. (1-800-552-3553), rated A++ by A.M. Best and AA by S&P, and USAA Life Insurance Co. (1-800-531-8000), rated A++ by A.M. Best and AAA by S&P.

* If you do buy cash-value insurance through an agent, insist on a policy that offers a first-year surrender value equal to at least 50% of the premium. Also make sure that the policy has level annual premiums — some policies provide a 50%, first-year surrender value based on an inflated initial premium, which means you really get no savings at all.

* Ask about "vanishing premiums." High-interest earnings, if continued in the future, can permit a policy to become paid up after 5 years or so.

* Always deal with an independent agent — one who can offer you a choice from among the policies of several different companies, rather than just one. That way, you can compare benefits and policy provisions, as well as rates, without having to run all over town.

* If you need advice about your insurance needs, there are "fee-only" insurance counselors who will work only for you, rather than taking a commission from an insurance company. These advisors charge around $125 an hour, but if you're dealing with a major policy it could be worth the money. If you can't find a fee-only advisor in your area, you can call the Life Insurance Advisors Association at 1-800-521-4578 for a referral.

SAVE UP TO 50% ON YOUR TERM LIFE INSURANCE

Even if you carefully follow all the advice we've just provided, you can probably still get a better deal on a life insurance policy by using the services of one of the national quote comparison companies. These companies take a minimum amount of information from you — including age, sex, whether you smoke and how large a policy you feel you need — and feed it into their computers, which match it up with the lowest rates offered from among all companies rated A+ or A++ by A.M. Best, America's leading evaluation service for insurance companies. The evaluations — which you can request by either phone or mail and which usually take only 24 hours — are free for both you and your spouse. You are not obligated to buy, nor will you be contacted by a salesperson. However, if you need more information or want to purchase a policy by phone, the quote companies do have representatives available to answer questions and take orders from you. The two leading quote services are:

* SelectQuote Insurance Services, 140 Second St., San Francisco, CA, 1-800-643-5115. SelectQuote's service covers most states, though only state-licensed companies are quoted for residents of New York and Minnesota. Minimum policy size is $50,000.

* InsuranceQuote Services, 3200 N. Dobson Road, Bldg. C, Chandler, AZ 85224, 1-800-972-1104 or 602-345-7241 in Arizona. Insurance Quote also serves most states and observes state licensing restrictions. Minimum policy size is $100,000.

WHEN YOU DON'T NEED LIFE INSURANCE

Though a salesman will never admit it, not everyone needs life insurance. People who can do without personal coverage include non-income-producing spouses with no dependents, young single individuals and retirees without dependents whose holdings are small enough to avoid estate taxes when they die. Self-employed individuals should also make sure they have adequate disability or income-replacement insurance before spending a lot of money on a life-insurance policy.

Exception: If you are young and single, but plan on marrying and raising a family later, you may want to take out a small policy now to ensure that you will be insurable in the future. Pass the insurance physical now, and you will be able to later renew the policy or convert it to a different type without having to take a new exam.

...AND WHEN YOU START NEEDING LESS

Life insurance is not intended to be a financial windfall for your survivors. Rather, it is meant to allow your family to maintain its lifestyle even though you are no longer around to bring home a paycheck. As such, if you handle your financial affairs wisely, you should need less and less insurance as you get older. As your savings grow and you build a quality portfolio of investments, your accumulated assets can replace your insurance, generating a cash flow that will offset any loss of income for your family should you die. Another factor in tho equation is the reduced length of time over which your family will need protection. When you are young, with small children, you need more insurance because the proceeds will have to carry your family for many years. However, once your children are grown and you approach retirement, you need only enough coverage to ensure the well-being of your surviving spouse. Thus, you can once again reduce your coverage without any great loss in protection.

GETTING COVERAGE WHEN YOU CAN'T PASS THE PHYSICAL

If you have health problems and have failed one or more life-insurance physicals, there's still no reason to give up on getting the coverage you need. The key is to find an independent agent who knows the health standards of a number of different insurance companies. How can he help? Well, though you may not know it, health standards vary substantially from company to company. Thus, the independent agent can ascertain your specific problem and identify the company with the most lenient standards in that particular area. For example, many companies will refuse a middle-aged, 6-foot man who weighs more than 250 pounds. Others will insure him, but will add a substantial surcharge on the premium. However, a few will accept such a person without a surcharge, so long as he has no other obvious health problems. The independent agent can compare standards and find those companies. Good agents also know how to word applications so that your health problems are presented in the most favorable light.

Alternative: If your health problems are so bad that even a good independent agent can't find a policy for you, there's a good chance that you can still get coverage under a group policy. Many social clubs, fraternal orders, professional associations, churches and other organizations offer group policies to their members. If you can't get insurance any other way, you may do well to join such a group — the membership fees will be a small price to pay to get the coverage you need.

RATING THE BIGGEST INSURANCE COMPANIES

When it comes to life insurance companies, bigger isn't always better. However, according to a survey of the 4 leading insurance rating services — A.M. Best, Duff & Phelps, Moody's Investors Service and Standard & Poor 's — at least 15 of America's 20 biggest companies also get exemplary safety ratings. They are: Prudential Life, Metropolitan Life , Aetna, Teachers Insurance & Annuity, New York Life, Connecticut General, John Hancock Mutual Life, Northwestern Mutual Life, principal Mutual Life, Massachusetts Mutual, Lincoln National, IDS Life, Allstate Life, Variable Annuity Corp. and Nationwide Insurance. The other 5 companies in the top 20 are also considered safe, but they do have concerns in one or more areas, such as the quality of real estate holdings or risk levels on bond portfolios. These 5 companies are: Equitable Life, Travelers Insurance, Mutual of New York, New England Mutual Life and Mutual Benefit Life.

...AND FINDING OUT ABOUT YOUR COMPANY

Most public libraries carry the reports of 1 or more of the 4 leading insurance-rating services — once again, A.M. Best, Duff & Phelps, Moody's Investors Service and Standard & Poor's — and will make those reports available for your review. Your independent insurance agent will probably also have a ratings report on all of the companies he or she handles. If you'd rather check on your own, you can also contact A.M. Best directly by calling 1-900-420-0400 — a call that will cost you about $5 to $7 for each company you want rated. Be aware, however, that Best changed its rating system in June 1992, adding several new categories. Thus, whereas A+ used to be their top rating, it's now second best.

Problem: Sometimes even the rating services miss the boat. For example, several of the insurance companies Best had rated as high as "A" were among the more than 120 companies that have failed since 1986. To protect yourself, you should learn the danger signs that indicate your insurance company may be in trouble. These include a low (or falling) level of loss reserves, cuts in shareholder dividends, a falling stock price, insider stock sales (as reported in the financial press) or a poor financial performance ranking in the annual study published by the National Association of Insurance Commissioners (usually available at your local library).

11 TROUBLED INSURERS YOU SHOULD AVOID

While political concerns are focused on the plight of America's banks and savings and loans, many people are overlooking the fact that a number of the country's leading insurance companies are also in severe financial trouble. According to a recent study by Weiss Research (407-684-8100), widely regarded as the nation's toughest insurance rating service, there are at least 11 companies that face at least the remote possibility of bankruptcy within the next year. Weiss says its rating doesn't necessarily mean a company will fail — in fact, the company says most could recover if the nation's overall economy improves. However, Weiss warns that you should avoid depending exclusively on any of them for your family's protection. The 11 companies, with their Weiss rating and total assets, are:

1. Executive Life (California, New York), F, $13.34 billion.
2. Fidelity Bankers Life (Virginia), F, $4.07 billion.
3. First Capital Life (California), F, $4.46 billion.
4. Monarch Life (Massachusetts), F, $4.48 billion.
5. Mutual Benefit Life (New Jersey), F, $13.48 billion.

6. Presidential Life (New York), E, $2.30 billion.

7. Mutual Life Insurance of New York (New York), D-, $18.00 billion.

8. Equitable Life Assurance (New York), D, $50.30 billion.

9. Anchor National Life (California), D+, $4.40 billion.

10. United Pacific Life, D+, $5.60 billion.

11. American International Life (New York), D+, $2.20 billion.

HOW INSURANCE COMPANIES RATE YOU

We've now explained how you can rate your insurance company, but you may also be interested in knowing how the insurance companies rate you — health-wise, that is. Following is a list of 14 interesting health, lifestyle and longevity facts the insurers have come up with, based on reviews of mortality statistics and actuarial probabilities:

1. The most dangerous kind of obesity is when a person's abdomen is larger than his or her expanded chest.

2. Smokers' at all ages have death rates more than twice as high as non-smokers.

3. The death of both parents before age 60 increases up to one-third the child's mortality risk.

4. Suicide rates are much lower among overweight people, but being lean generally increases one's lifespan.

5. Living alone is far more dangerous to your health than being in a stable relationship.

6. Rich people live longer — probably because they get better medical care, hygiene and nutrition.

7. Getting insurance is almost impossible for those who have a stroke after age 60, but a stroke before age 60 becomes a diminishing mortality factor the longer the person lives uneventfully after it.

8. Nearsighted people are prone to anxiety.

9. Obsessive-compulsive people are more susceptible to depression and suicide in later life.

10. Severe drunkenness — once a week or even once a month —

dramatically increases mortality risk factors.

11. Involvement in kinky sex increases the likelihood of violent death or suicide.

12. Doctors have found a correlation between susceptibility to fear and blood coagulation associated with phlebitis.

13. Insurers charge 1 applicant in 250 a surcharge because of occupation. Only 1 in 10,000 is refused outright because of an occupational hazard.

14. Among the best insurance risks — farmers, college teachers and Anglican ministers.

WHEN TO SURRENDER YOUR LIFE POLICY

Here are 5 situations when you should consider turning in your existing life insurance policy for its cash value, or changing to a less-expensive policy or one more suitable to your present needs:

1. You're in good health, with an old whole-life policy that has a cash value equal to 30% or more of its face value.

2. You have an old policy on which you've borrowed the full cash value, and you have no intention of paying back the loan. Replacing your policy in this case could have attractive tax advantages if you are not in a high tax bracket.

3. The premium on your current policy is high because of a surcharge for health conditions that have since improved, allowing you to qualify for a new policy at a lower rate.

4. You've had major changes in your economic or family situation. Perhaps your income has risen substantially, you've paid off your mortgage or your children have finished college.

5. You have several smaller policies and could save money by consolidating your coverage into a single large policy. Warning: Some high-pressure insurance salespeople may try to persuade you to turn in your old policy without reason. While many of the policies being offered today are better, you should first consider upgrading your old policies through your existing company. Many insurers offer such upgrades without commission charges.

SHOULD YOU BORROW AGAINST YOUR POLICY?

In all but two cases, the answer to that question is no — but not for the reason you may think. In virtually all situations, you are much better off to turn in your whole- or universal-life policy and redeem the cash value rather than borrowing it. You can then purchase a more economical term-life policy and use the cash value you've recovered for higher-yielding investments. The only time it is really smart to borrow against your policy rather than cashing it in is when your health makes it impossible for you to get a new policy. The other time you might want to borrow against the policy is when you would incur a large tax liability from cashing it in. Borrowing the cash value is a tax-free transaction (except in the case of some single-premium policies), while cashing in a policy subjects you to taxes on the earnings the insurance has accumulated (the principal you paid is returned tax free). Even then, however, you might do better by cashing in the policy and using the taxable earnings to purchase a tax-deferred annuity (under current tax laws, this qualifies as a tax-free exchange). Even a modestly performing annuity will likely produce higher returns than you'll get on your insurance policy — and you won't have even the small interest charge you would incur by borrowing against your cash value.

B. Better Protection for Your Home

ALWAYS BUY REPLACEMENT-VALUE COVERAGE

Even in today's depressed housing market, most real estate prices are still rising — which could cause big problems if something happens to your home and you have the wrong kind of insurance coverage. The key to proper protection is to buy replacement-value coverage — not market-value coverage — for both your home and its contents. Replacement-value coverage will pay whatever it currently costs to rebuild your house and/or replace covered items that have been stolen, damaged or destroyed. Market-value coverage, on the other hand, will pay only the current value of your assets — deducting for age and wear. For example, if you paid $800 for a TV set four years ago, a replacement-value policy would pay $800 if that set were destroyed in a fire. However, a market-value policy might pay only $150 or so. In addition to getting replacement-value coverage, you should also make sure your policy includes an appreciation clause. This will automatically increase your coverage each year to offset any rise in the value of your property due to inflation. Bonus: Though it's a much, much better deal, replacement-value coverage usually costs only $15 to $25 more a year than market-value coverage.

Warning: Much to their chagrin, many victims of California's devastating Oakland Hills fire and Florida's Hurricane Andrew in 1992 discovered that replacement-value coverage will not make up the difference if it costs more to rebuild your house due to changes in local building codes since the property was originally constructed. In the California case, many of the homes were 50 or 60 years old — meaning they couldn't simply be replaced, they had to be upgraded to reflect new building standards. Legal challenges may yet overturn this restriction — but for now, California insurers have sent notices to owners of older homes informing them they need a special rider in order to get full replacement value that includes code-mandated upgrades in construction.

LOW DEDUCTIBLES CAN MEAN HIGHER PRICES

As was explained in the Chapter 1 Section on Winning the Auto Insurance War, the selection of a deductible for your homeowner's policy can have a significant impact on its cost. The lower the deductible you choose, the higher your premium will be — and the lower your odds of making up the difference on potential claims. If your annual premium is $1,000 with a $250 deductible, increasing the deductible to $500 will cut your cost to approximately $880 — and raising it to $1,000 could drop the premium to around $740, a savings of more than 25%. The same no-fee credit card you use to cover any possible cash shortage on an auto insurance claim can protect you here as well.

BEWARE THESE POLICY TRAPS

Even if you buy replacement-value insurance for your home, it's a good idea to carefully review your policy in full — simply because it could still contain a few costly traps. We've already noted 1 of them in the lead item of this Section — the restriction against paying for construction upgrades mandated by changes in building codes. Here are some others:

* If your house burns down and you decide not to rebuild, your replacement-value coverage may be meaningless. Many insurance companies specify that they'll pay only actual cash value — meaning replacement value minus depreciation for age, wear and tear. Thus, if your house is worth $140,000, but is 40 or 50 years old, your actual settlement could be knocked down to as little as $70,000 if you don't rebuild. (Note: Depreciation tables used by insurance companies for residential properties differ substantially from commercial depreciation tables for tax purposes, so don't confuse the 2 types.) Solution: Be sure your policy has an endorsement by the insurance company agreeing to pay full replacement value, even if you decide not to rebuild.

* Many acceleration clauses make only a single inflation adjustment each year, based on the prior year's inflation rate. As a result, if inflation is running high and you have a claim late in the year, you could wind up with insufficient coverage — perhaps by as much as 10%. Solution: Ask for an endorsement in the policy that guarantees full replacement coverage, even if the stated face value is below the actual cost. * Many policies are full of exclusions, reducing them to little more than fire insurance. Solution: Seek the broadest range of

coverage possible within your budget, looking particularly at potential threats in your region. For example, if you live in a part of the country prone to tornados or hurricanes, you're wasting your money if you buy insurance that excludes wind damage. Note: Some coverages are available only at a substantial extra premium — as is the case in California with earthquake coverage. Likewise, flood coverage must be obtained separately in all states.

* Most policies have severe restrictions on coverage for such items as jewelry, furs, art work, collections, cash and securities. Solution: If you have such valuables, make sure their full value is covered by a special rider — and don't keep lots of cash or valuable securities in your home. That's what safe deposit boxes are for.

Best Bet: An "all-risk" policy. These cover nearly everything, making the insurance company prove that something isn't covered, rather than forcing you to justify a claim.

THE MORTGAGE COMPANY — YOUR POLICY PARTNER

If you have a mortgage on your house, you may be required to maintain certain types of insurance coverage by the holder of that mortgage, who will be listed on your policy as an "additional insured party." This designation means that the check for any damage reimbursement on the property itself will be made out jointly to you and the mortgage company — meaning they get their money first. (This keeps you from running off with the cash, leaving them to foreclose on a burned-out shell.) As such, you will have to abide by any coverage minimums mandated by the mortgage holder, who will automatically get a copy of any policy you buy and may object to high deductibles or a lack of full replacement-value coverage. It's best to check with your mortgage company to find out the accepted minimums before you start shopping for insurance. (Note: Don't make the mistake of thinking that the minimum amount required by the mortgage company is all the coverage you need. Most mortgage-company minimums are set by computer and don't take into account your individual circumstances. Remember, too, that the minimum set by the mortgage holder may cover only its interest in the property — leaving you out in the cold.

AVOID COSTLY OPTIONAL COVERAGES/SAVE AN EASY $75 A YEAR

While you want your basic homeowner's policy to be as all-inclusive as possible, there are a number of added optional coverages you should turn down, even though the insurance agent may push them (which is natural since they are high-profit items for the insurer). These coverages include:

* Tree and shrubbery coverage. These options reimburse you for

landscaping damage up to a maximum of 5% of the value of the property. However, most exclude wind damage, which is the major threat to plants.

* Fire Department surcharges. Many budget-strapped cities now charge a small fee if firefighters are called to your home. However, these charges are usually $250 or less, so you're better off paying them yourself than shelling out an annual premium of $25 or so for 20 or 30 years.

* Debris clearance or damaged-property removal. If you rebuild, the contractor will usually provide this service for free — and even if he doesn't, it's cheaper to hire day labor to clean up than it is to pay 20 years of additional premiums for the service.

* Temporary-repairs coverage. This pays for stopgap measures designed to prevent further damage to your property while it's awaiting repair. However, in most cases, the risk of such additional damage is slight — or protection can be provided by a few rolls of heavy-duty plastic sheeting — so why pay the premiums.

* Stolen credit-card coverage — Your liability is already limited by law to $50 if you quickly notify the credit-card issuer, so you don't need it.

THE BEST WAY TO PROVE YOUR LOSS

A photographic record of your possessions is the best means of establishing proof of loss — and speeding up an insurance claim in case of fire, flood or other damage to your home. How to do it:

1. Use an instant camera with color film.

2. Photograph everything you own. Even ordinary household objects can be costly to replace. Include all appliances, including water heater and pumps.

3. Write model and serial numbers on the backs of the photos.

4. Arrange small appliances together when photographing the kitchen.

5. Photograph silver and other quality objects against black velvet to enhance their appearance of value.

6. Don't forget the garage, where you likely have such items as expensive bicycles and costly power tools.

7. File the photos — along with receipts to prove the original value of the items — by room.

Quicker Alternative: Use a video camera to make a detailed tape of each room of your house, then store the tapes in a private security box along with receipts for the items shown (they do you no good if they're destroyed in the same fire that burns up the insured item). Most insurance companies will now accept tapes as proof of a claim, even if you don't have serial numbers and close-ups of each item.

COVER JEWELRY — BUT KNOW WHAT YOU'RE BUYING

While most homeowner policies offer coverage on contents equal to 50% of the value of the house, most also exclude high-value items such as jewelry, furs, fine art, coin collections, guns, etc. To get full coverage for these items, you must buy a what is known as a "rider" or "floater" — an addition to your policy specifically valuing and covering such possessions. These policies are worth the money, but you must be sure you know what you're buying. For example, since many of the covered items are appreciating assets, you need an clause that automatically increase coverage at a pace that at least matches the rate of inflation. You also need to make sure the policy can be easily amended — which you will need to do each time a member of your family purchases or receives as a gift a piece of jewelry or other covered item. Check, too, on appraisal requirements. If the insurer demands a professional appraisal each time you add an item to the policy, the cost can quickly become prohibitive. Purchase receipts and photographic proof of ownership should be sufficient for all but the most expensive items. Hint: Floaters to your homeowner's policy are usually the best buy, but if you have an extensive collection of rare items or own some unusually valuable pieces of art, you may do better by getting a private policy specifically for the collection or artwork. Trap: Some homeowner policies will replace jewelry and other items destroyed by fire at full appraised value, but will not cover them for theft . However, if you add a theft floater, the value set for that policy will override any other valuation for fire claims. For example, if a $15,000 necklace was destroyed in a fire, you'd normally get a settlement for $15,000 — but if you had added a floater in insuring the necklace against theft for $10,000, all you'd get for fire claim would be $10,000.

C. Overall & Specialty Strategies

DO YOU HAVE TOO MUCH INSURANCE?

When it comes to insurance, most people error the side of too much rather than too little — and the results are often costly, depriving them of money that could be better used for savings and investment. So, how do you avoid being over-insured? Here are some guidelines:

* Sit down a carefully review your family situation, making a list of the areas of risk that really affect you — and the likelihood of those risks becoming reality.

* Look for ways other than insurance to protect yourself against some of those risks, particularly if the cost involved is small or the likelihood of an occurrence is minimal. This is particularly crucial with respect to health and dental insurance, where premiums and deductibles are rising and coverage levels are falling. A more conscientious approach to preventative medicine and dental care may be enough to reduce your risks — and your insurance requirements.

* Automatically eliminate as many specialty coverages as possible — most are overpriced relative to the true level of risk.

* Review other sources of coverage, such as company life insurance, paid sick leave, state disability insurance, Social Security, etc., and adjust your personal policies to reflect those coverages.

* Look for cheaper ways to get the same coverage, such as adding to your company life insurance or disability policies at group rates, rather than buying private policies.

* Realistically assess how much you can afford to spend on insurance and still meet other needs (such as college savings or retirement), and then allocate that money to the areas of greatest risk.

* In all cases — especially with respect to auto and property insurance — be aware of the potential value you can receive relative to the payments you have to pay. If the annual premium is 25% or more of the maximum likely benefit you'll receive, you are far better off to put the money into a savings or investment plan for 4 or 5 years until you have enough cash on hand to be self-insuring with respect to that particular risk.

COVERING YOURSELF IF YOU ARE SELF-EMPLOYED

Insurance can be a major cost factor for self-employed people — and, as a result, many wind up with inadequate coverage. However, there are a number of ways to get quality coverage without draining your business of needed cash flow or your budget of necessary reserves. Among them:

* Check alternate sources. Nearly every businessperson can qualify for some type of professional association or trade group — and most of the larger ones offer group-insurance options for members. These rates can be as much as 50% cheaper than private policies providing the same coverage. Caution:

This isn't always the case, especially if you are young and healthy or don't have children. In such instances, you may well get a better deal on a private policy. Beware, too, of trade group representatives who use high-pressure tactics to get you to buy; many times, these tactics mask non-competitive rates. Another consideration is the yearly membership fee — if it is too high, it could offset any premium savings on insurance, leaving you in the hole unless you make substantial use of other member benefits. Church groups, fraternal orders and even social clubs sometimes offer group coverage for members, particularly in the area of life insurance. Check these out as well.

* Consider an HMO or PPO. These plans can offer big savings over regular insurance, even if the premiums are the same or slightly higher. Why? Because most have no deductibles (or charge only a flat $5 or $10 fee per visit) and require no co-payments for hospital care. Many even give premium rebates if you take better-health classes on nutrition, weight control, hypertension, etc., and most will reduce rates if you quit smoking. Bonus: Membership in some HMOs also qualifies you for group life insurance or disability coverage.

* Make use of a good agent or "fee-only" insurance consultant. These professionals will help you assess your actual insurance needs , and then check a wide range of companies and policies to structure the best overall coverage plan at the most reasonable price. For example, Wilkinson Benefit Consultants Inc. of Towson, MD (410-832-7503) will do a complete needs review for just $250 and then run your requirements through a data bank of more than 1,000 health-care plans for self-employed individuals, giving you a detailed analysis of the 3 least expensive options available.

* Check small-business pools. Group coverage options for self-employed people are now mandated by a number of states, and insurance companies have formed pools for small-business owners in other states. Many local and state chambers of commerce have also arranged coverage pools for members (the state chamber in Delaware and local chambers in Cleveland, Detroit, Milwaukee, Phoenix, San Francisco, Syracuse and Toledo offer plans that we know of). Some regional health-insurance pools have also been formed — among them the Alliance (303-333-6767) in Colorado; the Good Neighbor Alliance (401-946-1820) in Rhode Island and parts of Connecticut and Massachusetts; and the New England Business Association (617-332-7680) in the Northeast. * Don't forget the deduction. Owners of small businesses are allowed to deduct up to 25% of health insurance premiums for themselves and their families as a business expense, exclusive of the regular restrictions on medical deductions. Attention to this detail can make the cost less burdensome.

"SWITCHING SECRET" TO SAVE 25% ON LIFE INSURANCE

So long as you remain in good health, you could save money on your term life insurance by switching companies ever 3 to 4 years. The reason: Many companies offer the first 4 or 5 years of term coverage at a reduced rate in order to attract new business, then make up for it with higher-than-average premium hikes on subsequent renewals. Using this strategy will take a little extra time every few years, but it could save you 25% to 30% on your life insurance premiums. Drawback: You'll probably have to get a new physical each time you switch — but then you should get a physical exam at least that often anyway. Caution No. 1: Don't drop your existing coverage until you've been approved for the new policy, just in case you should fail the physical. Caution No. 2: Be sure the new policy you switch to offers guaranteed renewal — just in case health problems should develop that would prevent you from getting new coverage.

INSURANCE AS PART OF YOUR ESTATE PLAN

Life insurance can play an important role in estate planning. For example, if your estate is large enough to be subject to estate taxes (currently $600,000 or more), a life insurance policy is a good way to provide funds to pay those taxes, eliminating the possibility that your heirs might have to liquidate family assets. Estate taxes are due 9 months following death, and most life insurance claims are settled well within this time frame. There are several ways to handle life insurance policies so that the proceeds are not counted in the estate itself:

* Buy a policy on yourself and give it to someone else as a gift. For gift-tax purposes, life insurance is valued at its cash value at the time of the gift — not at its face value. Since most people buy term insurance for estate-planning purposes, it will have no cash value — thus it can be given away with no tax consequences. Warning: You must live at least three years after giving away a life insurance policy on yourself. Otherwise, the proceeds of the policy will be counted as part of your estate.

* Have someone else buy the policy and pay the premiums. If one of your children or your spouse is the owner of the policy and makes the premium payments with their own funds, the proceeds of the insurance policy are not considered part of your estate. However, you must surrender all claim to the insurance in order for someone else's ownership to be valid — meaning you cannot borrow against the policy, cancel it or change the beneficiaries.

* Place the insurance policy in a trust. By making a trust the owner of the policy, you can retain control over both beneficiaries and the means by which the proceeds are disbursed, while still having the value excluded from your taxable estate. This is a particularly valuable strategy if you have a surviving spouse or minor children and want to make sure the policy proceeds are distributed according to your wishes. For example, you can set the trust up so that all the insurance is held in an income-generating account for the benefit of your

surviving spouse until his or her death, with the remaining proceeds then divided among other surviving heirs. * Insurance, in combination with a trust, can allow you to make sizable bequests to charity while still providing for your heirs. (See the Chapter 4 Section on "Helping Your Cause — and Your Heirs.")

* Buy-sell insurance. This is an important tool for small-business owners — particularly if partnerships are involved. The insurance is set up to provide the necessary cash for the surviving partner to buy out the deceased partner's interest. In the case of sole proprietorships, insurance can also be used to replace lost income and/or hire professional business managers to keep the firm operating until it can be sold. For best tax results, each owner in a business should be listed as an owner of the others' policies, but not as an owner of his or her own. An alternative is to have the business itself own the policies, though that could subject a portion of the proceeds to taxes on the estate of the deceased.

For more information on how to maximize life insurance benefits and minimize tax consequences, consult with an estate-planning specialist or an attorney whose practice is devoted to trusts.

D. Getting Your Claims Paid

ARRIVING AT A FAIR SETTLEMENT

Some insurers pay off fairly and quickly. Others are difficult and slow. With a difficult company, you may need legal help to negotiate a favorable settlement. What you need to know:

* When large out-of-pocket expenses are involved due to pain and suffering, it's best to hire a lawyer who can point out losses you're not aware of.

* Find out what your claim is worth. Ask your insurance agent or a negligence lawyer.

* Be willing to take a discount. The insurer should be given an incentive to settle a claim. If you negotiate without a lawyer, a quick settlement may be offered to avoid legal expenses. Decide what you're willing to settle for.

* Some insurers play hardball — offering nothing until you actually take them to court. Even then, the size of a settlement offer may depend on proof of coverage, damages, documentation, recent court rulings and the caseload of the court you sue in.

* If your company is unreasonably delaying your claim or acting in bad

faith, complain to your state insurance regulatory agency.

* If that does no good, go ahead and have your attorney threaten a suit. You probably won't have to actually file as the threat alone may be enough to pressure the company into a faster settlement or one more to your liking. If you are forced to go ahead and in initiate a lawsuit, you may be able to collect not only for actual damages but also for a multiple of your claim in punitive damages.

THE IMPORTANCE OF GOOD DOCUMENTATION

Insurance companies love paperwork — and the more you can provide in support of your claim , the more likely you are to get a fair and rapid settlement. From the moment of your accident, injury or property loss, save copies of all police or fire inspection reports, medical reports, communications with insurance company personnel (including notes on phone conversations), repair or replacement estimates, etc. If property loss is involved, also retrieve your receipts and photo records proving ownership. Create a specific file for the case and a separate file for duplicates of all documents, which should be made immediately. It's also a good idea to immediately review your insurance policies — including the fine print — so you'll know exactly what kind of documentation is needed before you miss the opportunity to get it. If you know your policy provisions well and have full documentation to support your claim, the insurance company will have a difficult time dragging its feet.

HOW LONG IS TOO LONG TO WAIT?

Settlement times vary depending on the type of insurance and the size of the claim. As a general rule, however, the following maximum times should apply:

* Automobile collision claims — 7 to 10 days.

* Automobile property damage liability claims — 10 to 14 days.

* Automobile personal injury claims — 14 to 21 days.

* Automobile injury liability claims — 21 to 28 days.

* Homeowner's insurance claims — 10 to 14 days. * Business insurance claims — 14 to 21 days.

* Health insurance claims — 45 days.

* Disability claims — Too many variables and policy specifications to

make a general estimate.

* Life insurance claims — 60 to 90 days.

In all cases, claim periods will likely be extended if there are unusual circumstances, such as an on-going police investigation or some indication of fraud. However, for routine claims, you should probably suspect the insurer of unwarranted foot dragging if you can't get at least a claim approval, if not a full settlement, within the specified time periods.

E. Insurance Odds & Ends

BEWARE OF TV INSURANCE OFFERS

In spite of how good — or how cheap — the announcers make it sound, most insurance advertised on TV and sold by phone or mail is a bad deal. The rates quoted (i.e., "a dollar a week") are usually for a minimum base policy (sometimes as little as $1,000 face value), meaning it will cost substantially more to get enough coverage to offer even modest protection. In addition, even when the policies do offer substantial face value for the premium, they tend to have multiple exclusions that eliminate coverage in the most common circumstances. Firms that provide mail-order health or accident policies are even worse, with bad records for denying claims or excluding illnesses. Another Trap: Low introductory rates that are quickly raised once you are dependent on the coverage. Best Protection: Check with your state insurance commission to make sure the company is licensed and has not built up a thick file of complaints.

DOUBLE INDEMNITY CAN PREVENT DOUBLE TROUBLE & SAVE YOU HUNDREDS A YEAR

A double-indemnity clause is a provision in a life insurance policy that doubles the face value in the event of accidental or violent death. For young families, a double-indemnity clause can provide the additional coverage needed without a substantial increase in premiums. The reason is that most people calculate total potential need without considering the likelihood of why they might have to collect on a policy. A young father might feel he needs $500,000 to adequately protect his family, even though such a policy would be a huge strain on his budget. What he overlooks is that the greatest life risk he faces at his age is from an accident. Thus, he could cover his greatest risk by simply buying a $250,000 policy with a double indemnity clause, which might add only $10 or $15 to the annual premium. Caution: If you do get a double-indemnity policy, make sure the clause doesn't contain too many exclusions with respect to the greatest risks you face (e.g., we've seen some that apply to accidents in public carriers, but not to accidents in your own car).

Another Savings Option: Fear of a chronic or disabling illness that could wipe out a family's assets is another reason many people cite for buying excess insurance. However, you can provide additional low-cost protection for your family against such an occurrence by simply buying an "excess" major medical policy with a deductible equal to the maximum benefit under your current health plan . Because of the high deductible, the premium cost will be much more reasonable than if you bought a full-coverage policy for the s same total amount.

2 TYPES OF INSURANCE YOU SHOULD ALWAYS DECLINE

We've already covered several types of insurance that are bad value for the money . Here are a couple more you should always avoid:

1. Travel insurance sold at airports. Though your chances of dying in a commercial airline accident are remote, you may still feel the need for travel insurance. If so, buy directly from an insurance company — the coverage will be much less expensive.

2. Insurance to pay off loans or installment debts if you die or are disabled. This insurance is exceptionally expensive and many of the disability provisions are excessively restrictive. You can get the same coverage for 40% to 50% less by simply buying a decreasing easing-term life policy for the duration of the installments.

$150 A YEAR CAN SAVE YOU FROM LOSING EVERYTHING

An "umbrella" liability policy is the best bargain in the insurance business in today's sue-crazy world. This policy covers you for all types of personal liability (except professional malpractice) when damages exceed the limits on your auto or homeowner's policies. You can usually get $1 million in umbrella coverage for between $125 and $175 — and a $2 million policy (the largest most companies will issue) will run only about 60% more. However, if you also lower the maximums on your regular liability policies, you may actually be able to save money with an umbrella policy. Catch: Most insurance companies will sell you an umbrella policy only if you also buy both your auto and homeowner's (or renter's) policies from them.

INSURANCE YOU MAY NOT KNOW YOU HAVE

Here are 6 types of insurance coverage you may already have — or get when you make certain purchases — and not even know about:

1. Your homeowner's policy will usually cover lost luggage, stolen purses or wallets and property taken in car break-ins. It may also cover unusual accidents — such as damage by vandals or motor vehicles — and property lost or damaged while moving.

2. If you buy an airline ticket with most major credit cards, you automatically get from $25,000 to $100,000 in free travel life insurance.

3. American Automobile Association (AAA) members have automatic hospital and death benefits if hurt in a car accident.

4. Membership dues for many fraternal organizations and service clubs entitle you to minimum life- or health-insurance benefits under group policies.

5. If you are in a car accident, you may be able to collect twice on your injuries — first via your health insurance and again through a medical-payments provision in your auto policy.

6. Family health policies usually continue coverage for children, even if they are away at school. Check before you buy separate policies for them. Many colleges and universities also include a small amount of automatic life and/or health coverage in their tuition charges or mandatory fees, and others provide free health services for full-time students at campus infirmaries.

BEWARE THIS CASH-SURRENDER TRAP

Many whole- and universal-life insurance policies advertise a high surrender value in the early years, but are really only giving you your own money back because they overcharge on the first-year premium. For example, we recently saw a quote for a $500,000 policy for a 40-year-old man that claimed to have a first-year cash surrender value equal to 50% of the premium. The premium for the first year was $5,920 — meaning the cash-surrender value was $2,960. That sounded pretty good until we checked a bit more closely and discovered that the annual premium for each of the next 4 years was just $3,156. Thus, the true first-year surrender value was just $196 — the remaining $2,764 simply being an excess charge on the initial premium!

CHAPTER 8

INVESTMENT SECRETS

A. The Best Investment Planning Ideas

THE EASIEST WAY TO BEGIN — PAY YOURSELF FIRST!

All the investment advice in the world won't do you any good if you have nothing to invest — and, you will never build a pool of investment capital unless you specifically set out to do so. Those who say they will save and/or invest the money they have left over after covering their monthly expenses invariably find there's nothing left over — regardless of how much money they make. Thus, the only way to actually begin the savings and investment process is to grant yourself a higher status than you afford your creditors. In other words, pay yourself first! Even if it's only $5 or $10 a week, you must set that sum aside before you pay any other bills or spend money for any other purpose. Adjust payments on your other bills if need be (though our experience has shown you'll actually get used to living without the money in a very short time) — or, if necessary, join a credit union and have the money withheld directly from your paycheck. But pay yourself first! And, remember, this money is untouchable! It isn't an emergency fund or even a regular savings account. It's strictly for investments — and vital to your future. Ideally, your goal should be to set aside 10% of your net income for yourself — but don't be discouraged if you feel you have to start smaller than that. Even at just $5 a week, you will have $100 in 20 weeks — and that's enough to make an initial investment in many no-load mutual funds. At $10 a week you'll have more than $500 at the end of a year — enough for 100 shares in a low-priced growth stock. If you can set aside the full 10%, your opportunities expand even further — but, whatever your starting level, the important thing is simply to start!

INTRODUCING THE `RULE OF 72' (OR IS IT `76'?)

Once you begin the process of investing, the first thing you'll likely want to know is what kind of progress you can expect to make. To that end, there is a tool known as the "Rule of 72," which can be used to determine how long it will take to double your money at a given rate of return. It works quite simply — all you have to do is divide the number 72 by the annual yield on your investment. The result will be the number of years it takes your money to double. For example, if you get 6% on your investment, it will take 12 years to double your money (72/6 = 12) — but, if you get a yield of 9%, it will take just 8 years to double up (72/9 = 8). (Note: Though the accuracy of the Rule of 72 has been accepted for many years, some experts have recently challenged it, claiming it works only with fixed-interest investments such as savings accounts. They contend that, for investments with variable rates of return — such as mutual funds or stocks — a more accurate gauge is the Rule of 76, which works exactly the same way, but compensates for the lack of monthly compounding. Thus, if you want to be on the safe side in making your calculations, divide the number 76 by your expected annual rate of return to get the doubling time for your investment.)

TAILOR INVESTMENTS ACCORDING TO AGE

Investing is a life-long process, but that doesn't mean you should keep the same investment throughout your life. ~In fact, your age is one of the two most important factors in determining the types of investments you should consider — the other being your personal tolerance for risk, which comes into play regardless of your age. Thus, when you begin your investment program, you should first assess your own idea of acceptable risk and then tailor your portfolio based on your age and the goals you consider most important at that time in your life.

Assessing Your Tolerance for Risk: Most people have a fairly good idea of the level of risk they can accept in their investments and still be able to sleep comfortably at night. However, if you have any doubts, try taking the following short test developed by Michael Lipper, president of Lipper Analytical Services. To score, total the number of the answers chosen. A score of 9 or 16 means you are a moderate risk taker, and a score of 16 or more means you don't mind taking risks.

A. My investment is for the long term. The end result is more important than how I go about achieving it.

1. I totally disagree.
2. I can accept variability, but want no loss of capital.
3. I can accept reasonable amounts of price fluctuation in total return.

4. I can accept an occasional year of negative returns in the interest of building capital.
5. I agree with this statement.

B. Current income is:
1. Essential and must be known.
2. Essential, but I'm willing to accept uncertainty about the amount.
3. Important, but there are other factors to consider.
4. Desirable, but it can be a modest amount.
5. Irrelevant.

C. Rank the amount of decline you can accept in a single quarter.
1. None.
2. A little, but not for the entire year.
3. Consistency of results is more important than superior returns.
4. A few quarters of decline is a small price to pay to be invested when the stock market takes off.
5. Unimportant.

D. Rank the importance of beating inflation.

1. Preservation of capital and income are more important.
2. I'm willing to beat inflation, but other investment needs come first.
3. It's essential to get a real return on my investments.

E. Rank the importance of beating the stock market over both up and down economic cycles.

1. Irrelevant.

2. I prefer consistency.

3. Critical.

Once you have evaluated your tolerance for risk, you should spell out any specific needs (e.g., college savings for two children), as well as your overall objectives (e.g., retirement with a comfortable income). Then, you must look at the amount of time you have available to achicvo those goals (this is where age becomes an important factor) and choose the appropriate mix of investments. Unfortunately, there are no exact rules for selecting the best mix of investments. As a general rule, however, most experts say:

* Small-capitalization stocks or stock funds are best for maximum growth.

* A balance of growth stocks and fixed-income investments and/or growth and income funds is best for stability (with some international stocks or funds for

diversification).

*A mix of bonds, high-dividend stocks and other fixed-yield vehicles (or funds of the same type), including a money fund, is best for income-oriented investors.

Given these pre-qualifications, there are 4 basic age (or need) categories that should primarily influence your choice of investment vehicles and portfolio mix. They are:

1. The younger, growth investor. At this point, with plenty of full earning years ahead and few family responsibilities, you should be willing to accept greater risks in return for higher long-term growth. Preservation of capital isn't as important as profits, and income usually isn't a major consideration either. At this point, a good portfolio mix might have 35% of your cash in small-cap stocks or funds, 50% in growth and income stocks or funds, and about 15% in international stock funds for diversification.

2. The family years. At this stage, some growth is needed, but risk is a much larger concern. With college funding needs ahead, retirement savings a growing priority and current expense levels high, most people in this group can't afford substantial loss of principal, so a more conservative tone becomes necessary. A good mix at this point would be 15% in small-cap stocks or funds, 25% in growth and income stocks or funds, 40% in international funds and 20% in money funds or short-term bonds. Experts say the biggest danger at this age level is either chasing too much yield, with high associated risk, or being too conservative, keeping too much money in CDs and savings accounts with the resulting loss of earnings.

3. The pre-retirement period. At this age, the kids are through college and out on their own, and only a few years remain until retirement. Likewise, only a few peak earning years remain, so preservation of capital becomes the primary concern, though some growth is still desirable. The best strategy at this point is to increase diversification so you get maximum protection from a loss of value in any one area and a wide range of opportunities for growth. A suggested portfolio mix would be 30 percent in growth stocks or funds, 15% in international funds, 10% in inflation hedges (real estate, gold, etc.), 10% in cash equivalents and 35% in bonds or bond funds, broken down by thirds into short-, medium- and long-term maturities.

4. The post-retirement years. At this stage, income becomes the primary concern, with preservation of capital close behind. However, because of inflation — particularly in health-care costs — some growth is also needed. In fact, the biggest mistake among people in this age group is generally being too conservative, putting all their money in CDs or bonds. For better results, experts suggest a portfolio mix of about 20% in growth stock funds, 20% in utility stocks or income funds, 10% in money funds or cash equivalents and 50% in short- and

intermediate-term bonds or bond funds. This allocation should provide growth of 2% to 6% a year, as well as adequate income.

Obviously, these are general guidelines and will have to be adjusted to reflect your individual financial situation and your short- and long-term goals. However, they illustrate the importance of keying your investments according to age as well as to objective.

THE BIGGEST INVESTMENT MISTAKES YOU CAN MAKE

One reason many people fail to achieve their maximum investment potential is that they make needless mistakes — not just once, but over and over again. Here are 10 of the most common investment mistakes, and some tips on how to avoid them:

1. Running with the crowd. While the fact that everyone likes an investment doesn't automatically make it bad, there is strong evidence that a herd mentality often prevails in the markets — usually to the benefit of no one. If you buy or sell only when everyone else is doing so, your performance will be average, at best — and worse than average if you're among the last to hop aboard the trend. Studies have shown a contrarian approach — buying solid investments that are temporarily out of favor and then selling them when everyone else gets excited about them — can reap substantial dividends.

2. Not understanding the relationship between risk and reward. Though the rule of higher potential reward entailing higher possible risk is repeated almost daily, many people fail to grasp its true meaning. They either focus on high returns, ignoring the inherent risks, or they eschew all risk, and wind up with below-par returns. A good investment plan calls for a careful review of both sides of the equation, basing choices on a balance between the amount of return needed and the amount of risk you can tolerate. Recognition of the fact that an occasional loss is acceptable is also important. The best plan involves setting a range of expected returns and choosing investments that will perform within that range (as well as eliminating those that fluctuate outside the boundaries). For example, if you want to average an 8% return, you might set a risk limit of 5% and profit target of 20%, holding investments that continue to produce returns within that range and selling those that reach either boundary.

3. Chasing higher yields. This has been a particular problem the past year or two, with CD and money market rates down in the 3% to 4% range. The usual solution to low yields on risk-free instruments is to look for investments with longer maturities. However, when interest rates rise, such investments always fall in price, meaning their total return drops, wiping out the supposed

advantage. The best approach is to create a balanced portfolio with a variety of investment vehicles (CDs, money funds, stocks, bonds, mutual funds, etc.) so that falling yields on one segment will be offset by higher returns on another, thus providing the steady overall return you need.

4. Failing to properly diversify. Too many people put all their eggs in one or two baskets and then get killed when somebody drops the basket. As explained in No. 3, a good portfolio should include a variety of different investments that move in opposite directions in response to changing economic conditions. That way, the overall return remains fairly stable from year to year, and you are protected against major setbacks such as those seen by stock investors in 1987.

5. Failing to look overseas. Despite the increasing global nature of investments and economics, too many people still restrict their investments to U.S. securities. Every portfolio today should have an international component — perhaps as much as 25%, depending on objectives — to provide protection against domestic volatility.

6. Failing to adopt a regular investment plan. The majority of people invest either in fits and starts, buying a stock here and a bond there as they find an appealing story, or all at once, trying to time market tops and bottoms. A better approach is to buy according to a regular schedule, regardless of the price, using a method such as dollar-cost averaging (investing a set amount each month or quarter) or value averaging (investing a sum each period sufficient to make your total portfolio grow by a certain amount). Such plans tend to smooth out market performance and lower your overall cost per unit.

7. Basing decisions on fear or greed. Too many people react rather than act when it comes to investing, getting scared out of positions too early for fear of a big loss or hanging on to positions too long in hopes of making a killing The best approach is to follow the above guidelines for structuring a balanced portfolio of investments with preset risk limits and targets, and then stick to them. You may never triple your money on any one stock, but if you've tailored your investments to your objectives, you'll reach those goals without losing any sleep.

8. Searching for a "guru." Money managers, newsletter writers and market advisors all claim to have the answers you need — and will show you track records to prove it. However, it's highly unlikely any of these people will be making recommendations based strictly on your personal needs (nor will you have the money to buy everything they suggest). Thus, it's better not to be a slave to any one advisor. Rather, you should establish your own plan and then look to a variety of advisors for ideas on particular issues or investments that will fit into that plan.

9. Investing strictly on the basis of tax consequences. This becomes a problem for people with rapidly rising income levels, as well as for older individuals worried about estate-tax consequences. They start looking more at

the tax impact of an investment than at the merit of the investment itself — and the results can be disastrous if tax laws or economic conditions change (just ask all the people holding virtually worthless units in real estate partnerships). While year-to-year tax planning with respect to taking investment profits and losses is an important consideration in maximizing returns, the actual selection of investment vehicles should be based on their relative merit and the role they will play in your overall portfolio, not strictly on their potential tax benefits.

10. Failing to keep good records. If you don't know exactly what you own and exactly how much it cost, it will be virtually impossible to determine how it's performing and if it's contributing what it should to achieving your overall investment objectives. Though it requires some time and effort, keeping good, up-to-date records is vitally important to your investment success, facilitating buy and sell decisions, overall portfolio adjustments and tax planning. Thus, before you do anything else regarding your investments, take the time to get organized.

CHOOSING THE PROPER PORTFOLIO MIX

For those investors who have trouble determining an appropriate range of risk versus reward as discussed in No. 2 above, financial columnist Jane Bryant Quinn did a study of how portfolios would have done between 1947 and 1989 when split in various proportions between stocks (as measured by the S&P 500) and long-term government bonds (or mutual funds investing in those vehicles), assuming annual compounding and reinvestment of dividends. Here are the results, as published in her book "Making the Most of Your Money," to help you chose a mix that might be suitable for you:

	Largest	Largest	Average
Portfolio Mix Return	1-Year Loss	1-Year Gain	
100% Stocks	-26.5%	+52.6%	+13.5%
90% Stocks, 10% Bonds	-23.4%	+48.1%	+12.7%
80% Stocks, 20% Bonds	-20.3%	+43.5%	+11.8%
70% Stocks, 30% Bonds	-17.2%	+39.0%	+11.0%
60% Stocks, 40% Bonds	-14.1%	+34.4%	+10.1%
50% Stocks, 50% Bonds	-11.1%	+31.6%	+9.3%
40% Stocks, 60% Bonds	- 8.0%	+32.82	+8.4%
30% Stocks, 70% Bonds	- 6.1%	+34.7%	+7.6%
20% Stocks, 80% Bonds	- 5.8%	+36.6%	+6.7%

10% Stocks, 90% Bonds	- 5.9%	+38.5%	+5.9%
100% Bonds	- 9.2%	+40.4%	+5.0%

A quick look at the table shows that a bias in favor of stocks has offered the highest long-term return, but also the most severe short-term volatility. By contrast, portfolios more heavily weighted toward government bonds have been the best protected against short-term risk, but the returns have also been substantially below par. The best mix for protection against both short-term loss and wide fluctuations in performance appears to be a combination of about 40% stocks and 60% bonds, though the 8.4% average return may not be enough to suit the needs of many investors.

3 KEYS TO PROTECTING YOUR INVESTMENTS NOW

While many areas of the country are still having severe problems, overall U.S. economic numbers are showing improvement. However, with a new Democratic president moving into the White House and bringing along almost certain changes in fiscal policy, the environment for investing today can still best be described as confusing. For that reason, it's important to retain a cautious attitude with respect to both the individual elements in your portfolio and the balance among types of investments. Here are 3 key guidelines for protecting your investments in an uncertain economic environment:

1. Monitor fixed-income investments closely. With interest rates at or near a bottom, bonds of all maturities are at high prices, meaning there is capital risk should interest rates begin to rise. The default risk on both corporate bonds and bank CDs is also higher now than at any time in decades. As a result, you must keep a close watch on each of your fixed-income issues and be prepared to sell or shift to other investments at the first sign of bad news. You can't afford to wait and hope — particularly where there's a risk of default — because things can go from bad to worse in a hurry.

2. Avoid new equity investment. Despite the uncertain economy, stocks — particularly those of smaller capitalization growth companies — have stayed near their all-time highs. As a result, their prices have outstripped their earnings and many issues must be considered overvalued. This doesn't mean you should begin unloading your stock holdings, as both individual issues and the market as a whole could still move higher. However, you must monitor each issue carefully, looking for any sign of disappointing performance (e.g., a slowing of sales or earnings growth) that could trigger a price decline and be prepared to take your profits. You should also avoid making new commitments to stocks as the risk at current price levels is significantly higher than the potential reward. If you do

have a large sum of money available for equity investments, try to space out your purchases over at least a year — and preferably a year and a half — investing in a quarter to a sixth of your funds at a time.

3. Fine tune your portfolio for maximum protection and return. Obviously, the exact proportions will depend on your individual goals and tolerance for risk. However, a good balance for the first half of 1993 would probably be a 50-50 split between stocks and fixed-income investments, broken down as follows:

* 25% in individual stocks sited in strong or recession-resistant industries such as beverages, cosmetics, drugs, food, health care (particularly those companies focusing on cost containment), liquor, telephones and tobacco products. Avoid issues in the airline, auto, banking, media, metals, mining, real estate and textile sectors, all of which tend to be volatile in uncertain markets.

* 10% in mutual funds investing in a balance of growth and income-oriented stocks. 2 funds to consider are Selected American Shares (1-800-553-5533), which averaged a return of 15.60% over the past 5 years, and Berger 101 Fund (1-800-333-1001), which turned in a 5-year average return of 12.76%

* 10% in mutual funds investing in aggressive-growth and/or small-capitalization issues. 2 possibilities here are Pacific Horizon Aggressive Growth Fund (1-800-332-3863), which charges a 4.5% load but averaged a return of 22.59% over the past 5 years, and Twentieth Century Ultra (1-800-345-2021), which returned 27.55% over the past 5 years.

* 5% in international mutual funds, such as T. Rowe Price International (1-800-638-5660), which averaged a 16.26% return over the past 5 years.

* 10% in individual municipal bonds.

* 10% in short- to medium-term U.S. government securities

* 5% in top-rated corporate bonds.

* 25% in a mix of actively managed mutual funds investing in municipal, corporate and international bonds. 3 possibilities here, with 5-year average returns, are General Municipal Bond Fund (1-800-645-6561), 7.92%; T. Rowe Price International Bond Fund (1-800-638-5660), 10.85%; Value Line Income Fund (1-800-223-0818), 11.96%

With this degree of diversification you get maximum protection and your individual holdings are small enough that you can easily make shifts as conditions mandate, particularly among the suggested funds, all of which allow cost-free switches to other funds within the same family.

HOW TO GET EXPERT FINANCIAL ADVICE FOR FREE

Actually, it's not hard to get expert financial advice for free. Nearly every brokerage firm, financial planner and investment advisor offers some type of free seminar to the public on a regular basis, and many also provide a variety of free informational publications. Of course, there is a catch: The information is invariably biased toward products or services offered by the sponsoring firm or person — and you nearly always get a sales pitch along with the facts. Succumb, and the price of your "free" advice goes up considerably. Universities and colleges also often offer financial seminars, but many of these either require small fees or are co-sponsored and presented by brokers, which once again taints the impartiality of the information. Fortunately, there are some fairly objective financial publications — many prepared by professional associations, government agencies or consumer groups — that you can get for free (or nearly so) without any strings attached. Here are some of better ones:

* "9 Tax Tips for Mutual Fund Investors," published by GIT Investment Funds, 1655 Fort Myer Drive, Ste. 1000, Arlington, VA 22209, or call 1-800-336-3063. Free.

* "Consumer Credit Handbook" (Item No. 441Y), published by the Consumer Information Center, Pueblo, CO 81002, explains how to fix errors on your credit report and what to do if you're turned down for a loan. 50 cents.

* Selecting a Qualified Financial Planning Professional," published by the Institute of Certified Financial Planners, 7600 E. Eastman Ave., Ste. 301, Denver, CO 80231, or call 1-800-282-7526. Free.

* Shaping Your Financial Fitness," published by the National Association of Life Underwriters, 1922 F St. N.W., Washington, DC 20006, discusses the basics of annuities, MediGap coverage and other insurance-related financial products. Free.

* A Common-Sense Guide to Taking Charge of Your Money," published by Fidelity Investments (1-800-544-4774), explains the mechanics of lump-sum pension distributions and outlines rollover options. Free.

* Investment Swindles: How They Work and How to Avoid Them," published by the National Futures Association, 200 W. Madison St., Chicago, IL 60606, or call 1-800-621-3570. Free. The NFA also offers free copies of the "Investors' Bill of Rights," which explains the items brokers must disclose before selling you an investment product.

* "The Consumer's Almanac," published by the American Financial Services Association, Consumer Credit Education Foundation, 919 18th St. N.W., Ste. 300, Washington, DC 20006, explains the basics of money management and budgeting, with worksheets to help you out. $2.00. AFSA also offers a booklet explaining "What You Should Know Before Declaring Bankruptcy" for the same price.

* "How to Get Safety Information From Your Financial Institution," published by Weiss Research, 2200 N. Florida Mango Road, West Palm Beach, FL 33409, details what you should ask banks, insurance companies and brokerage firms to gauge their safety and rate their investment policies. $2.00.

* "A Single Person's Guide to Retirement Planning," published by American Association of Retired Persons, Fulfillment Dept., 60 E St. N.W., Washington, DC 20049, provides information on investing, insurance and other concerns of those preparing for retirement. Free. The AARP also offers a variety of other useful publications, including "Money Maters," which offers guidelines on choosing and working with financial services professionals.

* "Can You Afford to Retire?" published by the Life Insurance Marketing and Research Assn., P.O. Box 208, Hartford, CN 06141, or call 1-800-235-4672, discusses various sources of retirement income, with worksheets. $1.50

* "Getting Out of Debt," published by Bankcard Holders of America, 560 Herndon Parkway, Ste. 120, Herndon, VA 22070, offers budgeting strategies and guidelines for better credit-card use. $1.00

* "Your Money & Your Home," published by Countrywide Mortgage Co., 1-800-669-6064, explains step by step the process of applying for and getting a mortgage. Free.

* "Phone Fraud, We All Pay," published by the National Association of Consumer Agency Administrators, 1010 Vermont Ave., N.W., Ste. 514, Washington, DC 20005, explains how to deal with phone sales scams, calling-card abuses and other telephone rip-offs. Free.

THE BEST SOFTWARE FOR TRACKING YOUR INVESTMENTS

With personal computer prices coming down, PCs are becoming fixtures in more and more U.S. homes — and more and more people are using those computers to both plan and monitor heir financial affairs. Programs are now available to do everything from the simplest household budgeting to the most complex investment analysis, and many even offer tie-ins to on-line quote services or data bases so that the prices of your holdings can be instantly updated and your portfolio values quickly recalculated. We've reviewed a number of these packages — from highly technical market-specific software offered by Dow Jones & Co. to more consumer-oriented products such as Andrew Tobias' Managing Your Money program. However, in terms of value for the money — and maximum efficiency for all your investment planning and monitoring needs — our vote for best software currently available goes to a new product called Smart Investor. Designed by Reality Technologies and both endorsed and marketed by Money Magazine, Smart Investor provides personalized investment guidance, analyzing your needs and objectives and suggesting specific solutions. The program identifies specific mutual funds, money market fund, CDs and other investments to suit your risk tolerances on performance goals; provides automatic portfolio tracking and updating; gives access to on-line information services; and even connects you to electronic brokerage systems, allowing you to enter buy and sell order from your own computer. The package retails for just $99.00, but is available from discount stores (such as Egghead, 1-800-344-4323 for mail orders) for as little as $59.99. The program is currently available only for the IBM-PC and clones using DOS operating systems, but the makers hope to have a version for Apple computers ready sometime in 1993.

B. The Ins & Outs of Mutual Funds

THE ADVANTAGES OF MUTUAL FUNDS

By far the easiest way for most people to begin a serious investment program is through mutual funds. That's because mutual funds offer a variety of advantages for individuals unavailable in any other type of investment. Here are 12 of the most important advantages of mutual funds:

1. Buying shares in a fund is easy. With most funds, you can open a new account or add to an existing one by mail, phone or bank wire. You can also arrange for automatic investment plans, having funds transferred from your checking or savings accounts at regular intervals.

2. You don't have to have a lot of money. While some mutual funds require an initial investment of $2,500, most let you open an account with $1,000 or less — in some cases as little as $250. And, you can then add even smaller amounts to your account — usually as little as $50 at a time.

3. Equal opportunity. The fact that you are a small investor doesn't hurt your chances of making large returns with mutual funds. Because all monies are pooled and then invested in a diversified portfolio of securities, with shares valued according to the total holdings of the fund, you can earn the same return whether your investment totals $1,000 or $100,000.

4. Funds are ideal for systematic investment plans. Dollar-cost averaging and value averaging are extremely easy with funds — and can improve your returns by lowering your overall cost basis. You also eliminate the problem of trying to time your investments to get the best price — one area where most average investors are woefully inadequate.

5. Funds offer diversification that would otherwise be unavailable to smaller investors. If you try to buy individual securities when you have only a small sum to invest, one bad call can wipe you out. With funds, our money is spread across the full spectrum of fund holdings, even if you have only a few hundred dollars

invested. Thus, the failure of one stock or bond will have only a minimal impact on your overall performance.

6. Funds employ professional managers and analysts. Even if you had more money to invest, you probably wouldn't have the time to hunt out the best investments. Funds, however, have full-time research staffs that evaluate opportunities and professional managers who make the trading decisions. Because they handle millions of dollars, they also have access to the latest information and can make trades on the largest and most cost-effective scale.

7. If you want to take a more active role in your investments, most funds that belong to so-called "families" offer telephone-switching privileges that enable you to move your money from fund to fund, taking advantage of bullish trends and avoiding bearish moves.

8. Funds offer low trading costs. Commissions are a major drain on the returns of small investors, easily wiping out $2 or $3 of per-share gains on transactions of 100 or 200 shares. Mutual funds, on the other hand, trade in blocks of thousands or tens of thousands of shares, meaning per-share costs are reduced to a minimum and returns are increased proportionally.

9. Funds offer reinvestment plans, making it easier to increase your returns through compounding. If you make a $5 gain on a $10 stock, that's great — but then you have to turn around and find another promising $10 stock if you want to keep reaping the same return. That, as you know, is not easy. In addition, very few individual stocks offer dividend-reinvestment plans, meaning the income your holdings generates must be put into some other investment (or, more likely, it gets spent). With funds, dividend payments and capital gains distributions can be automatically reinvested, buying additional shares that will in turn produce more profits. This can make a tremendous difference over time. $1,000 invested at 9% for 10 years without compounding will grow to just $1,900, but with annual compounding it will grow to $2,367 — increasing your overall return by almost 50%.

10. Most funds have special provisions for retirement plans such as IRAs and Keoghs. This tailoring makes it easy for you to build a nest egg — and the other advantages offered by funds help that nest egg grow.

11. Fund investments are highly liquid. You can cash in your shares at any time with little problem. Many funds even offer check-writing privileges, and others will transfer money directly to your bank. Even if those services aren't available, the others will get your money to you within a couple of days after receiving a phone call or wire.

12. Most funds offer automatic withdrawal plans. This is a great benefit for retirees who want to keep the bulk of their money working while still getting monthly or quarterly income. It also eliminates the danger of having to sell out your holdings at a market bottom — in essence reversing the concept of dollar-

cost averaging.

HOW TO FIND A WINNING FUND

Despite the disclaimers printed on investment prospectuses to the effect that "past performance is no guarantee of future results," past performance is indeed the best way to evaluate a prospective mutual fund. Many of the leading financial publications — including Investor's Business Daily and Money Magazine — include regular and annual rankings of mutual fund performance. However, if you'd like quicker and more comprehensive performance rankings to help in making your selections, there are 4 major sources:

1. The Investment Company Institute, 1775 K Street N.W., Washington, DC 10006.

2. Lipper Analytical Services, 74 Trinity Place, New York NY 10006.

3. No-Load Mutual Fund Association, 655 Third Ave., New York, NY 10017.

4. Wiesenberger Investment Companies Services, 870 Fifth Ave., New York, NY 10019.

Each of these services provides comparative fund listings, showing performance rankings over the past 1, 5, 10, 15 and 20 years.

KEY THINGS TO LOOK FOR IN A FUND PROSPECTUS

Most mutual fund prospectuses run 40 or 50 pages of depressingly dull text, printed in a type size that can only be described as eye straining. That's why most people never bother to completely read them before they invest their money — and why some of those people wind up with investments that aren't really suitable for their needs. Fortunately, it's not essential to read every word of a fund prospectus, so long as you make sure to check on certain key points. Here are the most important questions you want answered when you read a prospectus:

1. What kind of performance record has the fund compiled? Prospectuses will usually feature a review of performance over the past several years as compared with major market indices. If you're looking for an income fund, you want to see a performance record that has consistently produced returns of at least 2 to 3 percentage points above the average market yield. If you're shopping for a growth fund, you want to see a record that has equaled or surpassed the performance of the S&P 500 in both up and down markets.

2. Does the fund's stated investment philosophy match your personal goals — and does the fund's list of holdings accurately reflect that philosophy?

Some funds that rank at the top of the performance listings do so by building portfolios of highly volatile issues or employing excess leverage to improve returns. That's fine when the market is moving in the right direction, but such policies can expose the fund — and you — to much higher risk if prices move the wrong way.

3. Are there limitations on types of investments the fund can make? Most funds are required to maintain diversified portfolios and limit their use of margin and options. However, others — particularly so-called sector funds — are allowed to invest almost exclusively in stocks of a single industry or market segment, as well as make more liberal use of leverage and options. As a rule, these specialized or leveraged funds carry higher risks than do diversified funds.

4. Does the fund stay fully invested most of the time, or does it move money into cash equivalents during down markets? Even though funds that take cash positions in down markets may rate lower on the performance charts, they are generally less volatile, meaning you face less risk if you are investing for a shorter term.

5. Does the fund charge a front-end load or sales commission? With only a few exceptions, long-term performance records show that no-load funds do just as well as those with fees, so there's little reason to sacrifice from 4% to 9% of your money to sales charges before it's even invested. If you do have a particular reason for selecting a load fund, make sure it's one with a performance record that justifies the added expense.

6. Are their any additional fees imposed when you open or close your fund account? Some funds charge a back-end load (one assessed when you sell your shares) of 1% or 4%, while others impose administrative or registration fees. However, with all the funds available today, there's really no reason to pay such fees.

7. What's the minimum amount required to open an account, and the minimum for additional deposits. As a general rule, the lower the limit the better — especially if you intend to employ some type of systematic investment plan.

8. Is the fund a member of a family of funds — and, if so, does the group offer reasonable fund-switching privileges? At a minimum, you want a fund that will let you switch into a money market fund — and, if you are a more aggressive investor, you may desire a much wider selection of funds into which you can shift your money. The best fund families allow you to switch your money with a simple phone call, and most allow 2 or 3 switches per year without a fee. If the fund family you're considering charges fees for switching, make sure they are not unreasonable.

9. Does the fund have special terms or conditions for retirement plans? Most funds offer lower limits for IRA or Keogh accounts, and some even have automatic deposit plans that will take money directly from your bank account for

monthly or quarterly share purchases. If discipline isn't your long suit, this can be an important advantage.

10. Does the fund offer an automatic withdrawal plan? This can be a very helpful feature if you are saving for retirement and want to ensure an orderly disposition of our money.

A GREAT INVESTMENT YOUR BROKER WON'T MENTION

Many of the nation's leading mutual funds have turned in outstanding performance records over the past 20 years — and, given their money management and stock selection expertise, it seems likely they will repeat that performance in the future. However, if you don't go looking for them, you may never find out about these top performers because they have no front-end load — meaning your broker will never tell you about them because he or she gets no commission for selling them. To give you an idea of what you may be missing in the no-load fund field, let's look at the performance of just one leading fund — Twentieth Century Growth Investors Fund. This fund returned a phenomenal 69% for the 12-month period ending Dec. 31, 1991 — and has averaged an annual return of almost 21% over the past 20 years! To put that in dollar terms, a $1,000 investment made on Dec. 31, 1971, would be worth $43,863 today, assuming all dividends were reinvested. In these days of 3% CD rates, it's hard to argue with performance like that. For more information about the Twentieth Century family of no-load mutual funds, write to the company at P.O. Box 419200, Kansas City, MO 64141, or call 1-800-345-2021 for a prospectus.

THE HIDDEN LOAD IN NO-LOAD FUNDS

More than half of the mutual funds that advertise themselves as no-load funds actually charge a small fee to cover the costs of marketing and distribution of shares. Called "12b-1" fees (named for the section of the Investment Company Act of 1940 that authorizes them), these charges can total as much a 0.25% of average daily net assets per year — which can lower your expected return by reducing the amount of capital you have at work in the fund.

5 FUNDS `FOR WINNERS ONLY' MUTUAL FUNDS

If preservation of capital is your prime concern, you may want to consider a mutual fund that concentrates on avoiding losses in all types of markets. How do you find such a fund? Actually, you can choose from a pretty short list — of the 264 stock funds in existence at the start of 1978, only 5 have been able to equal or surpass the S&P 500's 15.5% annual return without suffering through a single losing year. These funds, with their compounded annual gain (including reinvested dividends) since Jan. 1, 1978, are:

1. Phoenix Growth Fund, 20.2%, 4.75% sales fee, 1-800-243-4361.

2. Merrill Lynch Capital A, 16.9%, 6.50% sales fee, 1-800-637-3863.

3. Investment Company of America, 16.6%, 5.75% sales fee, 1-800-421-9900.

4. John Hancock Sovereign Fund, 15.6%, 5.00% sales fee, 1-800-225-5291.

5. CGM Mutual Fund, 15.5%, no load, 1-800-345-4048.

'CHURNING' FINDS ITS WAY INTO THE FUNDS MARKET

The practice of needlessly buying and selling stock in client accounts for the sole purpose of generating extra commissions is a dishonest broker practice almost as old as the brokerage business itself. Known as "churning," this technique victimizes individuals who give brokers discretionary power to make unapproved trades for their account. In the past, the practice has been largely limited to the trading of stocks and/or bonds. However, because of the rapid growth in the number of mutual funds, there have been an increasing number of complaints in recent years of churning among funds with front-end sales loads. In one case involving the account of an elderly Arizona woman, a broker made more than 100 shifts between funds in just 8 years, generating more than $100,000 in commissions. Actually, according to Michael Criden, a Miami attorney who specializes in securities arbitration cases, churning of mutual funds is a lot easier — and more lucrative — than churning accounts containing stocks. "For one thing," Criden says, "brokers who churn stocks run the risk that the market will turn against them, causing them to lose substantial amounts of client money. However, the risk to clients' principal is much smaller with funds because one fund is often being replaced with something similar, and the overall performance doesn't change that much. What the broker is actually doing is stealing your interest, in the form of commissions." Criden says the brokers also stand to make much more money churning funds since they get from 2% to 4% of the amount involved in a transaction, compared to just 0.5% to 1% on most stock trades. Finally, he notes, rules involving stock churning are very clear, making the practice easy to detect. With funds, which aren't as closely tracked, the risk of getting caught is much lower.

How To Protect Yourself: There are 2 basic ways to keep from getting burned by a churning scam:

1. Don't give your broker discretionary trading power over your account. If

you make all your own fund-switching decisions, there's no way the broker can get away with unauthorized trades.

2. Make sure you're dealing with a reputable broker. You can get the full disciplinary record of any stockbroker by calling the National Association of Securities Dealers at 1-800-289-9999.

A NEW WAY TO SELL FUND SHARES

How would you like to have someone pay you an extra $100 when you sell your mutual fund shares? Sellers of front-end load funds can do just that by redeeming their shares through the San Diego-based discount brokerage firm, Jack White & Company, rather than through their regular broker. And, if you want to buy shares in another load fund, White & Co. may also be able to give you big discounts on the next round of commissions. Under a program called the Connect System, White & Co. is making a secondary market in more than 100 funds that carry front-end loads, matching buyers and sellers and providing value on both sides of a transaction. So you can see how it works, let's assume you want to invest $20,000 in a fund with a 5% front-end sales fee. Buying the shares through a broker would mean paying a $1,000 commission. However, White & Co. charges only a $200 flat fee, meaning you have $800 more to invest in the fund. White keeps $100 of the fee for its service and passes $100 on to the seller of the shares as an incentive to redeem them through White, rather than through a broker or financial planner.

Drawback: Because the Connect System is still in its infancy, it's often difficult to find a seller of a particular fund on the same day a buyer calls in an order. However, White & Co. is attempting to get the National Association of Securities Dealers to list the firm's fund offerings and orders on its Bulletin Board, which would encourage more people to use the system and improve liquidity. For more information about the Connect System, call White & Co. at 1-800-233-3411.

C. Beating Today's Low Interest Rates

SHOP OUT OF STATE FOR BETTER CD RATES

If you're not happy with the rates your own bank is offering on certificates of deposit, you may be able to beat them by as much as a full percentage point by shopping in other states. The Wall Street Journal and Barron's list the top-yielding CD rates around the country every week. If you want more details, including safety ratings, you can also subscribe to a newsletter that specializes in interest rates. Two of the best are 100 Highest

Yields (8 weeks at $34, 1-800-327-7717) and RateGram ($10 per issue, 415-479-3815). RateGram also has a fax service (RateFax) that you can get for $25 by calling the same number. Catch: You won't always be able to get the yield you see quoted since rates sometimes change daily. If you mail your check, you'll get the rate that's in effect on the day the check arrives. If you have your bank wire the money, you'll get that day's rate — but you may have to pay a $10 to $15 transfer fee.

SHOULD YOU ABANDON YOUR MONEY MARKET FUND?

In a word, the answer is "no" — at least not entirely. While money market yields are near their lowest level since these popular funds came into existence, many of the alternatives aren't yielding enough to offset the loss of convenience and liquidity. If you want higher yields with the same low risk, you'll have to tie your money up for a longer period and may miss the opportunity to improve your returns should interest rates move up. And, if you go the other route — accepting higher risk in order to get a better yield — you could wind up losing enough principal to offset the increased yield if you have to liquidate at the wrong time. The best approach now is to maintain a minimum liquid reserve in your money market account and spread the rest of your capital over instruments of differing maturities to improve our overall return. For example, you might keep a third of your cash in a money fund, collecting the recent average yield of about 4%, put a third in a short-term bond fund (recently yielding around 6%), and a third in a conservative growth stock fund (yielding about 8%). What you don't want to do is lock your money up for a long period. For example, a 5-year CD is currently yielding only about 5.80% — better than the money market account but not enough to offset the opportunity risk you take in not having funds available should conditions improve.

HIGH-YIELD FUND AND STOCK STRATEGIES

One of the easiest ways to beat low CD and money market rates is with high-yielding funds and high-dividend stocks. By structuring a portfolio containing such instruments, you should be able to easily beat money market rates by 2% to 3% — and, if you're willing to take on a little more risk, you could wind up earning 10% to 11% overall. Here are some guidelines on choosing investments in these categories:

* High-dividend stocks — These are usually Blue Chip issues or utility companies that offer both price growth and steadily increasing dividends, thus providing a high total return. Best choices are companies with dividend yields of at least 4%, plus a steady record of earnings increases and raised dividends. Some examples, with recent dividend yields in parentheses, include Allegheny Power (6.7%), Bristol-Myers Squibb (4.3%), Boatmen's Bancshares (4.3%), Dow

Chemical (4.4%), Hanson Corp. (6.6%), IBM (7.1%), Ipalco Enterprises (5.6%), Mobil Oil (4.9%), Northern States Power (5.8%), Syntex (4.3%) and Teco Power (4.6%).

* Total-return funds — These mutual funds are the ideal alternative for people who don't have enough cash to maintain a diversified portfolio of individual stocks. They typically invest 50% to 60% of their assets in growth stocks and the remainder in government securities or other fixed-income instruments that provide a stabilizing effect on fund values. The result is a combination of growth and yield, that results in a total return of 8% to 12% or more. Some choices in this category, with recent average annual return in parentheses, include USAA Income Stock Fund (16.2%), no load, 1-800-531-8181; Financial Industrial Income Fund (18.7%), no load, 1-800-525-8085; Wellington Fund (16.6%), no load, 1-800-662-7447; Selected American Shares (15.6%), no load, 1-800-553-5533; and Twentieth Century Balanced Fund (12.4%), no load, 1-800-345-2021.

* Growth stock funds — These go more for capital appreciation and less for income, but the better funds have managed average returns of around 12% to 14% without substantial risk. Some alternatives in this category include Berger 100 Fund (25.4%), no load, 1-800-333-1001; Janus Twenty Fund (21.9%), no load, 1-800-525-8983; MainStay Capital Appreciation Fund (17.2%), no load, 1-800-522-4202; and Pasadena Growth Fund (21.5%), 5.5% load, 1-800-882-2855.

* International stock funds — These funds provide good returns and an added element of diversification when teamed with your domestic fund holdings. Some possible choices in this area include Scudder Global (14.6%), no load, 1-800-225-2470; Templeton Growth (13.2%), 8.5% load, 1-800-236-0738; T. Rowe Price New Asia Fund (15.2%), no load, 1-800-638-5660; and Smith Barney International Equity (11.5%), 4.5% load, 1-800-544-7835.

* Bond funds — These stress income, but also provide some growth potential, though the risk is higher than normal because of current low interest rates (rising rates would cause bond prices to slide). Some possibilities here include Value Line Income Fund (11.9%), no load, 1-800-223-0818; Income Fund of America (11.2%), 5.75% load, 1-800-421-0180; Vanguard Bond Market (12.2%), no load, 1-800-662-7447; Wellesley Income Fund (10.2%), no load, 1-800-342-5236.

A Strategy for Beating the Dow: For investors who like Blue Chip stocks and are content with consistently beating the performance of the Dow Jones Industrial Average, there's one additional strategy you may want to consider — though it takes a bit of money to put it into action. It's called the Dow Dividend Strategy and it involves constructing a portfolio comprising the 10 highest-yielding stocks from the 30 included in the Dow Industrials. Since Jan. 1, 1972, the Dow Industrials have produced a compounded annual total return of 11.5%. However, a portfolio made up of only the 10 highest-yielding Dow stocks has returned 15.8% — a 4.3% advantage. For the year ending Sept. 30, 1992, the Dow gained 5.6%, but the 10 dividend leaders returned 10.6% — almost double. The strategy can be initiated at any time and your total cash should be divided equally among the 10 stocks. At the end of October 1992, that would have meant buying equal-dollar amounts of the following stocks:

I. International Business Machines (IBM), 7.1% dividend yield.

2. Union Carbide (UK), 5.5% dividend yield.

3. Texaco Inc. (TX), 5.2% dividend yield.

4. General Motors (GM), 4.9% dividend yield.

5. Westinghouse Electric (WX), 5.6% dividend yield.

6. American Express (AXP), 4.9% dividend yield.

7. Sears, Roebuck & Co. (S), 4.8% dividend yield.

8. Eastman Kodak (EK), 4.7% dividend yield.

9. Exxon Corp. (XON), 4.6% dividend yield.

10. Chevron Corp. (CHV), 4.5% dividend yield.

All stocks should be purchased on the same day and the portfolio should be readjusted annually, selling stocks that have fallen out of the top 10 and replacing them with the new dividend leaders.

`MUNI' BONDS MAY GIVE YOU HIGHER YIELDS

With yields on taxable securities at low levels, many people in the highest tax bracket can actually boost returns by going into tax-free municipal bonds or municipal bond funds. To compare the yield on a municipal bond or bond fund, take the tax-free yield and divide by 1 minus your federal tax bracket. If you are in the 28% bracket, most tax-exempt funds today will generate the equivalent of an 8% or 9% taxable yield — and the yield will be even higher if you live in a high-tax state and buy bonds or funds that qualify for your home-state exemption. If you buy individual bonds, look for those rated A or better and offering a yield to maturity in the 6.3% to 6.5% range. Also beware of early redemption (or call) features, which could wind up hurting you if you pay a premium to the call price and the bond is redeemed early. Some good choices in the fund category, with recent yields in parentheses, include USAA Tax Exempt Short Term (5.3%) 1-800-531-8181; General Muni Bond Fund (7.9%) 1-800-645-6561; Value Line New York Tax Exempt (7.6%) 1-800-223-0818; and Flagship All-American Tax Exempt Fund (7.4%), 4.2% load, 1-800-227-4648.

D. The Art of Picking Winning Stocks

HOW TO ALMOST ALWAYS MAKE MONEY IN THE MARKET

The key to repeated success in the stock market can be expressed in a single word — discipline. Find a time-tested method for selecting successful stocks (there are any number from which to choose), adopt a strict loss-limitation rule and plan a strategy for closing out your profitable trades — and religiously stick to all three — and your odds of making money year after year will be quite high. This kind of discipline has been demonstrated by each of Wall Street's most successful investment managers, even though their individual stock picking methods vary greatly, as do their risk tolerances and objectives. One of the best examples of the value of discipline is William O'Neil, who used it to rise from a job as an entry-level stockbroker to president William O'Neil & Co. and founder of Investor's Business Daily, the nation's second largest financial newspaper. Since 1959, O'Neil has used the same 7-step process for selecting wining stocks — defined by the acronym CANSLIM. Here's what each letter stands for, and the criteria O'Neil considers indicative of future success:

C — Current earnings per share. O'Neil says there's absolutely no reason for a stock to rise in price if the company's current earnings are bad. Thus, the stocks he buys must have current quarterly earnings at least 20% to 50% above those for the same quarter in the prior year.

A — Annual earnings per share. O'Neil says his biggest winners over the years have also shown average annual earnings growth of 24% over the 5 years prior to their major move. Thus, he looks only at stocks that have shown a 5-year pattern of annual earnings increases.

N — Something new. O'Neil says major gains are usually triggered by some change — such as introduction of a new product or service, a better outlook for the industry or a shift in management or management philosophy. However, he says the most frequent "new" item he considers is a new high in the stock price. "We've found that 98% of investors are unwilling to buy a stock that has just hit a new high," O'Neil explains, "yet one of the great paradoxes of the stock market is that what seems too high usually goes higher and what seems too low usually goes lower." Thus, most of the stocks he buys are at new all-time highs.

S — Shares outstanding. O'Neil says the average capitalization of his most successful stock picks has been just 11.8 million shares. Thus, he usually limits his purchases to stocks of companies with under 25 million shares outstanding.

L — Leader or laggard. O'Neil says the 500 top performing stocks from 1953 through 1989 had an average relative strength of 87 before their major advance actually began. (Relative strength measures a stock's price performance over the past year relative to all other stocks; for example, a relative strength rating of 85 would mean the stock outperformed 85% of the stocks in the market during the past 12 months.) Thus, he selects only stocks that are already among the market leaders — i.e.,those with a relative strength rating of 80 or higher — and ignores the laggards.

I —Institutional sponsorship. O'Neil says institutional buyer (money managers for mutual funds, pension funds and insurance companies) are the single largest source of demand for stocks. Thus, he looks for stocks that have begun to attract the attention of some institutional buyers, but that have not yet been acquired by a majority of institutions. That way, there will be plenty of remaining demand as more institutions move into the stock, as well as less risk of a major sell-off due to institutional dumping should something go wrong.

M — Market. O'Neil says 3 out of 4 stocks will go in the same direction as major moves in the leading market averages. Thus, he monitors the overall market and does most of his buying when the overall market is in an uptrend.

O'Neil admits his formula is highly restrictive, noting that, at any given time, fewer than 2% of the stocks in the entire market will meet his requirements. However, he says the effort it takes to find hem is worthwhile because nearly 70% his stock purchases produce profits — and 10% to 20% wind up producing gains of 100% or more.

O'Neil also maintains a rigid stop-loss rule on all new purchases — closing his position on any loss of 7% or more from the initial price. He admits this is a fairly restrictive stop, noting that most money managers use 10% to 14%, but says it works because of the efficiency of his selection method. "If I buy at exactly the right time, based on the CANSLIM formula, the stock is usually not going to go down to my maximum 7% stop-loss point," he claims.

He also claims there is no such thing as an inherently good stock. "The only good stocks are those that go up in price. If they go down, nothing else matters — not earnings, not management, not forecasts — and you have to cut your losses fast. The secret to success in the stock market is not being right all the time. In fact, you should be able to profit nicely if you are right only half of the time. The key is to lose the least amount of money possible when you are wrong. And my 7% stop-loss level guarantees that."

What about taking profits? O'Neil says he usually holds a stock as long as it continues to perform well based in the same CANSLIM categories. If a stock keeps showing quarterly and annual earnings increases (even smaller ones), makes new highs, shows good relative strength and retains its institutional support, he will continue to hold unless the overall market begins to show signs of topping out. Then he will sell — and not look back. "I never feel badly if I sell a stock and it winds up going higher. It's ridiculous. Your goal is to make substantial profits on your stocks. If you do that, you should be happy. Kicking yourself when a stock goes higher after you sell is a waste of energy that could better be spent looking for new buying opportunities."

Our Recommendation: Even if you prefer not to use O'Neil's methodology, you should at least recognize the value of his discipline — and follow the same rigid standards regardless of the stock-selection method you choose. That's the true key to almost always making money in the markets.

8 MISTAKES STOCK INVESTORS REPEATEDLY MAKE

Another benefit of following a rigid discipline in your trading is that you will avoid the mistakes most often made — over and over again — by the majority of stock investors. According to Stan Weinstein, professional investment advisor and publisher of The Professional Tape Reader, 8 of the most common mistakes are:

1. Buying depressed stocks. If a stock has gone down sharply in price, there's always a reason — even if you can't see it. Rather than trying to "bottom fish" — looking for stocks at or near their lows — it's better to buy stocks that are already showing good performance (i.e., high relative strength).

2. Averaging down. Too many investors refuse to admit their mistakes. They buy a stock at $25 a share and, when it falls to $20, they think it must be an even better bargain. Thus, they buy more. This lowers their average cost per share to just $22.50, which supposedly makes it easier to get even and make a profit. However, in most cases, the stock went to $20 for a good reason, meaning it's less likely to rebound even to $22.50 — and you are exposed to double the risk on any further decline.

3. Buying stocks based on good news. Insiders and market analysts know ahead of time when something good is going to happen, and they buy stock in anticipation of it, driving the price up. If you wait until the headlines finally appear, you may have already missed most of the move, setting yourself up for a quick loss when earlier buyers cash in their profits.

4. Holding a stock without a stop-loss order. Stop losses provide an extra measure of discipline, giving you a means to cut your losses and protect your profits. Use them on every stock position.

5. Selling a stock too quickly. Rather than employing stop losses to lock gains, giving a sock a chance to continue its advance, most investors get scared that they will lose a portion of their gains and sell out too soon. This leaves their repeated small profits vulnerable to a single large loss, and prevents them from

ever recording the really big gains needed to produce outstanding overall performance.

6. Buying a stock without a potential target in mind. Whenever you buy a stock, you should consider both the possible risk and the potential reward. Ideally, you want stocks that offer 3 times as much upside potential as risk — e.g., if you buy a stock at $30 and feel it could go as low as $25, you would also want it to have the potential to reach at least $45, and that should be your initial target.

7. Trying to stay fully invested. Too many investors want to have all their money in stocks at all times. However, there are certain times — particularly in established bear markets — when cash is the best investment available (or rather, a cash-equivalent money fund).

8. Being afraid to sell short. Very few investors take advantage of the opportunity to sell short, fearing the possibility of unlimited losses should a stock take off. However, short selling is a perfectly viable technique in weak markets, and can be just as rewarding as buying if you set reasonable profit targets and protect yourself with what are known as buy-stop order (orders that will be filled by buying the stock if it rises to a certain price).

APPLY THIS TEST BEFORE BUYING ANY STOCK

Regardless of the methodology they use in selecting stocks, almost everyone in the securities business gives special attention to a company's earnings — with good reason. If a company is not making money — or at least showing a pattern of steadily shrinking losses (in the case of R&D firms and start-up firms) — it cannot pass profits on to shareholders. And, without the hope for profits, there is no reason to own the stock. That translates into a lack of buying demand, without which a stock simply cannot go up in price.

Thus, before you make any new stock purchase, you must evaluate the company's earnings. If they are flat, or have been declining, the likelihood of a major price advance is remote, and the stock if probably a bad buy. Likewise, if a company is losing money, there is little chance of its stock making a major up-move until it becomes profitable (the exception being certain technology and health-care research firms, whose stocks often advance on expectations of large future returns).

As a rule, the best opportunities lie in companies that have shown at least 2 consecutive quarters of solid earnings — and 5 quarters of steady earnings growth is even better. Most market analysts place heavy emphasis on the price-to-earnings (P/E) ratio — and if earnings are rising, stock prices will almost invariably follow. For example, if a company in an industry group whose members normally have P/E ratios of around 20 earns $1 per share, its stock price should be around $20 (20 x $1 = $20). If earnings subsequently rise to

$1.50 per share and the same P/E norm prevails, the stock can be expected to rise in price to $30 (20 x $1.50 = $30). If it doesn't, the stock would be considered undervalued.

In fact, one of the most popular investment strategies is to search out stocks with P/E ratios below those of other stocks in the same industry or market sector, the expectation being that they will soon rise in price to bring their P/E ratios in line with the rest of their group.

WHAT TURNS INSTITUTIONAL INVESTORS ON

As noted earlier in the comments by William O'Neil, institutional investors provide the bulk of the buying power in today's equity markets. As a result, if you hope to make profitable stock selections, it's essential to know what institutional buyers think is important in judging a company's potential. Here are 10 factors they consider, in descending order of importance: Price/earnings ratio; current earnings; projected earnings; management competence; health of balance sheet; share price (institutions don't buy stocks priced under $5 a share and rarely purchase those under $10); long-term earnings record; product quality; industry group; and the overall state of the economy as it impacts the company's business.

7 RULES FOR SELECTING COMMON STOCKS

According to investment advisor Al Frank, a successful mutual fund manager and publisher of The Prudent Speculator newsletter, you can improve your chances of selecting winning stocks if you always follow 7 basic rules:

1. Look for stocks that have a price/earnings ratio below that of the S&P 500 Stock Index.

2. Focus on companies with a solid record of growth. Sales, earnings and dividend payouts should have all increased consistently for at least 5 years, and a doubling over the past decade is desirable.

3. Try to find companies with a book value equal to or very near the current price of the stock.

4. Look for companies with a leadership position in a strong industry — preferably one where there is only a limited amount of competition.

5. Search for companies where management has a large ownership position. In a few cases, this can be detrimental, but as a rule, managers who have an ownership stake work harder to keep the company growing and the stock price rising.

6. Avoid companies with a heavy debt load, particularly if other

companies in the same industry carry much lighter debt burdens.

7. Avoid companies in industries that are a major component of government economic statistical bases such as the Gross Domestic Product or the Producer Price Index. When times get tough, such industry groups — autos, steel, energy, food, etc. — become easy targets for pressure from politicians looking to appease unhappy voters.

9 KEYS TO FINDING QUALITY GROWTH STOCKS

The rules for selecting a quality growth stock are similar to those just listed, but there are a few other considerations. According to J. David Stewart, an Canyon Lake, Calif., analyst and broker specializing in low-priced growth stocks, here are 9 things to look for:

1. A leading position in a growth industry.

2. High profit margins.

3. A record of steadily rising earnings (or steadily diminishing losses).

4. The ability to pass on cost increases to customers.

5. A good research program and a strong commitment to development of new products.

6. An experienced management team.

7. A solid balance sheet with low or steadily declining debt.

8. A product line that's generally not subject to government regulation or consumer activism.

9. Some awareness among institutional investors.

AVOID GOOD STOCKS IN BAD INDUSTRIES

No mater how good an individual company, its stock will have difficulty bucking a downward industry trend. For that reason, you should always check out overall industry ratings before buying a stock. It's also helpful to know which industries do best in differing economic environments. Here are some guidelines:

* When the economy is in recovery, the most volatile industries — i.e., those hurt worst by the prior recession — tend to be the best performers.

* When inflation begins to pick up as a recovery progress, the natural resource stocks — i.e., precious metals, oil and gas, timber — tend to do the

best, while utilities, banks and other interest-sensitive sectors are the most vulnerable.

* When a recession begins to set in, the strongest performer are the drugs, cosmetics, food groups and other makers of essentials, while the weakest sectors are autos, steel, chemicals, textiles, appliance manufacturers and other producers of durable goods.

* When a recession begins to bottom out, the above situation quickly reverses — i.e., cyclical stocks such as autos and chemicals anticipate the turnaround, while the defensive groups such as drugs and food begin to lag.

Match your good individual stock picks with strong industry trends, and you significantly improve your chances of stock market success.

4 SAFE STOCKS THAT ARE DUE FOR A DOUBLE

If, in spite of all the tips on selecting stocks that we've just outlined, you are still a bit nervous about making your own choices, here are 4 stocks that our analysts currently like and feel could be poised for a doubling in price over the next 18 months to 2 years:

1. Walt Disney Co. (DIS), NYSE, $40 — Disney CEO Michael Eisner received a lot of attention when he exercised his stock options, cashing in millions in profits in advance of possible higher tax rates under Democratic President Clinton. However, according to most analysts, he earned every penny of his gains by making Disney one of the strongest companies in the entertainment sector. A string of successful movies, including Pretty Woman, Beauty and the Beast and Aladdin; a move into retailing (there are now almost 200 Disney stores in upscale malls around the world); expansion of the theme park business worldwide; the company's huge library of classic movies and cartoons; and enormous potential from licensing of popular cartoon characters have all contributed to Disney's growth. That growth also produced a significant rise in the price of Disney stock — but there's plenty of room for more now that a 4-for-1 stock split has made the shares affordable to more investors. Growth has also provided a thick cushion to protect the stock against downturns. (Note: If you like the Disney image, but want a cheaper alternative, you might consider EuroDisney, recently about $12 a share. The company manages Disney's new European theme park outside Paris, and the stock recently made a new low based on weaker-than-expected first-year attendance and earnings linked to the poor economy. However, with times improving, the company — and the stock — should come charging back.)

2. Fuji Photo (FUJIY), OTC, $43 — Japan's economy was much slower than that of the United States to feel the effects of the worldwide recession. That explains why the Japanese stock market performed so poorly in 1991-92, losing 57% from its post-1987 highs before stabilizing in late summer, while U.S. stocks

remained near all-time highs. Now, the Japanese government has taken steps to spur the economy and bolster the market, and many Japanese companies appear poised to rebound sharply as the recovery progresses. Fuji, the world's second biggest producer of photographic film behind Kodak, should be among the leaders in this new advance. And, with a price/earnings multiple of just 14, there's very little room for downside risk.

3. PHM Corp. (PHM), NYSE, $29 — As the economy begins to improve and interest rates stay low, this major U.S. home builder (formerly known as Pulte Homes) should enjoy a major spurt of growth. With operations in 12 states, including California and several growing Southeastern states, PHM concentrates on the single-family market, though it does pull in about 27% of its $1.2 billion in annual sales from the apartment sector. With projected 1992 earnings per share of $2.05 and a P/E ratio of just 14.1, well below market averages, the downside risk seems slight, while the a doubling in price seems perfectly attainable.

4. Black & Decker (BDK), NYSE, $19-5/8 — The same conditions that bode well for PHM should also power up sales for this U.S. leader in the personal power tool field. Also beneficial is BDK's new DeWalt unit, which specializes in making heavy-duty tools for professional carpenters and builders, a $400 million annual market. With projected 1992 earnings of $1.35, the P/E ratio of 14.5 is well below the average of 18 for the S&P 500, and any catch-up bid could double the stock price within 2 years.

RECOGNIZING STOCKS READY FOR A REBOUND

In spite of all the advice on picking winning stocks based on strong industry positions, solid earnings records and breakouts to new highs, many investors still like to practice the art of bottom-fishing — looking for depressed stocks ready to bounce back. And, the rewards in this area can be significant if you learn how to recognize the signs of a pending turnaround. Here are some guidelines recommended by Robert Ravitz, research director at the New York investment-management firm David J. Greene & Co., for recognizing stocks likely to rebound:

* The stock price is depressed because of a failed merger. The fact that one company saw enough value to attempt a merger, even if it failed, could be an indication that another company will come along and try the same thing.

* The stock plunged because the company cut or eliminated its dividend. In such cases, conservative investors usually rush to sell, driving prices lower than they really should be. In addition, a reduction in dividend is a good sign that a company is working hard to deal with its financial problems rather than merely holding the line and hoping for the best. Thus, a rebound becomes more likely should the bottom line improve as a result of the reduced

pressure to meet dividend payouts.

* The company has been hit by wave after wave of bad news to the extent that nothing bad remains to be revealed. This increases the odds that any new information coming out will be positive, and could spark a rally.

* The company's problems have been caused by one poor product line or one losing division, and plans are announced to sell, close down or otherwise get rid of that product or business. When the loser goes, results could improve — and the stock price could rebound.

* The company has been overburdened with debt, but is selling off assets to improve the situation. Servicing debt is expensive, and eliminating such costs greatly increases chances the company's results will improve, pushing the stock price higher.

* Poor management has been to blame for may of the company's problems, but a new management team is coming on board. The reasoning here is obvious.

* Management has begun buying shares of the company's stock. This usually means no new bad news is likely to come out and a plan is in place to improve the company's fortunes.

A TIP ON PLAYING THE TAKEOVER GAME

Though the action is more subdued now than in the leveraged-buyout frenzy of the mid-1980s, plenty of companies are still being taken over every year — and plenty of shareholders are making large profits on these deals. So, how do you pick out potential takeover targets? The first step is to identify companies that are severely undervalued relative to either their assets (book value) or their earnings potential. Once you've found some likely candidates, watch the so-called 13D filings with the Securities & Exchange Commission (SEC), reported in most financial newspapers and many newsletters and also available directly from the SEC. Both companies and individuals are required to file 13D reports within 10 days of making a stock purchase that brings total holdings in a company to a level greater than 5% of shares outstanding — a good sign that further purchases, or a takeover bid, are likely to come. To find out how to get copies of 13D filings, call the SEC office in Washington, New York, Chicago or Los Angeles. If you're more serious, there are also a couple of firms — Bechtel Information Services (1-800-231-3282) and Disclosure Inc. (1-800-638-8241) — that will monitor 13D filings for you, watching for specific companies to appear on the lists.

STOCK SPLITS CAN MEAN ADDED PROFIT

Investors holding stocks that split in price usually have a very profitable record, both before and after the split. Studies have shown prices typically rise 14% to 25% within 3 to 6 months after a split — on top of even bigger gains that occurred before the split. So, how do you identify stocks that are likely to split? Here are some things to look for:

* Stocks that are trading above $75 a share, but have historically been priced at lower levels. Stocks at that price are too expensive for many buyers, but a split would take them into the $25 to $50 range — a more attractive level for smaller investors.

* Companies that need to attract additional financing. A split often sets the stage for a secondary offering at or near the lower post-split price.

* Stocks that have split before and have risen steadily to a level near the price at which the earlier split occurred.

* Over-the-counter stocks with strong earnings and under 1 million shares outstanding. Companies in such a position may be ready to apply for listing with the American or New York stock exchanges, but they will need more shares in order to qualify.

* Companies whose dividend payout levels have risen to new highs, meaning they'd still be able to offer strong per-share dividends even after a split.

* Companies with lots of assets and few management shareholders. By splitting the company's stock, managers whose livelihood depends on their jobs instead of their ownership position can broaden the shareholder base, making a potential unwanted takeover attempt more costly.

SETTING A STRATEGY FOR SELLING

The world is full of people willing to tell you when to buy a stock, but finding someone who'll tell you when to sell is a different matter. That's why it is essential to establish a selling strategy at the time you buy a stock. For starters, you should never buy a stock unless you have a good idea of its upside potential, given growth and earnings projections. As explained earlier, you should look for stocks with at least a 3-to-1 reward-to-risk potential — and that should provide your initial target on any stock purchase. However, that target should not be an absolute — meaning there will be times when you should sell before it is achieved, and times you should hold after it is reached. So, what's the key to making those decisions? The answer is the stock's performance. As long as the stock keeps rising on steady or improving earnings, you should continue to hold, even if your target is surpassed. However, if the stock begins to top — as indicated by a rally that stalls without reaching a new high — or some other bad news (e.g., a downgraded brokerage house recommendation or a drop in earnings by 10% or more from projections) comes out, go ahead and sell.

Safety Valve: Always enter a stop-loss order on every stock you buy. As soon as your buy order is confirmed, place the stop 7% to 14% below the purchase price (depending on your own tolerance for risk) — and stick with it. In other words, if the stock goes down, never lower your stop. Just take your loss and move on to the next opportunity. However, if the stock goes up, raise your stop-loss level each time the price of the stock increases by 10% or so, keeping it 7% to 10% behind the share price. That way, you will lock in a portion of your gains, yet leave your upside potential open.

POTENTIAL 10% BONUS FOR SMALL STOCKHOLDERS

Because it costs as much for a company to keep track of 10 shares as it does 1,000, many publicly held firms will pay a bonus of up to 10% over the market price to buy back so-called odd lots (holdings of under 100 shares). Getting rid of such small stockholders reduces the cost of printing and distributing annual and quarterly reports and simplifies proxy solicitations and recording. Bonus: There are no sales fees or commissions when you sell shares directly back to the company.

GUIDELINES FOR UNLOADING YOUR LOSERS

There's really only 1 rule for getting rid of losers: Do it! If you buy a stock and it goes down, hitting your pre-determined loss limit, go ahead and sell, taking your loss. (A stop-loss order will provide the discipline to do this is you can't manage it on your own. Always use them.) If it doesn't hit your loss limit, give it a bit more time — then sell, even if it means taking a small loss. Obviously, your initial judgment about the potential of the stock was in error — or your timing was very, very wrong. In either case, you'll make much better use of your money trying some new investment than waiting for a rebound in the original stock to get your money back. Never let pride or a fear of admitting you were wrong play a role in your investment decisions. If you are wrong, take the loss and go on to something new.

DOUBLE YOUR RETURN BY BUYING ON MARGIN

In these days of low interest rates — and, for more aggressive investors, even when rates are higher — a good way to increase your investment returns is to take advantage of U.S. securities laws allowing the purchase of stocks on margin. When you buy on margin, you are required to put up only a portion of the purchase price, with the remainder being paid by your brokerage firm and charged to your account as a loan. Under current regulations, stocks priced above $5 can be purchased on margin of up to 50% — meaning you can buy a $50 stock by putting up just $25 per share. The advantage of doing this, of course, is that you double the buying power of your investment capital — and, in effect, double the return (minus any charges for your margin loan) on your profitable stock purchases. For example, if you buy a $50 stock and it goes up to $55, your $5 profit represents a gain of 10% (less commissions, of course). However, if you buy that same stock on margin, putting up just $25, the same $5 gain represents a 20% return on your money (again, less commissions, and minus any margin interest charge — which, at recent rates, will run about 7% of the borrowed sum on an annualized basis). The downside? Your percentage risk also doubles — with a $5 stock-price decline representing a 20% loss on a $25 margin purchase, plus commissions and margin charges. However, if you are more aggressive and want to almost double your potential returns, buying stocks on margin is one way to do it.

2 WAYS TO MAKE MONEY IN DOWN MARKETS

Most average investors do one of two things when the market declines — both of them bad. Either they sell out and move their money into risk-free or cash-equivalent investments — or worse, they hang on and let the market decline erode a large percentage of the value of their holdings. Really successful investors, however, view market declines as opportunities to add to the gains they made during earlier rallies, usually employing one of two strategies — short selling or buying put options. Here's a brief description of how both techniques work:

* Short selling is really just a reversal of the old "buy-low, sell-high" theory of investing. Rather than buying a stock in the expectation that it will rise in price, short selling involves selling a stock in the expectation that it will fall in price. What makes the process confusing — even to some experienced investors — is that you are selling something you don't actually own. That, however, doesn't really matter — your broker simply loans you the stock, charging you interest on its value for the duration of your trade (you also have to make up any dividends paid to the buyer during the period). If the price of the stock does fall, you buy it back for an amount less than you were originally paid, give the stock back to the broker (this is actually all done on paper) and keep the difference, less interest charges, as profit. If the stock goes up after you sell short, you have to buy it back at a higher price and you lose money.

For example, let's assume IBM stock was trading at $75 a share, but — because of a general market decline and poor performance by the computer sector — you felt the price was likely to fall. You'd like to profit from that expected decline, so you tell your broker you would like to sell 100 shares of IBM short at $75. The broker enters your order and, if it is filled, supplies the stock to the buyer. The $7,500 received from the sale goes into your account, where it is held as security for the broker's loan of the stock. You also have to put up an additional margin deposit equal to 50% of the stock's value to secure the trade.

Now let's say that two months pass, during which time IBM stock falls in price to $65 a share. You feel the decline is over and decide to "cover" your short position. You enter an order to buy 100 shares of IBM at $65, and it is filled. $6,500 is withdrawn from your account to pay for the stock, which is then returned to the broker. You are thus left with $1,000 in profits (minus commissions and any interest charged on the loan) on a stock you never owned! Instead of buying low and selling high, you have simply reversed the process — selling high first, and then buying low.

If it's so simple, why don't more people sell short? The major reason is the general confusion regarding the process, but there is also a high degree of concern about the theoretically unlimited risk. When you buy a stock, all you can lose is the amount paid because the price can never go below zero — but, when you sell a stock short, your risk is potentially open ended because there is no limit to how high the price can rise. In reality, however, this concern is unwarranted. If you use a disciplined approach, setting realistic risk limits and targets at the time of the sale, your risk is no greater than it would be in buying stock — and, you can also protect yourself by using what is known as a "buy-stop order" (an order that is automatically triggered if a stock's price rises to a certain level). There is also one mechanical hindrance — the so-called "uptick" rule. This rule, imposed by the stock exchanges to keep short sellers from arbitrarily driving down a stock's price, mandates that short sales are allowed only when the previous trade moved the stock to a higher price (an "uptick"). Thus, though you can buy a stock at any time, you can sell it short only in a stable or rising market.

* Buying put options is a simpler, but more expensive and riskier method of playing a down market. A put option is an investment vehicle that gives you the right to sell 100 shares of a stock at a given price at any time during the life of the option. For example, a July 1993 IBM put option with a "striking price" of $75 would give you the right to sell 100 shares of IBM stock at a price of $75 per share any time prior to the third Friday in July of 1993. Put options have a number of uses, but the most common is speculating on an expected decline in a stock's price. What makes them expensive — and risky — is that you have to pay a "premium" to the seller of the option in exchange for his agreement to purchase the stock at the specified price. A large portion of that premium (sometimes all of it) is a payment for the time you are given in which to make a decision on selling the stock. This portion of the premium is called "time value," and it will steadily decrease over the life of the option because it will have less and less time remaining — no matter what happens to the price of the

stock.

This means the stock could actually move in your favor, and you would still lose money. For example, if IBM was trading at $75 a share and you thought it was due for a fall in the near future, you could buy a 6-month IBM $75 put option — which would give you the right to sell IBM at $75 a share any time in the next 6 months. At recent prices, you would have to pay about $3.50 for that option — or $350 per 100-share lot (the minimum option size). In this case, the entire amount would be time value (with the stock at $75 a share, an option giving you the right to sell it at $75 would have no real, or "intrinsic," value.) That $350 would also be the most you could lose, no matter what happened.

However, making a profit is not as simple as it might seem. If you were wrong about IBM, and the stock rose in price or stayed the same, you would lose the full $350. If you were right, and IBM went down — but only to $72 — you would still lose money ($50, plus commissions). Only if the stock fell below $71.50 a share — the strike price of $75 minus the $3.50 paid for the option — would you make a profit. And, if the price fell to $65, as in our earlier example, you would make a profit of $6.50 ($75 - $65 = $10 - $3.50 option cost = $6.50), minus commissions.

Thus, though put options offer an alternative way to play a down market, they offer less potential profit (though a much higher percentage return) than selling short, and the risk of a loss is greater (approximately 80% of all option buyers lose money because the stock fails to move enough to compensate for the loss of time value).

OPTIONS — POWERFUL TOOLS FOR STOCK INVESTORS

While buying put options as a means to speculate on a market or stock decline has certain drawbacks, that does not mean that investors should shun options entirely. Options are powerful tools with a variety of uses for both aggressive and conservative investors. We'll briefly describe some of the basic techniques — but let's first take a quick look at the nature of stock options themselves. (Note: Options are also available on a variety of other investment vehicles, ranging from gold to currencies to futures contracts to major market indexes. However, for purposes of this discussion, we'll focus specifically on options linked to stocks.) For starters, there are 2 types of options — calls and puts:

* A call option gives its owner the right to buy 100 shares of a specific security at a specific price for a limited period of time. For example, a July 60 IBM call gives its owner the right to buy 100 shares of IBM stock at a price of $60 per share any time between the purchase date and the third Friday in July.

* A put option gives its owner the right to sell 100 shares of a specific security at a specific price for a limited period of time. Thus, a July 55 IBM put would give its owner the right to sell 100 shares of IBM stock at a price of $55 per share any time between the purchase date and the expiration date (the third Friday of July).

There are certain terms unique to options trading that you should know before using them — terms that primarily describe the specifics of each individual option contract. To help explain these terms, let's assume you just bought the above-mentioned July 60 IBM call option at a price of $4.00:

* The underlying security — This is the item the option gives you the right to purchase or sell — in this case, 100 shares of IBM common stock.

* The strike price (also called exercise price) — This is the guaranteed price at which you can "exercise" your option — in other words, at which you can buy or sell the underlying future. In this case, the guaranteed price at which you can buy 100 shares of IBM stock is $60 per share.

* The expiration date — This is the date on which your option expires — in other words, the date after which you can no longer buy or sell the underlying security at the guaranteed price. Stock options expire on the third Friday of the expiration month. Thus, a July IBM call option would expire on the third Friday of July.

* The premium — This is simply the price you pay to buy an option. In this case, the premium was $4.00 per share — or $400 for the entire option contract ($4.00 x 100 shares = $400). There are two major factors that determine the premium of an option — its "intrinsic value" and its "time value." All options have time value, but not all of them have intrinsic (or real) value. All options have time value because, as long as there is time, there is always the possibility that the price of the underlying security will move enough to give the option real value — right up until the last moment before it expires. Time value is variable, but as a general rule, the more time remaining before an options expiration date, the higher its time value will be. In addition, as the price of the underlying security moves away from the options strike price, the option will have less and less time value. An options intrinsic value, if it has any, is always the actual cash difference between the strike price and the current price of the underlying security. For example, if IBM's stock were selling at $62 a share, the July 60 call option would have an intrinsic value of $2 a share, but the premium of the July 60 put would be made up entirely of time value. Conversely, if IBM's stock were at $58 a share, the July 60 IBM put would have an intrinsic value of $2 a share, but the premium of the July 60 call would consist only of time value. Options with no intrinsic value are said to be "out of the money," while options that have intrinsic value are described as "in the money."

Now let's look at the basic ways smart investors use options. By far the most popular — though not always the most rewarding — use of call options is as a vehicle for highly leveraged speculation on rising stock prices. The easiest way to explain how this works is with an example, so let's quickly walk through one. Assume it is January and an investor feels the price of IBM stock, currently at $58 a share, is likely to rise in the next few months. If he wants to profit from this expected rally, he basically has 3 alternatives — he can buy the stock itself, putting up $5,800 for every 100 shares he buys; he can buy the stock on margin, putting up $2,900 for each 100 shares purchased; or he can buy a July IBM call option. Based on recent prices, this latter alternative would require an investment of about $650 ($6.50 per share) for an option with a striking price of $55 or $400 ($4.00 per share) for an option with a striking price of $60.

Let's now assume that IBM stock does indeed rise in price — moving to $70 a share by the third Friday in July. Had the investor bought the stock, his gain would have been $12 a share and his profit $1,200, meaning he would have earned a return on his investment of 20.69% before commissions. Had he bought on margin, his gain would have been the same, but his profit would have been reduced by about $100 in margin interest charges. However, since he put up only $2,900 of his own money, the $1,100 net profit (before commissions) would have represented a return of 37.9%. That's outstanding — but it pales compared to the results on either option. With IBM stock at $70 a share, the July $55 IBM call would have had a price of $15 and a value of $1,500. Thus, the investor would have made a profit of $850 (before commissions) — a return of 130.8% on his $650 investment. And, the return on the July $60 IBM call would have been even better. It would have been worth $1,000, meaning the investor would have made a profit of $600 — a return of 150% (before commissions) on his $400 investment.

That huge potential return — coupled with the low initial cost — explains why options are such popular speculative vehicles. They also have the advantage of offering a lower level of absolute risk (though that risk is total). For instance, continuing with the above example, let's assume that, instead of rising $12 a share to $70, IBM stock fell $12 to $46. Both the stock buyer and the margin buyer would have lost $1,200 per 100 shares (not to mention the commissions and the margin interest charges), whereas the option buyer would have lost just $650 or $400, depending on which option he selected.

Unfortunately, there is one other element that keeps the buying of options from being the ideal investment strategy — and that also explains why about 80% of option buyers lose money. That element is the time value that makes up a major portion of every options premium. With the IBM $55 call option cited in our example, $350 of the options $650 premium was time value and only $300 (the difference between the stock's $58 price and the options $55 striking price) was real, or intrinsic value. And, with the IBM $60 call option, the entire $400 premium was time value, with no real value, since the striking price of $60 was above the actual $58 price of the stock. Why is that so important? Because, no matter what happens to the price of the underlying IBM stock — whether it goes up, down or stays the same — time is going to pass, and the buyer of those options is going to lose that time value. Thus, for the buyer of an option to make money, he must not only be right about the direction a stock's price is going to move, but he must also get a move large enough to offset the inevitable erosion of the time value. In this case, the buyer of the IBM $55 call had to have IBM stock rise in price to $61.50 (the $55 strike price plus the $6.50 premium) just to break even on his trade. And, the buyer of the IBM $60 call had to have the IBM stock price climb a full $6 a share to $64 in order to break even. Thus, because of the time-value erosion, option buyers — whether bullish (using calls) or bearish (using puts) — must not only be right about the direction of an expected move, but they must be very right about the magnitude of that move. Otherwise, they will lose money — as most of them do.

Some option traders minimize the negatives by using more conservative combination strategies such as spreads, wherein you buy one option and sell another, hoping to profit from a change in the price relationship between the two. In this instance, a speculator expect IBM stock to rise in price might do what is called a bull call spread — purchasing the IBM $55 call and selling the IBM $60 call. The cost (and the maximum risk) would be the difference between the 2 premiums — or $2.50 ($250) per spread (the $6.50 premium of the option purchased minus the $4.00 premium of the option sold). Unfortunately, most spreads also have a maximum profit — the price you pay for the lower cost and risk — which in this case would be $2.50 ($250) per spread (the $5.00 difference between the striking prices of the 2 options minus the $2.50 cost of the spread). In this particular spread, the maximum loss would be incurred at any IBM stock price below $55 (at the time the options expired), while the maximum profit would be made at any IBM stock price above $60 a share.

The savviest (and most profitable) option traders are those who sell, rather than buy options. Option sellers have an advantage because time works in their favor. In other words, they sell time value — which will always erode, regardless of what happens to the underlying stock or security. There are two types of option selling — or "writing," as it is called by veteran option traders. The first is known as "naked writing" — which means that you sell an option without owning the underlying security. Naked writing is extremely risky and the losses are potentially unlimited. As such, only the most experienced traders should attempt it.

On the other hand, the second form of option selling — known as "covered writing" — is considered a fairly conservative strategy, and is used by many stock owners to improve the returns on their portfolios. With covered writing, an investor actually purchases shares of a stock — such as IBM, GM or any of the more than 400 others on which listed options trade — and then sells out-of-the-money call options in order to bring in additional money and increase the income stream from his investment. For the sake of consistency, let's use the same IBM options we've been discussing in an example. As before, IBM stock is selling at $58 a share — but this time the investor feels the stock is likely to remain fairly stable, not rising significantly or falling sharply. Still, the $4.00 per share dividend represents an attractive 6.90% yield, so he buys 300 shares. Then, to make the return even better, he sells 3 July $60 IBM call options, collecting $400 for each of them (less commissions), or a total of $1,200. If IBM stock remains below $60 a share when the options expire, the investor keeps his stock, collects his dividends and also keeps the full $1,200 he received for the call options. He can then turn around and sell a new set of options, continuing to collect the dividends and keep the option premiums received so long as IBM stock stays below $60 a share. At these prices, this strategy increases the investor's annual return on his IBM stock to around 20% — even if the stock never goes up. The catch? If IBM stock rises above $60 before the call options expire, the calls will be exercised and the investor will have to sell his stock at $60 per share — regardless of how his the price may have actually risen. Thus, in exchange for generating the additional income and higher return, the investor forfeits any appreciation potential in the stock above the level of the option striking price.

Covered Writing Bonus: If the stock price falls, the money brought in through the sale of the call options provides additional downside protection against loss. In this particular instance, the $400 received for each call option sold represents $4.00 in downside protection — meaning the price of the IBM stock could fall to $54 a share and the investor would still break even (or actually make a bit of money if you consider the dividends).

...AND FOR PROTECTING YOUR PORTFOLIO GAINS

Speaking of protection, options also have another valuable function — that of insuring against loss or locking in profits on positions you are not yet ready to sell (for tax reasons or to preserve a dividend stream, for example). These strategies involve the purchase of put options — either on the specific securities you own, or on a major stock market index, such as the S&P 500 or the S&P 100. For example, if you bought IBM stock at $58 a share in July and it went to $70 by November, you would have a healthy gain. However, if you took that profit, you would have to pay short-term capital gains taxes in the current tax year. So, you'd prefer to hold until January (or even longer) before selling. The danger of doing so, of course, is that the stock could turn lower again, costing you your gains. However, you can protect yourself by purchasing a January $70 IBM put — an option that guarantees you the right to sell IBM stock at a price of $70 a share any time until the third Friday in January Such an option might cost you $2 per share ($200 per 100-share lot), which would reduce your guaranteed profit — but it would also protect the majority of your gains against a pullback prior to the new year when you would prefer to sell.

For those with large, diversified portfolios of individual stocks, put options on the major stock market indexes can provide a similar protection. While these index options do not give stockholders the right to sell individual stocks at a guaranteed price, they can generate sizable profits on any pullback in the level of the index — profits that can be used to offset any concurrent losses in the individual stocks in your portfolio. Use of such defensive option strategies can make it easier to build longer-term portfolios, ensure a steady dividend stream for income-oriented investors, lower commission costs and take the worry out of holding stocks that have already shown substantial appreciation, but which seem to have remaining potential. Don't hesitate to use them if you are an active investor in individual stocks.

A LOW-RISK WAY TO DOUBLE BLUE CHIP PROFITS

There's one other type of option that should also be mentioned since it can be an extremely valuable tool for getting substantially higher returns on investments in Blue Chip stocks. It's called a LEAP — which, in the peculiar vernacular of Wall Street, stands for "Long-term Equity Antici-Pations." LEAPs are long-term options with life spans of 2 to 3 years. They were first introduced in late 1990 and are currently available on around 50 of the leading U.S. companies. The most effective strategy for using them involves buying deep-in-the-money LEAPs, which have very little time value, rather than buying the stocks themselves. Because of the deep-in-the-money feature, the price movements of the LEAPs have a very high correlation to those of the stocks themselves — i.e., almost dollar for dollar. However, since the LEAP can be purchased for around a third the cost of buying the stock, the return on any appreciation in stock price (or depreciation if you use puts) will be almost three times as high. For example, if IBM stock were selling for $58 a share, you could probably buy a 3-year IBM LEAP with a striking price of $40 (meaning it was $18 in the money) for about $20 (or $2,000 per option). If IBM stock moved up to $70 a share, the $40 LEAP would most likely rise in price to around $31.50. Thus, an investor who had purchased the stock at $58 would make $12 a share — a return of 20.7% (before commission). However, an investor who had purchased the LEAP would make $1,150 on his $2,000 investment, a return of 57.5% — almost triple the stock buyer's return. There is one drawback to buying LEAPs instead of stock — you don't get any dividends. However, that can be offset by writing covered short-term options against the longer-term LEAP.

DO STOCK MARKET ADVISORY LETTERS REALLY HELP?

Not all that much is the sad answer for publishers and the advisors whose economic wares they push. According to several industry studies, stocks recommended by newsletter advisors often underperform the Dow Jones and Standard & Poor's 500 averages. Even stocks recommended by the best advisors only slightly outperform the averages. Advisory letters are also biased toward buy advice, neglecting a pick that's on the decline — and, they are woefully late when the time comes to sell. The letters will push a stock hard, then leave readers to decide on their own when to get out — or, if they do issue a firm "sell" recommendation, the lag time in the publication schedule will allow a big drop in price before the readers have a chance to react and sell the stock. The best advice on advisory letters is to make selective stock purchases based on the recommendations of top-performing advisors who are backed up by top-performing industry forecasters — and then do your own analysis with respect to getting out, based on your own objectives.

E. How Your Stockbroker Really Works

YOUR BROKER ISN'T A FINANCIAL ADVISOR

One of the most common mistakes both beginning and veteran investors make is placing too much trust in the advice offered by their stockbrokers. Though they may go by any number of names, from account executives to investment consultants, there is one thing stockbrokers definitely aren't — unbiased financial advisors. While brokers are quick to make recommendations, they may not be so quick to make sure the recommended items are right for you. The reason is that, above all else, brokers are salespeople — which means they have quotas to meet and are under constant pressure to promote securities their firms are underwriting. In addition, of course, they need to make sales in order to generate income for themselves. As a result, no matter how much you might like your broker, you should take his or her recommendations with a grain of salt. Consider both the merits of the investment itself and whether it is right for you. If you like it on those grounds, go ahead and buy. However, if you don't, don't feel like you have an obligation to buy just to make your broker happy. Say thanks for the idea — but no thanks on the purchase.

HOW YOUR BROKER MAKES MONEY OFF YOU

Having said that a broker's primary purpose in life is to generate commissions from your trading, it should be noted that commissions are by no means the only way brokers make money off of you. In fact, in today's modern world of "financial services," only about 45% of a broker's income actually comes from retail commissions on stocks and bonds, and only about 15% of a brokerage firm's revenue comes from that source. So, what else do brokers and brokerage firms do to bring in the bucks? For individual brokers, the big money comes from the sale of mutual funds, annuities, limited partnerships and other financial products that carry much higher commissions than those on stocks and bonds. And, for the brokerage firm, there are myriad other revenue sources, including:

* Mutual fund management. Brokerage firms operate more than 630 mutual funds investing in everything from stocks and bonds to precious metals and rare coins. These funds had more than $305 billion in assets in mid-1992, generating around $4 billion in annual management fees for their sponsors. They also generate substantial commissions or "loads" — as much as 8.5% of the amount invested in some cases — which are split between the firms and the individual brokers who are urged to sell them. That makes them a doubly bad deal since a recent study found that mutual funds managed by brokerage funds underperformed their competitors by an average of about 20%.

* Investment banking services. Brokerage firms handle virtually all new stock offerings in this country, earning both underwriting fees and big commissions on the sale of the new shares. They also get hefty fees for creating and marketing other types of securities (e.g., CATS, TIGERS, strips, straps, PINs, PERCs and dozens of others you may have heard of). These activities account for about 36% of a brokerage firm's earnings.

* Trading for their own accounts. Brokerage firms are their own best customers, buying and selling an estimated $600 billion in stocks and bonds each year for their own accounts. This activity generates big profits — representing about 28% of a typical firm's earnings — and it can also be costly to you if you're not careful. The reason? When brokerage firms make a mistake and wind up holding a stock they don't want, they will often turn around and recommend it to smaller retail investors, selling off their own shares to clients who neglect to check up on the merits of the companies.

* Margin loans to customers. When you buy a stock on margin or sell a stock short, you are in essence taking out a loan from the brokerage firm — and you pay interest on those loans. While the rates are competitive, they also generate substantial profits for brokerage firms — accounting for roughly 5% of annual revenues. Where do they get the money they lend? Why it's yours, of course — excess cash you have sitting in your stock account or money you have on deposit in the broker's money market or cash management account, earning less than what the broker is charging other customers who borrow it.

* Research services. Most brokerage firms maintain research departments, and they sell that research to mutual fund managers, institutional investors (such as pension funds and insurance companies) and other brokers. For some of the bigger firms, research activities generate as much as 5% of annual income.

* Asset management services. In addition to making recommendations, many brokerage firms actually manage money for individual clients, as well as for some smaller institutional customers. These activities generate either flat management fees or commissions (or both), accounting for as much as 10% of the earnings of some firms.

Thus, as you can see, neither your broker nor your brokerage firm is solely dependent on your commissions for their livelihood — so don't feel compelled to buy something just because the broker is pushing it. Even without your commission, he'll still make a living.

DO YOU NEED A FULL-SERVICE BROKER

If you trade in specialized bonds, preferred or convertible stocks, mortgages, tax shelters or commodities, or if you have less then $2,000 to invest, a full-service broker is probably right for you. Although discount brokers generally charge 35% to 85% less in commissions than full-service brokers, they don't usually give investment advice — and they are targeted toward a client dealing in large numbers of shares or someone buying on margin. Savvy clients with their own investment contacts or retirees who have time to do their own market research often benefit from a discount broker. However, most discount houses only handle stocks, bonds and options, so if you have other investment needs, a full-service house may be your only alternative.

3 MOST COMMON WAYS BROKERS RIP YOU OFF

First and foremost, you should know that most brokers are basically honest — they don't set out to rip you off; they just want to make a living. However, since there are some brokers who set their own profit-making ahead of your profit-making, here are some signals that might indicate a broker isn't acting in your best interest:

1. The broker recommends a stock you've never heard of and fails to provide a prospectus or other supportive documentation as required by law. A security is never so hot that it gets ahead of its regulatory paperwork, so don't buy any unknowns based solely on the broker's word. Note: This is a common sales ploy with small over-the-counter (OTC) stocks or new issues, so beware of brokers who consistently push such vehicles without respect to your personal financial interests.

2. The broker recommends an investment that will be profitable only through heavy trading. This is usually just a cover for churning, meaning the broker will make lots of money in commissions — and you won't make any money at all.

3. The broker pushes low-activity investments such as Ginnie Maes or other cash-equivalent securities even though your tolerance for risk and need for profits is higher. What's happening here is that you're giving the broker or his firm a loan. They're paying you minimum rates to hold your money, then using it as part of the firm's asset base to make more lucrative investments. It's also best to avoid putting big chunks of your investment capital in any brokerage firm's cash-management account unless you really are just holding it there temporarily

while waiting for a new opportunity. If you're not, you can usually get better rates elsewhere.

If you have any doubts about whether your broker is shooting straight when he or she makes a recommendation, here are 6 questions you can ask:

1. How much will you make from my investment? Commissions usually run between 1% and 3% on large NYSE or Amex stocks, but can go as high as 5% on thinly traded over-the-counter issues. For bonds and some OTC stocks, you pay a spread instead of a commission — meaning the brokerage firm sells the stock to you at a higher price than it pays. Spreads also range from 1% to 5%. On mutual funds sold by brokers, commissions typically run from 4.5% to 8.5% (with the broker getting a third to a half and the firm getting the rest), while commissions on some annuities can run as high as 8% to 12% and on limited partnerships up to 20%. Obviously, you'd prefer to be charged rates at the lower end of these averages — and, if you aren't, don't be afraid to ask for a reduction.

2. Why are you recommending this investment? If the broker can't give you some good fundamental reasons, odds are he or she is pushing the item for another reason. For example, some mutual fund companies pay brokerage firms big annual retainers to give their funds extra promotion. Some firms also give brokers awards — such as trips, cars, etc. — for selling certain funds or products (usually those created or operated by the brokerage firm). Finally, some brokerage firms maintain underwriting or venture capital arrangements with certain companies and recommend their stocks in order to cement business relations.

3. Is there a comparable investment that would cost less? There may be a no-load alternative to a load mutual fund that would serve your needs just as well. Or, you may be able to get a better fundamental buy on an existing stock than on a new issue. Make sure the broker can give you a compelling reason for paying the higher price for what he's trying to sell.

4. Can I get a discount on commissions? Most firms will let brokers give customers who ask a discount of up to 20% on a stock transaction. However, if you are an active trader — making 10 trades a year or more — you should be able to get as much as 50% off the standard rates.

5. How much does the investment have to rise before I break even? If you pay 8.5% in upfront fees on an investment, your remaining money has to earn 9.3% merely to make the commission back — and that can be a tall order these days.

6. What other fees will apply in this investment? Mutual funds routinely charge annual management fees of 0.25% to 0.75%; some charge redemption fees if you close out before a certain amount of time passes; and some impose back-end fees regardless of when you exit. Some brokerage firms also charge

both activity fees (designed to cover bookkeeping costs) over and above the commission charges, and others charge inactivity fees if you don't do a minimum number of trades per year. Be sure you know what you investment is actually going to cost.

Protective Tip: To make sure you are dealing with a reputable broker at a reputable brokerage firm, request his or her full disciplinary record from the National Association of Securities Dealers. Just call 1-800-289-9999.

CHOOSING THE BEST DISCOUNT BROKER

If you do decide to forego full service and try your luck with a discount broker, you should exercise care in the selection process. In fact, it's not a bad idea to interview a prospective discount brokor the same way you would interview a job applicant. Check out his or her educational background, industry experience, prior employment and references. Even though you will do most of the research and select your own investments when you work with a discount broker, you still want someone who is qualified and will understand what you are trying to do when you call to place your orders. You should also ask about fees as even discount brokers give special rates to active customers. If you plan to trade on margin, make sure you inquire about margin rates as well. A good discount broker should not only offer lower commissions than a full-service house, but lower margin rates as well. Finally, ask about the broker's accounting services to find out how long you can expect to wait for confirmations, how often you get statements (some firms now send them out only quarterly) and what the firm's settlement procedures are (how long you have to send in money for a purchase and how long you'll have to wait to get your money when you sell).

BEWARE OF DECEPTIVE DISCOUNT CLAIMS

The best thing about discount brokers is their competitive commission rates. The worst thing is that you must be very careful about believing their advertising claims. Discounters sometimes compare their charges with the higher fees generated by full-service brokers before deregulation of commission rates. Also be wary of undisclosed minimum commission rates — meaning a minimum charge per trade is required. If you trade in small lots, such minimums can boost your cost percentages and eat up your commission savings in no time. Most of the big savings touted in discount broker ads are based on large trades — 500 shares or more — so you may not get those rates on smaller lots. The best tactic is to describe the type and size of trades you'll usually be doing and ask for specific prices on trades of that nature. If they seem high, try another discounter since commissions do vary — even at the discount houses.

SAVE MONEY BY USING THE RIGHT ORDER

Almost every investor is familiar with the basic buy, sell and stop-loss orders. However, there are a few other orders that, when used properly, can save you a lot of money:

* Limit order — This specifies an exact price above which you will not go when buying a stock or below which you will not go when selling.

* Good-till-canceled (GTC) order — This is a limit order that stays in force until it is either filled at the desired price or you cancel it.

* Fill or kill orders — This means the order will be either filled or canceled immediately.

* All or none — Simply stated, this order demands that an entire order be filled at a limit price, or that no shares at all be bought or sold.

* Not held — This order gives the floor broker the authority to use his own discretion in the execution of an order. However, if the broker chooses wrong, the investor must accept the loss.

* Stop-buy order — This order is used for protection when you have a short position, directing the broker to buy stock to cover your short if the price rises to a certain level. Investors who rely on technical analysis may also use stop-buy orders when they want to purchase a stock only if it "breaks out" above a certain price level.

* Clean-up basic — This order usually applies to a heavy seller who wants to buy stock at a specific price only if the purchase leaves no more stock available at that price.

* Short or short exempt — This order is used when an investor is holding securities or bonds for conversion into common stock. The investor can sell short the amount of stock into which the convertible issue can be converted without waiting for an uptick.

Don't be afraid to use a specialized type of order if it suits your needs. While market orders ensure that you get the position you want, they often fall far short of guaranteeing that you get the price you want.

WHEN TO IGNORE YOUR BROKER'S ADVICE

There are several instances when you should consider saying no to your broker's advice:

1. When the broker thinks a stock will go up because of some forthcoming good news, rather than because it has solid current fundamentals.

2. When the broker tries to get you to buy into a sliding market because "the stock looks like a real bargain" at the new lower price.

3. When the broker tries to talk you into "averaging down" — which means buying more shares of a losing stock in order to lower your average cost. It's better to just take your loss and look for a better opportunity elsewhere.

RECOVER YOUR INVESTMENT LOSSES NOW

Thanks to new SEC conduct and arbitration rules, it's now much easier to recover your investment losses if they are the result of broker malfeasance. You don't even need an attorney, and you won't be locked up in years of litigation. If you think you've been a victim of misrepresentation, unsuitable recommendations, unauthorized trading, churning or commission abuses, you should find out about this option. IAS Inc. has a FREE brochure explaining why, how and what you can recover. Call 1-800-678-8185 to get a copy.

F. Tips on Other Key Investment Vehicles

KEYS TO EVALUATING UTILITY STOCKS

Utilities are often good stable income stocks. However, there are a few things you should consider before buying into one:

1. Make sure the utility is located in a state with a favorable utility climate. A good measure is that at least two-thirds of the utility requests for rate increases are approved by the state regulatory agency.

2. Does the utility have enough income to pay interest on its bonds? Typically, the utility should be earning at least 2.5 times the interest payments due on corporate notes — and hopefully more.

3. Make sure the utility can cover any projected dividend payments, and that the company isn't paying out too high a percentage of earnings in dividends (65% to 70% is the norm).

4. Check out the share price as it compares to book value. The higher the book value relative to the price, the better.

5. Finally, does the utility have a large debt? This should be easy to find out by examining the balance sheet for asset-to-liability ratios. The higher the ratio the better.

BUY TREASURIES AND BONDS ON YOUR OWN AND SAVE BIG

You can save 3% to 5% when buying government bonds and Treasury bills by cutting out the broker. To buy a T-bill, T-note or government bond on your own, send a letter to the Federal Reserve Bank or one of its branches. Include the type of security you want and specify how it will be registered. Include a check of $10,000 minimum for T-bills, $5,000 for 2- to 5-year notes and $1,000 for long-term bonds. Make sure your letter is postmarked by midnight the day before the next securities auction. You will receive a receipt for the security, as well as a refund of the discount from the Fed.

WHEN A GOVERNMENT GUARANTEE ISN'T

Just because a security comes from the government, don't expect it to be risk free. Some government securities are merely sponsored by the government — not backed by it. Others, such as Farm Credit System securities, are issued by agencies or insurance funds that are currently insolvent and unable to meet their debts. Therefore, when shopping for a government security, be sure what you're getting is really a government-issued security, not just one sponsored, insured or loosely guaranteed by a government agency.

PICKING THE BEST MUNICIPAL BONDS

Municipal bonds have grown in popularity now that returns on other low-risk investments have fallen to 30-year lows. In many cases, the taxable-equivalent yield on tax-free munis is now higher than the after-tax yield on other income-oriented securities. They are also a good way to preserve capital, since default risk is fairly low. However, some caution is needed when shopping for munis. The most important items to consider are quality, price, yield and maturity. Here are some of the most popular ways to invest in tax-free bonds:

1. Unit Investment Trusts — These are portfolios made up of diversified investments that qualify for double tax-free status (either state and local or state and federal). There is no professional portfolio manager, and the securities, once purchased, are held until maturity. Monthly, semi-annual or annual interest payment options are available.

2. Managed Bond Funds — These are also diversified portfolio, but they have professional managers who buy and sell bonds in an effort to generate capital gains as well as tax-free interest payments. These funds usually have a higher yield, but they also have a management fee. They offer the same payment options as unit investment trusts and most also allow for the reinvestment of interest payments.

3. Individual Bonds — These are individual securities issued by states,

localities and local government agencies (such as school districts, etc.) They are rated for safety by both Moody's and Standard & Poor's independent rating services. If you are concerned about default, stick to bonds that are insured by a state or national insurance association.

4. General Obligation Bonds — These provide you with the most security since they are backed by the full faith and credit of the issuing government entity, which usually has general taxing power.

5. Revenue Bonds — These are bonds issued for a specific purpose, such as road, bridge or sewer construction, and they carry more risk since they often rely on income from the completed project to pay off the debt.

Tip: If you are investing for the long term, look for tax-free bonds that are trading at a discount to face value. These provide both the stated yield and a guaranteed capital gain at the time the bond matures. Though you will probably be able to sell these bonds quite easily if you have to, it's still a good idea not to invest any money you might need for other purposes in discounted bonds. After all, the discount could get bigger if interest rates begin to rise, meaning you would suffer a capital loss that could wipe out your interest income.

G. Specialty Investment Rewards & Risks

CLOSED-END FUNDS ARE DIFFERENT ANIMALS

There are 2 basic kinds of pooled investment funds — open-ended funds, more commonly known as mutual funds, and closed-end funds. However, any investor who confuses the two is making a big mistake because closed-end funds are entirely different animals. Mutual funds sell units or shares to the public on a continuous basis and invest the proceeds in a portfolio of securities according to a published statement of objectives or investment policies. The "open-end" designation refers to the continuous distribution of new shares, and to the fact that the issuing fund will always buy back (redeem) the shares on demand. Shares of open-end funds are purchased by the investor at the net asset value per share (plus, in some cases, a load or commission) and are sold by the shareholder at the net asset value per share at time of redemption. Closed-end funds on the other hand, do not sell units or shares continuously to the public. Instead, they issue a set number of shares at the time the fund is formed (although they may, with regulatory approval, issue new units from time to time), and the units are traded on the secondary market much as shares of a common stock would be.

Like a mutual fund, the closed-end investment fund puts its assets in a portfolio of securities according to a predetermined investment plan or strategy. Closed-end funds are typically specialized, holding portfolios in such specific areas as precious metals (BGR Precious Metals, United Service Gold Shares); stocks of single foreign countries (The Germany Fund, Brazil Fund); foreign currencies (First Mercantile Fund), etc. Some, however, hold diversified portfolios of U.S. or international securities.

Since closed-end fund shares are traded rather than redeemed, they sell at a market-determined price, reflecting supply and demand. This price is rarely equal to the fund's net asset value per share, sometimes trading at a premium, but more typically at a discount to the actual value. In recent years, the discount for a typical closed-end fund has averaged between 10% and 20%, and is currently around 13%. However, some very specialized funds can trade at discounts of as much as 45%.

As a rule, well-managed funds of high-quality, fairly liquid securities, trading at a large discount (say, 25%) to net asset value per share represent a bargain for investors. After all, you are paying only 75 cents on the dollar for value. As a result, if the underlying portfolio contains a high proportion of dividend-paying securities, you have a higher dividend yield than the implicit rate in the secondary market. In addition, there has been a recent trend toward "open-ending" — i.e., the managers obtain permission to change the closed-end fund to open-end status, thus pushing the price directly to the net asset value. These factors make deep-discount closed-end funds interesting investments, and we generally recommend their purchase. However, you should be cautioned that the discount to net asset value can prevail indefinitely. In addition, open-ending doesn't always accomplish what investors expect. After absorbing costs for legal and accounting services, unitholder information packages, solicitations for approval and other such costs of the open-ending process, the unitholder often finds that he or she is no better off than before — particularly when back-end (or exit) fees are introduced.

The issue of why closed-end funds typically sell at discounts to net asset value is intriguing. A number of reasons have been cited for the discount, all of them subject to some argument. Among these are the cost of liquidating the portfolio and distributing the proceeds to investors; the implicit management fees or other expenses of the fund; the unrealized underlying stock appreciation and corresponding embedded tax liability in thefund; the lower commissions for closed-end funds, which reduce the incentive brokers have to sell them; the lack of active sales promotion, which reduces the relative demand for the funds; the lack of favorable tax treatments which are awarded to some open-end funds. In our view, however, the key factor underlying the discount is that the investor has two sources of risk and return on a closed-end fund — that associated with the portfolio itself, and that associated with the variance about the premium or discount.a result, we consider these funds appropriate long-term investments for aggressive investors, particularly those interested in specific sectors such as precious metals. However, more conservative investors should probably stick with traditional open-ended mutual funds.

WHEN TO INVEST IN A `NEW ISSUE'

If 1992's record pace of initial public offerings (IPOs) is any indication, new issues could be the hot investment game of the '90s, much as leveraged buyouts (LBOs) were in the '80s. However, investing successfully in new issues requires careful selection and timing. Here are some helpful guidelines to help you make the best choices:

* Invest in a new issue only if the company is a part of a successful and growing industry.

* The managing underwriter should be well known. If any of the leading investment banking firms are involved, it adds weight to the value of tho offering.

* Check out the underwriter's payment arrangement. It's a positive sign if the underwriter takes warrants or options to buy shares at a higher price than the initial offering price.

* Look for offerings from companies that have an established management team and a proven track record for making money.

* Look for companies with a proven record of growth and a plan for using the IPO proceeds for expansion rather than existing operations.

* Check out the company's board of directors to see if any respected individuals are included. Note, too, if any successful venture capitalists are involved with the company.

* Finally, for best results, invest in a new issue only when tho stock market as a whole is in an uptrend, not when the mood for stocks is bearish.

Warning: If your broker calls pitching a new public offering, your best move is probably to say "no thanks" unless you are a very good customer or the broker owes you a special favor. The reason? On really hot new offerings, the local offices of big brokerage firms involved in the IPO usually get only 500 to 1,000 shares to be doled out as rewards to special clients (when Apple went public, demand was so high many brokerage offices got just 100 shares). If a broker has to call pushing an IPO, it probably means the issue is not being well received by savvy investors or financial pros and the underwritor is having trouble unloading the shares — meaning you don't want them.

Selling Tip: When you buy shares in a new issue — either on the IPO or in the open market shortly after the shares begin trading — plan to sell within 3 months. Studies have shown that many IPOs fall in price after that because they can't meet high investor expectations.

7 RULES FOR VENTURE-CAPITAL INVESTMENTS

The field of venture capital — investing in new companies or start-up situations — can be both exciting and very, very rewarding. However, it is also fraught with risks, including the almost 50-50 chance that a new business will fail completely, costing you your entire investment. Here are 7 general rules to consider before investing in venture-capital deals:

1. An inverse relationship exists between the amount of pre-product publicity and the company's success. If everybody's talking about a new venture, it's probably not the best opportunity.

2. If a venture-capital investor doesn't see any problems — he has a problem. All new financing arrangements run into snags, and one that doesn't probably hasn't been fully thought out.

3. The most important thing in any new business is a positive cash flow. If the company can't project one fairly quickly, beware.

4. An inverse relationship exits between the size of the president's office and the success of a small company. Money should be poured into the business, not perks for the businessman.

5. A long-winded investment proposal generally equals a short shot at success. Most quality deals are clearly and succinctly explained, with no attempt at obfuscation and no more legalese than is legally required.

6. There is no such thing as an over-financed company, but all too many start out life with inadequate capital. Make sure the venture capital deal is big enough to really meet the needs of the business.

7. There is no limit to success in the venture-capital field — as long as you don't mind who gets the credit. Be happy with healthy profits; don't demand an active role in operations unless you have talents or energies the company really needs.

2 TRICKS FOR IMPROVING `PENNY' STOCK PROFITS

Because of their low price ($5 per share and below), so-called "penny stocks" are attractive to many new investors or investors with smaller trading accounts. However, these stocks usually have low prices for a reason — most often because the company is either new or in trouble — so the risk factor is fairly high. However, if the potential for large returns on a small investment appeals to you, there are a couple of tricks you can use says J. David Stewart, an independent Canyon Lake, Ca., analyst and broker who specializes in low-priced stocks:

* The "Spec-Pack" Approach — Stewart likes to split his clients' money

equally among 10 low-priced stocks — creating what he calls a speculative package. He uses the same criteria in selecting all 10 companies, focusing on quality management, a good product or idea and growing revenues (profits aren't essential, but a pattern of dwindling losses is attractive). However, even with careful selection, he's a realist about the likely results. "Of each 10 companies I pick, 3 usually go bust for one reason or other," Stewart says, "most usually undercapitalization or a failure of management (many smaller companies are started by inventors or idea people who turn out to be dismal at day-to-day operations). Five others will break even or show small gains — and 2 will wind up going through the roof." The net result? An overall gain on the full portfolio of 30% to 50%. "The key with these stocks is same as with any portfolio," Stewart notes. "The more you diversify, the lower your risk. The big difference with low-priced stocks is that the winners tend to be much bigger, so diversification also improves your odds of finding a rocket, which increases your overall return."

* The Capital Preservation Approach — For investors who don't have the cash to put together a Spec-Pack (Stewart suggests a minimum of $5,000), or the time to hunt for 10 different penny stocks, Stewart advises an alternate approach designed to maximize capital preservation while still leaving the door open for the really big gains. This involves buying round lots of 400 shares or more and playing for a double, which is not that hard to achieve with low-priced issues. Once you get the double, you sell half your shares, which guarantees a break-even on the position, regardless of what later happens. You're then left with a growing portfolio of "free" stocks, which you can hold for possible price explosions, and you still have your original stake available to put into new opportunities as they arise.

THE PERILS OF PRECIOUS METALS

Investing in gold, silver, platinum and palladium can be intriguing — as well as providing a hedge against inflation and world turmoil — but you should be careful. Gold has pulled back sharply during the recent period of reduced inflation, and the weak economy has cut into industrial demand for the other metals, sending their prices lower as well. This could make now a good time to buy, particularly if you believe the shift to a Democratic administration could result in renewed inflation. However, if you do decide to play the metals game, be sure to deal only with reputable bullion dealers or registered commodity brokers. There are numerous illegal dealers out there selling both non-existent bullion contracts and fraudulent gold and silver futures contracts. These scam artists often hire high-pressure phone solicitors to make the deals. The fraudulent futures scams are particularly insidious because they usually strike more than once. Customers are roped in; then, when their "investments" fail to pay off in a short time — usually 120 days — they are offered a second chance, being pushed to "roll over" the contract for an excessively high fee. Those unfortunate investors who try to close their accounts find it impossible to get their money back. Savings Note: When you make your metals investments through with a registered commodities broker, don't hesitate to negotiate for a lower commission. As with stock brokers, most futures trading firms allow their account representatives some leeway in setting commissions.

BEWARE COMMODITY FUND VOLATILITY

Trading commodity futures is a fast-paced game that offers high leverage and big potential profits — but the risks are also tremendous, especially for casual players who can't watch the markets constantly and make decisions within minutes after some new piece of information becomes public. For that reason, many people have chosen to hand their speculative money over to the managers of commodity pools or funds — and many have done quite well on their investments. Be aware, however, that there are still plenty of ups and downs with commodity funds — often in a short period of time. Unlike managers of stock mutual funds, who diversify widely in an effort to minimize big value swings, commodity fund managers tend to concentrate huge sums of money in a single market — scoring spectacular gains when they're right and taking equally large losses when they're wrong. As an example, look at the 1992 experience of one of the best-known commodity fund managers — Paul Tudor Jones, founder of the Tudor Futures Fund. Tudor's fund (in which a $1,000 investment in 1984 would have grown to more than $55,000 by the end of 1991) was down about 13% in mid-1992. However, he put more than half his fund's $885 million in assets into European currencies in the third quarter — and wound up earning about 25% for the full year.

By contrast, John Henry, manager of the $619 million Financial and Metals Portfolio Fund, was well ahead at mid-year based on a good soybean call. However, he missed the mark during the second half, and his fund finished 1992 with a 7.84% loss. The Moral: If the fast-paced commodity market appeals to you, you are probably best served by trusting your funds to an established commodity fund operator. However, don't expect a sure thing — and be ready for some very wide swings in the value of your holdings.

CHECKING UP ON YOUR COMMODITIES BROKER

If you have any doubts about your commodities broker's record, there's now a free hotline you can call to clear them up. Sponsored by the National Futures Association, the hotline will tell you whether the broker in question has been the subject of complaints or disciplinary action by a regulatory agency. The NFA's data bank features reports on over 11,000 disciplinary actions taken by regulatory agencies, and includes information on around 10,000 firms and 150,000 individuals. The toll-free number is 1-800-676-4632. The NFA also offers a mediation service that will attempt to resolve any conflicts you may have with your commodities broker. The rulings are non-binding, but the NFA mediators have a good record of dealing with problems before they have to go to arbitration or turn into law suits. For more information about the service, call 312-419-4650 or 212-725-6160.

DIAMONDS CAN BE ROUGH

Diamonds may be a girl's best friend, but they certainly are not an investor's. Although the precious stones have edged up in price since their lows in the mid-1980s, they're still an unwise choice as investments. Specialized expertise is required to evaluate them, and mark-ups are extremely high so it takes many years to recover your initial cost. It's also almost impossible to resell them as there is no established secondary market. So, if you like diamonds, buy them as jewelry or collector's pieces — but not as an investment.

BIG PROFITS FROM INTERNATIONAL INVESTING

When it comes to profits, opportunity knows no borders. Success always awaits astute investors somewhere in the world — even when American markets are collapsing and the U.S. economy is besieged. In other words, if you hope to truly succeed in today's ever more integrated financial world, you must adopt a global perspective on investing. The New York Stock Exchange is no longer the undisputed Capitol of capitalism nor is the U.S. the unchallenged king of the world's free-market hill. Other investment markets — both here and abroad — regularly outperform the NYSE, and other countries regularly challenge America's financial superiority. In fact, the capitalist system has made such strides around the globe that American stocks now account for just 28% of the world's total market value, based on capitalization (which is the share price times the number of shares outstanding). That means that if you limit your investment choices to the United States, you are willfully excluding yourself from more than 70% of the investment opportunities the world has to offer. And, if you stick solely to the large-capitalization stocks that trade on the NYSE, you reduce your opportunity set to just 15% of the world's potential investment winners. Even for the most proficient picker of individual stocks, that's a heavy handicap to overcome

Performance results for 1992 — which was actually a fairly good year for U.S. stocks in spite of America's troubled economic outlook — provide a perfect example of the risks inherent in maintaining either a single-market or single-country focus when it comes to investing. The Dow Jones Industrial Average — still the world's most closely watched investment indicator — gained a mere 4.2% in '92, while the NYSE as a whole advanced just 4.7%. By contrast, the Standard and Poor's index of mid-sized U.S. stocks showed a gain of 9.3%, and the NASDAQ Composite Index — which measures the activity of America's smaller, over-the-counter stocks — advanced by a more than respectable 15.5%. Thus, by merely limiting yourself to one market within the United States — and choosing the wrong one — you could have reduced your return by almost 11% on average. And, the contrasts were even greater when you look beyond America's borders.

Investors who stuck solely to the French market in 1992 broke just about even on the year, but those in Great Britain lost 7.4%. Even worse, those in Germany dropped 11.9%, those in Canada gave up 14.7% and those who played exclusively Japanese stocks lost a whopping 22.1%. However, lest you think that's an indictment of overseas stock investing, just look at the other end of the spectrum, where investors in Mexican stocks gained 20.1% and those putting their money in issues making up Hong Kong's Hang Sing Index picked up an extraordinary 27.4%.

The point, however, is not that Hong Kong was the place to be in 1992, but rather that there is a world of opportunity out there for investors — opportunity you will never recognize or be able to take advantage of if you fail to adopt a global perspective. In fact, if you have been investing solely in U.S. markets over the past 15 years, you have already suffered a substantial loss of return relative to the gains possible in other markets. According to Morgan Stanley Capital International, stocks in the United States — despite one of the longest bull markets in American history and a persistent series of new record highs — ranked a very weak 12th in average market performance during the period from 1976 through 1991. Including dividends, the average annual compounded rate of return for U.S. stocks over that time was 13.8%, almost 6 percentage points behind the results achieved by stocks in Great Britain, the world leader during that period. Barely missing the top spot was Sweden, with an average return of 19.2%, while the Netherlands ranked third, returning 18.4%. Other leading countries included France, Hong Kong, Japan and Belgium, all of which had average returns in excess of 17%; followed by Italy, Denmark, Australia and Singapore, all of which returned 14% or more. Lagging the United States were such countries as Norway, Spain, Germany, Austria, Canada and finally Switzerland, where stocks averaged an annual return of just 11.3%.

Again, however, the point is not to use the benefits of hindsight to single out any one market or country as better than all others. Rather, it is to stress the necessity of looking at all of them — of taking a truly world view when seeking out both new investment opportunities and diversification against the perils of an uncertain economy. Perhaps the best analogy was provided by Sir John Templeton, founder of the Templeton family of mutual funds and one of the earliest proponents of maintaining an internationally diversified investment portfolio. Though we cannot cite his exact quote, we clearly recall the essence of his reply when asked to explain his investment perspective. "I try to visualize myself as sitting in a space ship far above the Earth," he said, "where no borders or boundaries can be seen. And, as the globe spins, I target the best opportunities I see, wherever they may be."

Templeton's analogy is also useful in overcoming an all-too-common misconception that arises when many American investors hear someone speak of taking a global view. A global perspective does not mean a foreign perspective. Anyone building a true global portfolio would be foolish not to include U.S. securities — and, depending on world economic conditions, such investments might even dominate the portfolio. In fact, Templeton himself was recently quoted as saying he felt many of the best opportunities for the '90s would be in U.S. markets, a significant shift from the late '80s, when he excluded most American stocks in favor of foreign issues.

As with investing solely in U.S. securities, the primary element of global investing is the selection of a good stock — not the easiest task regardless of where you look. There are, however, some additional problems that go along with investing on a worldwide scale. These include a lack of quality information about companies in many foreign countries; different accounting and financial reporting standards; arbitrary and sometimes excessive transaction costs; a lack of liquidity in some overseas markets; withholding and other tax considerations; and government restrictions on foreign investment. Two other major risk factors involve currency exchange rates and political stability of foreign governments.

These factors can often lead to a higher personal cost in terms of time spent on research, analysis and monitoring. However, they also suggest the existence of market inefficiencies that can provide abnormal returns to the astute investor. And, the additional safety gained through international diversification more than offsets the risk of loss due to systemic factors. Besides, the difficulties in monitoring and tracking investments on a global scale are no longer that great. Thanks to advances in communications and computer technology, an investor with the right equipment can follow any market in the world, regardless of where he or she is physically located. In addition, both The Wall Street Journal and Investor's Business Daily publish daily listings of world stock market indexes, and Dow Jones has recently created a World Stock Index, which will be maintained and published in much the same fashion as the Dow Industrials are handled. This index will help provide investors with daily information they need to assess political, economic and financial forces affecting global markets, enabling them to determine quite easily when the best opportunities lie elsewhere.

Even with that public flow of information, however, the best choice for most investors looking at international diversification is the mutual fund. At the start of 1993, there were over 250 SEC-registered funds investing internationally. Thus, you do not have to go overseas nor do you have to send your money out of the country in order to participate in foreign investments. Most of the leading mutual fund families have at least one international fund, and some have several, focusing on different investment objectives. These funds are perfect for smaller investors or investors who don't have the time, experience or inclination to handle their own global portfolios.

Depending on the size of your portfolio and your desire to become a global investor, you can also consider several other alternatives. These include direct foreign investments through U.S. brokers, as well as investments in selected foreign issues represented by American Depository Receipts.

These so-called ADR's trade on U.S. stock exchanges, in effect giving you a foreign investment without the trouble of investing directly in shares traded on a foreign stock exchange such as those in London or Hong Kong. Of course, in order to protect yourself, you must be certain that your stockbroker or asset manager has the information systems needed to monitor the foreign securities and overseas market conditions underlying the values of these U.S.-traded ADR's.

Among all the options, however, international mutual funds still offer the most advantages. They provide total liquidity and eliminate many of the problems associated with converting your dollars to a foreign currency and then back again. You are also relieved of the need to conduct day-to-day research and make crucial decisions, leaving the management to professionals knowledgeable about overseas markets and individual foreign stock selection. A mutual fund enables even a small investor to diversify adequately — both among countries and within individual markets — and the results can be spectacular.

Sir John Templeton started his Growth Fund in 1954 as a vehicle to give smaller American investors access to opportunities outside the United States. Had you invested just $10,000 in the Templeton Growth Fund at its inception, you would be a multi-millionaire today. No other mutual fund in the United States — or, indeed, the world — can top that performance, so why not join the ever-growing crowd emulating Templeton and begin taking your own global perspective toward investing!

H. Investments You Should Consider Now

YOUR NO. 1 INVESTMENT STRATEGY TODAY/$45 A MONTH TURNS INTO $124,100

Regardless of how good you are at picking stocks or selecting mutual funds, there's one strategy that will almost certainly produce bigger returns than those investments in today's low-interest-rate, low-inflation marketplace. What is this exotic play? Don't be disappointed, but it's really not exotic at all — it's simply paying off your debts. After all, what sense does it make to earn 10% on a mutual fund and then turn around and pay 12% on a car loan — or, even worse, 18% on a credit-card account. This negative equation is compounded when you consider that state and federal taxes probably reduce that 10% fund yield to around 6%. By applying your money directly to paying off those debts, however, you can effectively double or triple your return. In fact, because early payment reduces the term of your loan — and thus the overall interest cost — your return is actually even higher over the long term. This strategy even applies to loans with tax-deductible interest for some more conservative investors. For example, if you're in the 31% tax bracket and have a 10% home mortgage, your effective after-tax interest cost is 6.9%. That's fairly low — but it's still more than you can earn from safe investments such as bank CDs, Treasury bills or money market funds.

In fact, as you'll learn about in greater detail later in the Section on Real Estate Realities, paying off a mortgage early can be a highly effective investment strategy regardless of your tax situation. For example, an extra "investment" of $45 per month on a 30-year, $90,000 mortgage at 10% can cut the term of the mortgage by about 7-1/2 years and save approximately $53,000 in interest payments. To compound the return even further, continue making the regular monthly mortgage payment of $790 into a savings account for the remaining 7-1/2 years, and you'll build up a balance, without earning any interest at all, of $71,100. In essence, that gives you a profit of $124,100 on the $45 investment and that understates reality since the money you save during the 7-1/2 years will obviously earn at least some interest. What other $45-a month investment can produce returns like that!

So, in summary, if you have money to invest, your No. 1 strategy in the current economic environment is most likely to pay off existing debts rather than looking for the next super stock or star mutual fund.

EARN INTEREST FROM 2 MONEY FUNDS AT ONE TIME

For those whose aversion to risk is keeping them in ultra-safe investments even in these low-yield times, it may seem like there are few options for improving returns. However, if you are nimble, there is one way you can boost returns on money market funds — simply collect interest on your money from 2 funds at the same time. How is this possible? It involves switching money from one fund to another and taking advantage of the so-called float — the time between when a deposit is credited to your account and when the money actually shows up. For example, if you have $25,000, you could split that money among 5 funds, each with checking privileges. Then, each week, you could mail a check for $2,500 from one fund to another, timing your mailings so that the checks arrive at the fund on a Thursday. That will ensure that the new deposit is credited to your account on Friday, even though the withdrawal from your other fund probably won't actually be made until the following Tuesday. The end result? For 4 days each week, it will appear that you have $7,500 in each account, rather than just $5,000 — and you'll earn interest on the full amount. This may seem like a lot of work, but it can increase your total money fund return by 25% to 30% — which is fairly lucrative pay for writing a few checks.

SURPRISING `MARKET' INVESTMENT EARNS 33%

Want to make consistent returns of 33% in the market? Of course you do. And, you can! Almost every week! The only thing is, the market we're talking about is the supermarket. All you have to do is watch for the sales on staple items such as detergents, paper products, soda, canned goods, toothpaste, etc., and buy them in bulk at the lower prices. Each time you manage to get $50 worth of goods at 25% off, you in effect make a 33% return on the $37.50 you invest. Caution: Don't buy items in bulk unless you are sure you will use them. A bargain price is no bargain if it's on something that will later spoil or go to waste.

THE 3 BEST SAFE INVESTMENTS TO MAKE NOW

Looking for some current investment opportunities that combine both safety and great potential? Here are 3 of our top choices — which might just surprise you:

1. Residential real estate. Many recognized advisors contend that real estate is a terrible investment right now, thanks to the combination of a weak market and low inflation, which could inhibit price gains. However, we have difficulty following that line of reasoning. It's true that the market has been weak, but it also has almost surely bottomed, leaving residential real estate in most parts of the country undervalued or, at worst, fairly priced. Interest rates are also quite low, mortgages are easy to get and residential real estate remains one of the few areas in which individual investors can easily employ the principle of OPM — other people's money — to increase their leverage. Real estate appreciation almost always keeps up with the rate of inflation. Thus, even at the current low 3% inflation rate, a 10% down payment on a home will grow about 160% over the new 5 years — a return of 21% per year. And, if inflation heats up again, the gains should be even larger.

2. Quality pharmaceutical stocks. This is another area that has been beaten down by current events. President Clinton promised he'd reform the wasteful health care system, and that led many nervous institutions to sell any stock even remotely connected with health care. In the case of the drug companies, however, this was a mistake. These stocks, which have long been among the safest and most consistently profitable you can own, are currently selling at their lowest price/earnings multiple relative to the market in more than 25 years. However, the drug companies should continue to roll up superior earnings in spite of government policies. The reasons? First, drugs account for

only 5% of every health-care dollar spent today, down from 9% 25 years ago. Thus, drugs aren't the reason for soaring costs and shouldn't be a prime target for reform — at least not until serious cuts have already been imposed on hospital charges and doctors' fees. Second, even if the government puts heavy controls on U.S. health-care costs, the drug companies should continue making lots of money because they do so much business overseas, where they have even higher profit margins (despite years of socialized medicine in many European countries). Finally, if Clinton and the Democrats succeed in establishing some form of national health insurance, that will bring an additional 35 million U.S. families into the health-care system, producing a skyrocketing demand for pharmaceutical drugs as doctors treat millions of new patients and send them home with prescriptions.

3. Japanese stocks. We're doing a little bottom fishing here, but the opportunity seems too good to pass up. Since its high in 1980, Japan's Nikkei Index of 225 leading stocks has dropped 57%, from 38,985 to 16,755. In recent months, however, the Nikkei has successfully tested the 15,000 level 3 times and appears to be forming a solid technical base. Though the Japanese economy is currently in worse shape than America's, a recovery here should quickly spark a similar rebound there since U.S. consumers have such a heated love affair with Japanese products. Warning: Even in their currently depressed state, many of the top Japanese stocks have price/earnings ratios higher than their American counterparts. However, in the past, they have demonstrated growth sufficient to justify these high PEs — and they should do so again in the future.

...AND 7 TO AVOID AT ALL COSTS

Having listed some investment areas we currently like, we'll now add some that we think should be avoided given present price levels and economic conditions:

1. Gold. Even though the price is currently at 7-year lows, there's very little likelihood of a major rally so long as inflation remains in check. In addition, the end of the Cold War has seemingly reduced the demand for gold as a turmoil hedge. It will take a major conflagration somewhere in the world to restore this role for the yellow metal. Another negative factor is the necessity for Russia and other former Communist Bloc nations to sell gold in order to get hard currency with which to buy badly needed supplies and technical services from the West.

2. Silver. Not only is silver handicapped by spillover downward pressure from gold, but it is also suffering from America's weak economy. Silver has many more industrial uses than gold, but with manufacturing slow, demand has been low — and it will remain that way until the recovery picks up steam.

3. Agricultural commodities. Another victim of the current low-inflation

scenario and the inability of foreign customers to pay for U.S. products or meet or current requirements for export credits. Barring major problems related to the weather, the odds of a surge in commodity prices is very low over the near term.

4. Oil and oil-related products (except natural gas). Per-capita use of gasoline continues to fall in the United States and the mild weather has lowered demand for heating oil. So long as the OPEC cartel remains unable to stick to an agreement reducing production quotas and lowering output, there's very little likelihood of a rise in petroleum prices failing a major armed conflict involving Saudi Arabia and the other leading producers.

5. Commercial real estate. While we like the prospects for residential property — particularly single-family homes — the same can't be said for the commercial sector. Both the office and retail markets were already overbuilt when the recession hit, further reducing the demand for both corporate and store space — particularly in prime downtown areas and high-end shopping centers. With many Japanese investors feeling a cash crunch at home, they are also unloading many of the high-profile properties they bought in the '80s, and that's adding still more pressure. It may be years before this market fully recovers.

6. Long-term bonds. Yields on long-term bonds (20 to 30 years) are fairly low in absolute terms, but very high in real terms (adjusted for inflation). Despite that, they carry substantial risk of capital loss since prices will fall rapidly at the first sign of a boost in market rates or a realignment of the yield curve. Losses on the resulting price pullback could quickly wipe out any current yield advantage and leave investors who thought they were being conservative holding the bag.

7. Large-capitalization U.S. stocks. The stock market has been fairly steady for the past year, trading in a range of just 7% or so from high to low during 1992 and making several new highs. As 1993 began, Wall Street was closely watching for more details on what new President Clinton had planned for the economy and the investment markets. Since it seems highly unlikely Clinton will be able to fulfill all his campaign promises, the stock market could become disenchanted with the new administration by mid-year, reacting with a sell-off of at least 15% or so. Investors should be safer in small-cap stocks, which have far outperformed the major indexes in recent months — and should hold up better in any pullback given the stronger recovery under way in the small-company sector of the economy.

CHAPTER 9

LEGAL SECRETS

A. Protecting Yourself in Legal Matters

SURVIVING IN A LITIGIOUS SOCIETY

When it comes to legal matters, that old football saw still applies: A good offense makes for the best defense. Here are 3 quick ways to protect your legal interests:

1. Put it in writing. Before doing work for someone — or employing someone to work for you — have a written agreement that details what each of you expects the other to do, and how and when payment will be made. Nothing fancy. No legalese. Just one side of a page will do. Important: Include a sentence stating that all disputes will be handled in the courts of your state — or you may wind up defending yourself somewhere else. To protect whatever you may win in court, also provide that if you win the dispute, the other side will pay your legal fees.

2. If "they done ya wrong," sue. The intimidating, time-guzzling cost of our judicial system scares off many from seeking legal redress. But if you develop a reputation as someone who is not afraid to sue, people will think twice before trying to take advantage of you.

Cheap 'n' Easy Alternative: Small claims court — the court of choice for routine claims under $2,500. Since small claims proceedings are hearings, not trials, no lawyers are required and no complicated rules of evidence are enforced. The injured party merely provides a statement to a court-appointed examiner. Sessions are generally held at night to avoid conflict with daytime jobs. You'll find small claims courts listed in your local phone book as part of the court system.

3. Buy an excess liability insurance policy. As explained in both the Auto and Insurance Sections of Money $ecret$, most insurance companies will sell you a $1 million to 2 million "umbrella" policy that generally covers any liability for which you might be sued — save malpractice or libel — in excess of any coverage under your homeowners' or auto policies. The cost is usually quite reasonable — sometimes less than $100 a year. Important: Specify in the policy that the duty to defend against lawsuits rests with the insurer, not with you. Then, if you are sued, you simply turn the legal papers over to the insurer to handle.

THINK TWICE BEFORE FILING BANKRUPTCY

Although filing for bankruptcy is easier and less traumatic than ever before, the protection it offers from harassment and dunning by creditors while you get your financial house in order comes at a price. As such, it should be your last resort to keep creditors from suing and/or garnishing your wages. Why? It stays on your credit record for 10 years, making it difficult (though not impossible) for you to obtain credit during that time. It can also be surprisingly expensive — retaining a good bankruptcy attorney can cost from $350 to $1,500; maybe more if your case is complex. Also, Chapter 7 — the most severe form of consumer bankruptcy — forces you to sell off most of your property to pay off debts. Your home may be one of the few "exempt" assets you get to keep. And while Chapter 13 may be "kinder and gentler," it only allows rescheduling of debts if you have a steady job, less than $350,000 in secured debt and can eventually pay off your bills. Alternative: If you're not in such dire straits or you feel you can "restructure" your debts (credit cards, auto loans, other installment loans), try working with a credit counseling service first. They're experienced at negotiating with creditors to set up livable repayment plans. The National Foundation for Consumer Credit Counseling, 1-800-388-2227, can help you locate a counselor nearest you.

YOU CAN BE LIABLE FOR YOUR KID'S PRANKS

Who's legally responsible if your child injures someone or damages another's property? Are you automatically responsible for a child's actions simply because you are the child's parent? The basic answer is no. State case law decisions have generally established that, by age 12, a child is old enough to be tried in juvenile court. A 17- or 18-year-old can usually be tried as an adult. Exceptions:

1. If it's proved a child was committing a crime under a parent's direction, the parent can be tried for that crime. (Example: pickpockets who train kids to do their dirty work.)

2. A parent can also be held responsible if it is demonstrated that he or

she neglected to control the child's behavior. This concept is called "vicarious liability" and, depending on the state, it could require a parent to pay property damages up to $10,000. Approximately half the states hold parents liable for personal injuries their child may have done to others. Example: New Jersey parents can be liable for up to $1,000 worth of damage done by their child to a public utility, plus court costs. The penalty is actually an alternative to a charge of juvenile delinquency. Many parents are willing to pay to keep their children from getting a police record. Bottom Line: Paying for a child's vandalism may make family sense. However, for more serious crimes, hire a lawyer.

SHOP AROUND FOR LOWER CONTINGENCY FEES

If you have to use an attorney, you don't have to pay top dollar. Since most liability cases are handled on a contingency-fee basis (the attorney gets a cut of whatever he gets you), many attorneys will negotiate a 40% to 50% fee down to 20% to 35% if you've got a good case. At your initial meeting (for which you should not be charged), ask what the attorney charges. If it's 40% or more, ask to negotiate. If he won't — walk. Others will gladly take your case for less — and probably work harder to make it more worth their while — all the better for you!

5 WAYS ATTORNEYS CAN STEAL FROM YOU

Your lawyer is supposed to protect your interests. Unfortunately, some attorneys are more interested in protecting their own earning power than in winning your case. Here are 5 common ways attorneys can rip you off:

1. By claiming to have a contact who can "fix" your case in exchange for a flat fee (make that read "bribe"). In the first place, such "fixes" are illegal, so you wouldn't want to get involved in one. In the second place, the attorney is probably making the offer only because he has reviewed your case and thinks it's so solid he can't possibly lose. What he is really doing is asking for extra money, which he'll pocket since no fix is needed.

2. By padding expenses in contingency cases. Many lawyers, especially those who handle personal injury or negligence cases, agree to take your case on a contingency basis, accepting 25% to 40% of any final judgment you win. The lawyer says that, if you don't win, the suit will cost you nothing — except for expenses. He then proceeds to pile up a lot of bogus expenses, charging you for "research" or other items that aren't really needed. Get "expenses" in writing before you hire an attorney.

3. By cutting deals with insurance adjusters. Attorneys in negligence cases have also been caught making side arrangements with insurance companies to the detriment of their clients. For example, if an attorney and an

insurance adjustor agree that a settlement should be $15,000, the attorney might offer to accept $14,000 if the adjuster will tell the client they really settled for $13,000. This allows the lawyer to pocket the extra $1,000 before splitting the settlement with the client.

4. By inflating billable time in cases where the client is charged by the hour rather than on the basis of the settlement received. Many law firms expect their attorneys to bill 100 or more hours per week, which means the lawyer has to charge you for every second he even thinks about your case in order to meet his quota.

5. By commingling client funds. Many attorneys collect a settlement from an insurance company and then put the money in their own accounts, rather than in an account for the client. The attorney then stalls paying the settlement to the client in order to interest on the money.

If you have cause to deal with an attorney — particularly one who is taking your case on a contingency basis — make sure all of the cost and settlement considerations are spelled out up front. If you have any questions, don't sign until they are answered to your satisfaction.

B. Making the System Work for You

5 KEYS TO SUING — AND WINNING

A great attorney helps, but there are at least 5 other things you can do to strengthen your case:

1. Have your facts straight. Be clear on dates, phone calls and conversations. Get names of witnesses or people you speak with. Write down addresses, time of day, order of occurrence, etc.

2. Be specific about how you were wronged and what you want in return.

3. Ask your attorney a lot of questions and tell him everything. The more information he has, the better a case he can build.

4. Be businesslike in your attitude in and out of court. Make it clear you expect satisfaction. Recount the facts and your demand for compensation firmly. Communication works. Hysteria works against you.

5. Be willing to negotiate in good faith. If a reasonable offer for settling out of court is proposed, be open to at least considering it. In terms of time and expense, it might work out to your advantage to take it.

HOW TO COLLECT ON THE JUDGMENT YOU'VE WON

A legal judgment is worth no more than the paper it's written on if you can't collect. And, nearly 75% of all judgments go uncollected. How can you fight that dismal statistic? Here are a 11 pointers:

1. Sue the right person. The county clerk's office or business-licensing bureau will have the actual name in which the business is registered. Don't go by the name on the front door.

2. Sue the name or entities that have the assets to pay your judgments. You can sue more than one party.

3. When you get a judgment against a business, visit the site and take a look at office equipment, machinery and other assets.

4. If you're suing for more than the small-claims limit, get legal help to arrange for an asset search.

5. A lawyer can also guard against unscrupulous debtors who go out of business in one name and open up under a new name, using the same equipment and inventory.

6. To forcibly collect a judgment, you'll have to hire a marshal, sheriff or constable — then point them at the debtor's assets.

7. An enforcement officer can attach a debtor's salary (once informed where the debtor works). Depending on state laws, you can collect up to 25% of the debtor's paycheck.

8. There are some things you won't be able to collect, including a debtor's household appliances, TV and stereo systems, clothing and items necessary for employment.

9. Things you can take in settlement of a judgment include cars, bank accounts, stocks, bonds, jewelry, antiques and real estate.

10. A debtor's home is exempt up to a certain amount. However, the home is untouchable if your judgment is against only one spouse and the home is jointly owned.

11. Don't hire a collection agency. They prefer large accounts. And, in any case, to actually collect assets, you'll need an enforcement officer.

WHEN TO USE SMALL-CLAIMS COURT

Got a minor grievance? Been wronged, but not seriously damaged? Small-claims court may be your court of last — and best — resort. Most states limit the money stakes to $1,000 (though some let you go as high as $2,500 and a couple even go up to $10,000), but the spiritual satisfaction may be worth a great deal more. Here's when to file a suit in small-claims court:

* If a monetary settlement means less to you than justice. * If the money, even though small, represents a significant sum to you.

* If you have the time — at least a month for a case to be called. * If you don't mind airing your grievance in public — or actually want the public's attention called to the problem.

YOUR LEGAL RIGHTS AS A CONSUMER

Though many people feel helpless when facing problems with retailers and many others fall hopelessly victim to buyer's remorse, you really don't need to fear if you understand your rights. Purchases — even impulse buys — needn't be binding, and you should never consider yourself stuck with a purchase that could turn out to be financially fatal. Here are some guidelines regarding consumer rights in various situations:

At-Home Purchases — Under Federal Trade Commission rules, you have 3 business days to change your mind for purchases of $25 or more. These rules also apply to "party" sales at hotels and other locations, but they don't apply to sales made by mail or phone, or sales of real estate, insurance, securities or emergency home repairs. What you need to do:

1. Always ask for two copies of a dated cancellation form showing date of sale and dated contract with seller's name and address. Make sure the contract specifies your right to cancel.

2. To cancel the sale, sign and date the form, keeping the second copy. Send the cancellation notice to the company by registered mail (receipt requested).

3. The seller must respond within 10 days, returning any signed papers, down payment or trade-in and arranging for pick-up or shipping of any goods (at their cost).

4. For pick-ups, you must make the goods available. If no pick-up attempt is made within 20 days of your dated notice, the goods are yours to keep.

5. If you fail to comply with the conditions for returning the goods, you can held responsible for the original contract.

Retail Recourse — Stores are required by law to post return policies at the check-out counter in full view of the customer. If the store fails to make good or adequately compensate you, call a consumer agency. State offices are generally listed under the heading for the attorney general's office. The Better

Business Bureau also has over 140 offices nationwide and more than 100 consumer hotlines. Hotline listings are available from Call for Action, Inc., 575 Lexington Avenue, NY 10022. Additionally, local newspaper, TV and radio stations often sponsor consumer-advocate centers that get quick results. If you can attach a monetary value to your loss, you may be able to get a judgment levied through small-claims court. Trade groups and professional associations can also be effective in dealing with problems if the company is a member organization.

TAKING YOUR LANDLORD TO COURT

Having problems with your landlord? The best way to get what you want from a non-responsive landlord is through a tenant organization. Here's how to organize one:

1. Talk to the tenants in your building. Pass out flyers for a meeting at which you elect a committee of tenants. Ask all tenants to fill out a questionnaire, listing things that need fixing in their apartments.

2. Collect and review the questionnaires, then call the landlord and suggest a meeting to negotiate the complaints. The implied threat: a collective withholding of rent. Most landlords will opt to negotiate.

If negotiation fails, go ahead with a rent strike — depositing the tenants' rent each month in an escrow fund or with the court until repairs are made. Consult a good lawyer before embarking on this final course.

DEALING WITH DIFFICULT NEIGHBORS

If you live in an apartment complex, you may find you have more problems with neighbors than with the landlord. For example, suppose a tenant in your building is dealing drugs, involved in other types of crime or disturbing the peace with riotous parties. What are your alternatives? Here are some suggestions:

1. Take out a legal summons, claiming assault or harassment. The court will usually instruct the tenant to stop causing a disturbance. Sometimes this works; often it doesn't.

2. Sue in civil court for damages. You may just win; but collecting your judgment is up to you.

3. Try to get your landlord to evict the tenant. This will usually work, though a landlord has the right to rent to whomever he chooses, so it may not. However, if you have a strong tenant organization, he might comply — especially if the undesirable tenant is endangering other people or destroying the

property.

4. If all else fails, you can break your lease and move to a new apartment without penalty. It's your legal right if you're being harassed by another tenant.

FILING SUIT FOR A BODILY INJURY CLAIM

Have you been hurt or injured on someone else's property or as a result of another person's negligence? If so, here are 5 things you need to do or know before filing a claim against insurance companies for bodily injury:

1. Document your injury and suffering. Medical reports and photographs are most effective.

2. Document every facet of your life affected by an injury. Don't forget hobbies and family relationships.

3. If your injury is non-serious and you live in a fault-governed state, you can negotiate for more than out-of-pocket expenses. You can't do that if your state is no-fault.

4. Inventory your damages. Don't leave anything out.

5. If your disability isn't permanent, demand from your insurance company at least twice your actual expenses. However, if you've suffered permanent disability, all bets are off. For instance, if you lost an eye, your medical expenses might be only a few thousand dollars, but a jury could easily award you several hundred thousand or more.

GETTING INJURY COMPENSATION FROM THE GOVERNMENT

If you suffer a disabling injury, you don't have to depend solely on the courts for relief. Many states have disability programs to which you can apply, and the federal Social Security also has 2 disability programs. Here is a brief overview of the 2 federal programs:

1. Supplemental Security Income (SSI) Program — This program is a nationalization of welfare benefits for those unemployable due to physical disabilities.

2. Old Age and Survivors Disability Insurance (OASDI) — This program applies to working people and is funded by what you pay through the FICA taxes withheld from your paycheck.

For both programs, the rules for acceptance are the same. However, you are automatically eligible for OASDI if you've worked and paid into the system for 5 out of the last 10 years and have the necessary years of work credit, depending on age.

How the Process Works: File an application with your local Social Security office. A claims representative will ask about your disability — and look for any evidence of such disability. He sends his findings to a state disability examiner, who contacts your medical sources. Depending on the medical information you've submitted, the agency may send you to a consulting specialist — at the government's expense. Then, if you've met the stringent medical disability requirements, you'll be granted benefits.

Proving Your Disability: Your doctor must submit precise medical information, including all test results. Social Security won't accept your doctor's conclusions. It wants the medical evidence that led to the conclusion. You and your doctor should take a look at Social Security's long list of impairments. It might help you avoid a visit to the agency's consulting physician.

Exceptions and Appeals: Even if you don't meet all medical requirements, you may still qualify. Age, past work experience and education are also taken into account. If benefits are denied, you can appeal the decision or reapply.

Filing an Appeal: You can go back to the Social Security office and file for a reconsideration — basically, a review of your case.

Further Appeals: Even if that is denied, it's not over:

1. You can take your case to an administrative law judge within Social Security's Office of Hearings and Appeals. The reversal rate at this level is 50% to 60%.

2. If denied again, you can go to the Appeals Council and then up through the courts. The chances of reversal improve at each level.

YOUR LEGAL RIGHTS IF YOU'RE DISABLED

If you are physically disabled, you have certain legal rights. Even if you are incapable of functioning, you can delegate power of attorney to a person with financial expertise to handle your business and financial affairs. However, if you choose this course, there are several things you need to know:

* You are liable for anything the proxy does in your name. * Some people may be disinclined to deal with the proxy.

* In some states, the power of attorney ends if you become legally incompetent.

* It ends in all states when you die. You also have numerous other legal

options in the event of a disability. For example, you can:

* Arrange a standby trust that is activated by a specific event, such as an illness. When your disability ends — or when you die — the trust automatically terminates. This avoids probate.

* Name yourself as trustee of your assets. If you are incapacitated, responsibility automatically passes to a substitute trustee. This prevents you from being subjected to judicial guardianship, thereby avoiding expensive, periodic court-ordered accountings by the trustee. Again, if you die, this arrangement avoids probate.

THERE IS HELP FOR VICTIMS OF CRIME

Victims of muggings, assaults or other criminal injuries often feel helpless. However, in many cases, it's possible to get something more than sympathy. Here are some of the other potential resources available to victims of crime:

* Some homeowner's policies cover financial losses suffered as a result of injuries incurred during a mugging or assault.

* People who have had difficulty purchasing homeowner's insurance privately can apply for up to $10,000 in federal crime insurance against financial losses.

* Anyone mugged or assaulted on the job or while traveling during the work day on company business may be covered by workers compensation. (Note: Injuries suffered during the daily commute are not covered.)

* New York offers mugging insurance for medical care, mental anguish and property loss — and several other states are considering it.

* A growing number of states have victim's-assistance programs that provide financial compensation to crime victims who have no insurance, as well as to low-income victims whose own medical or unemployment insurance is fully depleted as a result of the criminal injuries.

* If you can prove the injuries suffered in the crime were the result of negligence on the part of the city, a building owner or a business, you may be able to collect on a lawsuit.

C. Winning the Divorce Wars

4 COMMON DIVORCE MISTAKES MOST PEOPLE MAKE

"No-fault" may have led divorce law into a new era of "no victor to whom the spoils belong," but it doesn't mean there aren't any victims. To avoid becoming one:

1. Detach yourself emotionally. He who seeks revenge can be done in financially under equitable distribution. Self-Protection Help: Psychotherapy, at least on a short-term basis.

2. Build a business support system. Hire experts, like an accountant and real estate appraiser, especially if a business is involved.

3. Don't go for the jugular — make them an offer they can't refuse. Who wants the IRS and their spouse's attorney digging through business records if it can be avoided? A "wronged" ex may seek to attach a higher value to your assets (or business), inviting a visit by the taxman. It pays to be generous — and alimony is tax deductible.

4. Keep the financial issues separate from the custody ones. Divorce is tough enough on kids. Don't make it worse.

GETTING THE BEST LAWYER FOR YOUR DIVORCE

A good lawyer is essential in almost any divorce proceeding. Here are some guidelines on finding and working with a divorce lawyer:

1. Ask for recommendations and advice from friends or associates who have also gone through a divorce.

2. Never use a company lawyer or a general-purpose lawyer.

3. Check out any lawyer carefully to make sure there are no personality conflicts and the two of you can communicate adequately. This will save a lot of time and aggravation later.

4. Get any financial arrangement in writing

5. Have your lawyer keep you steadily informed of all the legal maneuvering.

6. Include your spouse's attorney in any agreement between you and your spouse.

PROTECT YOUR ASSETS BEFORE THE DIVORCE

If you own a business, divorce can blow-up into a battle between accountants and appraisers. You might even lose your business just to satisfy a settlement. Here are some suggestions on how to cover yourself before it goes that far:

1. Keep your spouse informed about your company's financial affairs. An unrealistic sense of value may lead to an ex who feels cheated.

2. Craft a good shareholders' agreement for your company. Provide for buyouts in case of divorce, and spell out the process for establishing the company's value.

3. Request a prenuptial agreement. These can be invaluable — even in first marriages — when one of the marriage partners is involved in a prosperous family business. To make sure the prenuptial agreement will hold up in court:

* Both parties should be represented by their own attorneys.

* The agreement should be signed before the wedding.

* Each party must disclose all assets and their values.

* The policy should be consistent — i.e., each individual who marries into the family should be asked to signed a similar agreement.

* Have the family business attorney send a letter to the engaged couple suggesting the agreement.

HOW TO GET THE BEST SETTLEMENT

Under modern no-fault laws, divorce is simply the dissolution of an economic partnership. In most states, community property laws and 50-50 splits have been replaced by an indefinable standard called "equitable distribution." Here are some effects of this:

1. Since nobody knows what equitable or fair means, distribution proceedings can be drawn out and costly.

2. Women generally get less under "equitable distribution," and receive alimony only for a limited time.

3. A working wife may get no alimony, even though she may have earned much less than her husband.

Here are some tips on other issues that may come into play in a divorce:

Mediation — This is recommended over a legal battle if large sums of money aren't involved. However, you should check out the mediation firm carefully. Does it have a proven record of equitable rulings? How about business expertise and access to qualified counseling? Some poorly qualified people have hung out their shingle as mediators.

Custody — Joint custody is the trend, but judges usually only award it where spouses can agree amicably. Keep financial issues separate from custody issues — and work to spare the kids as much trauma as possible.

Negotiating Tips — Revenge will cost you emotionally and financially. Make a genuine attempt to resolve emotional conflicts.

Get Business Help — An accountant or real estate appraiser can help you accurately value a business.

Settlement Offer — A little generosity may keep the IRS or a spouse's lawyers from intruding in your financial affairs.

3 KEYS TO CHANGING YOUR SETTLEMENT

Situations change — and may affect your ability to pay alimony and/or child support. The courts will not demand you work overtime or stay on a job to maintain a pre-adjudicated level of support if you can:

1. Prove recessionary impact on your Income.

2. Show sincerity in a desire to change occupations to a lower-paying career, or a desire to receive more schooling or training.

3. Demonstrate undue hardship presented by financial demands of the settlement, or adverse impact on your work and living conditions.

If any of these situations apply, don't hesitate to go back to court and ask for relief.

D. Will, Estate & Inheritance Secrets

HOW TO WRITE A LEGAL WILL YOURSELF — AND SAVE

No one likes to think about it, but we're all going to die sometime. And, since you worked hard for your money, you've earned the right to dictate where it goes when you go. That means you have to have a will — but it doesn't mean you have to shell out big bucks for a fancy attorney. In fact, you can do it yourself quite easily — and save the attorney's fees. For a very nominal fee, most legal aid centers now offer a standard will-writing kit that can guide you through the do's and don't's like a pro, as well as telling you where and how to file. There are also are variety of commercial will-writing kits available at bookstores, and several computer programs are now being marketed to help you create a legal will. If you have doubts about the result, you can always have your attorney review the will you create — which will cost considerably less than having the attorney draft it from scratch.

OFTEN-OVERLOOKED NECESSITIES IN A WILL

In the aftermath of your death, you won't be available to make your last wishes perfectly clear to anyone. Here are some guidelines on how to keep your will simple and sane, as well as heading off the possibility your heirs may decide to contest it:

* Include a simultaneous-death clause. This dictates how property will pass to survivors in the event you and your spouse die together in a common disaster. It prevents beneficiary battles, as well as possible litigation.

* Consider adding a non-contest clause. If a disappointed beneficiary challenges your will, this clause says his or her share is automatically forfeited.

* Tailor bequests to the age, experience, financial sophistication and personal peccadilloes of the beneficiary. In other words, leave property to each in the form he can best handle. This may require setting up trusts or custodianships.

* Bequeath tax shelters or other complicated investments to those financially sophisticated enough to handle them.

* Don't leave property in joint ownership if one of the co-owners would likely run roughshod over the other.

* Undivided fractional interest in a property may seem like an equitable gift — but if your beneficiaries have vastly different views on management or market value, you're setting them up for war. Instead, transfer the property to a corporation and give your beneficiaries voting shares.

* Percentage. Percentage. Percentage. In inflationary times, an estate can turn out to be worth much, much more than anticipated. Bequeathing a dollar amount — no matter how generous — could turn out embarrassingly small in relation to the size of an inflated estate.

WHICH IS BETTER — A WILL OR LIVING TRUST

Contrary to popular belief, the use of a living trust seldom reduces significantly the costs for settling an estate. The services of both legal counsel and trustee in preparation of tax returns and the management and administration of assets are virtually the same, whether your estate is disposed by will or by creation of a living trust. There are, however, some distinct advantages provided by a living trust over a will given certain circumstances. Before we discuss them, however, just what is a living trust?

In simplest terms, it's a trust created during your lifetime. It can be drafted so you can amend it (change it), revoke it (call the whole deal off) or call it irrevocable (not subject to change whatsoever). To create such a trust, all you have to do is transfer property (such as life insurance, cash, securities, real estate, etc.), by an agreement, to a trustee to be held by the trustee for the use of the beneficiaries as prescribed by the agreement. This living trust may, in fact, be created by your will.

Consider creating a living trust if:

* You have a large life insurance portfolio. Many states exempt policy benefits from estate taxation. The proceeds can also be made available through the trust to your executor for the payment of debts, funeral expenses, taxes, etc. — or to avoid the forced sale of a property or business.

* You are entitled to retirement benefits (other than lump-sum benefits) from as a pension, profit-sharing plan, Keogh or IRA. If you die before retirement, the benefits payable to the trust are entirely exempt from the federal estate tax.

* You have a large estate. By placing substantially all of your property in the trust, you can be relieved of the worries of managing it. Remember, you can always name yourself as one of the trustees. Or, if the appointed trustees do not perform to your expectations, you can always revoke the trust.

* You live in a different state than your children. In many cases, they would not be eligible to qualify as executors and trustees under your will. Under a living trust, however, you can name as trustee either your children or a bank (for example) in the community where your children live.

* You want to avoid tho delays of probate and publicity about either the size of your estate or the beneficiaries you've named. Living trusts do avoid these problems.

Note on transfers of property to an established living trust: The deed of transfer need not be recorded to be valid, which can allow you greater flexibility during your lifetime to sell or refinance the asset. In such an event, the unrecorded deed could simply be torn up as though it never existed and the property sold, refinanced or otherwise disposed of. However, recording the deed ensures it will not be lost — and a simple reconveyance of the property from the trust to your personal ownership could be executed before selling or refinancing the asset.

Important: If a living trust is revocable, the property in the trust will continue to be a part of your estate for death tax purposes. You will probably also want to write a "pour-over" will, which automatically passes all residual assets of your estate over to the trustee of your living trust at the time of your death.

HOW TO REVOKE YOUR WILL

Revoking a will sounds easy, but there are pitfalls. Some wills are even revoked against their maker's wishes. For instance:

* A will may be automatically revoked whenever a testator (person making the will) gets married or divorced, has a child or there is a death of a principal beneficiary.

* After a death, there can be confusion about whether a will was revoked. It may have been destroyed in the presence of a witness who has also died. Or people may be looking for a document that no longer exists.

To avoid these pitfalls:

* Consult a lawyer when any family event could trigger automatic revocation.

* Write a separate document of revocation and keep it where the will would have been.

NAMING A GUARDIAN FOR SURVIVING CHILDREN

As part of your will-drafting and estate-planning process, you and your spouse should name a guardian to take care of your children in the event you are both killed in the same accident. If you don't, and the tragic event occurs, a probate judge must make this critical decision. Here are some tips on how to proceed:

1. If the decision isn't clear-cut, draw up a list of possible guardians. Rate them as to responsibility, age and lifestyle, personal and temperamental compatibility with your children and other factors you deem important.

2. Meet with the candidates. Sound out their willingness to assume guardianship of your children.

3. Narrow your list to those who meet all your criteria. You should name

alternates in case your first choices later become unable or unwilling to take on the responsibility.

4. Meet or talk with the potential guardians as time goes by to keep current on your respective situations.

5. Prepare written instructions for the guardians, and update them periodically. List matters such as your children's health needs, medical history and personality traits, along with any strong preferences you have on child rearing.

6. Include your wishes about how the guardians should spend estate funds to achieve short-range and long-range goals for your children, such as a college education.

7. In your estate planning, determine a minimum monthly allowance to be paid to the guardians for your children. Your trustee should be able to increase these amounts as needed.

ESTATE PLANNING HAS ITS LIMITS

Before drawing up a will or estate plan, you should be aware of what the law says about inherited property. Allowing for variations by state, here are some general guidelines:

* Most states have held that a spouse is entitled to a minimum portion of a partner's estate — say 35%. A survivor who gets less can sue. A few states also allocate a certain minimum percentage to minor children.

* The property of a person who dies intestate (without a will) is distributed to the next of kin according to rules that vary from state to state. Intestacy laws can also apply if a will is found legally flawed — lacking the minimum number of witnesses, for instance.

* It's important that you make provisions for contingent or successor beneficiaries. Otherwise, if a beneficiary dies before you do, the property goes to tho "remainderman" — the person named to get what's left after all specific bequests have been honored.

* To combat erosion by inflation, make all bequests in estate percentages rather than fixed-dollar amounts.

* Be aware of state laws restricting certain bequests — such as to tax-exempt organizations if made less than 30 days prior to death.

* There can be heavy tax penalties for restrictions on property left to a surviving spouse. Check with your tax advisor.

* Some corporations offer group insurance policies that limit the ability of the employee to designate who will benefit financially from his or her death.

* If the deceased owed back taxes, the IRS can attach the cash-surrender value of any of his or her life insurance policies.

BEAT THE ESTATE TAX LAWS

The simplest way to reduce estate taxes is to reduce your taxable estate. It's easier than you think, and you don't have to be a financial genius to do it:

* Take advantage of the annual $10,000 gift-tax exclusion ($20,000 when gifts are made jointly by a married couple). You can make any number of gifts of this amount to separate recipients each year.

* Living trusts, as described earlier, do a nifty job of cutting the taxman out of a share in your estate.

* If your estate is considerably larger than your spouse's, a marital deduction will (MDW) will do nicely, too. You can leave the greater of a) all; or, b) any part of your adjusted gross estate (total taxable estate, less debts, funeral expenses and administration costs) to your spouse, and that bequest will be free from U.S. estate taxes at your death. However, your spouse's beneficiaries will be taxed on his or her share of your estate when he or she dies unless you establish some form of trust. An MDW has more holes in it than a 5-pound slab of Swiss cheese, but the fundamental theory does, at least, exist on the tax books. You can write a MDW any one of three ways:

1. Bequeath the entire deductible portion outright to your spouse.

2. Create an estate trust, or power of appointment trust.

3. Leave your spouse a life estate with remainder to your children upon your spouse's death.

* Create a family trust — especially if a) your spouse has an estate of his/her own; b) you are unwilling to give your spouse the power to decide where your taxable estate goes; or, c) you don't want your spouse remarrying and giving away the family farm.

ESTATE-PLANNING MISTAKES INVOLVING GIFTS

As we've stated, gift giving can be one of your most effective estate-planning tools. There's plenty of good incentive: The federal estate tax rate starts at 37% for taxable estates over $600,000, and rises to an even steeper 55% once you get into the millions. You may not consider yourself rich, but the

IRS certainly places a high estate value on your home, IRAs and insurance policies. Giving while you're living reduces your taxable estate and benefits your heirs directly. Improperly dispersed, however, your gifts could wind up taxed to the hilt. Avoid these big mistakes:

* Not Giving Property Away Completely — That is, keeping "strings" attached to retain some benefit from its use or the income it produces. For example, continuing to live in a house you give your child — but not paying fair rent. Or, declaring the gift of a bond while continuing to hold it and collect the interest it pays. As the IRS sees it, if you still benefit from it, you still own it. To avoid such problems, don't retain possession even "for convenience." Set up a trust or a UGMA account, if necessary — and name a third party as trustee. Anything less may be challenged.

* Improperly Setting Up a Uniform Gift to Minors Act Account — If you have over-funded, you may encounter problems when the child takes over control at age 18 and may not be able to handle substantial sums. You may want to limit your contributions. Important: Name someone other than yourself as custodian. If you die before the child reaches 18, the funds revert to your estate.

* Retaining "Incidents of Ownership" in Life Insurance — Proceeds of a life insurance policy will be taxed to your estate if your policy allows you to change beneficiaries or borrow against it. You can remove the policy proceeds from your estate by giving away the incidents, even if you continue to pay the premiums.

* Exchanging Your Property for an Unsecured Annuity — If you've made such a deal in return for a lifetime annual payment, your children may become financially unable — or unwilling — to pay.

* Giving Away An Undivided Fractional Interest In Property — You may be able to give away an annual $10,000 (or $20,000) undivided interest in land or a building you own, but having several owners can create management problems since everyone has to agree on actions (such as a sale, refinancing, improvements, etc.) that affect ownership rights. It's better to set up a partnership or S corporation to own the property, and then donate voting shares annually.

* Giving Away Voting Shares in a Family Business — If you do, you lose. Consider recapitalizing instead. Or retain control by giving away non-voting shares. Or by giving voting shares away only to those children actively involved in the business; non-voting shares to those who aren't. By keeping preferred shares (set value) and giving away common shares, you may also be able to "freeze" your taxable estate by shifting appreciation to the next generation.

LIVING WILLS AND YOUR RIGHT TO DIE

More and more states have "living will" legislation. This honors an individual's written statement that he or she doesn't wish life artificially prolonged with no hope of recovery. Here are some keys to enforcing a living will:

* Make sure the doctor is aware of a living will and that it's on the patient's medical chart.

* If medical opinion is that the relative will never return to his or her former condition, ask why the hospital is maintaining the patient. The doctor must answer this question.

* Ask that a "do-not-resuscitate order" be put on the chart.

* If the doctor won't do what you want, find out why.

* Talk to the hospital's patient representative.

* Try to get a more cooperative doctor assigned.

* Try to get the person transferred to another hospital.

* Finally, notify the hospital attorney that your relative did not give consent for whatever procedures you're objecting to. If this is correct and the staff doesn't take the patient off the equipment, you can sue the hospital.

* Finally, you can take the person home to die. A hospital can't hold a patient against his or her will. However, you should never pull the plug yourself, no matter how desperate you feel. That's homicide. Even though so-called "mercy killers" are rarely found guilty in this country, such a trial is a terrible ordeal.

NOTES

CHAPTER 10

MONEY MANAGEMENT SECRETS

A. Getting More (Some?) Money to Manage

START WITH A FAMILY FINANCIAL REVIEW

Before you can figure out where you are going financially, it is essential that you know where you are. For that reason, the first step in good money management — whether the end goal is purchase of a home, college funding, retirement savings or just day-to-day survival — is a complete family financial review. This process involves 2 basic steps — construction of an income and expense statement and compilation of a net worth statement.

Preparing an Income & Expense Statement: This is a fairly simple process, but it is essential in determining just where you are financially, which you must do before you can begin planning how to change. The first step involves listing all or your monthly income from sources such as salary, commissions, tips, bonuses, gifts, savings interest, stock or mutual fund dividends, trusts, annuities, government payments (pension or disability), etc. While there are many sources of income, most people have only a few — and listing them and totaling them up is fairly easy. The expense side is a little more difficult since very few people keep track of their spending as closely as they should. Fortunately, it's not really necessary to account for every penny. Merely list your major monthly bills — such as mortgage payment or rent, utilities, car payments, other loans, typical credit card payments, grocery bills, etc. — and then allocate a monthly portion of annual or quarterly expenses for such things as taxes, insurance premiums, etc. Don't forget seasonal items such as vacations or school expenses, and make an estimated allocation for entertainment funds. Once you have both lists complete, total them up — and then compare them.

If you have more income than expenses, then that's your starting point for savings and investment. If you don't, then you are going to have to sit down and take a close look at ways you can either increase income or cut expenses in order to create some money to manage. In either case, the real purpose of this exercise is to give you a better awareness of your current money picture so you can begin the process of making adjustments — the first of which is to put regular savings and investment allocations at the top of your expense list, rather than making them on a piecemeal basis or waiting to fund them with whatever is left over.

Preparing a Net Worth Statement — This is important because it not only helps you figure out where you are in financial terms, but because it also helps identify the areas on which you need to focus in achieving the goals you will be setting for your financial future. Once again, you will be using a comparative process — first listing all your assets, and then totaling up your current liabilities. Assets will generally fall into one of 9 distinct categories:

* Cash or cash equivalents, including money in checking and savings accounts, money market accounts, money market mutual funds and certificates of deposit.

* Securities, including individual stocks, individual bonds, mutual funds, unit trusts, limited partnerships, etc.

* Retirement accounts, including 401(k) or 403(b) plans, IRAs, Keoghs, annuities, and cash values in company profit-sharing or pension plans.

* Life insurance cash values from variable, whole or universal life policies.

* Real estate, including your primary residence, vacation homes and any investment properties in which you may have an interest.

* Personal property, which includes cars and household items (put low values on both since that's what you'd get if you had to dispose of them), jewelry, furs, collectibles (such as stamps, coins, firearms, etc.) and other miscellaneous items with a reasonable resale value (such as TV and stereo equipment, cameras, sports equipment, tools, etc., but not clothes, books, dishes and other garage-sale-only disposable items).

* Equity or ownership share in any personal or family business.

* Items held in trusts to which you or other immediate family members are beneficiaries.

Your liabilities will also fall into distinct categories, but there are really only 4 important divisions. These are:

* Housing loans, including first and second mortgages on your primary residence, home-equity loans or balances on equity lines of credit, mortgages on vacation homes and loans you may have taken out on any investment properties in which you have an interest.

* Installment loans, including those for automobiles, recreational vehicles, boats, educational expenses or any other type of unsecured bank loan.

* Revolving debt, which includes the outstanding balances on all your credit cards.

* Other debt, which might include such things as loans against your insurance policies or pension and retirement accounts, margin loans for securities you've purchased and private loans from friends or family members.

Once you've totaled both assets and liabilities, subtract the latter from the former and you'll have a pretty good idea of your estimated net worth — which should serve as a guide in setting your savings and investment goals, as well as pointing up key areas on which you need to focus in achieving those goals. (Note: If you want more detailed help in preparing a net worth statement or calculating income and expenses, there are a numerous books that will walk you through the process. Check the financial section at your local book store or library, paying particular attention to books on personal financial planning. In addition, there are a variety of computer programs available to help you, such as the Money Magazine endorsed WealthBuilder program, available for around $100 from Reality Technologies, 1-800-346-2024, ext. 4801. A number of brokerage firms and mutual fund companies will also do a free financial analysis and investment review for you. One of the best services is offered by the Dreyfus mutual fund family. Call 1-800-782-6620, ext. 4600, to request the form needed for the review.)

If you'd like an idea how you stack up relative to the rest of the U.S. population, the following table gives the median net worth for Americans of different age and income levels, based on 1990 data collected by the U.S. Census Bureau:

Annual Household Income:	Age Group: 16 to 34	$ 35 to 44	45 to 54	55 to 64	65 and up
$20,000 to $30,800	$ 6,440	$ 20,008	$ 38,295	$84,627	$141,811
$30,801 to $46,600	$ 15,420	$ 39,983	$ 65,794	$96,066	$201,562
$46,601 to $75,000	$ 37,817	$ 88,293	$130,867	$198,987	$343,015
$75,000+	$ 82,500	$175,000	$250,000	$355,000	$600,000
All Household	$6,078	$33,183	$57,466	$80,032	$73,471

*—Based on estimates. **—Median income for all households is $23,796.

MAKE MONEY MANAGEMENT A WAY OF LIFE

Many people are put off by the idea of "money management," resenting the notion that they might have to account for every penny they spend. However, good money management is nothing more than basic day-to-day financial planning — and it requires little more than some basic common sense. Just follow the KISS formula — "Keep It Simple ... Sweetheart." Many people also feel they don't earn enough money to warrant managing it. However, you don't have to earn a doctor's or a lawyer's salary to achieve financial security. Anyone, regardless of job or income, can become financially independent as long as he or she follows these 8 simple principles of money management:

1. Spend less than you make. This sounds incredibly basic, but unfortunately most people can't manage to live within their means. Obviously, you cannot become financially independent if your spending regularly exceeds your income — unless you marry or inherit wealth (but that's not something most people can count on). Trap: Budgets are almost always sabotaged by human nature. You tell yourself you're budgeting for your needs, but what happens is that you wind up budgeting for your wants. Do you really need that winter vacation in the Caribbean, or a new car for your business? Or do you simply want those things so much that they have become needs? Very few people budget successfully, and most of them aren't much fun to be around.

2. Pay off your credit card balances. The interest on these balances, like the interest on personal, installment and car loans, is no longer tax deductible. And, at annual interest rates of 18% or more, eliminating these debts is one of the best financial moves you'll ever make.

3. Buying a house is still a good investment — even though it's unlikely the double-digit growth in real estate values we saw in the 1970s and early '80s will be repeated. Trap: Too many people in the past felt a home was the only investment they really needed. Not true. A home is just one element in fashioning a sound approach to investing — and has to be done in conjunction with other financial planning.

4. Aim to save at least 10% of your net income. That's the money left over after you've paid federal, state and local taxes. Saving 1/10th of that amount may seem like an impossibly ambitious undertaking, but if you use the next 2 suggestions, after a few months, you won't even miss the money you're stashing away to invest for financial independence.

5. Pay yourself first. This sounds simple — and it is. You can't spend what you don't see, so if you automatically divert some of your paycheck into savings each month, you quickly become accustomed to making ends meet with less income than before. The money you save goes into building a portfolio that can be used for a retirement nest egg, a down payment on a house, a college education fund for your children, etc.

6. Use payroll deductions or pre-authorized bank withdrawals for painless savings. The 401(k) plans many companies now offer are the ultimate in the payroll-deduction approach to savings. These plans allow you to reduce your income (and your income taxes) by automatically making monthly contributions to a tax-deferred savings plan with a variety of investment options, ranging from stocks to bonds to insurance contracts. Bonus: Many companies will match your contributions, up to a certain point.

7. Be an owner, not a loaner, over the long term. If you have a decade or more to go before retirement, contribute the bulk of your savings to stocks, not bonds or bank certificates of deposit. Reason: Over the long term, equities have had a much higher rate of return than fixed-income securities, and that pattern should continue in the future. Even though the U.S. has huge deficits, major environmental concerns and serious social ills, these problems will likely be addressed over the next 20 to 30 years, with the solutions representing some of the greatest investment opportunities ever. And, the only way to share in the successes of the companies involved is through ownership. Best Approach: Invest in a carefully selected mutual fund, where you buy into a diversified portfolio of stocks and gain access to a professional money manager who has those qualities you need to succeed in the market. Consistently selecting individual stock winners is much more difficult, requiring a rare combination of guts and brains — and most people can't manage it.

8. Don't try to time the market. Market timing requires using key indicators to predict major shifts in the stock and bond markets — and to shift your money from one investment to another. In theory this sounds great, but in practice it seldom works — except for brokers, who reap big commissions from

such trading. Most people do better with a long-term buy-and-hold approach.

5 MISTAKES THAT KEEP MOST PEOPLE POOR

There are 5 major things most people do that keep them from advancing financially. Most of these were covered in the 2 previous capsules, but we're going to repeat them here — just to emphasize their importance:

1. Living paycheck to paycheck — Obviously, if there's always month left at the end of the money, you'll never get ahead financially, meaning you're going to have to make some lifestyle changes. The easiest way to alter this situation is by delaying gratification. In other words, whenever you are considering whether to spend money on something that's not an absolute necessity, choose not to — at least for a while. By cutting out the luxuries and putting the money into savings or investments, you let your money do some of the work for you and start building up wealth.

2. Failing to plan ahead — Wealth building doesn't just happen. You can't do it by just promising to save what's left at the end of the month, because nothing will ever be left. You have to plan ahead, budgeting money for both savings and investment — and paying those items first, as if they were your most important bills (which, in terms of your long-term financial well-being, they are).

3. Failure to set reasonable goals — Many people get discouraged at the slow rate at which their money grows in the early years. It seems as if they will never reach their ultimate goal, so they slack off in their efforts. A better way is to set small goals along the way — and thereby reinforce your commitment to wealth building as each is achieved. Remember, as an esteemed financial planner once noted: "$1,000 left to earn interest at only 8% per annum will grow to $43 quadrillion in just 400 years — but the first 100 years are the hardest!"

4. Failure to adjust investments — Too many people take a "set it and forget it" attitude with their investment plan, but no plan is good forever. Review your plan and your individual investments regularly — at least once a year — to make sure both that the investments are still worthwhile and that they will still get you where you want to go. Such reviews are particularly important whenever you have a change in your family (such as a birth, death, marriage, divorce, etc.) or financial (promotion, bonus, job loss, career shift, etc.) situation.

5. Paying too much in taxes — Even though it's more difficult than it used to be to shelter income from taxation, there are still plenty of ways to earn investment profits free of taxes (at least for now). And, nothing increases the compounding power of your money more than having it work on a tax-deferred basis. For example, $10,000 in a taxable account at 9% annual interest will grow to $15,814.30 in 10 years and $25,009.40 in 20 years, assuming a 33% total federal and state tax rate. But, $10,000 invested in a tax-deferred account at 9%

annual interest will grow to $19,671.50 in 10 years and $38,696.80 in 20 years — a difference of $13,687.40.

SIMPLE WAYS TO SAVE MONEY FAST

Most people who are living paycheck to paycheck say it's impossible for them to save money because they don't even have enough to meet their monthly expenses. However, if you are really interested in beginning a savings and investment program, you CAN save the money you need to get started. The key is to religiously take the money you save — even if it's small — and set it aside for your savings and investment program. Here are just a few ideas — some of them remarkably simple — for squeezing come extra money out of your budget:

* Delay gratification — As mentioned earlier in this Section, this is the most effective way to start a savings program. Each time you consider a discretionary purchase, just say no — at least for a while. For example, if you want a new TV that would cost $400 and you would normally purchase it using a credit card, simply delay the purchase for 3 months and instead put the $40 per month you would have paid on the credit card account into your savings account. If you still want the TV after 3 months, go ahead and buy it — and at the same time put the $120 you saved into a mutual fund.

* Take advantage of discounts — When you use coupons at the grocery store or buy products in bulk, take the money you save and set it aside for investment. A good way to get in the habit of doing this is to keep a jar for coins (or an envelope for bills) in the kitchen and add the saved money to it as soon as you put away the groceries. When you get $100, put it into your mutual fund.

* Use 2-for-1 coupons for entertainment or dining out — Nearly every city has some kind of entertainment or dining guide (usually sold by civic or charitable groups for around $25 or $30) that contains 2-for-1 offers from local restaurants, movie theaters, stage events and athletic events. Make full use of these coupons — and immediately put the money you save away (you can use the same envelope you use for your coupon savings).

* Comparison shop by phone rather than by car — This will not only save you money on your purchases, but you should be able to put aside 50 cents or so for each call that you would have otherwise spent in gas. (Get in the habit of putting the money in your jar or envelope as soon as you get off the phone.)

* Be frugal around the house — There are dozens of things you can lift from household hints books that will save you small amounts. For example, you

can make liquid dishwashing soap by putting the slivers from your used soap bars into a jar of water and stirring occasionally. A bottle of dishwashing liquid costs about $2.50, which you can then put aside each month. You can also save the cost of plastic garbage bags by asking for the heavy brown paper bags when you buy groceries and using them for trash instead. Making your own greeting cards and wrapping paper (the comics pages are good) can also save $4 or $5 a month.

Whatever you do to save money, you must remember that you really aren't saving if you go ahead and spend the money on something else. The key is to immediately set aside any money you save in a jar, envelope or savings account — and then put it into an investment account as soon as you have enough to meet the deposit minimum.

CHEAP ADVICE ON CUTTING EXPENSES

If you want to save money but seem to be having difficulty figuring out how, you might be able to get some ideas from a new book called "1,001 Ways to Cut Your Expenses." Written by Jonathan D. Pond, a certified financial planner, the 288-page book is published by Dell and is available at most book stores for around $7.95. Using a light, easy-to-read style, Pond offers money-saving tips on subjects ranging from car buying and baby-sitting to utility bills and funeral planning. Though many of the ideas will be old hat to experienced savers, there are enough fresh ideas to make it a valuable resource if you really want to cut your expenses — especially at the low $7.95 price.

YOU'VE GOT MORE MONEY THAN YOU THINK

Another way to increase the amount of money you have available for investment is to make better use of the money and other assets you have. For example, if you have money sitting in a passbook savings account earning 3% interest, move it to a money market account and earn 4% or 4.5% instead. The extra interest won't amount to much on a monthly basis, but it will add up over the course of a year. Here are some other ideas:

* Review your investments to see if your goals have been met — Many people buy a stock and hold it until they've forgotten why they originally bought it. If you take a careful look at your holdings — be they stocks, bonds or mutual funds — and find that your goals have been met, or that, for one reason or another, you would no longer consider buying them, then you'd probably be better off to sell and put the money into something else that offers more potential.

* Take advantage of low-cost loan sources and use the money to earn higher returns — If you can borrow against an insurance policy at 3% to 6%

annual interest and invest the money to earn 10% to 12%, go ahead an do it. Even after taxes, you'll still be netting 3% to 4% that you wouldn't be earning otherwise.

* Manage your own escrow accounts — If you have a home and are paying on a mortgage, the lender may be collecting money from you each month to pay your annual insurance premiums and property taxes. This means the lender is collecting interest on your money for 11 months out of each year — interest that you should be getting yourself. If you owe less than 80% of the value of your house (most mortgage companies insist on withholding tax and insurance money on loans larger than 80%), contact the lender and tell them you want to start maintaining your own escrow accounts. That way, you can collect interest on the money you set aside each month. Warning: Be sure you DO set aside the money each month, rather than waiting until the bills are actually due and then trying to come up with the money.

* Sell unwanted or unused items — Many people buy expensive hobby or recreational items and then lose interest in the activity, leaving the equipment to sit idle. If you have cameras, ski equipment, an ATV, a boat, a snowmobile, exercise equipment, etc., that you don't use, sell it and put the money to work in a productive investment. The same goes for smaller items of used household goods; hold a garage sale and put the money you bring in directly into a savings or investment account.

* If you are self-employed, make maximum use of the tax advantages — Keep good records and deduct all allowable business, entertainment and travel expenses, including use of personal autos, computers and other items that do split duty. Also make full contributions to your tax-deferred retirement plan each year. This money comes right off the top of your earnings, before taxes, and then grows on a tax-deferred basis as well. You should also keep all business money possible in interest-bearing accounts, or even CDs if you have reserve funds you won't need for at least 3 months.

If you sit down and look at what you have — which we showed you how to do at the start of this Section — you should be able to spot other ways to make that money work harder for you. Don't delay; start the process today.

B. Making Your Money Work for You

REDUCING DEBT MAY BE YOUR BEST INVESTMENT

As we note in Chapter 8, Investment Secrets, and referred to earlier in this Chapter, it's highly likely that the best use you can make of your money in today's low-interest-rate climate is in paying off debts — especially credit-card accounts and high-interest personal or auto loans. If you use money you'd normally be putting in safe investments earning 4% to pay off credit-card accounts that charge 18%, it's like earning an extra 14% on your investment with no reduction in safety. In many cases, it even makes sense to pay extra on your mortgage, though that interest continues to be tax deductible. As we've noted a couple of times before (and will discuss further in the Chapter on Real Estate Realities), paying extra on your mortgage not only saves tens of thousands of dollars in interest charges, but it also shortens the payoff time on your debt, freeing up the monthly payment amount for use in investment or for retirement savings. As soon as you finish compiling your net worth statement, examine each of your liabilities and see if paying them off would provide a better return than you could get by investing the money elsewhere. It might just be the best investment you can make today.

25 EASY WAYS TO MAKE YOUR MONEY GROW

Just like the tree in your back yard, you want your money to grow ... and grow ... and grow. Here are some easy ways to get it to do just that:

1. Refinance your home mortgage. If you can find a mortgage rate that's at least 2 points below the one you have presently, and plan on owning your home for another 3 years, refinancing can save you money. Then take the difference between your old mortgage payment and your new one and invest it.

2. Use your company savings plan. Remember, you can contribute up to $8,745 in pre-tax dollars to your company's 401(k) plan. If you have a 403(b) plan, you can contribute up to $3,500 a year tax free. With a Keogh plan you can contribute up to 20% of your earnings. This adds up and will save you big money at tax time.

3. If you don't have a pension plan through your company, open an IRA. You can make tax-deductible contributions up to $2,000 a year for singles and $4,000 a year for couples filing their taxes jointly.

4. If you're married and file a joint tax return, take the withholding allowances for the spouse with the highest income.

5. Put your money in tax-free municipal bonds instead of conventional CDs or savings instruments.

6. Nothing beats a U.S. Treasury security for safety. You can buy them commission-free through the Federal Reserve and its branch banks.

7. If you pay any points on a mortgage, be sure you write a separate check to your lender. Otherwise, you can't deduct the points on your taxes.

8. Use money market mutual funds that can increase your yield by an extra 0.75% to 1.5% on your short-term savings.

9. If you buy stocks, whenever possible, buy them directly from the company in order to save the commission. If you're not comfortable with that, consider using a discount broker who offers substantially lower commissions than a full-service broker.

10. If you have no dependents, you don't need to buy life insurance. If you need life insurance only to cover the financial needs of your dependents, buy term insurance. It's significantly less expensive. Paying your premium once a year instead of monthly can save you even more.

11. You can save as much as half the cost of bank checks if you buy them from outside your bank. There are several nationwide vendors that offer this service.

12. If you put a car alarm in your auto, you can save over 5% on your auto insurance. You can save an additional 20% if you install a device that shuts down the engine should someone attempt to break into your vehicle.

13. Increasing your insurance deductibles can save you money. If you increase the collision deductible on your auto policy from $250 to $500, you can save up to $200 a year — and raising the deductible to $1,000 is even more lucrative.

14. Think about increasing the deductible on your tenant's or homeowner's insurance policy. Once again, you'll save up to 25% of your premium cost.

15. If you're shopping for insurance, you can save 5% to 15% if you buy your auto and homeowner's policies from the same company. If you install smoke detectors and fire extinguishers in your home, you can save an extra 2%.

16. Buy no-load life insurance and annuities.

17. Invest in no-load funds that don't charge you 12b-1 sales and distribution fees.

18. Find no-load funds that have relatively low expense ratios.

19. If your IRAs aren't earning what you'd like, look at stock mutual funds. Granted, they are riskier, but the returns are far better than bank instruments.

20. Pay cash whenever possible. This includes paying off your credit cards monthly. Shop around as well to find the bank that has the best combination of fees and rates on checking and interest-bearing accounts.

21. Use your bank's ATM instead of doing business at a regional or national ATM network. You'll save 50 cents to a dollar with every transaction.

22. Deposit checks when they come to maximize the interest, and wait until the last moment to pay your bills.

23. Use this principle of "floating" in your money market mutual funds, moving cash from one to another to collect interest from both at the same time during the period while the funds are in transition.

24. Learning how your interest earnings compound is another way to increase your investment returns. For example, a CD that compounds monthly rather than quarterly, semiannually or annually is a much better investment.

25. Manage your money fund, CD or money market accounts more efficiently. When interest rates are high, put your money in other short-term investments.

ALLOCATING YOUR ASSETS FOR LIFELONG SECURITY

The key to achieving financial security is setting and then obtaining the correct investment goals. Unfortunately, the world of money is full of alternatives, so it's not always easy to properly allocate assets to get the results you want. In addition, each person's situation is unique — depending on age, the amount of starting capital, income and other factors — making it impossible to provide exact formulas. However, we can offer some general guidelines for allocating your assets, depending on your age and the level of risk you tolerate. As a rule, the more money you have to start and the more time you have for your money to grow, the less risk you need to assume in order to achieve your goals. But, as the amount of time available shrinks, the level of necessary risk rises. Following are 3 suggested asset-allocation models, based on risk tolerance:

* Low risk — 30% cash or cash equivalents, 20% high-grade bonds, 20% Blue Chip stocks, 10% income stocks, 10% aggressive-growth stocks and 10% foreign stocks.

* Medium risk — 25% Blue Chip stocks, 20% cash or cash equivalents, 20% high-grade bonds, 15% foreign stocks, 10% aggressive-growth stocks and 10% income stocks.

* High risk — 25% Blue Chip stocks, 25% aggressive-growth stocks, 25% foreign stocks, 10% cash or cash equivalents, 10% high-grade bonds and 5% income stocks.

In all cases, mutual funds can be substituted for individual investment vehicles, and you should take advantage of tax-deferral options whenever possible (i.e., fully fund your 401(k), Keogh or IRA and make your investments through those accounts before you put money in outside accounts). In addition, these models assume you already own or are in the process of purchasing your own home. If you're not, then that should be a priority. As mentioned in Chapter 8, Inside Investments, we do not currently recommend allocating assets to commercial real estate, precious metals or inflation-sensitive commodities, including partnerships investing in oil drilling or reserves. However, if interest rates rise and inflation increases, those asset classes should come into play, beginning with the high-risk model and progressing into the medium- and low-risk models as inflation rises.

SHOULD YOUR CHILD'S MONEY BE IN A TRUST?

Many times, the return on investments in a child's name can be enhanced by putting them in a trust, which will provide tax and control advantages otherwise unavailable (this is especially true of the child has enough assets to bring the "kiddie tax" into play). The easiest way to accomplish this is through what is known as a Totten Trust, which can be established simply by filling out a card at the bank where the child's account is held or with the fund family that handles the child's money market or other investment accounts. Because the parent has control of the funds, a Totten Trust lacks many features of a true trust account, which would be controlled by an independent third-party trustee. For example, because the parent can control the account funds, any income taken out of the trust is usually taxable to the parent. In addition, in many states, the account is subject to creditor claims against the parents. On the plus side, a Totten Trust allows the parent to use the funds while the child is a minor, but still guarantees that the parent will be accountable for the funds when the child gains control of the account at a specified age, thus protecting the child's interest. (This can be particularly important in case of a divorce or family dispute over assets.) In addition, if the parent dies, the child receives any Totten Trust funds outside the will or probated estate. If you think you or your child might benefit from this simplified trust format, discuss it with the trust officer at your local bank or call the account services desk at your mutual fund family.

PROTECTING YOUR WEALTH AGAINST FINANCIAL RISK

With all the S&Ls collapses, bank defaults and insurance company failures, it's imperative to protect your money. First and foremost, never allow your account balance to exceed the FDIC's insurance limit. And, since more banks are in jeopardy all the time, make sure your money is registered with appropriate regulators. Diversify your savings and distribute your money among several banks or institutions. Here are some general guidelines for protecting your assets:

* Never put more than $100,000 in any single institution.

* Use money market funds for your hard-earned cash. Stick with taxable funds that invest in highly secure Treasury Bills.

* Know your investments — especially stocks. Don't buy stocks at a peak, but instead buy small amounts of stock on a regular basis by dollar-cost averaging.

* Know your broker. Many investors have lost all or part of their savings to fraudulent or incompetent brokers. Investigate their background and make sure your planner or advisor is registered with the SEC and/or your state's securities commission. In the case of a financial planner, ask to see Parts I and II of their ADV document, which outlines their credentials and details any disciplinary actions they've been subject to. Brokers should be members of the National Association of Securities Dealers (NASD) and the Security Investors Protective Corp. (SIPC). Look into their past for any disciplinary actions.

* Even your retirement accounts may be in jeopardy. Make sure they are held by trustees or financial services companies that are highly ranked by major ratings firms. And, once again, diversify.

* Review your retirement plan's documents, especially the annual report for anything suspicious.

* Your health is one important way to protect your wealth. Be sure to provide a long-term disability plan that will replace your income should you be unable to work for some time. If your company provides disability coverage, consider yourself lucky. If it doesn't, buy an individual policy that features guaranteed level premiums, the option of buying more disability without an medical exam and the assurance that the policy cannot be canceled as long as you pay the premiums. Insist on residual benefit coverage. This means you'll continue getting partial payments should you return to work part-time.

* It also goes without saying that you should have medical coverage. Lacking adequate coverage could wipe out your savings in no time. Buy a policy that features a lifetime benefit ceiling of at least $500,000 or more, and a catastrophic or out-of-pocket limit that caps your share of medical bills at $2,500 a year. Raise your deductible to keep policy costs down or join a health maintenance organization.

* If people depend on you, buy life insurance — but stick to term insurance, which provides only a death benefit.

* Be sure you have adequate insurance on your home. Base the amount of coverage on the full replacement value of your home. Even though you'll pay a little more for this coverage, it's worth it should you lose your home to any disaster. Be sure, too, to include full replacement cost on the valuables within your home. Raise your deductible, if you need to keep costs down.

* If you live in an area with high earthquake, flood or mud slide danger, consider expanding your coverage in these areas.

* To further protect yourself, increase the personal-liability segment of your homeowner's and auto policies to insure against lawsuits.

PLANNING AHEAD FOR ROUGH TIMES

Most analysts are now calling for a slow but steady recovery in the economy. However, times are still rough — and many people will still fall victim to cutbacks, layoffs and other situations that could dramatically impact their financial well-being. So, how do you protect yourself against such a possibility? Here are a few guidelines:

* Pay off debts as quickly as possible, starting with those that charge the highest interest rates, not those that have the least time remaining.

* As you pay off debts, resist the temptation to spend. Instead, use the excess money to build up cash reserves. In normal times, it's a good idea to have the equivalent of 6 months' worth of net income in reserve. However, in these tough times, many professionals are finding it can take as much as 12 to 15 months to find a new job comparable to your current one. As a result, we advise trying to build a liquid reserve equal to at least a year's total expenses — and a reserve fund equal to a year's income would be even better.

* Pay close attention to what is going on in your company. If you see signs of trouble, don't just blithely assume things will get better. Instead, start looking around to see what's available elsewhere. It's a lot easier to get a new job while you're still employed than after you've already been laid off. Safety and Savings Tip: If it appears your company is in really bad shape and might wind up going under, making it unable to fulfill obligations, you should immediately stop making contributions to company profit-sharing, pension and 401(k) plans. (If the plan would prohibit you from joining again later, just cut to the minimum contribution so you'll maintain your eligibility should the firm recover.) Do not, however, start spending this money; set up accounts of your own and make the same contribution (or a higher one since you'll be losing some tax-deferral benefits) to them.

* If you need to borrow money now — or think you might in the near future — go ahead and apply for a home-equity credit line. Interest rates on these credit lines are low, they are generally tax deductible and they cost you nothing (except for a small annual fee in some cases) if you don't use them. Because business is slow, many banks are offering special deals (e.g., no points, no application fees, no appraisal fees, etc.) on these credit lines. In addition, if you think your job might be in jeopardy, you'll have a lot less trouble getting approved while you are still employed than after you get laid off.

* Delay as many purchases as possible, particularly on large items such as cars or major appliances. Make repairs instead, and put the difference in your reserve account.

* Shift to a more conservative investment strategy aimed at capital preservation with steady income. The last thing you need if you lose you job is a large investment loss. Don't, however, make the mistake of chasing high yields

so that you let yourself get locked into deposit accounts with long maturities. You're better off to take a percentage point or 2 less and keep your funds liquid.

* If you already have CDs or own individual Treasury securities that you will need to roll over soon, make sure you adopt a "laddering" strategy (see Chapter 2, Banking Secrets). This will allow you to get higher yields by taking slightly longer maturities while still ensuring that you'll have adequate liquidity (funds available at least every 6 months).

* Protect yourself against a reversal in the U.S. economy but putting a portion (10% to 25%) of your portfolio in foreign investments or mutual funds investing in international stocks, bonds or foreign-government securities.

C. Miscellaneous Money Matters

WHO SHOULD OWN YOUR INVESTMENT ACCOUNTS

Though most people give it very little consideration, the way in which your bank and investment accounts are held — i.e., the account ownership — can be extremely important, affecting estate taxes as well as allocation of assets in a divorce or in a dispute with adult children. Couples generally have 3 choices when setting up account ownership:

* Independent ownership — The account is held in the name of one spouse only and the other has no ownership rights whatsoever (a legal document may need to be filed specifying this in community-property states). Funds or assets held in such accounts usually include monies owned prior to a marriage, interests in a family business or partnership, inheritances received by one spouse only and insurance policies (by having your spouse the sole owner of your insurance policy, it is excluded from your taxable estate).

* Joint tenancy — This is most common type of account ownership for couples. It specifies that both spouses are full co-owners of the property in the account and have complete right of survivorship, meaning the money automatically passes to the surviving spouse in the event of the death of the other. Some assets belonging to business partnerships also are held in joint tenancy accounts.

* Tenancies in common — This specifies that each of the listed owners of an account owns an equal portion of the assets in the account. If one person dies, his or her share goes into his estate and the other person or persons retain ownership of their shares.

There are a number of variations and exclusions to these designations. For example, in community-property states — Arizona, California, Idaho, Louisiana, Nevada, New Mexico, Texas, Washington and Wisconsin — all assets acquired during a marriage are assumed to be owned equally by both spouses and attempts to designate ownership otherwise may require legal maneuvering. There is also an ownership designation known as tenancy by the entirety, which is the same as joint tenancy except that one partner cannot dispose of his or her share in an asset without the permission of the others (this type of ownership is only available in about 30 U.S. states).

There are also some general guidelines on ownership of other types of property that you should consider in order to protect yourself against lawsuits and estate complications. For example:

* Your primary residence should be held in the name of only one spouse, generally the one with either the lowest income or the least exposure to lawsuits. This is particularly crucial in the case of professionals such as doctors and lawyers, who may be targets in malpractice suits.

* Out-of-state properties or vacation homes should be held jointly with right of survivorship. Otherwise, if the spouse in whose name the title is held dies, the property might have to go through probate in the state where it is located, unnecessarily complicating the estate and delaying inheritances. If both spouses own the property jointly, no probate is required until the surviving spouse dies.

* Automobiles should be held solely in the name of the person who drives the car most often. That way, if that person is involved in an accident, the assets of the entire family won't be subject to lawsuits for damages. This can be costly when it comes to insuring vehicles for teen-age drivers, but it may be necessary if you have substantial assets that could be targeted by greedy contingency attorneys.

* Valuables such as jewelry and collectibles should be individually owned and specific instructions for inheritances should be included with the owner's will. That will prevent family disputes over who gets what and will also keep you from having to sell heirlooms or other personal items in order to split the proceeds among feuding heirs.

RETRENCHING IF YOU LOSE YOUR JOB

You've just gotten a notice that your job will be eliminated in the next round of cutbacks at your company. So, what do you do? Here are some tips on how to deal with such issues as pension plans, retirement accounts and separation benefits:

* Many people assume they must cash out their retirement plans —

IRAs, 401(k)s, 403(b)s, etc. — in a single lump sum in order to give themselves protection and ensure that they have enough money to tide them over during their period of unemployment. This is actually the worst move you can make. Here's why. Unless you are over age 59-1/2, the money will be subject to both ordinary income tax and a 10% early withdrawal penalty. This could wipe out as much as 52% of the distribution amount, depending on the state in which you live. This will not only hurt your ability survive in the short term, it will devastate your retirement plans. The best alternative is to take money from all other sources — money markets, investment accounts, even CDs with early withdrawal penalties — first, preserving the tax-favored treatment of the pension plan. In many cases, you will be able to leave your funds in your old employer's plan. However, if you cannot, roll it over into an IRA, being careful to avoid penalties on that transaction as well (IRA rollovers will be discussed in detail in Chapter 12, Roads to Retirement). If you must take money out of a pension plan, take only what you think you will need and roll the rest into an IRA (assuming your employer's plan allows partial withdrawals). The portion taken out will still be subject to taxes and penalties, but the tax rates could be lower since you'll be dealing with a much smaller base amount.

* Another option is to start receiving annual payments from the plan. These payments will be subject to taxes, but there will be no penalty, regardless of age. The annual payments will be based on your life expectancy and can continue penalty free for 5 years or until you reach age 59-1/2, whichever is longer.

* If you have stock options or preferred stock in the company as a result of your employment, review the terms of the stock agreements carefully. Some require you to exercise conversions within 6 months of leaving the company and failure to do so could cost you big bucks, depending on how the stock is priced and how it reacts to the cutbacks. If exercise would prove profitable, it's probably worthwhile to do it even if you have to take out a loan.

* Don't forget your accumulated vacation pay. Most people expect to get severance when they are laid off, but they forget that they may have earned current-year or following-year vacation credits for time already worked. You are entitled to payment for such credits, so make sure you get it. The same is true for unused sick leave if your company has a plan that pays employees for the time they don't use.

* Ask for extra benefits. Companies are required to offer you a continuation of medical and dental insurance benefits, but you are usually required to pay the premiums. Ask the company to pick up the tab for 3 months or so. Many companies will also provide outplacement services to help top-level people find new positions, and some will even give you the use of an office and a secretary to help you in your job search. However, you'll have to ask because the company probably won't offer otherwise. Ask for anything else you can think of as well, such as continued use of a company car or a home-based computer

for a limited period. It doesn't even hurt to make what might otherwise seem like totally unreasonable requests. The company just might say yes and you've got nothing to lose by trying. After all, what can they do — fire you?

DO YOU REALLY NEED A LOAN?

The first inclination many people have when faced with unemployment — or with any crisis from car problems on up — is to seek out a loan. However, in most cases, you are better off not getting a loan — instead making temporary adjustments in living habits or reducing your lifestyle a bit. If you are unemployed, the last thing you need is another monthly bill to pay. And, even if you're employed, you're probably already having trouble with your bills — otherwise, whatever you think you need the loan for wouldn't seem like a crisis. In any event, before you go rushing off to get a loan, sit down and do an income and expense statement (as was described at the start of this Chapter). Then you'll be able to see exactly what impact the projected new loan payment will have on your budget. Ironclad Rule: Never take out a new loan if the payment would throw your income and expense statement into the red (i.e., more expenses than income). Even if you plan to use the loan for bill consolidation, you are far better off to temporarily adjust your habits in order to quickly pay off existing loans, thus freeing up needed money, than you would be with a consolidation loan, which just stretches your debt out over a longer period and increases your total interest cost.

OFTEN-OVERLOOKED LENDING SOURCES

If you do decide you need to borrow money, you may do better if you avoid the usual sources and look for some help from more unconventional and often-overlooked sources. Here are a few:

* Always check first for cash-value life insurance policies. These policies all have provisions for low-interest loans (some of which don't even have to be paid back). You may also do better to simply cash in the policy completely, taking out the full cash value and substituting a term policy.

* Check with your employer. Many companies have special, but mostly unpublicized loan programs for key employees. If your company has one, you might find you qualify — but only if you ask.

* Borrow from a qualified company retirement plan. Nearly all retirement plans have loan provisions, though some have fairly strict conditions. Check to see if yours does.

* If you have stocks or bonds for which you've paid full price, you can deposit these securities with your broker and take out margin loans against

them. In most cases, you can borrow up to 50% of the value of stocks and 80% of the value of bonds and 90% of the value of Treasury securities such as T-bills or T-notes. Interest rates are usually variable, pegged to the prime rate or other interest-rate index, but they're nearly always better than you could get at a bank or even a credit union.

* If you have long-term CDs at a bank or S&L, you can almost always get a loan against them. Since the bank has your money to secure the loan, approval is usually not a problem, and the rates are reasonable — usually only 2 percentage points or so above the rate being paid on the CD.

Any of these sources will beat a bank or finance company hands down — but, as we said before, the best approach is to avoid needing the loan in the first place if you can possibly manage it.

FREE HELP IN GETTING OUT OF DEBT

If you are already heavily in debt and need help, Budget Acceptance Co. of Bozeman, MT., may be willing to bail you out. The company makes new loans and also provides advice on how to structure bill-consolidation loans and payment-reduction plans. Bad credit ratings are secondary to your current ability to pay. For more information or an application, write Budget Acceptance Co., P.O. Box 970, Bozeman, MT 59771, or call 1-800-735-0443.

NOTES

CHAPTER 11

REAL ESTATE REALITIES

A. Your House Is More Than a Home

BUY OR RENT — WHAT'S BEST FOR YOU?

From a purely financial standpoint, it's hard to find a better use for your money than the purchase of a home. In spite of the current slow market, the investment value is still substantial, the tax benefits are exceptional and there's a sense of achievement and personal pride associated with home ownership that's hard to beat. However, there are a few good reasons why continuing to rent a residence may be the best option for you. Financially, there are 3 primary reasons for continuing to rent:

* You don't have enough money for a down payment on a home of your own (though, as you will learn later in this Section, it's possible to overcome this problem with creative financing).

* You don't have enough income to qualify for a mortgage loan. This is a bigger hurdle to overcome, but it is possible if you are willing to scale down your needs (perhaps considering a condo) in order to get started in the housing market. Besides, when you factor in the tax benefits, owning a home is often less expensive than renting if you can come up with the upfront cash (which will also be discussed later in this Section).

* Your employment situation is unstable. If there's a possibility you may lose your job in the near future, then the timing is obviously not right for taking on a new debt burden.

There are also several reasons outside the financial realm why you might want to remain a renter. Home ownership does carry with it certain responsibilities in terms of maintenance, upkeep and repair, and some people just don't have the disposition for these chores. They lack the time, the energy or the inclination and prefer staying in a situation where other people are responsible for the problems that routinely go along with property.

If you fall into this latter category, renting probably remains the best course for you. However, if you'd really like to be a homeowner and are being held back only by one of the financial conditions listed, there's almost certainly a way to eventually achieve your goal. For starters, keep reading this Chapter — and you just might find one.

8 WAYS YOU CAN AFFORD TO BUY YOUR FIRST HOUSE

In today's economy, the American dream of home ownership has become just that — a dream — for many people. Coming up with a down payment, typically 10% to 20% of the purchase price, plus closing costs on an average house selling upwards of $100,000 can frustrate even those who have been saving for years. The prices of homes have escalated faster than people could save. However, there are ways to beat this spiral of unaffordability. Here are just a few ideas on how you can make that long-awaited dream of home ownership a reality:

1. Lower your debt load so you can qualify for a mortgage. If you have credit-card debts, either reallocate funds on a short-term basis to get those with the highest interest charges paid off or consolidate with a low interest rate loan from a credit union or other source. Though consolidation costs you extra money over the long term, it may be a worthwhile strategy if it allows you to get into that first home.

2. Set a realistic goal with respect to how much you can afford. The guidelines used by lenders are:

* The price of the home should not exceed 2-1/2 times your annual gross income.

* Your total annual payments, including insurance and taxes, should be no more than 28% of your gross income.

* Add your projected house payment to payments on your other long-term debts and fixed expenses. Most lenders require that those payments should not

exceed 33% of gross income.

3. Consider buying a townhouse or condominium, which can reduce the cost of home ownership $10,000 to $40,000 in comparison to a single-family home in the same location. (Keep in mind, however, that you will be required to pay a monthly home association fee for maintenance — an additional expense that may actually compare favorably with the costs of maintaining a yard, trees and regular repair jobs.) Townhouses differ from condos in that they are rows of houses attached to each other, whereas condos are simply apartments that are owned by the occupants. Townhouses are often a better value than condos.

4. Ask your boss if there is a company assistance program to help employees acquire a home. For example, some firms have employee benefit programs that will help pay mortgage insurance premiums or closing costs. Employers may also help get local lenders to reduce their rates or allow you to borrow from your 401(k) plan for the down payment. Try to avoid withdrawing money from your company savings account as the penalties may be costly.

5. Check with public housing agencies. Sometimes state housing agencies may help those with average incomes acquire a house by subsidizing or lending money toward a down payment. Ask your real estate agent or your state housing agency for information. (A full listing of state housing agencies follows this Section.)

6. Find out the current lender on the property and talk to them. They already possess much of the information on the house, such as the title search and appraisal. By dealing with the companies that have previously done the work, you may be able to save on fees.

7. Negotiate closing points or loan-administration fees with the lender. Those fees are usually based on a percentage of the purchase price, but banks may reduce the points if you accept a higher mortgage rate over the life of the loan. This can save you money in closing costs, though you will wind up making a higher monthly mortgage payment.

8. Go to an auction. Foreclosed houses and properties are auctioned regularly by developers, banks, the Veteran's Administration, the FHA or law-enforcement agencies. Watch for ads in your local newspaper or check with the Board of Realtors, local banks, the Sheriff's Department or the Drug Enforcement Agency and get on their mailing lists. You may get a bona fide bargain.

LET THE STATE HELP YOU BUY

Every state in the Union has a housing agency, and most of them have special programs to help first-time homebuyers. Qualification standards and terms change frequently, so check with your state's housing agency. Here's a state by state list, with phone numbers:

Alabama Housing Finance Authority (Montgomery), 205-261-4310.

Alaska Housing Finance Corp. (Anchorage), 907-561-1900.

Arizona Department of Commerce (Phoenix), 602-542-5371.

Arkansas Development Finance Authority (Little Rock), 501-682-5900.

California Housing Finance Agency (Sacramento), 916-322-3991.

Colorado Housing and Finance Authority (Denver), 303-861-8962.

Connecticut Housing Finance Authority (Rocky Hill), 203-721-9501.

Delaware State Housing Authority (Dover), 302-736-4263.

District of Columbia Housing Finance Agency (Washington), 202-628-0311.

Florida Housing Finance Agency (Tallahassee), 904-488-4197.

Georgia Residential Finance Authority (Atlanta), 404-320-4840.

Hawaii Housing Finance and Development Corp. (Honolulu), 808-848-3230.

Idaho Housing Agency (Boise), 208-336-0161.

Illinois Housing Development Authority (Chicago), 312-836-5200.

Indiana Housing Finance Authority (Indianapolis), 317-232-7777.

Iowa Finance Authority (Des Moines), 515-281-4058.

Kansas Department of Commerce (Topeka), 913-296-3480.

Kentucky Housing Corp. (Frankfort), 502-564-7630.

Louisiana Housing Finance Agency (Baton Rouge), 504-925-3675.

Maine State Housing Authority (Augusta), 207-623-2981.

Maryland Community Development Administration (Annapolis), 301-974-3161.

Massachusetts Housing Finance Agency (Boston), 617-451-3480.

Michigan State Housing Development Authority (Lansing), 517-373-8370.

Minnesota Housing Finance Agency (St. Paul), 612-296-7608.

Mississippi Housing Finance Corp. (Jackson), 601-961-4514.

Missouri Housing Development Commission (Kansas City), 816-756-3790.

Montana Board of Housing (Helena), 406-444-3040.

Nebraska Investment Finance Authority (Lincoln), 402-477-4406.

Nevada Housing Division (Carson City), 702-885-4258.

New Hampshire Housing Finance Authority (Manchester), 603-472-8623.

New Jersey Housing & Mortgage Finance Authority (Trenton), 609-890-8900.

New Mexico Mortgage Finance Authority (Albuquerque), 505-843-6880.

New York State Housing Finance Agency (New York City), 212-686-9700; or State of New York Mortgage Agency (New York City), 212-340-4200.

North Carolina Housing Finance Agency (Raleigh), 919-781-6115.

North Dakota Housing Finance Agency (Bismarck), 701-224-3434.

Ohio Housing Finance Agency (Columbus), 614-466-7970.

Oklahoma Housing Finance Agency (Oklahoma City), 405-848-1144.

Oregon Housing Agency (Salem), 503-378-4343.

Rhode Island Housing & Mortgage Finance Corp. (Providence), 401-751-5566.

South Carolina State Housing Finance & Development Authority (Columbia), 803-734-8831.

South Dakota Housing Development Authority (Pierre), 605-773-3181.

Tennessee Housing Development Agency (Nashville), 615-741-2400.

Texas Housing Agency (Austin), 512-474-2974.

Utah Housing Finance Agency (Salt Lake City), 801-521-6950.

Vermont Housing Finance Agency (Burlington), 802-864-5743.

Virginia Housing Development Authority (Richmond), 804-782-1986.

Washington State Housing Finance Commission (Seattle), 206-464-7139.

West Virginia Housing Development Fund (Charleston), 304-345-6475.

Wisconsin Housing & Development Authority (Madison), 608-266-7884.

Wyoming Community Development Authority (Casper), 307-265-0603.

FREDDIE MAC CAN HELP, TOO

The Federal Home Loan Mortgage Corp. — more commonly known as Freddie Mac — also provides loan guarantees and down-payment subsidies to low-income Americans buying their first homes. The agency will also buy mortgages from banks if the borrower has shown a 2-year record of regular rent, utility and phone payments that is equal to or greater than the monthly mortgage payment amount. The agency has also authorized banks to consider any public assistance — including state disability payments or food stamps — in computing income for mortgage qualification. For more information about qualifying for a mortgage under Freddie Mac guidelines, check your local phone directory for the FHLMC office in your area.

DON'T FORGET THE GOOD OL' RTC

Thanks to the collapse of many savings and loan associations and banks in recent years, the government has wound up with lots of real estate it really doesn't want. In fact, so much real estate in default came along with the seizure of failed financial institutions that the government set up a separate agency to manage and eventually sell off the properties. Called the Resolution Trust Corp., or RTC, this agency regularly holds sales of everything from high-rise office buildings and shopping malls to single-family homes and condos. Many of these properties wind up being sold for near market prices, but many others turn out to be bargains, sometimes selling for as little as $20,000. If you want to make sure you're not missing out, you can call the RTC at 1-800-431-0600 to get a free listing of up to 150 properties for sale in a specific state. (The lists are updated every 3 months, and you can specify the types of property you're looking for.) The RTC can also mail you listings of properties nationwide for a fee. Categories include commercial listings ($25); single-family homes in Texas ($15); single-family homes nationwide (3 volumes at $15 each); land ($15); property with more than 5 units ($15); and condos, townhouses and 2- to 4-unit buildings ($15). This lists are updated twice a year and include a name and number to call for instructions on how to bid, how much deposit is required and other details. (Usually, you will have to send a certified check for the deposit along with your bid.) Note: Don't be dismayed if you see a notation requiring "all-cash sales only." This simply means the RTC must get cash at the time of settlement — which will be furnished by whoever you get to provide your mortgage.

NOTHING VENTURED, SOMETHING GAINED

It's not a myth — you really can buy property with no money down. In fact, it's not even hard to do — provided you know how. Here are some of the strategies:

1. Pay the real estate agent. If a seller uses an agent on the sale, he's obligated to pay the agent's commission. Strategy: Suggest the agent lend you part of the commission in exchange for a personal note guaranteeing to pay the money, with interest, at some future date. The agent may agree if you explain the sale depends on such an arrangement. If the agent balks, negotiate a small monthly payment, perhaps with a final balloon payment. Then subtract the agent's entire commission from the expected down payment.

2. Assume seller's debts. This works if, as is often the case, the seller is in a financial bind. Strategy: Make arrangements, with the seller's agreement, to make good on his outstanding debts. Relieved creditors may be willing to extend due dates or agree to a discount. Deduct the face amount (not the discounted amount) of the debts you assume from your down payment.

3. Prepaid rent. Perhaps you're in no hurry to move in and the seller is in no hurry to move out, but you'd both like to close the deal as soon as possible. Strategy: Agree with the seller on a delayed, but fixed date for vacating. Then, instead of charging the seller a monthly rent, subtract that cumulative rental amount from your down payment.

4. Satisfy the seller's needs. Suppose the seller needs appliances and furniture for his new residence. Strategy: Offer to buy them — delaying payment by using credit cards or store credit — then deduct the total expense from the down payment.

5. Purchase-money second. If the seller does not need the entire proceeds of the sale in order to finance his next home purchase, he may be willing to give you what is known as a "purchase-money second." In essence, what this does is have the seller loan you the money for the down payment, securing that loan with a continued interest in the property (a second mortgage). Be aware, however, that such arrangements may be frowned on by the primary lender (or first-mortgage holder) because it means more than 90% of the home's value is pledged to secure loans. The monthly payments on the second mortgage could also affect your ability to qualify for the first mortgage, as well as your ability to make the higher monthly payments. (Note: That's why many purchase-money seconds carry no monthly payments, but rather call for a balloon payment, including interest, in 3 or 4 years.)

CONDO-BUYING GUIDELINES & TRAPS

If you can't quite manage a single-family home yet — or want a second property for investment purposes — you may want to consider the purchase of a condominium or townhouse. However, buying a condo is not quite the same as buying a house. Here are some guidelines to help you ensure that you get a good condo deal:

* Evaluate the price carefully. Because condo prices are substantially lower than home prices in the same area, some people think they're automatically a bargain and rush to buy, only to find they paid more than the property was really worth. Avoid impulse buying.

* Study the "covenant of condominium" (often called the master deed or declaration of condominium). All clauses in this covenant are non-negotiable, and no participant can have a differently worded covenant. If you spot any of the following, you should think seriously about walking away from the deal:

1. Restrictions on Resale — If the condo association has a 30-, 60- or 90-day right of first refusal, you could lose a sale. Such resale restrictions rule out FHA, VA and other government-insured mortgages, thus cutting your resale market significantly.

2. Restrictions on Use — Can owners rent their units? This is obviously critical if you're buying the condo as an investment. Other restrictions can apply to children, pets, even mailboxes.

3. Sweetheart Deals — Does the developer own the common areas and lease them back to the association? Escalator clauses in such leases could increase your monthly association fees dramatically. It's better if the condo association owns all common areas. Management agreements with the condo association should also contain cost controls and spell out termination provisions.

Other Hidden Traps:

1. Subsidized Fees — To increase sales, developers sometimes keep management fees below cost. Then, after the condo association takes over, the owners' monthly costs soar. Check out similar condo associations in your area.

2. Construction Problems. Get an engineer to go over the property — and not just your unit. Here's why: If the condo association has to make expensive repairs, you'll have to pay your share. If your unit is in a converted building, ask the salesperson to show you the engineer's report.

A Final Tip: Prices are lowest during the pre-construction sale of new units, or early in a building's condo conversion. But be wary of buying too soon. If the other units don't sell, your investment suffers. Check sales of other condos units in the area.

BEWARE OF BUILDER COST-CUTTING

With the real estate market in the doldrums, many home-construction companies are looking for ways to maintain cash flows and profit margins in the face of falling sales — and that could mean trouble for you as a potential homebuyer. The most obvious builder cost-cutting method is downsizing — lower square footage, 3 bedrooms instead of 4 and unfinished basements instead of rec rooms. Smaller building lots are also becoming more common. These cutbacks are easily spotted, and are usually reflected in the price. However, other items are more subtle — and could cost you money if you're not aware of them. For example, many builders are putting in less-expensive appliances and fewer quality touches — e.g., manufactured fireplaces instead of custom masonry ones. Other substitutions include metal doors instead of wooden ones, foundations finished in stucco instead of brick veneer and lower-grade or lighter-weight shingles.

Possible Benefit: If the cost-cutting measures are reflected in the price

rather than hidden, it could put an otherwise unaffordable home in your buying range or allow you to look in neighborhoods you might have been priced out of a few years ago. However, check closely to make sure you're not paying for more than you're actually getting.

CHECKLIST FOR REDUCING CONSTRUCTION COSTS

Rather than buying a new home, some people are opting for building their own so they can control features and quality — or they are putting up additions to their existing dwellings. In either case, it's important to keep a close eye on the contractors to ensure that the work meets specifications and the costs are in line with the preliminary estimates. Here are some key areas to watch when monitoring construction work:

1. To control expenditures — and track expenses to offset future capital gains — set up a separate project bank account.

2. Check all preliminary plans against all deed requirements, and show them to any authorities that must issue any permits.

3. Make sure adequate utilities are available on site.

4. Budget for permits, professional fees, surveys, finance costs, bonds and insurance.

5. Get three bids (or more) for every part of the job — carpentry, plumbing, etc.

6. Never pay a contractor in advance.

7. Be sure no outdated drawings or specifications are left on the job site.

8. Get a knowledgeable person (not the contractor) to check work progress regularly.

9. Don't make final payment to the contractor until all corrections to completed work are made.

7-STEP PLAN TO SELL YOUR HOUSE YOURSELF AND SAVE

With the real estate market in one of its most sluggish phases in years, there's a strong economic incentive for homeowners to try to sell their properties themselves. Housing prices haven't risen substantially the past few years, so people in financial distress don't have profits needed to pay a 6% to 8% broker's commission when they sell. Fortunately, it is possible to do it yourself and save those expenses (the National Association of Realtors estimates 16% to 19% of annual U.S. home sales are "by owner") — though it does take patience, some basic knowledge and, in a lot of cases, luck. Here are 7 steps to take that will make selling a home yourself somewhat less of a challenge — and save you money in the process:

1. Get the house ready. Depending on the condition, this can involve some major repairs — or it may mean only some minor clean-up/fix-up that you can do yourself. The best way to begin the preparation process is to make a list of all the needed repairs, both inside and outside the home. Once you finish this list, you can determine how long you'll need for repairs, which projects are do-it-yourself jobs and which will need to be handled by professionals. For example, if you want to put the house on the market in April and repairs are expected to take 2 months, you should begin fixing up in late January. If you're going to have an appraisal done, the repairs must be completed before the appraiser comes. Since it takes 3 or 4 weeks to get an appraisal report, you'll need to start fixing up that much sooner. In many cases, you may even want to consider professional help for jobs you could do yourself (the cost has to be balanced against potential time savings and work quality). Typical fix-up projects could include:

* Painting — A fresh coat of paint is about the easiest way to add value to a home. Bright colors can make rooms appear larger, and new paint can hideyears of wear. Be sure to paint properly, which means sanding and patching before the first brush is dipped in the can.

* Kitchens — All appliances must be thoroughly cleaned. The best way to do this is with scouring powder and a toothbrush. Cabinets should be cleaned, and whatever can be thrown out should be removed to create a more spacious look. It may be worthwhile to move some kitchen items to the basement for temporary storage. Any drip damage beneath the sink, which is usually caused by condensation, should be repaired.

* Bathrooms — All sinks and tubs should be caulked. Tile grout should be replaced or cleaned (try bleach and a toothbrush). Accumulated hair and other obstacles should be cleaned from drain pipes. Washers should be changed if necessary. The toilet should be immaculate, and the holding tank should not "run."

* Basement — Junk should be removed. Moisture damage, if any, should be repaired. The entire basement should be aired out for as long as possible.

* General — Broken glass, torn shades, holed screens, dead light bulbs, etc., should be replaced, and other items — such as loose doorknobs or cabinet pulls and squeaky hinges — should be repaired. Floors and carpets should be cleaned, with machines if possible.

2. Settle on an asking price. This is one of the most difficult things for a sell-it-yourselfer to do, both because he doesn't have the benefit of knowing what other homes have been selling for and because he has an emotional involvement with the property that often leads to overpricing. The first problem can be overcome with a little research or the (free) help of a real estate agent. Many newspapers, especially small neighborhood shoppers or regional weeklies, regularly publish lists of recent home sales in their coverage area (these are a matter of public record), or your can get a list yourself from the County Recorder's Office. Many people who plan to sell themselves also have a couple of real estate agents come in and give listing presentations and then use the prices determined by the professionals. This might seem a bit underhanded, but the majority of real estate agents don't really mind it, figuring you'll fail at selling the house yourself and eventually give them the listing. With regard to the emotional attachment, there is really nothing you can do but mentally punch yourself a couple of times to ensure you realize that what you think about the house means nothing — it's what the potential buyer thinks of it that counts. As part of the price-setting process, you'll also want to identify any other conditions of the sale, inclusions or exclusions (e.g., appliances, above-ground pools, hot tubs, window air conditioners, etc.)

3. Prepare a brochure. Very few buyers purchase the first property they see — and, as they go from house to house to house, the characteristics of each begin to blur. For this reason, it is extremely important for you to prepare a brochure — or at least a detailed fact sheet — about your home. Such a brochure has 3 purposes: It is a selling tool; it helps distinguish your home from the many others on the market, reminding them of the features of your property;

and, finally, it provides a quick reference so buyers can easily contact you. A basic brochure should list your name and address, as well as telephone information (where to call you at what hours). State the asking price and any special purchase arrangements you would be willing to accept (such as a delayed settlement, VA financing or a loan assumption). Also, there should be a list of items that are not for sale or those which are "not included but available." The brochure should list your property taxes during the past year and provide a summary of winter and summer utility costs. Other useful information may include a floor plan, a picture, specific data about the house, such as the capacity of the electrical system or the type of flooring, a map to the property (valuable when mailing information), and a description of your garden or trees. If you are selling a condominium or a home purchased from a developer it may be useful to re-print some of the original sales literature if it is available (remove any information relating to your acquisition cost).

In developing a sales brochure, you must be certain that the material is wholly factual. False or incorrect information may provide the buyer with a wedge to end or modify a deal. For example, you should retain actual utility and property tax bills to support any claims made in the brochure, and make them readily available to potential buyers. They enhance your position by showing that you can support the claims you make. As potential buyers leave your home, offer your brochure and ask for their names, addresses, and phone numbers. This gives you the ability to follow-up on visitors — and to invite them back for a second tour of the property.

4. Prepare a good ad — and set aside the money to pay for it. The ad should be concise, but it should also include all the key features of your house. (This will cut down on bothersome calls from people who have special requirements your house doesn't include — though it won't stop all of them.) Some people advise against putting in the price, fearing it may scare away some potential buyers. However, our view is that the price should be stated as it's one way to pre-qualify potential buyers and it will also reduce the number of nuisance calls (which you don't need, since you'll have plenty of other nuisance factors during the course of the sale). As for the money, that's one thing that comes as a surprise to many self-sellers. Ads in major newspapers can run into several hundred dollars in just a few weeks — and they have to be prepaid. This cost is one of the first things that makes many people begin wondering if it wouldn't be better to have a broker handling the sale.

5. Utilize other marketing methods. These include a sign in front of the property, notices at high-visibility locations around the neighborhood (to attract the attention of buyers interested in relocating to that area) and possibly flyers placed at the personnel office or on the bulletin board at major employers in the area. This will give you at least a small shot at reaching the job-transfer market, which accounts for a large percentage of residential real estate sales. Another vital marketing tool is the Sunday open house. You'll need to hold one every

week, and it will generally be an all-day job. First, you have to get the house in shape so it doesn't look like you've lived in it all week. Next, you have to place open house signs on strategic streets around the area to direct shoppers to your property. Then, you have to race back to the house and throw some cookies or bread in the oven to give the place that "homey" aroma, put a smile on your face and get mentally ready for 5 or 6 hours of having people march through your home, point out its flaws and reject your charming sales overtures. Finally, you have to go back around the neighborhood and pick up your signs so you'll have them ready to use again the next week. And that's just on Sunday. If you hope to sell your house yourself, you'll also have to be prepared to make yourself available for showings every other day of the week when people respond to your ads, signs or flyers. (Note: It's not a good idea to show the home alone since you'll be dealing with strangers. Try to have a friend come over when prospects come during off hours. And, whether you're showing to a single prospect or holding an open house, always make sure all valuables are locked away safely out of sight.) Many people consider showing the home the hardest aspect of the home-sale process — and rightfully so. However, even with this effort, you're still at a major disadvantage because your home isn't featured on the Realtors' multiple-listing service and you have no access to broker referrals — 2 sources real estate surveys show account for two-thirds of allsales. However, if it works, it's worth it because the monetary rewards of selling yourself are so great.

6. Pay close attention to the finances. You can waste a lot of time and effort trying to sell your house to people who really can't afford it. Real estate agents nearly always pre-qualify buyers before showing them properties, but you don't have this luxury. As a result, you need to make every effort early in the negotiating process to find out about your prospect's financial resources. Get a book with amortization tables so you can quickly tell figure what monthly principal and interest payments will be (don't forget to add in money for taxes and insurance as well). Ask serious prospects early on if they can afford the house and demand an earnest-money deposit of at least 5% of the price of the house with any offer. This requirement will quickly weed out casual shoppers and those who aren't really serious but are merely fishing for a deal. Be aware, too, that you may have to take a stern negotiating stance. Many potential buyers think they should be able to get a better price because you're selling yourself and won't have to pay a commission. Others will simply assume you don't know what you're doing and try to run over you when it comes to price.

7. Get it all in writing. Once you've got a hot prospect, it's best to get some professionals involved. Some self-sellers suggest to buyers that they have their offer drawn up by their own attorney — and then they have another attorney review the offer. If you've never sold property before, it's not a bad idea to consult your attorney way back at Step 1, just to make sure you are aware of all the legal requirements before problems arise. You may also want to have your attorney prepare a generic purchase contract for you before you actually start showing the house. This contract should include schedules that anticipate

potential purchaser demands, such as the sale being conditional on home inspection, the securing of financing or the sale of the buyer's former home. You will also need to deal with other legal matters such as escrow provisions and accounts, title searches, document recording, etc., though your bank or the bank making the loan to the sellers should be able to help with many of these details. However, don't sign anything — or agree to it verbally — without running it by your lawyer first. This may cost you $500 or $600, but it will be worth the money if it keeps something from going wrong.

If you want more detailed information before deciding to sell your home yourself, there are a number of books on the market that can help. One of the classics is Gerald M. Steiner's "Home for Sale by Owner" (Hawthorn Books, New York). Another that has a comprehensive chapter on the subject of self selling is the "Complete Book of Home Buying" by Michael Sumichrast and Ronald G. Shafer (Dow Jones-Irwin, Princeton, NJ). However, the best if you can find it is probably the "30-Day Way to Sell Your Own Home" by J.R. Paine (Gold Key Press, Royal Oak, MI $19.95). Paine, a Realtor himself, incurred the wrath of other Realtors and was nearly drummed out of the profession when the book came out in June 1989. It provides complete step-by-step guidance through the entire process, telling you what to do and how and when to do it. It also includes samples of purchase agreements, deeds, final settlement statements, HUD forms, water and rent escrow forms, mortgage tables, sample ads, an open house register and advice on appraisals and negotiating tactics. It also lists the most common snags, surprises and snafus that can occur when dealing with buyers, lenders, Realtors, attorneys, agents and others who may seek to complicate things for you.

Finally, if you don't want to try selling the house yourself but still hate the thought of paying a hefty 6% to 8% commission, you may want to consider the use of a so-called "flat-fee broker." These firms — such as Phoenix-based WHY USA; Help-U-Sell (based in Salt Lake City); Sell Your Own Home (Kansas City) and Home Marketing Specialists Inc. (Southfield, Mich.) — don't charge a commission. Rather they charge from $990 to $3,500 to provide a wide array of services, from setting a selling price and developing a marketing plan to handling your closing. They also place houses either in exclusive weekly listings available to prospects seeking their services, or with local multiple-listing networks (if the network produces the sale, the commission broker typically collects 3%). What a flat-fee broker generally won't do is show your home, which is a serious drawback if you have neither the time nor the patience to provide prospective buyers enticing house tours.

6 WAYS TO GET A HIGHER PRICE FOR YOUR HOUSE

We mentioned the importance of getting your house ready for sale earlier, but this process can have such an important impact on the eventual selling price, we want to reiterate some of the key things to do. Here are 6 strategic improvements that can help your old house sell as quickly and easily as a new one:

1. Do a thorough cleaning, repainting or wallpapering. Buy new carpets or have them professionally cleaned.

2. Rid your house of cat and dog odors potential buyers may notice.

3. For selling to working couples, a 4-bedroom house can be advertised as 2 bedrooms, library and den.

4. To improve the critical first impression, repair the porch, repaint porch furniture, fix awnings and other entrance features.

5. Spruce up landscaping.

6. If you're not selling yourself, make sure you select a top real estate agent who will work hard to show your house. Review the description of your home on the multiple-listing service as well, as this listing is the main thing that attracts salespeople — and prospects — from other agencies to your property.

HOME IMPROVEMENTS THAT PAY OFF

Uncle Sam will help you pay for home improvements — allowing you to add their cost to your tax basis for the property — but only if they add value to the house. For example, converting attic space into a fourth bedroom, adding a bath or installing central air and heating would all qualify, but replacing an old furnace or bad plumbing wouldn't (these are classed as general repair and maintenance items by the IRS). If you have questions about whether a planned improvement will qualify, ask your tax advisor.

Photographic Proof: Protect yourself in the event of a future audit by taking both before and after photos of the improved area, just so you can clearly show exactly what was done.

HOW TO LEGALLY AVOID TAXES WHEN YOU SELL YOUR HOME

If you sell your home and don't buy another one, you'll pay tax on any gain from the deal — unless you're over 55 and the gain is less than $125,000 (a one-time exception that applies if you've lived in the house for 3 or the past 5 years). Gain is basically the difference between your cost basis and the selling price, less selling expenses. Your cost basis may include some or all of the following:

* Price paid in cash or other property, and by mortgage assumed or mortgage to which property is subject.

* Attorney's fees and expenses involved with the purchase contract and its closing or settlement; plus cost of searching, defending, or perfecting the title.

* Title search and title insurance.

* Fees for appraisal, recording of deed and mortgage survey.

* Cost of acquiring cash for purchase (mortgage broker's fees, lender's origination fee, title search and/or title insurance legal fees for drafting bond and mortgage), but not "points."

* Engineering and architectural fees, termite inspection.

* Capital investments for building restoration or long-term improvements.

* Cost of outside improvements, such as paving, landscaping, grading, wells, masonry.

* Seller's real estate taxes assumed by buyer as part of the purchase price.

* Insurance during construction.

* Purchasing commissions.

* Any "rent" paid under option to purchase and applied to purchase price.

Deductible selling expenses include:

* Broker's commission.

* Attorney's fees and other legal expenses.

* Advertising.

* Sales tax.

* Title abstract.

* "Points" paid by the seller to help the buyer get financing.

* Fix-up expenses if incurred within 90 days of the sale contract and paid within 30 days after sale. Keep an accurate record of any such items that will help reduce your tax liability.

Note: There's one other tax advantage that may apply to your home sale, even if you're not over 55. If you accept installment payments from the buyer and the selling price is less than $150,000, you can generally spread the tax due over a period of years, thus avoiding having to take a large gain all at once and possibly lifting yourself into a higher tax bracket. This break is available only to owner/occupants, not to real estate agents or commercial real estate investors.

FIGHTING FOR FAIRER PROPERTY TAXES

If you've watched your property taxes creep up over the past few years, you'd probably like some relief. Many fed up taxpayers have successfully challenged the system, and won cuts in their property taxes by proving that their home was over-valued for tax purposes. If you suspect this might be the case for you, the first thing to do is review your assessment. Check it over periodically like you would your insurance policy. Property taxes result from multiplying the assessed value of your home by the local tax rate. This rate is set by law and can't be changed, so the only hope for a lower bill means you have to beat down the assessment. Find out how the assessment is set — by full market value or a percentage of that value. The assessed value is supposed to relate to your home's market value, but the two may wind up being quite different. For example, many states set assessments at 80% of value at the time of sale. Then, communities are then allowed to raise assessed values on a regular basis, using a variety of different formulas. This is supposedly designed to keep assessed values in line with inflation, but when the housing market is slow, these automatic hikes tend to cause properties to become overvalued — meaning you become overtaxed. To correct this problem, you must prove that the description of your property is wrong or that the market value assigned to It is too high — and then either contact the assessor and informally request an adjustment or file a formal appeal.

To Determine an Overvaluation: Look at your property record card at your county assessor's office. Make sure the age, size, location, number of bathrooms and quality of construction are correct. Assessors make many errors in these areas — and these errors cost you money. After correcting any errors, your assessment can be rolled back. While you're looking at your property record card, also make sure that notations on easements, encroachments and the general condition of your home are correct. Review the math calculations and any other information on the card. Be sure your property is classified as residential, and that you are getting any exemptions you deserve. Now look at market value. The rules for market value vary from state to state, so check the rules for where you live. Take into account the price you paid for the home and the sale prices of similar properties that sold around the time you purchased yours. Find out if your purchase was near a time of revaluation; that could account for a big early jump in your taxes and could be the basis for an appeal. Find out, too, if you can appeal based on comparability — i.e., based on the fact that your home is assessed differently than comparable homes in your area. Many times, if you can show a large discrepancy, you can get the assessor to adjust your valuation without going through the process of a formal appeal. In fact, you can get an adjustment and still go through with an appeal seeking a larger reduction.

There's Help Available: It is not that difficult to request either an informal adjustment or file a formal appeal. However, if you are reluctant to try it yourself, most communities have consultants who can help. Simple check in the Yellow Pages of your phone book under the heading "Tax Consultants." Some of these pros charge a flat fee for appealing your assessment, while others will take cases on a contingency basis, charging 20% to 50% of your first-year tax savings if they win.

B. Take the Mystery Out of Mortgages

CALCULATING HOW MUCH MORTGAGE YOU CAN AFFORD

The general rule of thumb is that you can afford a mortgage equal to roughly twice your annual income. However, if you can do a bit of math, the following worksheet and table will give you a much better fix on how much mortgage you can really afford. The calculations are based on the assumption that you are taking out a 30-year, fixed-rate mortgage and that closing costs will equal about 4.5% of the purchase price:

1. Regular monthly pre-tax income from all sources: ______
2. The maximum amount most lenders will allow you to spend per month on your mortgage, property taxes and insurance (Line 1 times 0.28): ______
3. Regular monthly debt payments, including credit-card debt, car payments, etc. (If the result is greater than 8% or Line 1, the lender may require you to reduce your debt before approving a loan.): ______
4. Estimated monthly property tax and insurance cost on house you want to purchase: ______
5. The amount the lender will allow you to pay each month for mortgage principal and interest (Line 2 minus Line 4): ______

6. Total loan amount you qualify for (find the current mortgage interest rate on the top line of the table below; match the total from Line 5 to the closest number in that column; then read the mortgage amount in the column at the far right in the table.): ______
7. Price of house you can afford:
   A. With 10% down (Line 6 times 1.112) ______
   B. With 15% down (Line 6 times 1.177) ______
   C. With 20% down (Line 6 times 1.250) ______

30-YEAR, FIXED-RATE MORTGAGE TABLE

Interest Rate					Mortgage
7.5%	8.0%	8.5%	9.0%	9.5%	Amount
$350	$367	$384	$402	$ 420	$ 50,000
$420	$441	$461	$483	$ 505	$ 60,000
$490	$514	$538	$563	$ 589	$ 70,000
$560	$587	$615	$644	$ 673	$ 80,000
$630	$661	$692	$724	$ 757	$ 90,000
$700	$734	$769	$805	$ 841	$100,000
$770	$807	$846	$886	$ 925	$110,000
$840	$880	$923	$967	$1,009	$120,000

8 WAYS TO GET A MORTGAGE WITH 0% TO 5% DOWN

The biggest problem most people have when buying a new home is coming up with the money for the down payment. However, there are many ways to reduce or eliminate the need for a big cash down payment. Here are 8:

1. Ask the seller to help by providing what is known as a purchase-money second mortgage. In such an arrangement, a portion of the seller's equity provides your down payment, and you make monthly payments to him as well as to the holder of your first mortgage.

2. Apply for an FHA loan, currently available with 3% down.

3. Acquire private mortgage insurance. The insurance assures the lending company it will get its money, so it's more willing to accept a low down payment,

even though it means higher monthly payments for you. (Note: You can expect to pay from 0.5% to 1.0% in extra interest on the loan to get this insurance.)

4. Lease with an option to buy, applying an agreed-upon amount toward the down payment while you live in the house.

5. Borrow from relatives — or better yet, if they are willing, ask them to make you a gift. Catch: The lender may consider a loan from relatives as increasing your long-term debt, which could affect the determination of how much mortgage you can afford.

6. Ask the seller to pay for or loan the amount of closing costs. A motivated seller might pay for legal fees, a title search, transfer fees required by the registry of deeds and even the initial points on the mortgage, leaving all of your cash to be applied to the down payment.

7. If the seller is facing foreclosure, you can offer to take over payments on his mortgage if he will take a second mortgage for the amount of the down payment. You can also offer to assume his mortgage in exchange for a reduction in the sales price, taking out a new loan to make up the difference between the mortgage amount and the reduced selling price. This lets the seller get out from under the payments and salvage a portion of his equity (the rest is, in effect, your down payment), which he would have lost in a foreclosure. It also saves the mortgage company the trouble and expense of foreclosing on the property, which is why it will usually go along with the deal.

8. Check with mortgage bankers to find out if they hold any foreclosure properties. They are usually eager to dispose of foreclosed homes, and may be willing to accept only a small down payment in order to unload the property.

HOW TO GET A MORTGAGE WITHOUT PAYING POINTS

"Points" are loan fees charged by banks and other lending institutions to cover the upfront costs of making a new loan (and to give the lender some instant profit). These fees usually run from 1% to 4% of the amount of the mortgage — which means they can run into thousands of dollars on even a modestly priced home. By far the easiest way to avoid having to pay points on a new mortgage is to convince the seller to pay them as a condition of the sale. Failing that, however, you should be aware that these fees are negotiable — and some lenders are willing to waive them entirely in a competitive lending market, especially if you have a large down payment or an outstanding credit rating (meaning you'll have no trouble getting a loan elsewhere). When you begin discussions with the lender, don't hesitate to ask for a reduction in fees based on your good credit — and, if the lender won't respond, don't hesitate to walk out and try somewhere else.

Another way to handle the situation is to get one loan approval, then take it to another lender and ask them if they can beat the deal. If they really want your business, you'll likely win some concessions — and, if you don't, try somewhere else. Finally, some lenders will reduce or eliminate points if you are willing to take a higher interest rate. Check the figures on both methods to see which one better suits your needs (e.g., if you have a igh income, but not much cash, you're likely better off with a higher rate and no points.)

HOW TO FIND THE LOWEST MORTGAGE RATE RIGHT NOW

Reporting on the most competitive mortgage rates has become a major function of the financial media in recent years, so it's not that difficult to get a pretty good reading on the best deals in your area. Most major newspapers carry loan-rate tables weekly, and a number of popular magazines list the best rates around the country and give phone numbers needed to reach the lenders. You'll even find a listing of some of the best recent mortgage deals around the nation in Chapter 3 of this book. However, if you want to take a lot of the hassle out of shopping for a home loan, you may want to consider a new service being offered by Money Magazine. Called Mortgage Match, the service gives you everything you need to shop at home for a loan, including:

* A computer printout, updated weekly, with full information on the deals being offered by lenders in your area, including rates, points, fees, ARM indexes, margins, caps, etc.

* A second printout at a time you specify, up to 4 weeks later.

* A 44-page booklet titled "How To Shop for Your Mortgage."

* A special guide to discounts or premiums being offered by lenders.

* The most recent issue of "Homebuyer News and Tips," an informative newsletter containing useful articles, buying tips and news from the world of real estate and mortgage financing.

The entire Mortgage Match kit costs just $29.95 and can be ordered using your credit card by calling 1-800-243-8474.

DON'T USE A 40-YEAR MORTGAGE

Many banks and S&Ls are now offering 40-year mortgages, a reflection of the housing-price inflation of the '80s. However, using one of these mortgages can be a costly mistake for homebuyers — despite the lower monthly payment. On a $100,000, 40-year mortgage at 9.0%, the monthly payment would be just $767, compared to $805 on a 30-year, 9.0% loan of the same size — a savings of $38. However, over the full life of the mortgage, that $38 "bargain" would cost a total of $78,360 in extra interest payments ($268,160 vs. $189,800)!

SAVE $126,000 ON AN $85,000 MORTGAGE

If you already have a mortgage in place — regardless of its length — you can still save big money, simply by making an extra payment on your principal each month. On a 30-year mortgage for $85,000 with a 10% interest rate, the monthly payment will normally be around $746. However, an extra payment of just $5 a month will save you $57,283 in interest charges and shorten your pay-off time to 22-1/2 years. That means, for almost 8 years, you will have an extra $746 a month to put into your savings or investments — or merely to enjoy. (Most mortgage payment coupons have a space to indicate extra principal payments. However, if yours doesn't, you will have to write a separate check and note on it that

the payment is to go toward principal reduction.) For even bigger savings, boost the extra payment to $150. You will cut your pay-off time almost in half (to 15 years, 9 months) — and save $99,966 in interest payments. Finally, if you put in an extra $300 a month, you'll shorten the loan term to just over 11 years, saving a whopping $126,191 in interest charges!

One Warning: Paying ahead on your principal does not relieve you of the obligation to make your regular monthly payment when it comes due. Thus, you should always maintain a reserve big enough to cover at least 6 months' worth of expenses, just in case of a job loss or other financial problem.

BEWARE THIS ADJUSTABLE-RATE MORTGAGE SCAM

Some lenders advertise what they call adjustable-rate mortgages when what they are actually handing out are escalating-rate mortgages. A true ARM is linked to some popular index or market interest rate, and will go down as well as up, depending what happens in the overall interest-rate environment. While some legitimate ARMs do have an automatic increase built in during the early years to compensate for an artificially low introductory rate, they usually revert to the standard ARM formula for variable adjustments after a 3- to 4-year period. However, a few lenders have been caught handing out loans with rates that go nowhere but up. Usually, these loans are introduced at a very low rate, making them seem like good deals. However, instead of being linked to a variable index, they feature a fixed scale of interest-rate increases that will, within a few years, have you paying a rate well in excess of market rates — with no chance of having it drop again. Another scam involves giving borrowers an ultra-low initial rate, but scheduling adjustments on a monthly basis so that the rate can be boosted to a non-competitive level within a few months. The best way to protect yourself is to make sure you fully understand all the terms of your mortgage, checking on such items as the initial rate, the index or market rate to which adjustments are linked, the frequency of adjustments and the overall cap (or limit) on how much rates can be raised over the life of the loan. If you see anything in the terms that looks fishy or questionable, ask for an explanation — and, if you don't get it, head for another lender.

EVERYTHING YOU NEED TO KNOW ABOUT REFINANCING

When mortgage rates are falling, the decision to refinance a high-interest home loan is an easy one. And in 1992, according to the Mortgage Bankers Association of America, around 3 million mortgages were refinanced, saving consumers an estimated $6 billion annually. But as interest rates work their way upward, the decision becomes more difficult, the process more expensive and the factors more confusing. How can you decide if refinancing is right for you? And how do you find your way through the refinancing jungle? Here are some guidelines:

It usually pays to refinance if the difference between the old rate — on a 30-year fixed mortgage, say — and the current rate is 2 or 3 percentage points. However, other factors also enter in. You need to consider how long you plan to live in the house, then add in the total cost of refinancing (see the table below). For example, the refinancing boom has seen many home owners trade in their adjustable-rate mortgages for fixed-rate notes. But adjustables actually offer advantages — if you don't plan to stay long in your home. They are frequently capped at 1.5 to 2.0 percentage points a year and carry lower points than fixed-rate loans.

Add Up the Costs: Another consideration in deciding whether to refinance are the steep costs that may be involved. These include:

* Penalties for paying off the old mortgage early can cost 3% to 5% of the loan's outstanding balance. (FHA and VA mortgage don't have prepayment penalties, and some states ban or restrict them.)

* Application fees. As the refinance rush picked up speed, some lenders

began increasing their upfront fees, like tacking on $100 or more to their applications for refinancers. Application fees generally should not exceed $400. (To protect yourself, write for a free copy of "A Consumer's Guide to Refinancing Your Mortgage" by sending a self-addressed, stamped envelope to P.O. Box 65299, Washington, D.C. 20035.)

* Deposit fees. Many lenders requires a substantial deposit with applications — from 0.5 to 1.5% of the loan amount. The money is refundable if the lender rejects you — but not if you're approved, then decide to go with another lender.

* Legal fees. Another closing brings additional legal fees.

* Title insurance. You'll need a new search to see if there are property liens or title problems — even if you don't switch lenders. Expect to pay around $1,400 for attorney fees and title search.

* Credit check. Whenever you refinance, they'll do an up-to-the-minute review of your credit rating.

* Appraisal fees. Credit check and appraisal fees together usually come to around $600.

* Inspections.

* Mortgage recording tax.

To help with your refinancing decision, you should try and determine how soon the savings in monthly mortgage payments will equal your refinancing costs. Here are some rules of thumb:

* If the drop in interest rates in percentage points equals the points you have to pay the bank to get the loan, you can figure loan costs will be recovered in about a year. Other costs will be offset during the second and third year. After that, it will be pure savings.

* If you expect to move within a year, or if your mortgage is almost paid off, you probably shouldn't refinance.

* If you face a prepayment penalty, it will take longer to recoup your costs. However, even in such a case, refinancing should show a savings within 5 years.

Here's an illustration of how long it takes to make refinancing a $100,000 mortgage pay off at various interest rates:

If new rate is this	It will take
this much lower than the current rate:	this long to recoup the cost:
1%	41 months
2%	21 months
3%	14 months
4%	11 months

Shopping For the Best Deal: Naturally you want the best refinancing deal for the lowest cost — but not at the expense of financial solidity. Steer clear of lenders nobody's ever heard of. If you apply to a bank that subsequently fails, the acquiring institution isn't legally obligated either to process your application or refund any up-front fees. Often the best place to begin is with your current lender. Some may offer breaks on closing costs and points. To continue your search, make a list of firms offering the lowest rates and points. Ask the lender to quote an annual percentage rate, combining rates, points and other fees into a single figure. Don't forget to ask how long the approval process will take, if the interest rate is guaranteed in writing and for how long. To speed the approval process, take along your W-2 forms, pay stubs, account numbers, bank statements and addresses of creditors. Make sure you understand the figures. If you find personnel abrupt with you or unwilling to explain things to your satisfaction, cross the institution off your shopping list. Many borrowers save thousands of dollars in interest by making an extra principal payment each year or by paying off

the loan early. However, some lenders charge a penalty for pre paying on a mortgage. If the lender you're considering is one of these, take your business elsewhere.

Some Refinancing Options:

* No-points deals — Obviously, all things being equal, refinancing without paying points (1 point equals 1% of the mortgage) beats paying points. But on some deals, all things aren't equal. A mortgage with a slightly higher rate and no points might be a better deal than one offering a lower rate with 1 point — for 3 years, say. But, after that, you might be better off paying the point to get the lower rate for the life of the loan. Always run the numbers — or get someone to run them for you.

* Lower rates vs. higher payments — Your monthly payments will obviously increase if you refinance a 30-year loan to a 15-year loan with a lower interest rate — but they won't double. Because the principal will be paid down more quickly — and because lower rates are available on shorter loans — your payments may be only 15% to 25% more. Or, instead of making higher monthly payments to pay off the mortgage earlier, you may want to consider putting the money into other long-term investments. To decide which way to go, subtract your tax deduction on the mortgage interest. Is the resulting mortgage rate more or less than you can earn on alternate investments after taxes? Remember, mortgage interest is probably the largest tax write-off available. Refinancing to a lower-rate mortgage with a shorter term could nullify tax advantages and offset any hoped for savings.

A mortgage Refinancing Trap: Points can generally be deducted in the year in which they're paid, provided the mortgage is for the "purchase or improvement" of a taxpayer's principal residence. However, the IRS says points paid to refinance a mortgage loan are not deductible because the new mortgage is actually for repaying an existing debt — not for purchasing of a residence. So, the points have to be amortized and deducted over the entire period of the loan. Example: You pay $6,000 in points to refinance a $200,000 mortgage over 20 years. You cannot deduct the $6,000 this year. You can only deduct $300 a year over the 20-year period.

Borrowing on the Cheap: Depending on the size of your mortgage and the value of your house, you can use refinancing as a cheap way to borrow money. With a $25,000 mortgage on a house worth $100,000, you could take out a new lower-rate loan for $50,000 and have $25,000 to invest.

LOSE YOUR JOB AND STILL KEEP YOUR HOME

In these perilous economic times, not even the most secure job with the biggest company is truly secure. For that reason — and because they have a vested interest in trying to light a fire under the sluggish real estate market — a number of developers, realty companies and even lenders around the country are now offering job protection for new home buyers. Call it recession insurance — which, in essence it is, since many of the programs are actually underwritten by insurance companies (including the famed Lloyds of London).

How the Plans Work: In most cases, the coverage applies for a period of 1 year after you buy a home. Should you lose your job within that period, the mortgage insurance will make your payments (up to a certain limit) until you find a new job (again, up to a certain limit). Typical policies we've seen will make payments of up to $2,500 or a period of up to 1 year. Some don't specify individual payment or time limits, but have an overall cap on the amount of coverage (usually $7,500 to $10,000). As a rule, no screening is required for the insurance — meaning anyone who buys a home through a sponsoring firm and can qualify for a loan will also automatically qualify for the insurance.

Warning: If such a plan interests you, you may have to hurry to take advantage. Some developers are already considering dropping the programs, saying that, with the economy picking up a bit, buyers are becoming more interested in upgrades and added features than in recession coverage. As a result, the value of these programs as marketing tools may be short-lived.

BUYING MORTGAGES AS AN INVESTMENT

With money market and CD rates stuck in the 3% to 4% range, you may also want to take a look at mortgages from the other side — as a lender. Many lenders regularly sell off mortgages to private investors as part of their risk-balancing or capital-raising processes — and some of these investments offer returns of as much as 12% to 15%. Of course, they offer substantially higher risks as well. As a rule, you will find 2 types of loans available in the private-mortgage market — those originated by mortgage brokers, who place them with private investors after taking out a loan-acquisition fee; and so-called purchase-money mortgages, which are first or second mortgages taken by home sellers in order to facilitate the sale of their properties. They then sell off these loans in order to get their money in a lump sum, rather than a month at a time, and also to avoid having to service the loan. Loans for sale are often advertised in the Classified or Real Estate sections of local papers under such headings as "Trust Deeds for Sale" or "Money Wanted — Real Estate," though they are sometimes also sold through real estate agents. The reason you can get such high returns is that many loan sellers are willing to discount the face value of the loan in order to get a large sum of cash. For example, you might be able to buy a $20,000, 10%, 10 year second mortgage for as little as $15,000 — which would give you an effective yield of around 17% per year.

Evaluating the Risks: Unfortunately, even the safest of these investments — first mortgages on single-family homes — carry high risks. After all, you are essentially assuming the role of the lender — and you've seen the kind of trouble that has gotten the banks and S&Ls into. In addition, the likely reason the loans were made in the first place was because the buyer couldn't meet the financial requirements for a regulation bank or thrift loan, so the risk of default is high. Unless you have lots of money, you're also stuck in a situation where you have no diversification. If you buy a $20,000 note and the borrower defaults you could be wiped out, or you could have to sue to get control of the property from other creditors (a suit you could lose, meaning you'd wind up with legal fees on top of your loss). The best way to protect yourself is to both inspect the property and interview the borrower before you buy a mortgage. Don't simply take the word of the person trying to sell the loan that it's on a good property with a stable buyer. Be sure, too, to avoid loans on properties where the borrower lacks sufficient equity — e.g., he owes almost as much on the house as it is worth. A lack of equity makes it that much easier for a borrower to default if he gets in trouble. A final note: If you don't feel the projected yield justifies the risk, don't hesitate to make a counter offer. Often, you can get an additional 5% to 10% discount from the face value without too much negotiation — and that will boost your effective yield substantially.

C. Real Estate as an Investment

DON'T INVEST FOR TAX SHELTER ALONE

It used to be that real estate offered so many tax benefits, the quality of the property wasn't all that important. Today, however, things are different (thanks largely to the Tax Reform Act of 1986). You can't afford to buy a property based on the potential tax benefits alone — the property also has to make sense from a business standpoint. You also have to pay careful attention to the details, since operating losses no

longer automatically translate into tax deductions. Here are some potential areas of concern to consider when investing in a real estate tax shelter:

* Cash flow projections assuming complete rental of an apartment house are unrealistic. Even a 95% occupancy rate in a low-vacancy area is optimistic. That 5% difference must be subtracted from projected cash flow, diminishing the investment return.

* Rental income projections may also be inflated. Check with area brokers for realistic rent projections.

* Does the shelter management company get fees for selling the project to the group, and for selling the property at the end?

* Does the shelter management receive a profit share on the final sale?

* Are the fees reasonable? Management fees should not exceed 5% to 6% of gross rents.

* Are the managers getting more than what you consider their fair share from the project?

* Do the managers get their fees up front? It's preferable if managers ride along with investors and get their fees as they go along.

CHECKING OUT A PROPERTY'S INVESTMENT VALUE

Some of the same concerns just listed apply to determining the investment value of commercial properties, such as office complexes, retail buildings or even strip shopping centers. However, there are also several other factors to review before putting your money down. Here's what to check:

1. High-paying tenants. Are they affiliated with the seller, or party to agreements that make it difficult to raise rents?

2. Operating expenses. Is the seller keeping these low by operating the building himself? If you don't want to assume that task, you'll have to add a management fee to operating expenses.

3. Assessments. Ask the local assessor to show you the building's

assessment and when it was assessed. If it was assessed recently and no major additions have been made, reassessment may not hurt you. However, if there's been no assessment in recent years, you could face a major tax boost. Check the property description carefully. If the seller claims 20,000 square feet are being sold, but the assessor's tax card says 15,000 square feet, structural add-ons may not have been recorded and therefore not yet assessed — or there could be an assessment error that will cost you in taxes when corrected.

4. Insurance premiums. Ask to see the policy and find out what's covered. Is coverage too low for the building's assessed value? If so, how much more will proper coverage cost?

5. Energy efficiency. Check with local utilities to nail down actual energy costs. Don't rely on the seller's claim. While you're at it, check with regulatory commissions to see if utility companies will soon be increasing their rates.

THE BEST STARTING PLACE — SINGLE-FAMILY HOMES

Though many people overlook the fact, the very best starting place for novice real estate investors is a single-family house. You only have one tenant and one set of problems with which to deal, which gives you a chance to decide whether property investment is suited to your temperament and time availability. However, even this area contains some traps if you're not careful. Here are some things you should check or be aware of before investing in a single-family house:

1. Is there an active rental market for homes in your area? What are the odds of finding and keeping a good tenant for the rental price you need?

2. Home mortgages may be several percentage points higher than financing for commercial properties.

3. There's a significant risk of cash drain with single-family houses bought as rental units. They can go empty for months.

4. The investment should make economic sense without tax benefits.

QUICK GUIDE TO INVESTING IN CONDOS & COOPS

With the housing market still sluggish, condo and co-op investments remain a good alternative. But how can you avoid the errors made by real estate investors in recent years? Here are 7 crucial lessons:

1. Avoid investing in condos or co-ops surrounded by rental apartments. Prime locations are next to single-family housing.

2. Look for units going for considerably less than comparable-sized homes nearby. Rule of thumb: Co-ops should sell for 25% less than the lowest-priced houses in the area.

3. Avoid over-built areas. In housing gluts, co-ops or condos can remain vacant for months or even years.

4. Watch the housing market. When homes become cheaper (due to lower interest rates, oversupply or zoning changes), apartments are harder to sell.

5. Look for an assumable loan. If you have to sell in a down market, buyers may be willing to take over payments on your loan.

6. Avoid investing in apartment units in outlying areas.

7. Be careful investing in resort condos. Seasonal rentals can be risky, and properties far from the investor's area are harder to manage.

A Hidden Benefit: Condos require less management than straight rentals, since condo associations handle day-to-day maintenance of the main building and grounds.

Cautionary note: Many people start with a condo investment, find they can handle it, and then make a move into ownership of a multi-family apartment building. This can make since because a multi-family apartment house is less risky than a single-family home or condo, assuming all are located in a good area. (An apartment house risks only partial vacancy, while a home or condo risks zero occupancy.) However, multi-family buildings can take a lot of management and maintenance, and professional building managers don't come cheap.

JUMPING ON THE REHAB BANDWAGON

Quick profits can be made by renovating and renting older buildings in areas undergoing "gentrification." To spot likely target areas, look for neighborhoods:

* Where at least a third of the buildings show signs of improvement.
* With a low crime rate.
* Near parks, lakes, colleges and good shopping.
* With owner-occupants, not absentee landlords.
* That promote community interests and activities.
* With visible police protection.
* Targeted by local government for cleanup.

* Where banks are willing to lend money for purchase or building rehab.

SHOPPING CENTERS & OTHER COMMERCIAL PROPERTIES

For wealthier investors, shopping centers can be a good investment — and an easy operation. Tenants handle most maintenance. For the rest, hire outside contractors. However, before you invest in an existing center with units leased on a 3- to 5-year basis, here are a couple of things you should find out:

* Are the tenants doing well? If so, they'll renew their leases and rents will go up — and so will the property's income and value.

* What are existing leases in the center going for? What are other new leases going for in the area? The difference between the figures is what you can count on when current leases expire.

NEW FDIC RULES ON LOAN LIMITS

In an effort to reduce the exposure of member banks to bad property loans, the Federal Deposit Insurance Corp. has adopted new limits on the size of allowable real estate loans. Under the new standards, banks will be permitted to lend no more than 65% of the value of

raw land, 75% for land development and 85% for improved investment property. The FDIC set no upper limits for loans on single-family homes, multi-family apartments with 4 units or less and home equity loans, leaving the lending maximums on those properties up to the discretion of individual banks.

BORROW YOUR WAY TO REAL ESTATE WEALTH

Despite the new FDIC lending limits, property is still considered one of the most secure forms of collateral for a loan — which makes it possible to greatly leverage your assets and increase your chances to build true wealth through real estate. In fact, according to a new book on the subject, today's depressed property market, which features flat or even declining prices in many areas, offers the best opportunity to "Borrow Your Way to Real Estate Wealth" in more than 15 years. The 300-page volume says it is still quite possible to borrow $50,000, $100,000 or even more to purchase investment real estate — and tells you exactly how to go about getting loans (even from bankers who would laugh at you if you wanted $5,000 to state a new business or make another type of purchase). The book explains:

* How to control land or property without actually owning it.

* How to prepare a loan-request package bankers will find impossible to resist.

* How to get loans for more than you need to buy the property — and pocket thousands in extra cash.

* Why you should start with single-family homes — and how to quickly make the move into apartment buildings and commercial property.

* How to "rent" collateral so you can qualify for a loan, even if you've had a bankruptcy.

* How to avoid the hassles of being a landlord.

* How to profit from rehab projects, foreclosures and other offbeat property deals.

To get a copy of the book, send a check for $15 to Discovery Publishers, Dept. 240-J, 11160 Veirs Mill Road, Wheaton, MD 20902.

FREE MONEY FOR REAL ESTATE INVESTMENT

Best-selling financial author Laurie Blum has a new book titled "Invest in Real Estate With Free Money." Blum's book shows you where to go for private-sector grants (many of which never have to be paid back) to help you buy residential, recreational or commercial properties. It also walks you through the tricky process of getting grant applications approved. The 296-page volume also includes sections on Fiscal-Sponsorship Funding and How to Get Federal Monies, as well as a chapter on charitable tax investments. The book costs $39.95, plus your local sales tax and $3.35 in shipping and handling charges. To get a copy, send your check to John Wiley & Sons, Inc., Dept. 063, One Wiley Drive, Somerset, NH 08875. The publisher will refund your money if you're not satisfied after a 15-day examination.

D. Other Pointers on Property

SAVE $2,000 OR MORE ON COMMISSIONS

If you're planning on buying another local home after you sell this one — either because you're trading up or you want to unload the big family house now that the kids are gone — you may be able to get a hefty break on your commissions. Most real estate agents will readily agree to lower the standard 6% to 7% fee by up to 2 percentage points if you let them represent you in both transactions. Assuming you're selling a $150,000 home, this could save you up to $3,000 in commissions ($7,500 at 5% vs. $10,500 at 7%). The broker still makes out nicely on the deal, since he also gets half the commission paid by the seller of the next home you buy.

7 TIPS ON DEALING WITH REAL ESTATE AGENTS

You may also be able to save big money just by knowing your legal rights in dealing with real estate agents. Here are 7 key pointers:

1. Shop for a Realtor and agent you feel comfortable with.

2. Read all brokers' contracts carefully.

3. Try to negotiate the commission rate. Some brokers will, others won't. The law doesn't require them to.

4. Make sure you understand the listing agreement before signing.

5. The most common listing offered is the exclusive right to sell. This requires you to pay full commission to the listing brokers, no matter who brings in the buyer — even if you find the buyer yourself.

6. Signing a contract and accepting "earnest" money from a buyer commit you to the sale — unless the buyer backs out and forfeits the money, or the contract is invalidated by some contingency.

7. If you back out after you've signed a contract, you could face a lawsuit from the buyer. Lawsuit or not, you may still have to pay the agent's commission.

WHEN YOU SHOULD USE AN AGENT TO SELL:

When the real estate market is slow and you absolutely must sell your home. Trying to save brokerage commissions when the market's bad and you're in a hurry is a losing proposition — and could wind up actually costing you money. Without the multiple-listing service, you won't get maximum exposure for your property, and you could wind up having to accept a bad offer out of desperation — if you get one at all. Agents have many more resources — including broker networks and display advertising — than do individuals when it comes to attracting buyers. In addition, according to real estate author Peter Miller, "brokers tend to hoard as many buyers as possible during slow times, greatly reducing your chances of attracting a prospect on your own."

Money $ecret: If a speedy sale is your first priority, but you'd still like a chance at a lower commission, ask the broker if he or she will take a lower percentage if the property isn't sold within a certain time period. Some brokers will agree to such deals — though they may do so only in exchange for a bonus if they sell your house within 2 or 3 days.

CONSIDER A SALE/LEASEBACK ARRANGEMENT

Instead of refinancing, consider selling your property, then leasing it back. Biggest Advantage: Immediate cash equal to 100% of the property's current value. A mortgage loan would probably yield only 75%. Here's how it works:

The seller (or lessee):

* Continues to use the property during the term of the lease.

* Pays deductible rent.

* Receives a taxable gain or loss on sale.

The buyer (or lessor):

* Puts up the cash (perhaps borrowing).

* Gets taxable rental income.

* Takes depreciation deductions.

At the end of the lease:

* There may be an option to repurchase the property at fair market value. Word of Warning: The IRS looks carefully at sale/leaseback deals, especially any with options to repurchase at less than market value. Such deals may be viewed as disguised mortgage loans. If so, the only "rent" deductible is the part considered to be "interest" on the "loan."

CHAPTER 12

THE ROADS TO RETIREMENT

A. The Time to Begin is Now

TURN $300 A MONTH INTO $1.15 MILLION!

Just in case you think you're too young to start worrying about retirement and plan on skipping this Chapter, we're going to begin with an example of the power of starting early. If you are 30 years old and put just $3,600 a year ($300 a month) in mutual funds, stocks or some other investment earning a fairly conservative 10% annual return, your holdings will be worth a whopping $1.15 million by the time you turn 65. However, if you wait until you are 40 and begin investing the same $300 a month, earning the same 10% rate, your portfolio will increase to only about $400,000 at 65. And, if you delay until you are 50, your investment of $300 a month at 10% will grow to a mere $125,000 or so. The moral? Start now!

5 SECRETS TO RETIRING IN STYLE

Want to live the good life in your golden years? Here are 5 keys that will help you do just that:

1. Set good retirement goals. How can you succeed in anything if you don't have a vision of what success means? As President Clinton's favorite oldie anthem says, "Don't stop thinking about tomorrow." What kind of lifestyle do you

want to have in retirement? Where do you want to live? How much do you want to leave behind for your heirs? When you've figured out how you want to live, you'll be ready to calculate how much you'll need — and how much you'll have to start saving to get there. Which brings up the second mistake in retirement planning:

2. Don't procrastinate. Remember, retirement is right around the corner! On the first day of rehearsals, some theatrical directors have been known to use a particularly alarmist expression: "Tomorrow's opening night." This may induces general panic — but also prudence. The longer you delay investing for retirement, the costlier it will be. For instance, put away $50 a month beginning at age 25 and you'll have over $75,000 by age 65 (assuming an average 5% after-tax annual return). But wait till age 55 to start salting away that same $50 a month, and by age 65 your nest egg will amount to less than $8,000.

3. Be practical and realistic in setting goals. Decide what's most important and attainable — then stick to it. Scattering your efforts will more than likely cause you to fall short of all your goals. And don't forget to weigh non-financial values in envisioning the retirement lifestyle you want.

4. Try to strike a sensible balance between safety and growth in your investment plan. Naturally, this is easier said than done. Most people want both — safety for their savings, along with the kind of big returns that usually entail some kind of risk. Here's a rule of thumb to help strike that balance: The younger you are, the more risk you should accept. If retirement is distant, you can invest in growth stocks, knowing you can always recover. If you have only 5 years before clocking out, your investments should be more conservative. And, naturally, if retirement is upon you, your portfolio should be targeted for security and income.

5. Pick a target retirement date sooner than your actual retirement date. If you employ this bit of self-trickery — and plan accordingly — you will automatically boost your retirement savings contributions. Then, if circumstances force you to retire early, you'll be prepared. If not, you'll have the pleasurable option to do so.

Worksheet for those on the glide path to retirement: People in the last decade of their working life — ages 55 through 64 — are generally in a position to have a much clearer idea of the kind of retirement they want. If you fall into this age category, the worksheet and table below will help you figure out if you'll be able to leverage the kind of lifestyle you're hankering after — by determining how much of your savings you can afford to spend in retirement each month. (The table assumes you will live to age 92, leave nothing to heirs, that your investments will grow by 7% annually and that inflation will average 4.5% annually.)

1. Estimate your annual Social Security benefit

at retirement age (call 1-800-772-1213 for a projection) ______

2. Your expected annual company pension income (consult your employee-benefits counselor for an estimate) ______

3. Total value of your savings and investments, including any lump-sum distributions, at retirement ______

4. Line 3 times the appropriate factor in the table below ______

5. Projected annual retirement income (Line 1, plus Lines 2 and 4) ______

6. Amount you can spend each month in retirement (Line 5, divided by 12) ______

CALCULATING YOUR RETIREMENT INCOME

Retirement Age:	Factor:	Retirement Age:	Factor:
55	0.0401	56	0.0408
57	0.0415	58	0.0423
59	0.0431	60	0.0440
61	0.0450	62	0.0460
63	0.0471	64	0.0483
65	0.0495	66	0.0509
67	0.0524	68	0.0540
69	0.0557	70	0.0576

AVOIDING THE 5 BIG RETIREMENT PLANNING MISTAKES

Most people hurt their chances of retiring with the kind of life they want because of simple mistakes. Here are 5 of the most common:

1. Failure to get an estimate of Social Security benefits in advance. Doing this should go without saying, but too many people wait till the last minute. If there are mistakes in your account (as there certainly can be), you need to know

about it early so you can correct them. And if the amount will be less than you assumed, you need to know that, too, so you can plan to supplement it. Besides contacting your Social Security office and asking them to compute your expected benefit, you should also check out various options. What are the consequences of drawing your benefits early? Or late? Find out as well if your company will reduce its contribution toward your pensions by the amount of any Social Security you receive.

2. Misunderstanding your company's retirement plan. The kind of pension mentioned above is called an "integrated" plan, under which the designated pension amount includes Social Security. However, there are many other questions you need answered from your employee-benefits department. For instance:

* What would you collect (and how much would you lose) if you left the company early? Left immediately?

* What is the vesting schedule?

* How are your benefits affected if you're fired? Laid off? Take an early retirement? Accept a buyout?

* Is it possible to estimate the fixed-dollar value of the pension you'll receive? Or, is the final benefit dependent on a profit-sharing plan under which the company's contribution to your pension can vary?

* Will your benefits be adjusted for inflation?

* How soon after retirement will payouts begin?

* Are any modifications to the company plan in the works?

3. Failure to look into your retirement rights as a spouse. A divorce or death of a partner may leave one spouse financially uninformed and unprotected. It's critical for both partners to know where all necessary documents are located. And both should know exactly what will happen to benefits in the event of divorce — and what survivorship options have been selected relative to any benefits. Note: Another important reason for advance planning in these matters is so that critical financial decisions do not have to be made under emotionally traumatic circumstances.

4. Failure to investigate your company life insurance. You may be able to convert your company term insurance into whole-life coverage without the necessity of taking a physical examination. If such a conversion benefit is available, you should consider it seriously. Remember, the older you get, the harder it may be to pass a physical required to qualify for insurance.

5. Failure to anticipate the cost of retirement health insurance. Some

companies provide retirement health benefits; some do not. If yours doesn't, you'd better figure in the cost of health insurance in your retirement investment program. Don't forget to look into nursing home insurance and Medigap coverage as well. These may not be the most pleasant topics to contemplate, but it's important to be familiar with such coverage. After all, none of us is growing any younger.

HOW TO RETIRE EARLIER THAN YOU THOUGHT POSSIBLE

There's no shortage of ways to finance a comfortable retirement — or even an early retirement. But, in order to access any of these creative solutions, you'll have to face one of the many hard truths of our financial era: You can no longer rely on the federal government or your employer to provide for your golden years. You'll have to do the job yourself. Gone are the days of generous company pension plans, escalating Social Security benefits and endlessly appreciating real estate — all the golden geese that provided retirement nest eggs for many of our parents' generation. Cutbacks in public and private retirement benefits are more and more prevalent and the housing boom of past decades is unlikely to resume. It's up to you to get busy now if you want some quality of leisure later. Here are 4 strategies for early retirement:

1. Take advantage of all company plans. One of the most effective and painless methods to amass the money for an early retirement is the 401(k) tax-deferred savings plan. If your employer offers it — and 40 percent of corporations with 100 or more employees do — sign up immediately. Typically, 401(k)s allow you to put away up to 6% of your pre-tax income in a variety of investments, from money-market accounts to stock funds. A monthly deposit of $500 in a 401(k) appreciating at 8% annually will, in 25 years, be worth $475,000. Most corporations also offer traditional pensions, which do not require employee contributions. Other employers provide retirement health care, and a few offer company stock-purchase or profit-sharing plans. Investigate all such company benefits — and make sure you know when you can retire with full benefits. Military and government jobs are often the most liberal. Then — and this is crucial — always contribute the maximum to your 401(k). Will a 401(k) be enough to provide for all your retirement needs? Not likely. Remember, inflation can eat away the purchasing power of any fixed pension. Since 401(k)s are generally fixed income investments, you will undoubtedly need supplementary savings. Thus, you should diversify in other areas, buying growth securities such as mutual funds.

2. Live on one spouse's income; save the other's. As obvious a strategy as this seems with around 33 million 2-income U.S. households at last count,

many couples may not have not taken a good hard look at it. In most cases it requires serious belt-tightening — cutting out luxuries, large and small, passing on big-ticket items, dining out, entertaining and expensive vacations. However, if the goal is important enough, the motivation will follow — exactly as many newlyweds scrimp and save for the down payment on their first house. The second paycheck can be funneled into a mix of growth investments and savings — mutual funds, a tax-deferred SEP (simplified employee pension), life insurance, etc. Note: If both incomes are absolutely needed to meet basic expenses, consider adding a third paycheck to salt away for your retirement. In other words, moonlight. The adage remains true: Where there's a will, there's a way.

3. Launch your own enterprise. What if you're self-employed, with no access to 401(k)s and other tax-deferred corporate largess? Despair not. With a Keogh account, you can put away as much as 20% of net income (up to $30,000 annually, if willing to commit to contributing the same percentage year after year), or up to 13% (if you wish to vary contributions). A SEP offers similar flexibility, also with a ceiling of 13% of net income. To consider starting your own business, take stock of the skills you employ on your present job. Many executives can use their expertise as a consultant. However, the best plan is usually to start a business in something you love that will allow you to continue working at least part time in retirement.

4. Invest in rental real estate. With the real estate boom no longer even an echo, you can't expect your home to provide you with retirement income. However, investments in rental housing can pay off handsomely down the road — and also give you a retirement home when you're ready for it. As with any kind of real estate, location is the critical factor in judging income property. Check out rental-vacancy rates in the areas you're scouting. Consider managing the property yourself for additional savings. And don't count on property appreciation to offset rental losses for empty houses or apartment units.

TURN $2,000 A YEAR INTO $314,870 FOR RETIREMENT

Perhaps understandably — but unfortunately — most young people (under 35) consider retirement impossibly remote. As a result, they postpone thinking about it for decades. The fact is, however, that starting to save early can be the best ticket to a comfortable retirement. For instance:

If you contribute $2,000 annually to an Individual Retirement Account earning 8% for the 10 years from ages 25 through 34 — without ever adding another penny — the magic of compounding will give you a retirement kitty of $314,870 at age 65. By contrast, if you wait until age 35 to start investing $2,000 annually — and keep it up for 30 years — you'll still have only $244,692. That's a difference of $70,178 — and it can make a big difference in your retirement lifestyle.

PLAYING CATCH-UP IF YOU'RE GETTING A LATE START

Ready for a cold shower? Most Americans retire shockingly cash poor. In fact, the median American family enters retirement with only around $11,000 in liquid assets — and with a retirement income of less than $17,000 a year. That's half what people in the 55- to 64-year-old age bracket make. Do diminishing living expenses in retirement compensate for this loss of income? Not really. Taxes, clothing and parking costs taper off, but health care, travel and entertainment costs generally increase. Consequently, many financial counselors advise people to strive to replace 100% of their working incomes in retirement. If you're among this sizable segment of the populace in their later working years, but financially ill-prepared for retirement, what can you do? Here are 3 possible catch-up strategies:

1. Consider dropping your life insurance policy. Many couples maintain life insurance policies with premiums that gobble up sizable chunks of their after-tax incomes. To free up that income for other — and better — investments, some financial planners advise buying only sufficient term insurance to replace a lost wage earner's income — taking into account reduced taxes and living costs after death. With lower-cost insurance in effect, you may be able to drop the previous policy (though it means accepting the loss of all those premiums paid over the years) and add its cash value to your savings.

2. Invest in a tax-deferred savings plans. One of the best ways to start building retirement savings is to contribute the maximum allowable amount to any tax-deferred savings plan offered by your employer. This is especially effective for people who lack savings habits, since the money is deducted directly from your paycheck. The contributions could be invested in mutual funds, then, on retirement, rolled into a conservatively invested Individual Retirement Account.

3. Calculate your monthly tax savings from the tax-deferred savings plan and invest that amount each month in another retirement account. This is money you'd be giving to Uncle Sam anyway, so it shouldn't be factored into your budget. Why not compound your own retirement savings by putting it to work in some other type of investment that provides diversification from the investments employed by the tax-deferred plan?

To help you determine just how much catching up you need to do, here's a worksheet for calculating the amount you should put away annually for a comfortable retirement. (Assumptions: you'll need 80% of your current income; inflation will average 4.5% a year; your savings will grow by 7% annually after taxes; you'll live to age 92; you'll leave little or nothing to your heirs. Amounts are in current dollars.)

1. Income needed when you retire (80% of current income)

2. Estimated Social Security and pension benefits (call 1-800-722-1213 for Social Security projections; ask your employee-benefits counselor to estimate your pension in today's dollars) ______

3. Extra investment income needed (Line 1 minus Line 2) ______

4. Amount you must save before retirement (Line 3 times Factor A below) ______

5. Amount you have saved already, including IRAs, corporate savings plans and other investments ______

6. Projected value of those savings at the time you retire (Line 5 times Factor B) ______

7. How much retirement capital you still need to set aside (Line 4 minus Line 6) ______

8. Annual savings needed (line 7 times Factor C)

9. Annual employer contributions to savings plans ______

10. Total you must save each year (Line 8 minus Line 9) ______

Age when you plan to retire:	Factor A	Years to retirement:	Factor B	Factor C
55	25.0	5	1.13	0.191
57	24.1	7	1.18	0.133
59	23.2	9	1.24	0.101
61	22.2	11	1.30	0.081
63	21.2	13	1.36	0.066
65	20.2	15	1.43	0.056
67	19.1	20	1.60	0.040
69	18.0	25	1.81	0.030

DON'T COUNT ON THE NEXT REAL ESTATE BOOM

If you're a young professional, you shouldn't plan to retire on the appreciated value of your house or condominium. It may have worked for your parents, but the population boom that triggered the surge in housing prices since 1960 won't be repeated.

GOOD BOOKS & OTHER PLANNING AIDS

Even with the planning guides we've given here, there's lots more you should known and do with respect to planning for your own retirement. Several books that can help you in the process include:

* "Can You Afford to Retire?" published by the Life Insurance Marketing and Research Assn., P.O. Box 208, Hartford, CN 06141, or call 1-800-235-4672. The book discusses various sources of retirement income, with worksheets. Cost: $1.50.

* "A Single Person's Guide to Retirement Planning," published by American Association of Retired Persons, Fulfillment Dept. (AARP), 601 E Street N.W., Washington, DC 20049. The pamphlet provides information on investing, insurance and other concerns of those preparing for retirement. Free.

* "How to Stretch Your Retirement Dollar" is a videotape/workbook package put together by Information Video Inc., 2 Wisconsin Circle, Ste. 700, Chevy Chase, MD 20815, or call 1-800-852-1355. It provides an overview of a variety of retirement strategies, and also discusses post-retirement issues such as going back to work, medical costs, etc. Includes worksheets. Cost: $29.95.

Also available is a visually stimulating retirement planning kit for your IBM-PC or compatible computer. Offered by T. Rowe Price, the big mutual fund family, the user-friendly program does "what-if" scenarios based on your assumptions, then displays the results graphically within seconds. Change an assumption, and the program quickly recalculates the probable outcome. The kit costs $15 plus local sales taxes and can be ordered by sending a check to T. Rowe Price, P.O. Box 15098, Worcester, MA 01615, or with a credit card by calling 1-800-541-3022.

SHOULD YOU GET PROFESSIONAL HELP? QUESTIONS TO ASK

A lot of people feel overwhelmed by both the math and the emotional strain associated with comprehensive retirement planning, so they call on the services of a financial planner or other professional advisor. Our view is that you generally don't need one unless you already have lots of assets and are concerned primarily with preparing to pass on an estate. For most other people, the time spent researching financial planners might better be spent researching investments — and drafting your own financial plan. However, if you think you want some paid professional help, here are some guidelines on finding the right person:

1. Shop around. Consumer advocates counsel people to move slowly when considering a financial advisor. Interview several planners before selecting one. Ask friends and co-workers. Ask for introductory, no-cost meetings. Be wary of meaningless credentials.

2. Learn about the field. It's useful to understand exactly how financial advisors are paid. Some earn commissions on the investment products they recommend. Others charge customer fees, but do not take commissions. And, a final category — comprising the majority — take both fees and commissions. Naturally, advisors who earn the bulk of their income from commissions are confronted by an obvious temptation to recommend products that make them the most money. Unfortunately, many people who present themselves as planners are no more than salespeople out to generate maximum commissions. Fee-only planners usually charge a higher initial fee, but the Consumer Federation of America and American Association of Retired Persons recommend that consumers looking for planners seriously consider fee-only advisors because of the absence of conflicts of interests.

3. Use planners as a resource, but make the final decisions yourself. This should go without saying since it's your money and your retirement. However, all too many people take the advice of planners as gospel and get led down a path that goes somewhere they don't want to be.

If you do decide to employ the services of a professional financial advisor, here are 11 key questions to ask during your initial consultation (and before you pay any fees or commissions):

1. Will I work with you, an associate, or both?

2. What is your education and experience?

3. Do you take continuing education courses to keep up with the latest investment options and tax laws?

4. Are you a full-time planner, or do you practice incidental to other activities — such as insurance or mutual fund sales?

5. How are you paid? Will you divulge the commissions you make on individual products?

6. Have you retained 50% or more of the clients you had 3 years ago?

7. After my financial plan has been implemented, what follow-up services do you offer — and what will they cost?

8. Will you provide examples of plans you've done for other clients?

9. Would you work for me on a negotiated fee-only basis?

10. Are you a member of any professional planning associations?

11. Will you provide references to other clients who have financial circumstances similar to mine?

B. Social Security & Pension Plans

CHECKING OUT YOUR STATUS WITH SOCIAL SECURITY

It's a truism that bureaucracies bungle. Why, then, should the Social Security Administration be any different? In fact, the SSA makes frequent mistakes in crediting contributions. Indeed, mistakes have occurred so frequently that, although the general time limit for correcting errors in credited earnings is 3 years, 3 months and 15 days, Congress has waived this for earnings between 1978 and 1984. To compound matters, most people never bother to check the accuracy of the large sums they've been depositing into their Social Security account — until retirement is upon them. To avoid any last-minute surprises, simply request, by phone or letter, a "Request for Earnings and Benefit Estimate Statement." It's easy to fill out and free (except for the postage stamp to return it). After mailing it back, you should receive your statement in 6 weeks or less. Then, if you spot anything that doesn't seem right, you can enlist the help of your employer or an accountant in getting it corrected. To request your form (Form SSA-7004), just call the SSA at 1-800-772-1213.

6 SECRETS TO GETTING THE MOST FROM SOCIAL SECURITY

Most people think the level of Social Security benefits they'll get is based solely on their contributions and that there's nothing they can do to improve the situation.

However, that's not the case. Here are 6 things you can do maximize your benefits under Social Security:

1. Time the start of benefits to maximize overall return. Traditionally, the

standard age to begin Social Security retirement benefits is age 65. Starting in the year 2003, that will increase by stages to 67. However, you have the option to receive benefits at a reduced rate as early as age 62 (60 for widows and widowers), or to go for higher monthly payments by delaying the start of benefits as late as age 70. Health is another factor in timing the start of benefits. If your health is not good or longevity does not run in your family, you may consider electing to start receiving Social Security benefits as soon as you are eligible.

2. Beware of earning too much in retirement. Deciding on when to take retirement benefits is often determined by how much you can earn by working after retirement — in a hobby, say, or part-time job or as a consultant. Additional earnings, of course, bring additional taxation. However, under Social Security, in extreme cases, you may keep less than one-third of additional earned income. For example, benefits paid to people under age 65 are reduced by $1 for each $2 earned over $7,440. For those aged 65 to 69, $1 in benefits is lost for each $3 earned exceeding $10,200. Only at age 70 and above are full benefits paid regardless of other income. If you exceed a second threshold — $32,000 for married people filing joint returns — a portion of benefits is subject to income tax. And, naturally, you must pay Social Security tax on your wages. This may be enough to make people think twice about working.

3. Calculate whether some of your benefits will become taxable. First, determine your Adjusted Gross Income (taxable income from pensions, interest and dividends minus payments for such items as alimony). To that figure, add any income from tax-exempt municipal bonds and foreign securities. If the total exceeds $32,000 for couples ($25,000 for singles), part of your Social Security benefits will be taxable. (The AARP offers a free booklet, "Are My Social Security Benefits Taxable?" Write: AARP, Fulfillment Dept., 601 E St. N.W., Washington, DC 20049.)

4. Register for Medicare before age 65. Even though you may not plan to use the health-care coverage right away, you may face a higher premium if you fail to register by the deadline.

5. Beware of "early" retirement. Regular retirement for Social Security purposes is either at age 65 or 67, depending on the recipient's year of birth. Those who retire before that age will get reduced benefits. Those who retire after will get increased monthly benefits. However, early retirement can reduce benefits in another way. Later years' earnings tend to weigh heavily in the calculation of your "primary insurance amount" — partly because a comparatively higher amount of wages were subject to Social Security taxes. So, before accepting early retirement, you should...

6. Call or write to the Social Security Administration to get a free estimate of your earnings and benefits. Don't wait for age 65 to check your benefits and then perhaps discover a mistake. Trying to prove contributions years after the fact can be a nightmarish task — and may cause you to forfeit some of your rightful

benefits. To avoid this, simply call the SSA's toll-free number, 1-800-772-1213 and ask for your free "Request for Earnings and Benefits Estimate Statement." (Note: a copy of this form, along with the mailing address, is reprinted here).

BEWARE THESE SOCIAL SECURITY TAX TRAPS

Here are some common mistakes many people make with respect to their Social Security benefits and potential taxation of those benefits:

1. Failure to check your Social Security records regularly. We keep harping on this, but there's a very good reason. The General Accounting Office has estimated that at least some earnings of nearly 10 millions workers may not have been credited to their Social Security accounts because of employee or government errors. Such errors, if undetected and uncorrected, can result in a partial loss or even denial of retirement benefits. To check your on the status of your account, simply call 1-800-772-1213 and ask for Form 7004 — or use the copy of the form reprinted here. Fill it out, mail it in, and the Social Security Administration will send you a Personal Earnings and Benefit Estimate Statement.

2. Failure to realize that tax-exempt income doesn't save you from being taxed on your benefits. If your retirement income exceeds a certain amount ($32,000 for couples, $25,000 for singles), and much of it is derived from tax-free municipal bonds, up to half of your Social Security benefits may be subjected to income tax.

3. Failure to recognize potential benefit cuts for ex-government workers who join the Social Security system. To prevent public-sector workers already eligible for government pensions from reaping double benefits after joining the private sector, Congress passed special legislation. It decreed a benefit cut unless former government workers join companies that have participated in the Social Security system for at least 21 years. These cuts can reach 40%.

4. Failure to plan for benefit erosion caused by inflation. People who retire today at age 62 must prepare for another 20 to 25 years of life. And, with increased longevity comes the necessity of coping with the likelihood of inflation — and the political unlikelihood that Social Security benefits will keep pace with the rising cost of living. So, it's more than ever essential that anyone planning for retirement supplement his or her pension and Social Security with other investments.

5. Failure to recognize the costs of early retirement. Thinking about joining the increasing ranks of people who retire at 62 instead of waiting until age 65? If so, you owe it to yourself to run some simple numbers before making your final

decision. For instance, for every month you retire before your 65th birthday, your Social Security benefits will be reduced by 5/9ths of 1%. For someone who retires at age 62, that adds up to a hefty 20% cut in benefits.

5 EXEMPTIONS FROM SOCIAL SECURITY WITHHOLDING

Having repeatedly told you the importance of checking to make sure all appropriate earnings are credited to your Social Security account, we should also note that there are several types of income that are not subject to Social Security taxes — and therefore won't be reflected in your summary of earnings. These include:

1. Health-insurance payments to employee accident, health or medical-reimbursement plans.

2. Educational benefits contributing to an employee's job skills.

3. Wages paid to your child under 18 — but only if your business isn't incorporated.

4. Loans taken out from the company by an employee or shareholder. However, if the IRS decides the loan is not legitimate and won't be paid back, tax will be levied.

5. Reimbursements for job-related moving expenses — when the move is more than 35 miles, and the employee remains at the new job location at least 39 weeks the following year.

FINDING OUT IF YOUR PENSION MONEY IS SAFE

Whether your pension is with a privately or publicly held company, you'll want to insure yourself of its safety. Here's how you can check:

1. Public companies — Basic information is available in the company's annual report. You may have to look in the footnotes, though, to find the size of its unfunded pension liability and of its past service liability. More detailed information can be found in the financial section of the firm's 10K report, which is filed with the Securities and Exchange Commission.

2. Private companies — Every participant of a qualified plan (i.e., one approved by the IRS) has the right to obtain information about his or her pension from the trustees of the plan. Unfortunately, this information may be gobbledegook to you. If so, enlist the help of a pension expert or accountant.

Here are some things to watch out for in examining the health of either public or private company pension plans:

1. A poor investment record. Compare market value of assets in the pension with book value. If book value is more than market value, the trustees have been investing unwisely. If such assets had to be sold today, there would be a loss.

2. Overstatement of funding assumptions. If the firm is funding pension plans over, say, 40 years, find out why. Ten to 20 years is a more practical figure. Actuarial assumptions made on a 40-year basis may not hold up. You should also beware of high projected returns. For example, if a company assumes a rate of return of 10% or more on its investments, it's unlikely it will be able to meet such an inflated expectation over the long haul. Also look to see if they are underestimating salary and wage scales. A solid plan will make provisions for an increase in employee compensation over the years.

When checking on your pension plan, you should also check on the vesting period. Don't assume you are fully vested for a maximum pension after only a few years. Companies can't afford to vest people fully with short service.

What if your company's finances are shaky? Trustees of pension plans have a fiduciary obligation to vested employees, and that includes protecting fund assets from creditors in a company bankruptcy proceeding. In fact, under some bankruptcy circumstances, the pension plan can be the first creditor in line to seize corporate assets. Also, in cases of gross mismanagement of pension funds, stockholders of a closely held company can be held liable.

BUILD A BETTER PENSION BY ADDING YOUR OWN MONEY

You can make your company pension grow much faster by adding your own money to that contributed by your employer. Here are 3 reasons why you should consider making voluntary payments (up to 10% of your salary) to your company's pension plan:

1. The interest your voluntary contribution accumulates is tax free — though it isn't deductible.

2. You won't have to pay taxes on the earned interest until you withdraw it at retirement.

3. When you do make a withdrawal, that part attributable to your voluntary contributions is tax free. (The exact percentage is calculated by a complex formula.)

THE MERITS OF SELF-DIRECTED PENSION ACCOUNTS

Very few Americans these days can hope to adequately fund their retirements exclusively out of Social Security and their employee pensions. In fact, more and more companies are either scrapping or drastically downsizing their employee retirement plans — forcing workers to begin managing their own pension plans. This is no cause for panic, however. For starters, if your employer puts your pension pursestrings into your hands, you'll likely have 90 days or more to phase out of your old

plan and into a new one — and the transition may even be longer. Secondly, there are actual advantages to taking these critical financial matters into your own hands. For instance, old-style company plans were often overly conservative and inflexible, penalizing or disallowing employees who frequently changed jobs. And, when firms went belly up, so did many uninsured pensions. Many such traditional pension plans were also vulnerable to corporate buyouts. By taking the retirement reins into your own hands — via a 401(k), say, or an IRA rollover — you not only create a portable pension that goes where you go, but you can choose higher-yielding investments. Yes, there are also drawbacks, the principal one being that many workers fail to contribute to a self-directed and voluntary plan. Others do invest, but far too conservatively for proper growth. They put all their retirement money in fixed-income investments such as CDs, money-market funds or government bonds. This sacrifices the growth potential offered by quality stocks or mutual funds.

Here are some other considerations with respect to managing your own pension funds:

1. Though self-directed pensions generally allow more frequent switching of investment options, it's better to devise a long-term strategy and stick with it.

2. While you don't want to be overly conservative, you also don't want to gamble with your retirement money. Look for high-yielding instruments or equities with potential for both growth and future dividends.

3. Don't overtrade your self-directed retirement account. Dollars in an IRA, Keogh or 401(k) are worth far more to you than regular dollars since earnings are tax deferred.

4. Another reason to minimize risk: You get no tax deduction from the government if you lose money in a retirement account.

5. A custodial, tax-deductible fee ($30 a year or so) is usually charged for self-directed retirement plans. Be sure to pay this fee separately, with after-tax dollars, rather than having it deducted from the tax-free dollars in your account, diminishing their earning power.

401(k) PLANS — THE BEST RETIREMENT OPTION AROUND

Without question, there is no better vehicle for building an adequate retirement account than a 401(k) account. These plans, created in 1978, allow the most generous contributions, give you immediate tax breaks for making those contributions, provide the best tax-deferred growth and, in many cases, a portion of your funds are even matched by employer contributions. Here's a brief description of how 401(k) plans work:

* An employer sets up a qualified profit-sharing plan or conforms its present plan to the tax law's 401(k) requirements.

* The plan allows employees to defer taking a portion of their salary — up to 25%, though most employers impose lower limits, usually between 11% and 15%. The deferred salary is put directly into the plan by the company, with an annual limit of $8,728 (for 1992), adjusted each year for inflation. (Other restrictions, based on the number of employees who participate in a plan and the overall salaries of all employees in the plan, may impact the limits, so check with your company for the exact maximums.)

* The employee is not taxed on this contribution. Income accumulated in the plan is tax-deferred, meaning you pay no taxes until you begin withdrawing the funds.

* In more than 85% of the plans available in 1992, the employer also made contributions to the plan, typically putting in 50 cents for every $1 deposited by the employee up to a maximum of 6% or 7% of the employee's salary. This money also compounds on a tax-deferred basis.

* Funds are invested by the company's plan administrator, usually in GICs

(fixed-income notes sold by insurance companies), money-market funds, growth stocks, the company's own stock or some combination of the above. Most plans give the employee the option to choose the type of investment he or she wants — and to switch between types once or twice per year.

* Distributions once you retire may qualify for 5-year-forward income-tax averaging, which can result in substantial savings.

The typical 401(k) plan, with its generous contribution limits and employer matching, offers retirement-minded employees much bigger tax benefits than Individual Retirement Accounts — and also provides for much faster growth. For example, a 401(k) contribution that earns 9% a year will return an almost unbelievable 63.5% per annum after tax benefits and a 50% company match are factored in. Thus, you should always participate in a 401(k) plan if one is available (though an estimated 30% of eligible American employees did not in 1992) — and you should do whatever it takes to make the maximum contribution allowed, even if you have to borrow occasionally to meet other needs. Here's another example of the power of a 401(k):

Assume you are 25 and make $25,000 a year. If you start a regular savings plan, putting away 6% of your annual salary each year and increasing your contribution each year as you get raises (assuming 4% annual salary increases), your investment will grow to just $472,778 at age 65 (assuming a 9% annual return and payment of all capital gains or income taxes along the way). But, if you put the exact same amount in a 401(k) plan earning the same return, the tax-deferral benefits will allow your nest egg to grow to $877,296 by age 65. And, if your employer matches 50% of your contribution, you'll wind up with a whopping $1,315,944 are retirement — or even more of the investments do better than a 9% annual return. Now do you see why maximum participation in your 401(k) account is so important?

Note: Even though a 401(k) is a powerful retirement savings tool, it shouldn't be your only investment. And, the investments you make outside the 401(k) should be diversified into areas not featured in the plan options. This gives you added protection against losses, and also increases the odds that you'll earn a higher long-term annual average return than might be possible with the plan's fairly conservative investment options.

Warning: Even if your 401(k) plan allows you to make early withdrawals for hardship circumstances, you should not take advantage of this option. If you do, you will have to pay a 10% penalty, plus income taxes on the money withdrawn. A far better alternative, if you plan permits it, is to borrow against your plan's assets.

KEOGHS KEEP SELF-EMPLOYED ON TRACK TO RETIREMENT

If you are self-employed, a Keogh plan offers all the same benefits as a 401(k) plan — except, of course, there is no employer match. However, that is offset somewhat by the fact that you can generally make larger tax-deferred contributions — up to 20% of gross income or $30,000, whichever is less. In addition, you are eligible whether your business is a sole proprietorship, partnership or corporation. There are 3 basic types of Keogh plans from which you can choose:

1. The defined-benefit type is designed to provide a specific level of income for you at retirement. Because it allows larger tax-deductible contributions in order to achieve the defined goals, it can grow much faster and produce a larger retirement fund. Because it generally covers a shorter time span, it's also less affected by inflation and less dependent on superior investment performance. This type of plan is preferable for those with 20 years or less remaining until retirement.

2. The money-purchase type is based on allowable contributions rather than

on desired benefits. Contributions are smaller and more manageable,

making this a good option if you can start your Keogh relatively early in life or have confidence in your ability to earn top investment returns.

3. Profit-sharing plans are like the money-purchase plans except contribution amounts are linked to the performance of the business. As such, tax benefits may be somewhat lower, though administration is generally simpler.

Warning: The law that created Keogh plans also mandated that the person setting up the plan make it available to eligible employees under the same terms. As a result, if you have employees that you must include in your plan, you may have to pick one that's less than optimum for you personally.

5 LITTLE-KNOWN SNAGS FOR IRA INVESTORS

Everyone knows April 15 is tax day, but it's also the deadline for making Individual Retirement Account contributions — which you should definitely do if you are eligible for tax-deferral benefits (and, perhaps, even if you aren't since even after-tax contributions will compound tax-free inside an IRA). However, here are 5 things you should know about IRAs before investing:

1. The law requires contributions in cash or check only. There are no deductions for stock transfers from an investment account into an IRA.

2. Stay within the contribution limits. If you exceed them, you could be slapped with a non-deductible excise tax (6% of the excess amount).

3. Beware of management fees, set-up charges and early withdrawal penalties (over and above the tax-law penalties).

4. Don't invest your IRA money in municipal bonds or a municipal investment trust. Two reasons: Income earned in an IRA is tax free until withdrawn, so tax-free interest on municipal bonds is of no value to an IRA. And, in any case, such bonds typically yield less than taxable bonds.

5. Don't invest your IRA in federal Individual Retirement Bonds. You can't redeem just a part of the bond, but must withdraw the entire Individual Retirement Bond in one piece.

C. When Retirement Time Arrives

HOW LONG YOUR RETIREMENT MONEY WILL LAST

This following table illustrates how long your money will last if you want to spend more than your retirement income. For example, if you withdraw 10% of the original capital each year and your savings earn an average of 7%, your money will last 17 years. If you need your savings to last 20 years and expect the money to grow an average of 8%, you could withdraw about 10% of the original capital each year.

How Many Years Your Money Will Last

If Your And You Withdraw This %age of Your Original Capital a Year:

Money Earns:	6%	7%	8%	9%	10%	11%	12%	13%	14%	15%	16%
12%	—	—	—	—	—	—	—	22	17	14	12
11%	—	—	—	—	—	—	23	17	14	12	11
10%	—	—	—	—	—	25	18	15	13	11	10
9%	—	—	—	—	26	20	16	14	12	11	9
8%	—	—	—	28	20	16	14	12	11	9	9
7%	—	—	30	22	17	14	12	11	10	9	8
6%	33	23	18	15	13	11	10	9	8	8	
5%	36	25	20	16	14	12	11	9	9	8	7

BEST IRA WITHDRAWAL STRATEGIES

The flip side of all IRA investment strategies is when — and in what amounts — to take your money out. Annual withdrawals are mandatory starting the year you reach age 70-1/2 — with a grace period on the first one until April 1 of the following year. After the first year, withdrawals are due by Dec. 31. Warning: Delaying your first mandatory

withdrawal until April 1 means you'll make 2 years' worth of withdrawals during the second year — which could push you into a higher tax bracket or expose more of your Social Security benefits. If you miss that deadline, Uncle Sam will relieve you of 50% of the amount you should have taken out — a penalty over and above the tax due on the money normally subject to taxation.

How Much Should You Take? The minimum withdrawal is based on your life expectancy. However, if you've named a beneficiary for your IRA, you should calculate your withdrawals on the basis of the joint life expectancy of yourself and that designated person. Here's the basic formula: Divide your IRA balance at the end of the previous year by the appropriate life-expectancy figure. For instance, let's say that a 70-year-old has a life expectancy of 16 years. So, the first required payout would be one-sixteenth, or 6.25% of the account balance. Subsequently, you may simply reduce the original life expectancy number by one each year — taking one-fifteenth the second year, one-fourteenth the third and so on — or you can completely recalculate your life expectancy each year. Once you pick a method, however, you must stick to it. The second method — recalculating life expectancy — will reduce the minimum withdrawals because the longer you live, the longer actuaries expect you to live. For instance, a 70-year-old is expected to live for 16 years, but a 71-year-old has a life expectancy of 15.3 years. The minimum payouts will also be reduced if you use the joint life expectancy tables for yourself and a beneficiary. A 70-year-old whose beneficiary is 65 might stretch IRA payouts over 23 years. For a table of life expectancies, call 1-800-829-3676 and request IRS publications 590 and 939. If you don't want to bother, the custodian of your IRA will probably notify you when it's time to start withdrawals and help you figure the minimum required.

What If You Have Multiple IRAs? You can withdraw from any or all of your IRAs, but the total taken out must match or exceed the required minimum. If you do have multiple IRAs, you must figure out the minimum distribution for each. This can be complicated if the accounts have beneficiaries of different ages. Once you figure out the total, you can withdraw that amount from one or more accounts, ideally from the ones with the lowest return.

SPOUSAL RIGHTS IN RETIREMENT

Even though you can figure your withdrawal schedule based on your life expectancy and that of your spouse, you do not have to have your spouse's approval to retire early and take your pension benefits. However, if the spouse is beneficiary, he or she must be consulted on how best to take retirement benefit payments.

AVOID PENALTIES ON POST-RETIREMENT EARNINGS

People who plan to work even part-time after retirement need to be aware of the potential penalties — and the ways to get around them:

* You lose a dollar in Social Security benefits for every $3 earned above $10,200 per year (for 1992) if you're over 65, but under 70. If you're under 65, you lose a dollar in benefits for every $2 earned above $7,440 per year. Add up

payroll deductions, related expenses and commuting costs to see if part-time work is really worth it. (Note: these figures change every year, so contact your local Social Security Administration.)

* You may not be able to collect your pension if you continue working part-time for the same company. However, if the company agrees, you may be able to quit as an employee and be rehired as a self-employed consultant.

* If you work past age 65, you may not be earning any more company pension credits — while losing Social Security and pension benefits.

Alternative: Instead of working part time, consider starting your own business — or converting a hobby you enjoy into a business.

5 WAYS RETIREES CAN EASE FINANCIAL WORRIES

Unfortunately, retirement doesn't mean an end to money management, or financial worries — especially with respect to pensions, taxes, health care and estate planning. Here are a few ideas for easing some of the typical retirement concerns that may arise:

1. Largesse to grandchildren — Instead of selling securities and other assets for cash gifts to your descendants, give the kids the securities and let them sell them. If the recipient is in a lower tax bracket than you, he or she will pay less tax on the gain than you would.

2. Rent a condo from your kids — If children buy a parent's retirement condo, then rent it back to the parent, they'll get tax deductions for mortgage interest and property taxes. And, if the kids charge a fair market rent, they can also take depreciation deductions on the condo.

3. Advance planning for nursing home care — Before the U.S. government will pay nursing home bills, the person has to have depleted the assets in his or her name. This can be done by putting the money in a trust that pays income but doesn't allow the person to touch the principal. Drawback: Check state laws — most won't accept a trust set up within 2 years of person's entering a nursing home.

4. Early tapping of Social Security can pay off — Reduced benefits usually add up to more in the long run. For instance, if full benefits are $750 per month for retiring at age 65, you get reduced monthly benefits of $600 by retiring at 62. You'd have to collect full benefits for 12 years to make up the $21,600 you'd receive during the 3 years of early payments.

5. IRA distributions — You have to start withdrawing money from your Individual Retirement Account by April 1 following the year you reach age 70-

1/2. Loophole: Check with the IRA trustee to see if a slower distribution schedule can be used for your payouts.

MENTAL STRESS CAN BE A CONCERN, TOO

The retirement years are supposed to bring an easing of all manner of stress. Too often, however, anxiety over living costs, health problems and other concerns can rob the retiree of this benefit of well-deserved tranquility. Here are a handful of ways to reduce retirement stress:

1. Lower living expenses — If your monthly cash outflow is a major source of anxiety, and the thought of moving doesn't trouble you, consider selling your house and moving to a lower-cost area. A little investigation will turn up many options, some quite close to home, and peace of mind may be the result. You can also make a game out of cutting other living costs — checking out flea markets, yard sales, factory outlets, seasonal specials for items you need and would otherwise have to pay retail for.

2. Meditate — Think of this as a mental and emotional relaxation break. For 10 minutes or so, just sit quietly, concentrating on your breathing, perhaps repeating a favorite proverb or prayer, or even a syllable. Let troubling thoughts drift away. Do this on a regular basis and you'll cultivate an inner calm — as well as mental energy — for dealing with daily problems.

3. Look after your body — Anxieties can affect your health and start a downward spiral. Make sure you sleep well, eat well and healthfully, and exercise regularly. A 5-minute stroll can be a better pick-me-up than a second cup of coffee.

4. Learn to focus — Scattering attention on different problems and projects brings mental and physical fatigue. The trick is to be more like artists and athletes. Shut out distractions and concentrate totally on the task at hand — even if it is mundane. When it is done, go on to the next thing.

5. Reflect on your life goals — A strong sense of inner direction — knowing what is of primary value to you and why — will help create daily energy and a sense of well-being.

RETIRE IN STYLE ON $18 A DAY

With snowbirds flocking south in vast numbers in search of sunnier retirement climes, are there any out-of-the-way, bargain havens left to be found? Yes, says publisher Ross Paron. Details are to be found in the latest edition of "Paradise Found: How to Live in North America's Best Climate for Under $500 a

Month." Paron offers a few provocative hints. His favorite hideaway is a 60-mile-long lake in the mountains of Mexico, offering low prices, clean air, good medical services and U.S.-style shopping. According to Paron, the place is ideal for Americans on Social Security and small pensions. To order a copy of the book, send $12.95, plus $3 postage and handling, to: United Research Publishers, 249 S. Highway 101, Solana Beach, CA 92075. If not satisfied, return the book within 30 days for a full refund.

RETIRING ABROAD? BEWARE THE TAX CONSEQUENCES

An increasing number of Americans are retiring abroad, especially to countries where the dollar remains strong and living costs remain low. However, before you join the exodus, here are some things you should consider:

* An American abroad remains subject to U.S. income tax, though you do get U.S. tax credits for taxes paid to a foreign government. You should also check out the foreign country's tax policies — some tax U.S. Social Security income for American retirees living within their borders.

* Even renouncing citizenship doesn't necessarily exempt an individual from U.S. taxes. Dividends and other passive income are still taxed at their source. And, if the IRS can prove that citizenship has been renounced within the last 10 years mainly in order to escape income taxes, the individual will be taxed as a U.S. citizen.

* To qualify as a foreign resident for U.S. income tax, you must live abroad for a full calendar year, or be outside the United States for 12 of 13 consecutive months. This will also exempt you from state and local taxes in the United States.

* Americans who earn income while legally residing abroad qualify for a U.S. tax exemption on the first $70,000 of earned income, plus a living allowance exclusion. That can be a real bonanza if the foreign country doesn't impose an income tax.

* Retirees may elect to keep a U.S. home as a place to stay stateside, or as a rental investment that can be depreciated to tax advantage while they live abroad. If used as a permanent abode fewer than 183 days a year, it won't be considered as a principal place of residence for tax purposes.

* A foreign home can qualify for the 1-time tax-free gain of $125,000 on the sale of a principal residence — if it has been used as a principal residence 3 out of the last 5 years.

* After selling a principal residence, a person moving abroad has 4 years (instead of 2 as in the U.S.) to buy a home of equivalent value and qualify for tax deferral on the gain.

* Rules on currency restrictions and capital gains vary from country to country. However, as a generalization, it's easier to invest abroad than to bring money back after a sale. This may be a reason to rent rather than buy a home in another country.

NOTES

CHAPTER 13

SCANDALOUS SCAMS

A. Protection Against Frauds & Phonies

9 WAYS TO AVOID GETTING RIPPED OFF

Most rip-off artists take advantage of a mark's inherent greed, grabbing the money and running. However, many also profit because of their victims' carelessness, ignorance or fear of trying to fight the system. The latter group is most dangerous, because they may not really be doing anything illegal — merely providing poor value or low quality for the money, and banking on the fact most people won't do anything about it. However, there are things you can do to both protect yourself from such people — and get satisfaction if you do get a bad deal on a purchase:

1. Shop wisely. Deal only with established, reputable businesses. Know what things are worth, and be suspicious of products or services that seem to be too much of a bargain. If you're dealing with a mechanic, contractor or other type of workman, your best protection is a recommendation from someone who has used the person and been satisfied. (The same applies to doctors, lawyers, accountants and other professionals.)

2. Buy with a credit card. If you're dealing with a store for the first time — or if you're buying by mail — your best protection is to use a credit card. That way,

if you have a problem with the product or service, you can legally refuse to pay the bill when the merchant won't give you satisfaction. The credit-card company will then credit your account for the amount in question, and check on the matter with the merchant. If your complaint proves valid, the credit will stand. Note: To fully protect yourself in these cases, you must explain your problem in writing to the credit-card issuer. Simply calling do the job.

3. Use the right return method. Faulty small appliances and electronics equipment, defective clothing items, etc., should be returned to the store from which they were purchased — preferably to the person who made the sale or the supervisor of the appropriate department. Problems with large items or in-home services should be reported first by phone and then by mail, with supportive evidence as photographs if possible.

4. Don't get angry. Regardless of how frustrated or upset you are — and how justified those feelings may be — don't let your anger show. Wait until you can discuss the problem calmly and rationally before you return to the store or sit down to make a call or write a letter. Ranting, raving, yelling or idle threats won't help your cause — and may damage your credibility.

5. Complain to the right person. As we've already noted, the best place to start is with the same person who sold you the product or service. Tell the person your name and ask his or hers. Then state your problem in general terms and ask for a resolution. If that person doesn't have the authority to resolve your problem, ask who does. If the person claims not to know, move on to his or her supervisor or ask to be referred to customer service. If you are dealing with a large company, this latter step may be a waste of time. In many big companies, the customer service division is merely a bureaucracy of mid-level managers whose job it is to defuse complaints rather than help the consumer. If you encounter an uncooperative person at this level, don't waste your time. Instead, get the name and/or phone number of the supervisor and immediately go to that person. And don't stop there — if necessary go all the way to the company president or chief executive officer.

6. Be specific about your problem. Explain the trouble with the product or service in precise terms. Speak slowly and clearly, whether in person or on the phone, and try to set up a congenial resolution to the problem.

7. Support your claims with good records. When you make your complaint, be sure to take along your receipt and credit-card slip, a copy of the ad you responded to if appropriate, the warranty and serial number of the defective product and any other information (such as records of service calls) about the product or problem. (Note: If you're writing, be sure to send copies, not originals.) As you progress through the complaint process, maintain a file of all information — including a record of dates and times of store visits, telephone calls and letters sent and received. Include the names and titles of all people you've spoken to at the company, as well as notes regarding the conversations.

Companies perceive complainers who are organized as credible and determined to win, and are thus more likely to resolve their problems.

8. Suggest solutions. Don't just complain aimlessly. Know what you want before you make your first contact, whether it's repair of the product, a full replacement, a store credit or a repeat of work done. You may also want to ask for a discount on future purchases or services as compensation for the problems you've encountered. However, be realistic — don't ask for something to which you're not really entitled.

9. Get someone on your side. If you have no luck complaining on your own, don't give up — get reinforcements. Sometimes merely telling a merchant you plan to take your complaint to a consumer agency or regulatory body will produce satisfaction. Other times, you may have to actually seek help from one or more of these varied sources:

* The Better Business Bureau (BBB) can not only help you resolve complaints but also lets you check up on stores before doing business with them. * The Consumer Affairs Office in many states will help you deal with retail and other consumer problems.

* The Department of Motor Vehicles (DMV) will hear complaints against car dealers and repair shops, and may revoke business licenses in some states.

* The Public Utilities Commission (PUC) can help with problems involving the phone company (including "900" number services), the gas company, the electric company and, in some areas, cable TV provides. Many cities and counties also have utility boards or commissions to hear complaints.

* The State Insurance Commission in most states licenses insurance companies and can help with problems in that area.

* Newspapers and TV stations in many cities have consumer reporters who will investigate your charges and do stories on rip-off artists. You'll find that, even though these advocates carry no legal weight, their ability to threaten public exposure of grievances can quickly lead to settlements.

* Your state Attorney General's office is the ultimate arbiter of consumer disputes. They can file both civil and criminal cases against merchants who abuse your rights under state consumer laws.

THE TOP 5 RECESSION RIP-OFFS, AND HOW TO AVOID THEM

Rip-off artists and con men are around every day, but when times are hard — such as during the current economic slowdown — they seem to multiply. Here are the leading recession-born rip-offs, and some tips on how to avoid them:

1. Phony loan scams. Most ads promising to get you credit or loans even though you're out of work and in debt are total cons. Respond to one of them and you'll get an application form to fill out, which you will have to send in with a processing fee of $199, $299 or some other such figure. However, if you actually send in the money, you'll never hear from them again. Be particularly wary if they ask you to return the forms and deposit via Federal Express or other overnight or 2-day delivery service, especially if they want amoney order rather than a check. This is usually a dodge to avoid the penalties for mail fraud. The easiest way to protect yourself is to remember that there are no magic solutions to your money problems. You can certainly ease them through legitimate means, but no one but you can make them go away — and if you pay money to someone who says they can, you're just getting yourself deeper in the hole.

2. Phony employment offers. These operate just like the loan scams. Con artists run ads promising you the inside track on high-paying jobs — if you will send them a fee of $100 to $250. However, if you do, you'll either get nothing back — or, at best, you'll receive a list of jobs copied from the newspaper Classifieds. The best protection is to ignore these ads altogether. Legitimate employment agencies almost always wait until after you get a job to collect their fees.

3. Home-loan rip-offs. This is a particularly insidious scam because it can actually cost you your home. It usually works like this. The con artists will approach an out-of-work homeowner with a paid-up mortgage. They promise to get the victim a loan of up to $25,000 with reasonable interest rates by taking a lien against the house. However, before approving the loan, they ask to see all papers relating to the property, including the deed. Then they switch documents during the signing of the loan forms and have the owner unknowingly sign over the house to them. The victim gets the loan, but after it's paid off and he goes to get the lien removed, he finds someone else now owns his house. Texas officials recently put away scammers who had stolen more than 200 homes this way, but many of the victims never got their homes back. The key to protecting yourself here is ignore anyone who knocks on your door or calls you on the phone and offers you a loan. Legitimate lenders don't work that way — you have to go to them and ask for money.

4. Auto scams. This is a combination of schemes No. 1 and 3. The operators run ads promising to get you out from under your debt load and save your credit rating when you are out of a job and can't keep up your car payments. All you have to do is pay $200 and sign over your car to them. They say you might as well since the holder of the car loan will repossess it anyway. So, you agree — but, soon after paying the fee and giving them the car, you learn the title to the car was never transferred. Thus, you're out both $200 and the car — and you still have to repay the auto loan. Once again, the best protection is to simply ignore ads that promise magical solutions to your money problems. If you're having trouble making your car payments, talk to your lender; it's possible some

form of alternate payment plan can be worked out.

5. Phony sales. Store sales that aren't really sales are always a problem — but they become more common in a recession. Retailers advertise big savings, but when you get to the store you find the price is only a dollar or so lower than it was before the sale — or the price was artificially inflated and then marked down again to the regular price. You can avoid getting burned by comparison shopping before you make any major purchase. Then you'll know what the fair price is — regardless of how big a discount the sale promoter claims you're getting.

BEWARE OF HOME-WORK SCHEMES

Most advertised work-at-home plans that promise high payments for addressing envelopes, assembling small consumer items or selling products to your neighbors are scams. The promoters either want you to pay them a "training fee," buy needed work materials or make a substantial deposit on essentially worthless merchandise.

PHONY PHONE COMPANY REPS CAN RIP YOU OFF

New York City police say a new telephone scam is making the rounds in the Northeast. Here's how it works:

You receive a call from someone who claims to be a fraud investigator for the phone company. The caller advises you that you will be getting a call from an operator, who will ask you to accept a charge call placed by a third party. The fake investigator requests that you accept the charges so the call can be traced, often promising you a "reward" for your help. Instead, it is really the phony investigator who's making the call, leaving you stuck with a big long-distance bill. Protect yourself by refusing to accept third-party phone charges from anyone you don't know.

NOT ALL `800' NUMBERS ARE TOLL-FREE

By now, almost everyone knows the perils of "900" and "976" numbers, which cost the caller a per-minute charge for the full duration of every call. Now, however, consumer-protection officials in several states are reporting complaints of abuses involving "800" numbers, which are generally assumed to be toll-free.

How It Works: You receive a letter or card announcing that you have won a prize and telling you to call an "800" number to claim it. The number is answered by a computerized voice, which gives instructions on how to get your prize. The catch? At some point in the call, the voice also says — somewhat unclearly —

that you will be billed if you stay on the line. At the end of the call, you find you've been awarded only a minor prize. Later, you get a bill — designed to look like a regular phone bill — charging you more for the call than the prize was worth.

Protection: Hang up immediately — or, better yet, don't call to begin with. If you win a prize in a legitimate sweepstakes, you'll receive an official notification telling you what you've won.

NO MORTGAGE HELP NEEDED!

As you've read several times in "Money $ecret$," one of the best ways to save huge sums of money and shorten the life of your mortgage is to make an extra payment on the principal each time you send in your check. Recognizing the marketing appeal of such big savings, a number of scam artists are getting into the "mortgage acceleration" business — offering to help people set up plans to pay off their loans early. According to the consumer group Call for Action, these grifters advertise that they will devise a payment plan, handle the math and bookkeeping, make the payments and provide statements showing how much you are saving. All you have to do is send your money to them each month, rather than to the mortgage company. Some actually perform the "services," but charge big fees — $1,000 or more per year. Others, more interested in a fast buck than a long-term swindle, simply keep your money rather than sending it on to the mortgage company — skipping town after they've gotten 2 or 3 months' worth of payments.

Protection: Most mortgage lenders allow you to accelerate principal payments by simply noting on the payment coupon how much extra you are enclosing. The principal reduction is then reflected on your annual or semi-annual statement. If your payment coupon doesn't have a space to note extra payments, contact the lender and ask what the correct procedures are.

YOUR SOCIAL SECURITY NUMBER CAN GIVE YOU AWAY

Look at the first 3 numbers on your Social Security card. You may not know it — most people don't — but the numbers aren't random. They're actually a code for the issuing state and can be useful to check on place of birth or employment history. If you want a particular Social Security card number decoded, a private detective may be able to do it for you — for a fee.

CHAPTER 14

SUPERSAVERS & FAB FREEBIES

A. How to Get Today's Best Bargains

TIMING CAN BE EVERYTHING

Finding bargains in the shopping jungle takes expertise — and a little help. Here's a list, by month, of when retailers normally put various items on sale:

January — Almost everything that didn't sell at Christmas, including toys and Christmas cards. Also, winter coats, fashion accessories, linens and white goods, books, appliances, furniture, carpets and rugs. Late in the month, you should also look for bargains in other merchandise as stores hold pre-inventory sales.

February — Used cars, furniture, lamps, silverware, dishes and other kitchen items, air conditioners, sportswear, sporting goods, TVs, stereos and toys (again).

March — Winter sports equipment, housewares, garden supplies, children's shoes and infants' clothing.

April — Women's shoes, lingerie, fabrics and paint.

May — TVs, luggage, jewelry, outdoor furniture, tires and auto accessories. Also watch for Mother's Day specials.

June — Men's clothing, floor coverings and bedding. Check out Father's Day specials as well.

July — Men's shirts and shoes, children's clothes, lingerie, sleepwear, furniture and summer sports equipment.

August — Curtains and drapes, men's and women's coats, linens, tires, bathing suits, fans and air conditioners. Also shop the back-to-school sales.

September — Fall fashions, hardware, new cars, bicycles, paints, dishes and glassware.

October — Fall clothing, fishing equipment, school supplies and major appliances. Many stores also hold storewide clearances to make room for Christmas merchandise.

November — Winter clothing, blankets and quilts, shoes and men's suits and coats.

December — Men's and children's clothing, resort wear and men's fashion accessories. Also check out pre-Christmas promotions and day-after-Christmas sales on cards, toys and specialty gift items.

A QUICK GUIDE TO SHOPPING THE OUTLET STORES

More and more factory outlets are springing up in the suburbs, often along interstate highways. In fact, in several places around the country, there are now entire shopping centers filled with nothing but outlet stores for various types of clothing and accessories. However, if you haven't tried these stores yet, be prepared for something a bit different. Instead of fancy displays, helpful sales people and orderly racks of clothes, you're more likely to find warehouse surroundings, makeshift fitting rooms, self service and limited return and credit policies — but the savings should compensate you for the lack of customary settings and services. Here are some tips on getting the best bargains when shopping outlets:

* Pick the outlet store of a manufacturer whose products you know and like.

* The best savings at a manufacturer's outlet will be on its own line.

At a Liz Claiborne outlet, for example, don't expect the same discount on other label clothing.

* Irregulars are fine if the defects are minor or easily repaired. Be wary of

packaged items that can't be opened for inspection.

* Always inspect products for defects. If buying clothing, check material for flaws, look at stitching, make sure plaids are matched across seams.

* Many larger outlet stores carry goods from a variety of manufacturers or designers, so comparison shop here just as you would at a retail outlet.

* If you need a particular item and want to ensure getting the best quality, check the department stores or specialty shops first, then look for a comparable (or even the same) item at an outlet shop to get a better price.

SAVING 40% AT EXPENSIVE STORES — WITHOUT SALES

Specialty stores depend on big mark-ups — always at least 100%, and sometimes as much as 150% — to pay for their classy overhead and make up for comparatively low sales volume. Many also disdain sales as not befitting of their image. However, that doesn't mean you can't get a price reduction from these stores. Shop during off-peak times, when the store isn't busy. Then, if you find something you like, ask to speak to the owner or the manager — and ask for a personal discount. Explain that you really like the item, but it's a bit much for your budget. Tell him you'd prefer to buy the item from his store — and will if he will give it to you for a lower price, say 25% to 40% below the marked price. However, if he can't accommodate you, you'll have to search for a comparable, lower-priced item elsewhere. In most cases, with a store empty of customers and a mark-up sufficient to still give him a nice profit on the sale, he'll say yes. And, if he doesn't, you haven't lost anything by asking.

EVEN LUXURY ITEMS CAN BE BARGAINS

It's possible to get good prices on virtually everything — even luxury items — but you have to know when and how to look for them. Here are some tips:

* Check out new specialty stores as soon as they open. Most set initial prices at much lower levels than they'll feature later in an effort to draw as many potential customers into the store as possible. Then, once they've built up traffic levels, they'll gradually escalate their prices to the levels they want to maintain over the long term.

* A luxury item is still a luxury item — even if it's not new. Resale shops (not to be confused with thrift shops) have become extremely popular in recent years by offering big savings on pricey items like suits and designer dresses that have been well maintained or only occasionally worn. These stores are particularly good sources for party dresses and other high-fashion items, which may have

been worn only once or twice. It's helpful to know something about brand names before shopping resale shops. Even then, check the item carefully, noting stitching, country of manufacture, etc., before trying on. And always check for damages.

* Before shopping for appliances, electronics or other big-ticket items, establish what you want — make, model, options, colors, ballpark prices — and then look for the best deal on precisely that. Don't let yourself be switched to a higher-priced or lower-quality item.

* For unmarked goods, ask the price — then for a cash discount price, or discounts for buying a floor model or taking immediate delivery.

* Consider smaller clothing stores where the owner is the buyer, perhaps selecting better quality and more distinctive fashions at lower prices than department stores.

* Don't overlook department stores. According to a recent survey, the major department stores sell only 35% to 40% of their merchandise at full price. The rest goes at sale or, eventually, at clearance prices — meaning you've got a 60% chance of getting a better deal on the best department store items.

BUYING FINE JEWELRY AT 55% TO 65% OFF

It's possible to buy fine quality jewelry at lower prices, but you have to know a bit about the business to get the best value for your money. For example, you can buy a lower quality stone and dress it up with a special setting, creating a piece with the overall impact of items selling for double or even triple the cost. This is an especially attractive option with diamonds, where the color of the stone can greatly reduce the cost. Specific Color Tips: Take a less-than-white diamond and put it in a white gold or platinum setting. The whiteness of the metal will reflect into the stone, making it look whiter, and thus more expensive. A similar trick works with yellowish diamonds. Putting them in a yellow gold setting will mask the yellowish tint of the stone, making it look brighter and whiter.

For those who didn't know, diamonds are graded according to the 4 C's — cut, color, clarity and carat (weight). Here are some tips on getting the best value in each category:

* Cut. Contrary to popular belief, this does not refer to the shape of the stone. Rather it describes the proportioning of the stone from top to bottom and the precision and care that was put into cutting the stone. There are 6 grades of cut, ranging from "ideal" (best) to "poor" (worst). However, since it's difficult to distinguish the quality of the cut from the top (the view most people get of a ring or necklace setting), you can drop down a grade or two and save 10% to 20%

without hurting the appearance of the jewelry.

* Color. Diamond color is graded on an alphabetical scale beginning with D for totally colorless (best) to Z. Grades D, E and F are generally considered colorless; G, H, I, J and K are consider near colorless; L, M and N have a slight yellowish tint; and O through Z are considered to be "tinted" diamonds. Once again, virtually no one can distinguish the difference between a D and a G diamond without a loupe, so you can get almost the same appearance for 15% to 20% less.

* Clarity. This refers to the absence of inclusions inside the stone, based on what can be seen through a 10-power microscope. Most jewelers believe their is no such thing as a totally flawless diamond (grade FL), so when you hear someone speak of a flawless stone, they are usually describing one that has inclusions, but none visible under a 10-power scope. This is the least important factor to consider when getting a diamond since the distinctions between the grades cannot be seen with the naked eye.

* Carat. This is the best known measure of diamonds, but many people mistakenly thing it refers to size when it actually refers to weight. To get the most for your money in this class, buy a "90-point" diamond (each carat is made up of 100 "points") rather than a 1-carat stone. Once it is set, no one will be able to tell the difference but you'll save 10% to 15%. You can also save money while getting the appearance of a larger diamond by clustering 2 or 3 small stones. You can also choose a size-maximizing shape such as a marquise, pear or duchess, rather than opting for a round shape, which shows off the stone but makes it look smaller.

Money $ecret: You can save as much as 75% on a piece of diamond jewelryby "juggling" the 4 C's. For example, once the stone is set, an E-color, SI-2 clarity, 90-point, round brilliant stone (about $6,000 retail) with look the same to the naked eye as a D-color, IF clarity, 1-carat round brilliant stone (about $25,000 retail).

For Bargain Hunters: Auctions can offer real savings — thousands of dollars in some cases — on all types of jewelry, but you have to know what you're doing. Here are some tips on how to become a shrewd bidder:

* Buy a 10x jeweler's loupe ($25 or less) and use it whenever you're examining jewelry.

* Condition of antique jewelry often counts more than design, workmanship or intrinsic value of gold and gemstones. Read the catalog description and drop your estimate if you see "repaired," "altered," "cracked," "later additions," "stone missing," "stone cracked," "lead solder marks," "enamel worn," etc.

* Check the back of a piece as well as the front. The front may be pink gold, but the reverse may be yellow gold.

* The value of modern pieces is almost completely determined by the gemstones. Divide the pre-sale estimate by the total weight of the stones to compare the value of similar pieces.

* Stone size as well as weight affects price. Two diamond rings may have the same weight, but the one with fewer and larger stones will be worth more.

* Look for soldering repair marks. Gold solder, carefully applied, won't alter a piece's value. Lead solder leaves gray residue and can cut the price by half.

* If the karat weight of gold isn't listed, it's 14K.

SECRETS OF SUCCESSFUL SHOPPING BY PHONE

Shopping by phone can save lots of time and money, but it's important to protect yourself so you don't get taken when you actually go in to make your purchase. Here are some key tips to help you avoid problems:

* Ask for prices and availability based on the specific make and model of the item you want — and double check to make sure that's what you get when you go to pick it up. Some stores will tell you they have an item just to get you into the store, assuming they can get you to switch once there. If that happens, refuse to buy anything and complain to the manager.

* If you can't get into the store right away, make sure you have a firm commitment on how long the price quoted over the phone will be available. * If quantities are limited, ask to have the item set aside for you if you can't go right in — or even if you can. It's absolutely amazing how often someone will decide to buy the last of something you want during the short period it takes you to drive to the store.

* Always get the name of the person you speak to about the item — and make sure that same person will be on duty when you want to go in. If he or she won't, ask for the name of another person you can ask for, and request that that individual be told to expect you.

EAT AT FINE RESTAURANTS FOR 50% OFF

Everyone enjoys a good meal as part of an evening on the town, but good meals can cost a bundle these days. Fortunately, it's not that hard to get discounts at many major restaurants. In fact, a lot of them advertise 2-for-1 specials in the local newspapers or tourist guides (you don't have to be a tourist to pick these up at any major hotel in the area), and many others participate in discount programs in conjunction with major credit-card issuers such as American Express and Visa. However, for consistent value all across America (and in Canada too), its difficult to beat the program of ENTERTAINMENT Inc., P.O. Box 1014,

Trumbull, CT 06611. ENTERTAINMENT publishes value books — each containing hundreds of 2-for-1 and discount coupons — for more than 100 cities or areas around the country. Each book has a section on fine dining, featuring 30 to 40 of the city's best restaurants, as well as sections on casual dining, fast food outlets, movies, theaters, sporting events, tourist attractions, car rentals and hotel and resort savings in nearby areas. In larger cities, such as Baltimore, Boston, Chicago, Detroit, Long Island, Los Angeles, north New Jersey, New York, Philadelphia, Seattle and Washington, there are even books for different areas of the city. The books are generally sold for $30 to $35 as part of fund-raising drives by local charitable and civic organizations. However, you can purchase up to 4 different books (only 1 per city) directly from the publisher for only $22, plus $3 shipping and handling. Just call 1-800-374-4464 and use your Visa or MasterCard to order.

SAVE 50% TO 70% ON NEW FURNITURE

If you've gone shopping for a new sofa, dining room set or breakfront lately, you know that there's been no recession in furniture prices. However, it's possible to save big money on many home furnishings — particularly finer quality items — by buying directly from the manufacturer. There are also a number of catalog outlets that buy manufacturer's overruns and sell direct by mail at substantial discounts. Similar price reductions are also available by buying direct on such items as drapes, shutters, wallcoverings, etc. Following are some good sources to check out:

* Ellenburg's Furniture is a catalog outlet for many lines of fine furniture, including Lexington, Henry Link, Link-Taylor, Lane, Pulaski, Hooker, C.R. Laine, National Mt. Airy and others. Their catalog costs $6 and you can request a copy by calling 1-800-841-1420.

* Cherry Hill offers discounts of up to 50% on more than 500 major brands of home furnishings, having provided nationwide delivery service for more than 50 years. For price quotes or a free brochure, write Cherry Hill Furniture, Box 7405, Furnitureland Station, C1, High Point, NC 27264 or call 1-800-328-0933.

* North Carolina Furniture Sales represents more than 100 prestigious lines, offering discounts of up to 50%. The company, in business more than 20 years, offers free brochures and optional in-home delivery. For information, call 1-800-248-6237.

* Arthur M. Welling features discounts on quality wooden furniture. For a copy of their catalog, send $6 to 117 Old Rutherford Road, Taylor, SC 29687 or call 1-803-877-0852.

* Designer Secrets offers savings of up to 75% on decorator fabrics, bedspreads, window coverings, drapes and furniture, and also provides a special "design-a-room" service to buyers. The company's catalog is available for $2 (refundable with you first purchase) by writing Box 529, Fremont, NE 68025, or calling 1-800-955-2559.

CALL THIS NUMBER TO SAVE 55% ON CARPETING

Cherry Hill Furniture also has a division that specializes in discounts of up to 55% on carpets and other interior and decorator items. To get more information or price quotes, telephone 1-800-888-0933. Numerous sources are also available for other types of floor coverings, including:

* K&D Supply Co. specializes in discounts on handcrafted braid rugs, as well as imported handwoven and machine-made Orientals. For a 75-page color catalog, send $3 to 1440-A Industrial Drive, Matthews, NC 28105, or call 1-800-477-1400.

* The World of Clothing, Hendersonville, NC 28792, has a catalog with

discounts on more than 500 rugs, including Orientals and braids. The cost is $7, but you get a $5-off certificate good with your first order.

SAVE UP TO 75% ON GLASSES & CONTACTS

Few things are more important than your eyes, so it pays to take care of them. However, there's no need to pay too much. A number of sources offer discounts on glasses and contacts, as well as on other medical and pharmaceutical items. Here are some examples:

* The Contact Lens Discount Center offers savings of up to 75% on such recognized name contacts as Bausch & Lomb, CooperVision and Barnes+Hind. Call 1-800-328-2220 for a free brochure.

* As mentioned in Chapter 6, a number of auto clubs, consumer clubs and shopping services give members special discounts of 50% or more on medical items, including glasses and contacts. One is British Petroleum's Horizon Club, which can save you up to 50% on glasses and 60% on contacts. For information on joining, call BP Customer Service at 1-800-321-9555.

* Another discount buying service that includes big savings on contacts and fashion eye wear is America's Choice Discounts. The program also offers reduced prices on scores of other products and services, including a full range of health, fitness and pharmaceutical products. Membership is $29.95 a year. For more information or an application, call 1-800-627-9479.

SLASH YOUR GROCERY BILL 40% — WITHOUT COUPONS

You don't have to go marching into the store with a grocery bag full of coupons to save money on groceries. Here are some tips on how to buy smarter and save more:

* Don't be suckered by ads for extra-strong paper towels. Typical economy brands handle mop-up jobs just as well.

* In fact, most generic or plain-wrap products are smart buys. This goes for soft drinks; canned soups, fruits and vegetables; paper goods; laundry products and soap.

* Buy the large, economy size of non-perishable products (though you should be sure to check the per-ounce cost as some of these larger sizes don't actually save you money over smaller sizes).

* If you really want to save, you can also reduce expenses by buying perishable items at quantity discounts, taking them home, preparing them and then freezing them in meal-sized portions for later use.

* If you use a lot of bread, cakes, cookies or pasta, trying baking or making your own instead of buying them. If you can spare the time and enjoy working in the kitchen, you can save 50% to 60% over the price of pre-baked goods. If making your own pasta is too much trouble, buy the dried commercial brands rather than fresh pasta — it's just as good and half as expensive.

* Imported mineral waters are overpriced. Buy domestic. You'll find a cleaner taste, less sodium — and save money.

* Milk in translucent plastic containers can oxidize under supermarket fluorescents, taste flat and lose vitamin C. Stick to cardboard containers, which are generally cheaper anyway. And buy by the gallon — you'll save 2 cents to 3 cents per fluid ounce.

* Finally, never go shopping without a list. Impulse buying drives up your grocery bill faster than anything.

INCREASING YOUR GROCERY PRODUCT AWARENESS

Phil Lempert is known as "the supermarket guru" because of his expertise on the subject of food shopping. His newsletter, "The Lempert Report," covers all aspects of the food industry, with an emphasis on helping consumers get the most for their grocery dollar. He says shoppers can not only save money, but also be more socially_responsible if they just increase their awareness of how and what they buy at the supermarket. Some of his suggestions:

* Always make a list before going to the store — and stick to it. If you're tempted to buy something not on the list, ask yourself: "Do I really need this."

* Read labels — and take the time to learn exactly what the various notations mean. "More and more people are reading labels, but that doesn't mean they understand them," Lempert says, "particularly when it comes to terms like `Light' or `Free' or a full comprehension of nutritional information and recommended daily allowances."

* Be skeptical. Don't buy something just because of what it says on the label or in the advertising. If something claims to have specific benefits with respect to other products, make sure you need those benefits, which nearly always come with an added price.

* Compare prices. If you really like a product, you should probably stick with it — even if something else comes along at a slightly lower price. However, if a product's just okay, always be willing to try a lower-priced alternative.

* Keep the environment in mind. Look at packaging. Excess packaging not only wastes resources, but usually wastes your money. Take your own canvas or mesh bag to carry home your purchases. It won't save you immediate money, bit it will lower store costs — which will lower your costs in the long run — and it's better for the environment than either paper or plastic.

* If you're not happy, complain. Talk with the department manager — or the manager of the supermarket. If you have a product complaint, check to see if the manufacturer has an 800 number and call your complaint in direct (it's also nice to call sometimes about great new products). You can also send any product complaints to Lempert, who will investigate and report in his letter. Write to Consumer Insight, P.O. Box 585, Montclair, N.J. 07042.

CUT YOUR DRY CLEANING BILLS IN HALF

The cost of keeping a wardrobe clean and in good condition is becoming one of the biggest personal expenses for business and professional people, running as much as $600 a year in some cases. However, there are ways to both cut your costs and get better service from your dry cleaner. Here are a few:

* The best way to reduce dry cleaning costs is to buy clothes that don't need cleaning. For that reason, you should think twice about buying garments made of silk — the most expensive fabric to clean. The same goes for pleated skirts or dresses. Many cleaners charge extra — sometimes as much as 60 cents a pleat — for the hand pressing they require.

* Don't pay extra to have work done at stores that claim specialized services such as "French cleaning" or that advertise "1-Hour Martinizing." The former is

just a fancy name for regular cleaning, based on the French origin of dry cleaning, while the latter is merely a brand name for a national chain of franchised dry-cleaning stores. All dry cleaning methods are basically the same.

* More important than the cleaning method is the “spotter” employed by your local cleaner. The spotter is the individual who handles the tough job — removing stains before the garment is actually cleaned — and there is a lot of difference between spotters. The best cleaning establishments send their spotters to school each year for refresher course on new techniques and improved chemicals. If you cleaner seems to have trouble with spots, you may want to change stores in search of a better spotter. Also, it never hurts to actually meet the person who handles this chore and find out a bit about how he works, perhaps putting in a request for special handling of your garments when you bring in a tough stain.

* For many years, cleaners have charged more for women’s garments than for men’s — even if they were basically the same. More and more states are now making that practice illegal, however, so don’t hesitate to complain if you see a price such as $1.50 for men’s shirts and $3 for women’s blouses. Unless the cleaner can justify the extra cost, you should get a reduction.

* If you don’t know exactly how to remove a spot or stain at home, don’t try it. Take it to the cleaners instead and tell him what caused the spot. That will improve your chances of saving the garment, and could also make the cleaner liable if he fails to do the job. Be aware, however, that cleaners often get a bad rap, getting blamed when the real problem was that the manufacturer mislabeled the material or you misidentified the stain.

* Be careful with sequins or beads, especially those in bright colors. The heat from dry cleaning can cause the beads to melt or the colors to run, either one of which can ruin a garment. Ask your cleaner to do a test on one sequin or bead before doing the entire garment.

* When you try out a new cleaner, don’t take in a special garment or a favorite sweater. Instead, test his work with a piece of clothing that you can afford to lose.

* As a final resort, seek outside help. If a garment was mislabeled by the manufacturer, write to the Federal Trade Commission, Correspondence Branch, Washington, DC 20508, and it will notify the manufacturer, who may give you a refund. If you need a garment analyzed to find out if it was mislabeled, you can send it to the International Fabricare Institute, 12251 Tech Road, Silver Spring, MD 20094. For problems with the cleaner, contact the Better Business Bureau or check the Yellow Pages for a local or regional dry cleaners trade group or professional association and complain to them about the bad service.

When You Deserve a Settlement: You should get some type of

reimbursement from a dry cleaner if your garment is lost or ruined — especially if the cleaner damages an article with a "do not dry clean" tag. The amount of reimbursement is negotiable, based on the original price of the garment or it's current replacement value, minus any depreciation for wear. If your cleaner won't give you satisfaction, keep your receipts and take them (or the damaged garment) to the local dry cleaning trade association or your city's consumer affairs department. Be aware, however, that a cleaner's failure to get out a spot isn't grounds for a complaint — and, in fact, you still legally have to pay for the cleaning job.

BIG BARGAINS IN BOOKS — EVEN NEW ONES

To quote a popular commercial for a chain of discount book stores, "books cost too much." However, if you're an avid reader, there are a number of ways to cut your book-buying costs. Here are a few:

* You can save 10% to 25% on new books — even best sellers — by shopping the discount stores rather than the retail shops. Among the best-known and most readily available are Crown, SuperCrown and Bookstar. Check your local Yellow Pages for the location nearest you.

* Both discount and full-price stores generally have bargain racks, with books marked down 50% to 75% — or even more. Crown and SuperCrown also have special racks labeled "Books Near a Buck" and "Books Near $3" — prices that represent even larger savings. Admittedly, some of the books on these racks are real dogs, but lots of them aren't. In fact, if you wait a few months after the release date, you may even find works by some of the most popular authors on the bargain racks — simply because the store ordered too many.

* Book clubs and mail-order publishers generally offer rates 25% to 33% below retail prices on the newest releases. Be aware, however, that you

usually have to pay shipping and handling charges, which could more than offset your savings on the price of the book.

* Many of the country's largest publishing houses not only supply retailers and book clubs, but also have their own catalogs, which usually offer discounted prices. The catalogs, which generally come out twice a year, also feature stock-reduction sales on books that were overprinted, offering savings of 60% or more.

* Wait for the paperback edition to come out.

* For really big savings, check the used book stores. More and more of these operations are popping up these days, and they usually feature a wide selection of fairly recent editions. Hardbacks normally go for about 25% of the original retail price, with paperbacks selling for around a third of their original

cost.

* Garage and yard sales can also be fertile ground for book shoppers, offering paperbacks for as little as a dime and hardbacks for a quarter.

BUY A COMPUTER BY MAIL & SAVE $400 OR MORE

Choosing a new computer also means choosing a computer store. Here are the leading sources, with some tips on choosing among them:

1. Full-service dealers: These ex-kings of the computer hill have been gradually sliding away. They offer the most in-store customer assistance, at-home set-up help, and post-sales service. However, marked prices are high and sales are infrequent. Buying Tip: Even though sales may be rare, don't hesitate to haggle with these dealers over price. In the face of a declining market share, most of them would rather take a smaller profit than lose a sale entirely. Another good strategy is to ask for at least limited no-interest financing — say paying $1,250 at the time you purchase a $5,000 system, and then paying the remaining $3,750 in 3 equal payments spread over the next 90 days. Another benefit you can request from dealers is additional training. Most full-service stores hold regular classes, and you should be able to talk them into letting you attend the ones that interest you without additional charge.

2. Department stores: Probably the worst place to buy a computer (unless you need to take advantage of almost automatic store financing). They offer only so-so prices — and less than so-so service.

3. Discount stores and mail-order houses: These have been dramatically increasing their market share. Disadvantages: Little service or support (though many hardware and software firms offer warranties and toll-free helplines). Still, if maximum selection and minimum cost is what you are after, the mail-order houses are a great deal. Standard catalog prices are usually 25% to 40% below those charged by full-service dealers — meaning you can save $400 or more on even a basic system costing around $1,600. And, if you go for a higher-priced configuration, your savings can be even bigger. To find a good selection of mail-order computer dealers, just go to your local newsstand and pick up a copy of any of the leading computer magazines. All to the top mail-order houses have ads detailing some sample prices and telling you how to get a copy of their catalog. For protection, it's a good idea to talk to a friend or associate who has purchased equipment by mail to see if they have any recommendations or warnings.

Buying Tip: Whichever source you choose, make sure you buy from an authorized dealer. This ensures your warranty will be honored and preserves your eligibility for discounts on future hardware and software upgrades. You should also refuse to buy unless the dealer will make the purchase subject to your satisfaction, giving you the option to return the system for a full refund within 30 days (some dealers may require a small non-refundable deposit when offering such terms).

CONSIDER A USED COMPUTER

If you are buying your first computer, or buying a second one for use by your children, you may be able to get a much bigger bang for you buck by shopping for a used system. With prices on new hardware dropping steadily, you can pick up good used systems for rock-bottom prices, though they may lack some of the bells and whistles of the newer models. Used systems also tend to be fairly reliable (if it's going to fail, most computer equipment will do so within the first 90 days after its initial purchase). Even so, there are things to watch out for.

1. Suspiciously noisy disk drives. This can signal a pending failure, or it may indicate a condition that would affect your ability to save or restore information.

2. Flickering monitors, poor image quality. Nothing will tire you out faster than struggling to read copy on a poor display terminal and nothing will ruin a good computer game quicker than a monitor that scrambles the graphics.

3. Sticking keys (check 'em all). Dead or unresponsive keys can render your computer virtually useless (though replacement keyboards are available for under $100). Also test the mouse to make sure the cursor responds well to your hand movements.

4. A good way to check the overall operation of the computer is to copy files. Try a few and notice the speed. Also check the copy to make sure all the data was replicated.

5. Try a telecommunications hookup to see if you can both send and receive files.

6. Check all ports and peripherals and send a few files to a printer.

7. If possible, attempt to run all the software you'll be using should you purchase the machine.

STOP THE MAIL-ORDER BLIZZARD

As convenient and economical as shopping by mail can be, there comes a time in most people's lives when both they and their mailboxes are overwhelmed with catalogs and other direct-mail offerings. If you've reached that point, there's a simple way to stop a big chunk of the advertising mailers you receive. Simply write the Direct Marketing Association, P.O. Box 9008, Farmingdale, NY 11735, and request that your name be removed from all lists (four times a year, DMA member companies check the requests and purge names from their mailing lists). For this to work, however, you must be sure to list your name exactly as it appears on catalog mailing labels — and, if it's listed more than one way, be sure to include all variations. There's no charge for this service. Catch: If there are 1 or 2 catalogs you'd still like to receive, you'll have to contact each company individually and ask them to keep you on their list — but to stop renting or selling your name to other mailers. This can be done by calling the "800" number on the catalog, or by sending a written request to the company, enclosing the actually mailing label from the last catalog you received.

CALL TOLL-FREE AND SAVE

Most of the major American companies, as well as many smaller operations, now have toll-free "800" numbers for both sales and customer service. If you have a complaint or simply need information about a company, a product or any other aspect of a business, find out if it has an "800" number before you spend your own money on a call. Just dial toll-free directory assistance at 1-800-555-1212.

B. There's No Better Price Than Free

INFORMATION FOR 29 CENTS OR LESS

Whatever you're trying to do in life, it's a pretty sure bet that someone, somewhere has produced an informational booklet that explains the best way to get it done. And, because the people producing these brochures are either consumer advocates or companies hoping to generate some additional business, the information is usually free — or, at most will cost you the price of a stamp and a self-addressed envelope.

Here are a variety of booklets you might want to send for, in no particular order and with no recommendations as to the value of the contents:

* Auto Repair — How to select the right repair shop for your car. Free, but enclose a stamped, self-addressed, business-sized envelope. National Institute for Automotive Service Excellence, 13505 Dulles Technology Drive, Herndon, VI 22071.

* Better Vision — A discussion of vision problems arising from the use of video display terminals. Free, but enclose a stamped, self-addressed, business-sized envelope. American Optometric Association, Communication Center, 243 N. Lindbergh Blvd., St. Louis, MO 63141.

* Books for Older Readers — A mail-order catalog of hard-to-find publications on subjects of interest to the over-45 crowd. Free. Thornapple Publishing Co., Box 56, Ada, MI 49301, or call 616-676-1583.

* Business Efficiency — How to get organized for improved productivity and reduced stress. Free. Kroy, Inc., Box 12279, Scottsdale, AZ 82567, or call 1-800-733-5769.

* Dealing With Dogs — A complete guide to basic obedience training for your puppy, with key do's and don'ts. Free, but enclose a stamped, self-addressed, business-sized envelope. ALPO Pet Center, Box 25200, Lehigh Valley, PA 18002.

* Funeral Costs — An examination of the pros and cons of prepaid burial plans. Free. American Association of Retired Persons, Fulfillment (EE0139), 601 E St. NW, Washington, DC 20049. Ask for Product Report D13188, "Prepaying Your Funeral?"

* Guide to Knives — A catalog with everything for the blade buff, from pocket knives to swords, with accessories. Free. Smoky Mountain Knife Works, Box 4430, Sevierville, TN 37864.

* Money Mistakes — A guide to the most common blunders people make with their bucks. Free. Aetna Insurance Co., 151 Farmington Ave., RWAC, Hartford, CN 06156.

* Moving Made Easy — An explanation of how moving companies work, how charges are determined and what you should do to get ready for a move. Free. Call Allied Van Lines at 1-800-367-6683.

* Piano Care — Explains how often to find good service for your piano, how often to have it tuned and how to care for the cabinet. Free, but enclose a stamped, self-addressed, business-sized envelope. Piano Technicians Guild, 3930 Washington St., Kansas City, MO 64111.

* Recycling — An educational comic book to teach kids the joys and value of recycling. Free. Office of Solid Waste, U.S. Environmental Protection Agency, RCRA Information Center, Mail Code OS-305, 401 M St. SW, Washington, DC 20460.

* 6 Steps to Free Publicity. Explains how to get media coverage for you or your business. Free, but enclose a stamped, self-addressed, business-sized envelope. Marcia Yudkin, Box 1310, Boston, MA 02117.

* Winter Warmup — Do-it-yourself guide to getting your car ready for cold weather. Free, but enclose a stamped, self-addressed, business-sized envelope. National Institute for Automotive Service Excellence, Box 347, Department BLW, Herndon, VI 22070.

UNCLE SAM ALSO LIKES BOOKS

If you don't like the free reading choices offered by private sources, the U.S. government also offers many helpful and inexpensive — or even free — publications. Some samples (with order codes):

* Recycling Used Oil (504Y) — How to change your oil — and what to do with the old stuff. 50 cents.

* Books for Children, #7 (149Y) — Lists more than 100 of the best recent books published for children preschool to junior high. $1.00.

* The Job Outlook for College Graduates to the Year 2000 (102Y) — Describes job opportunities for grads in the current decade. $1.00

* Getting Fit Your Way (109Y) — A 12-week program to help make exercise a lifelong habit, with emphasis on weight loss and building a stronger heart. $3.25

* Help Your Child Do Better in School (410Y) — Guide to helping kids improve their study habits. 50 cents.

* Thrifty Meals for Two (115Y) — A guide on how to shop for and prepare nutritious and economical meals; with menus. $2.50.

* Quackery — The Billion-Dollar "Miracle" Business (626Y) — Explains how bogus remedies for cancer, arthritis and the "battle of the bulge" can hurt you more than they help. Free.

* Headaches (117Y) — Headaches, their causes and treatment. $2.00.

To Order: Make check or money order payable to Superintendent of Documents and send with publication number and quantity desired to: R. Woods, Consumer Information Center-2D, Box 100, Pueblo, CO 81002. Note: There is a $1.00 service fee if you order free publications.

127 VALUABLE THINGS YOU CAN GET FOR FREE

Actually, there are a lot more than 127 things you can get for free — perhaps several thousand. How do you do it? Virtually every maker of packaged food products, household cleaners, personal-care items, laundry products, etc., offers free manufacturer's samples. If you see a new product at the store or in an advertisement, and think you'd like to try it, simply write the maker and ask for a sample. In almost every instance, the manufacturer will send you a small trial size — and, in many cases, samples of other products they make as well. Many manufacturers even include coupons in their ads or in special mailers so you don't have to write — you can just clip the coupon and trade it for a sample at your nearest store.

STOCKS THAT GIVE YOU MORE THAN DIVIDENDS

Are you planning to buy something at Radio Shack? If you can wait a month or so, you could save some money by calling your broker first and buying some shares of Tandy Corp. Tandy is Radio Shack's parent company and one of the benefits it gives corporate shareholders is a 10% discount on many Radio Shack products. That's just one example of the many discounts and free products companies give to their stockholders. Here are some others:

* Anheuser-Busch — Discounts of 10% at all 9 theme parks owned by the company, including the 4 Sea World locations around the country.

* Brown-Forman — A 50% discount on its Lenox holiday china patterns and crystal ornaments if ordered during November or December.

* ConAgra — Yearly discount coupons good for up to $40 off on company products.

* General Mills — Holiday gift boxes of company products are made available to shareholders at discounts of as much as 80%.

* Marriott Corp. — Discounts of from $10 to 50% off during non-peak times at selected Marriott Hotels and Courtyard and Residence Inns.

* Procter & Gamble — Discount coupons worth up to $80 a year for the purchase of company products.

* Ralston Purina — Discounts of 10% to 20% on lodging, ski rentals, lessons and lift tickets at Colorado's Keystone ski resort, which the company owns.

* Rubbermaid — Free product gifts to shareholders who attend the company's annual meeting.

* Sara Lee — Yearly discount coupons good for up to $40 off on company products.

* Walt Disney — Discounts of 10% to 40% on hotel rooms at selected Disney resorts, 10% discounts on Delta flights to Disney resort locations, 10% to 30% off National car rentals while there, 10% to 15% off Disney theme cruises

and 10% discounts on merchandise purchased at any of the more than 100 Disney stores around the country.

* Wm. Wrigley Co. — A free gift box containing about 20 packs of gum.

If you want to know whether a company in which you own stock has a shareholder discount, simply contact the company's shareholder services department. The telephone number or address should be in your latest annual report. Warning: In order to qualify for benefits, many companies require that you hold the stock in your own name, rather than in so-called "street name" — which means it's merely credited to you on the account books of your brokerage firm.

HAS YOUR CAR BEEN RECALLED? FIND OUT FREE

The National Highway Traffic Safety Administration maintains a complete list of recall notices for cars, trucks, vans and recreational vehicles. You can access the Auto Recall Hotline from your Touch-Tone phone by calling 202-366-0123 and punching in the make, model and year. There's no cost except for the long-distance toll.

C. A Quick Guide to Smart Shopping

PAY WITH CASH & SAVE

Any time you make a consumer purchase, ask the store manager if you can get a discount for paying cash instead of using a credit card. Many firms will knock 3% to 5% off the sales price because cash transactions save them the cost of credit card-related paperwork — and they also get their money sooner.

17 THINGS YOU CAN DO TO SAVE UP TO $1,800 A YEAR

Saving money really isn't that difficult, but it does take a little thought and some advance planning. Here are just a few examples (17 of them) of the many ways you can cut your everyday living costs:

* Do your laundry with warm instead of hot water. Water heating is the biggest cost factor in most household gas bills.

* Your refrigerator eats up more electricity than any other household

appliance, but you can cut costs by turning down the thermostat when the refrigerator is almost empty.

* Do your grocery shopping right after a meal. If you're hungry, you're more likely to buy items you don't really need just because they look good or the packages have attractive pictures.

* You may be paying for more cable TV services than you really need — or have time to watch. If so, cancel some of your subscription services.

* Take a Thermos of coffee to work rather than buying it from the office machine.

* Change clothes as soon as you get home from work. This will make your costly business wardrobe last longer.

* Resist the temptation to give in to status and get a gold or platinum credit card. Basic cards do the job just as well and fees are almost always cheaper because the don't offer all the benefits (most of which you won't use anyway).

* Limit the amount of cash you carry. If your pocket is full of money, you are more likely to spend it — probably on things you don't really need or could get a better price on if you took the time to shop carefully.

* When entertaining at home, serve fewer expensive items such as meat and instead learn to make dressed up versions of less-costly dishes such as stews, casseroles and pastas.

* Learn to give family members haircuts, home perms or dye jobs. Even if you have to buy kits, it's at least 75% cheaper than having it done at a salon or barber shop.

* Buy exercise tights in flesh tones rather than pantyhose or regular stockings. They look attractive and wear much better.

* Switch from expensive perfumes to bath and body oils. The fragrances are lighter, but they last just as long — and they are far less costly.

* Unless you are an avid practitioner, don't buy sports or vacation equipment. Renting — or, better yet, borrowing — can save you lots of money until you're ready to commit to serious participation.

* Consider buying jewelry with fake stones rather than real ones. Very few people can tell the difference, the pieces are every bit as attractive if you are careful in choosing a setting and you don't have to worry about insurance or theft.

* Don't buy fresh flowers for the holidays. Prices are usually higher then. Instead used dried flowers or silk flowers for occasions and treat yourself to

fresh flowers at other times, when prices are lower. Alternative: If you like working in the garden, grow your own fresh flowers.

* Take advantage of matinee prices at movies or stage shows. Savings can be 50% or more for the same film or production.

* If you have to host a reception for a wedding or other event, try to schedule it in the afternoon rather than the evening. Decorations can then be less formal, and food can be simpler and cheaper.

COMPLAINING — AND GETTING SATISFACTION

If it's broke, get it fixed. Here are some guidelines on how you can make good on bad merchandise:

* Save receipts, tags and copies of warranties so you can be certain about when you made the purchase and the price you paid.

* Explain to the salesperson or store manager exactly what's wrong, showing (but not surrendering without satisfaction) the relevant paperwork. Ask for what you want — replacement, repair or refund. Be polite but firm.

* File copies of all correspondence, along with notes on any conversations or telephone dealings. Those records may be crucial if you have to take your complaint elsewhere.

* If you get an excuse instead of satisfaction, repeat your demand — and keep doing it — with a reasonable deadline.

If the deadline isn't met, take your problem to a higher level:

* State your case concisely in a letter to the store manager or owner. If your letter is to the manager, mention your intention to contact his or her superior; if it's to the owner, explain that you're ready to go to the Better Business Bureau or your state's consumer agency. Enclose copies of relevant paperwork.

* Write directly to the company president, not the customer-relations department. Names of executives and addresses of companies can be found in Standard & Poor's Register of Corporations at the public library. Restate the facts and the demand for compensation, again with copies of paperwork. Send a "carbon copy" of this letter to the store's local manager.

If your problem still isn't resolved, try these courts of last resort:

* Consumer agencies, the Better Business Bureau or consumer hotlines.

* Trade associations can sometimes apply pressure to member companies.

* Local newspapers or radio or TV stations often have consumer reporters who might champion your cause.

* Small claims court. (Though you may get a judgment and psychological satisfaction, collecting can still sometimes be a problem.)

FIND MONEY IN FUNNY PLACES

Ben Franklin said "a penny saved is a penny earned," but most people don't really look for ways to save mere pennies — and it could be costing them real dollars. Here are a few savings suggestions — some of them admittedly offbeat — from The Tightwad Gazette, a newsletter published in Leeds, Maine, for the benefit of hard-core penny-pinchers:

* Wash and reuse your aluminum foil.

* Nail frozen juice-can lids to your kid's shoe heels instead of spending money on expensive tap shoes that will quickly be outgrown.

* Flatten toilet paper rolls before putting them on the roller, making it harder for them to turn and thereby discouraging the kids from spinning off unneeded extra feet of tissue.

* Save rubber bands from newspapers, grocery items, etc. If you're a real miser, you can even make two rubber bands by cutting in half the thick ones wrapped around some vegetable clusters (such as broccoli).

* Buy 15 or 20 pairs of identical socks when they're on sale. Then, when one sock in a pair wears out or gets eaten by the dryer, you'll always have a matching one with which to replace it.

If you are really into saving money around the house, there are a number of other newsletters that can also help you out. Here are some of the leading ones:

* Cheapskate Monthly, published by Mary Hart, P.O. Box 2135, Paramount, CA 90723, 310-630-8845. $12.95 for 12 8-page issues. Send a 29-cent stamp for a free sample.

* Lesko's Info-Power Newsletter, published by Matthew Lesko, Information U.S.A., P.O. Box E, Kensington, MD 20895. $128 for 12 10-page issues a year, or call 1-800-955-7693 for a free sample.

* Skinflint News, published by Melodie and Ron Moore, 1460 Noell Blvd., Palm Harbor, FL 34683, 813-785-7759. $9.95 for 12 8-page issues a year, or send a stamped, self-addressed, business-sized envelope for a free sample.

* The Penny Pincher, published by Jackie Iglehart, P.O. Box 809, Kings Park, NY 11754, 516-724-1868. $12 for 12 8-page issues a year, or send a 29-cent stamp for a free sample.

HOUSEHOLD ITEMS YOU CAN MAKE & SAVE 60% OR MORE

One of the best ways to save money is to make things yourself. Here are just a few examples of things you can make without too much talent or trouble:

* Instead of buying dishwashing liquid, make your own by dissolving the last slivers of your bar soap in a jar of water.

* Make your own hand-illustrated and lettered greeting cards instead of buying expensive commercial ones.

* Bake cookies, cakes and breads instead of buying them.

* Buy plain products and dress them up yourself. This can apply to everything from clothing (making a basic dress look special with belts, scarves, etc.) to food (buying plain cereal and adding raisins is cheaper than buying Raisin Bran or other cereals with fruits already mixed in).

* Since you're trying to save, you'll obviously want to use coupons — but you don't need an expensive coupon box or filing system. Envelopes and a small shoebox will do just as well.

* Make your own pizzas from scratch or by using pre-made crusts and adding your own ingredients. It's a lot cheaper than buying them or having them delivered.

* Make your own salad dressings using mayonnaise, catsup, lemon juice, vinegar, oil, etc. Most good recipe books tell you how, and home-made dressings are much less expensive than store-bought brands.

* Instead of buying cans or jars of commercial baby food, make your own. Thoroughly cook fresh fruits and vegetables and then blend them until they are easily digestible, even to tiny tummies.

* Use your blender to make your own juices from fresh fruit rather than buying it already squeezed.

* Pop you own popcorn rather than buying prepackaged bags. Its about 90% cheaper — and it tastes lots better.

* Save the juices when you cook vegetables and use them as the base for soups.

* Buy fruits and vegetables in season and freeze them yourself rather than

buying frozen foods.

* Don't buy expensive costume jewelry. Use beads, sequins, small stones, fishing line, etc., to make your own. Many hobby shops have books or classes that can show you how.

* Rather than buying expensive blankets or comforters, save scraps of colorful material from shirts, blouses and dresses — and then make your own quilt.

* When you visit friends, take a gift you've made yourself — such as cookies, preserves, canned fruits, etc. — rather than buying wine, flowers or other expensive items.

LET THE POSTAL SERVICE DELIVER SOME BARGAINS

Every few months in all major U.S. cities, the Postal Service auctions off lost, damaged or undeliverable merchandise. What turns up on the block? Anything that can be sent through the mail — TVs, electronic gear, radios, books, clothing, pots and pans, tools, coins, you name it. Call the main post office in your city for the next scheduled auction. Here's how it works:

* Similar articles are grouped together — boxes of books, 4 TVs, 5 sweaters, and so on — and must be purchased together. The groups are called "lots."

* Lots go on display the day before the auction. Nothing can be handled — and some are in badly lighted bins, so bring a flashlight.

* Lots are listed by number on a sheet given out on the inspection day, with a minimum acceptable bid beside it (never less than $10). Some lots are overbid, while others go for the minimum, often with no obvious relation to actual value. Here are some sample prices from recent auctions: A new Persian lamb jacket with mink-trimmed sleeves, $40; Brother electronic typewriter, $120; Oriental jewelry chest (very large and ornate), $85; a Sanyo cassette deck, $100; a Hamilton beach blender and hand mixer, $28.

* Lots are sold "as is" — meaning neither quality nor quantity is guaranteed — and all sales are final.

* To obtain a numbered paddle for bidding you have to pay a nominal fee the day before the auction (the fee is refunded if you don't buy anything, or applied to the price if you do). To bid, simply raise your paddle.

* You must deposit half the purchase price in cash or by certified check a half-hour after buying a lot. To avoid bringing large sums of cash, have several certified checks in different amounts.

How to bid: As you go through the lots in advance, write down your maximum bids. Do homework on going prices for items you're interested in. It's best to stick to lots that seem new or in good condition. Otherwise, figure in likely repair costs. Sit in back so you can see people bidding against you, listen carefully to the bidding and don't exceed your top price.

CHAPTER 15

TAX TIPS & TRAPS

A. Today's Top Tax-Saving Strategies

CHANGE STRATEGY WITH A NEW PRESIDENT

Democrat Bill Clinton's 1992 presidential election victory, ending 12 years of Republican rule, means you should probably reverse one of the classic tax-management strategies. With a Democratic Congress and a Democrat in the White House, history says both taxes and inflation will most likely rise over the next few years. As a result, rather than trying to defer income into the next tax year, you should now try to accelerate receipt of income into the current tax year. If tax rates rise 6% next year, you'll save around $4 on every $100 in gross income you can bring forward into the current year. Here are some of the possible tax-law changes (based on campaign statements) we may see during the Clinton presidency:

* An increase in the top tax rate from 31% to 36%. According to promises, this would impact only individuals who earn more than $150,000 annually and couples who bring home more than $200,000.

* An increase from 24% to 26% in the alternative minimum tax.

* A surtax of 10% on income exceeding $1 million annually.

* A tax credit of $150 for middle-class individuals and $300 for middle-class couples (middle class is yet to be defined).

* A reduction in the current estate-tax exemption from $600,000 to a mere $200,000. (This could be a particularly devastating change, forcing the sale of many small family businesses and the break-up of many family farms, not to mention the forced sale of many family homes.)

* A change in the gift-tax exemption. Currently an individual can give up to $10,000 per person per year with no tax implications, but it could be changed to a lifetime maximum of just 3 $10,000 donations.

WAYS YOU CAN SAVE UP TO $2,431 IN TAXES EVERY YEAR

Though changes in the tax laws over the past decade have eliminated many tax-saving opportunities, there are still a number of things you can do to reduce your annual liability to Uncle Sam. Here are a number of tips that can save you big money — in some cases $2,400 or more on an income of $50,000:

* Use the long form, even if you don't itemize. Filing the IRS short Form 1040EZ not only eliminates itemizing, it also prevents you from taking the Individual Retirement Account deduction (even if you're qualified) — which can cost you as much as $620 in extra taxes each year. Similarly, short Form 1040A doesn't let you deduct penalties for early withdrawal of a bank CD or other time deposit. Before using either short form, check Form 1040 and Schedule A for any deductions or other tax benefits you might miss.

* Claim every exemption. Each one is worth $2,150 — which will save you between $323 and $667, depending on your tax brackets. Most commonly overlooked exemptions are for parents or children who don't live with you.

* Use the right filing status. Tax rates are significantly lower for "Heads of Household" than for "Single" filers. Most married couples do best filing a joint return — unless one has much larger medical expenses or business-related deductions that would be wiped out by the joint AGI limits. Then, it makes more since to file separately and claim the expenses on the return of the spouse with lower earnings.

* Remember your medical-insurance deduction if you're self-employed. Youmay be allowed to deduct 25% of the premiums you pay for your own health insurance, depending on your overall income level.

* File on time — or file for an extension. Filing late extends the time in which

you can be audited and may embroil you in a lot of costly red tape. If you can't file by April 15, file Form 4868 requesting an extension. (Note: Even if you get an extension, you must still pay any taxes owed by April 15 or be subject to a penalty.)

* Double-check your W-2 Form. The amount should match that on your last pay stub for the year. Most Common Error: Employers fail to deduct the contribution to a 401(k) from the reportable income on the W-2.

* Pick the right method for deducting business meals. The IRS lets business travelers deduct a flat rate of $26 to $34 a day for meals instead of bothering with receipts. If you eat in cheaper restaurants when you travel, this flat rate could give you a bigger deduction than itemized meal costs. Trap: You have to elect one method for the entire year. You can't use the flat rate on a car trip to Modesto and the itemized method on a restaurant tour of San Francisco.

* Don't get trapped with a bad cosmetic surgery deduction. As of 1991, medical costs for cosmetic surgery are deductible only if the operation was required to correct a deformity related to a birth defect, a disfiguring disease or an accident.

* If you're self-employed and failed to get a Keogh retirement account set up by the end of the year, you can still set up a Simplified Employee Pension (SEP) until April 15. Don't fail to take advantage of one of these two retirement-savings options — which will also save you big tax dollars now.

* If you are required to take a medical exam by your employer, the cost can be deducted as an employee business expense rather than a medical deduction. This is important since employee expenses are deductible if they exceed 2% of your AGI (Adjusted Gross Income), while medical expenses are deductible only if they exceed 7.5% of AGI.

* Don't overlook credits for child-care expenses. If you hired someone to watch your kids so you could work, you may be eligible for the Child and Dependent Care Credit on Form 2441.

* Get full credit for mortgage interest paid. If you made a house payment late in December, it may not be reflected on the Form 1098 you receive from your lender. If it isn't, deduct the interest anyway and attach a note with your return explaining the discrepancy.

* If you take your spouse along on a business trip, don't credit him or her with a full half of the expenses incurred. Hotel rates for singles are usually the same, or at least 80% as much, as they are for doubles. Taxis also usually cost

the same for 1 person as for 2. The same goes for car rentals, valet parking, etc. It's likely meals will be the only item that requires a real 50-50 split.

* Claim all allowable mileage expenses. If you have 2 jobs, travel from one to the other is deductible. So is business travel to and from your home if it is your principal place of business, and travel from your regular workplace to a temporary work site. At the personal level, mileage for medical trips is deductible at 9 cents per mile, and mileage for charitable purposes is deductible at 12 cents per mile.

* Alimony payments are deductible; child support isn't. If you're getting a divorce, try to have as much of the monthly payment to your ex-spouse designated as alimony as possible.

* If you get lucky in Las Vegas, and have to report your winnings (casinos must tell the IRS any time you win a jackpot or wager of $1,200 or more), don't forget that you can also deduct your verifiable losses against thosewinnings. Most gamblers have more downs than ups, so it pays to keep a small book with your gambling winnings and losses, just so you'll be able to prove your losses should you need to offset part or all of a big win.

VALUABLE DEDUCTIONS MOST PEOPLE OVERLOOK

Many people fail to take advantage of some key deductions and longer-term tax-saving strategies. Here are some of the more common mistakes:

* Forgetting to keep track of expenses incurred in fixing up or improving a home. These expenses can be added to your cost basis, reducing your capital gain when you eventually sell.

* Failing to maximize the exclusion on capital gains taxes for home sellers over the age of 55. If 2 homeowners older than 55 plan to marry, and one has already taken the $125,000 exclusion on a home, then the other potential spouse should be sure to sell his or her residence before the wedding. This is a once-in-a-lifetime exclusion, and married couples are considered one unit for tax purposes. As a result, once the marriage takes place, the exclusion for the partner who hadn't yet used it will be wiped out. This single mistake can generate up to $35,000 in additional tax liability.

* Failing to keep track of property assessments. Special assessments for sidewalks, streets, sewers and other improvements that increase the value of your property can't be deducted from your income tax. However, they can be added to the cost basis for you home, reducing your taxable gain when you later sell.

* Failing to claim medical expenses for non-dependents. Just because you

can't claim a parent or other individual as a dependent doesn't mean you can't deduct any medical expenses you pay on their behalf. Just add the amount paid to your own medical expenses and deduct them (subject, of course, to the AGI limitations).

* Forgetting to tell the IRS when you move. In early 1991, the IRS had more than 72,000 tax refund checks worth about $41 million that had been returned because of incorrect addresses. If you move after filing your tax return, but before you get your refund, call 1-800-829-3676 and ask for Form 8822 to report your change of address.

* Incurring penalties for underpaying estimated taxes. The safest strategy here is to pay a sum equal to your previous year's tax liability. This saves the trouble of calculating quarterly estimates while still protecting you from being penalized, even if your liability rises.

* Failing to make the most of tax-free investments. If high taxes on investment profits are a concern, you can reduce your liability by investing in tax-advantaged securities such as Treasury bonds, bills and notes; municipal bonds, annuities, variable life insurance policies and certain limited partnerships.

* Failing to deduct hobby expenses from hobby profits. If you collect items such as coins, stamps or baseball cards, any profits you make from selling items from you collection are taxable. However, they can be reduced by expenses incurred in building and maintaining the collection.

* Failing to take a home-office deduction. Many people shy away from home-office deductions because they are considered to be a "red flag" to the IRS. However, if you use a home office to generate significant income, then you are entitled to take deductions for the specific area you use for business. The same logic applies to deductions for home computers and personal automobiles used primarily for business purposes.

* Paying unnecessary taxes on items produced by your business that you use for personal purposes. If your business makes products or provides services, you and your family are entitled to samples of those products or services without claiming them as income, so long as they don't add to the company's deductible expense.

3 WAYS TO CUT YOUR STATE TAX BILLS 40% OR MORE

If you live in a state such as New York, California or Massachusetts that has a high state income tax, you know that the IRS is not your only worry come April. However, you can substantially reduce the state tax bite on your income — particularly in retirement — if you carefully select your investments. Here are 3 investment ideas designed to cut state income taxes up to 40%:

1. U.S. Treasury obligations. Treasury bills, Treasury notes and U.S. government bonds are exempt from state income taxes (as well as being considered the safest investment in the world).

2. Series EE Savings Bonds. These government-issued bonds pay a guaranteed 6% return if held for at least 5 years. They are also exempt from state taxes, and federal taxes on the interest they earn is also deferred until they mature. Further deferral is possible by converting them to Series HH bonds at maturity. Series HH bonds pay interest in cash twice a year, and it is also exempt from state taxes (though not from federal levies).

3. Bonds issued by your home state or municipalities within your state are generally exempt from both state and federal income taxes (some agency issued bonds are excluded from state exemptions, so be sure to check). Note: It's possible to make capital gains on these bonds if interest rates fall, and those gains are taxable. Only interest payments are exempt. If you don't want to go to the trouble of selecting and managing your own portfolio of municipal bonds, there are many state-specific tax-exempt mutual funds that also offer largely tax-exempt interest payments (though some of these funds also generate some taxable dividends).

Warning: If you plan to move out of state after retirement, you could lose the tax exemption on your bond investments — and also have to pay taxes on deferred income earned in the state where you formerly lived. Be sure to check the tax laws for both the state you're moving from and the state you're moving to before you plan your retirement budget.

TURNING BUSINESS DEPRECIATION INTO PERSONAL TAX BREAKS

Business property that has used up most or all of its depreciation can still provide personal tax benefits if you use a gift-leaseback arrangement involving lower-income family members. Here's how it works:

* The owner gives the property to a family member, then leases it right back. The lease must be in writing and the leaseback rental rates must be reasonable when measured against commercial rates in your area.

* Rental payments are considered as business expenses and as income to the family members who now own the property.

* When a gift-leaseback deal is set, the donor must yield control over the physical property and relinquish all substantial equity interest in it (some minor equity positions are allowed under specific conditions).

* Expert legal and tax advice is essential in setting up such arrangements. If the IRS successfully challenges a gift-leaseback, the owner will be denied the

rental deduction and may be required to pay income tax on any rental payments he made.

B. Holding Your Own With the IRS

THE 7 MOST COMMON TAX FILING MISTAKES

Even if you are extremely careful about keeping records and claiming deductions properly, it's still possible to run afoul of the IRS. Here are the 7 most common mistakes made in compiling and filing federal tax returns:

* Adding up income totals incorrectly when you fill out your 1040.

* Using the wrong tax tables and coming up with the wrong amount of tax.

* Getting the earned income credit amount wrong. To avoid mistakes, follow the instruction booklet worksheet.

* Miscalculating the amount of taxable unemployment. Use the special formula in the IRS instruction booklet.

* Confusing withheld income tax with the Social Security tax that was withheld.

* Making errors in calculating child and dependent-care expenses. Follow Form 2441 and go over all calculations.

* Amazingly, many taxpayers are also confused about whether the IRS owes them or they owe the IRS. Double check the tax you owe with how much you've already paid through withholding or estimated tax payments.

6 KEYS TO AVOIDING AN IRS AUDIT

Want to triggor an IRS Audit? Here are some "red flag" deductions or mistakes that could just do the job:

* Expenses incurred in transactions involving relatives.

* Overstated casualty losses: Use IRS Form 4684 to make sure you don't go over legal limits on casualty deductions.

* Home office deductions: The room must be used solely for business and

be your principal place of business.

* Charitable donations of property or undocumented charitable gifts: List the dates of all property contributions, the fair market value and the name of the charity. Any property worth more than $5,000 must be independently appraised.

* Large losses on tax shelters: These almost always trigger an audit.

* Unreimbursed or overstated business expenses: Keep them well-documented and reasonable.

...AND WHEN YOU SHOULD ASK FOR ONE

Believe it or not, there are times you should ask for an IRS audit. Here are 3 instances:

1. It could be much better — and cheaper — to be audited right after a business is shut down, when records and key personnel are easily available, than to wait for a later date when people and documents are dispersed.

2. The sooner the IRS examines an estate the better for heirs who will be sharing after-tax proceeds.

3. If a particular year's tax return is in dispute, you can request a prompt audit (within 18 months). Otherwise, the IRS has up to 3 years to make its examination. Note: Either use Form 4810 to ask for the prompt assessment or state in your letter that your request for an examination is made under Code Section 6501(d).

DEFUSING IRS `LETTER' BOMBS

If you're like most taxpayers, you react adversely to getting an envelope from the IRS. Here's a list of likely IRS communications, and the appropriate response. (Note: In several cases, no response is required, but it's always best to check with your tax adviser on any IRS communication.)

Audit Notices: Usually no written response is needed. You may need to prepare schedules to respond to an IDR (Information Document Request).

Agreement Forms: These come after an audit. Sign only if you agree with the specified changes on your return.

Tax Bill: Officially a "Notice and Demand," this is like any bill. Pay on time — or face the consequences.

Penalty Notice: These are keyed to a specific penalty, and will include an explanation, along with the amount due and what exactly is required of you. Many penalties are reversible by prompt and proper action on your part.

30-Day Letter: You have 30 days to pay the amount requested or submit a written protest against the IRS adjustments detailed in the letter or pay the amount noted.

90-Day Letter: This deficiency notice allows you 90 days to file a petition with the Tax Court or pay the amount specified.

Request to Extend Statute of Limitations: Sign if you agree; ignore it if you don't. However, if you don't sign, expect a 90-Day Letter fairly soon.

Tax Shelter Notice: This is a pre-filing notification, warning you that a shelter's benefits are non-deductible and, if claimed, will subject you to penalties. No response is needed.

General Advice: When documents are requested, send Xeroxes, not originals, putting your name and Social Security number on each page to speed processing. Always send replies by certified mail ("return receipt requested") in time to meet IRS deadlines.

Trap to Avoid: Any time you make a payment to the IRS in response to a notice or other communication, be sure to designate which tax liability the payment is supposed to cover. If you don't make this clear, the IRS may credit the payment to some other liability, leaving those tax bills that carry the most excessive penalties unsatisfied. Payments can even be credited to liabilities that you haven't yet been informed of, leaving you in the awkward position of thinking you've paid a bill when you really haven't.

WHEN 2 RETURNS ARE BETTER THAN 1

A joint return usually brings tax savings because joint return rates are usually more favorable than rates for married persons filing separately, and child-care expenses can only be deducted on a joint return. However, separate filings do have advantages in some cases:

* If the husband or wife has hefty medical expenses, they are deductible only in excess of 7.5% of both spouses' combined income. A smaller income on a separate return might result in a deduction that wouldn't show up with the larger combined income of a joint return.

* In community property states, all community income and deductions are reported half on each return. This can result in lower tax-bracket filings.

* Some married couples file separate returns to keep private from a spouse the source and extent of their earnings.

* The tax savings from separate returns can be greater in certain states than the federal tax savings from a joint return.

THE BEST DAY TO FILE YOUR FEDERAL TAX RETURN

Actually, there are 3 best days, depending on what you are trying to accomplish:

1. If you have a refund coming, the best day to file is the earliest day possible. Why let the government keep your money any longer than you have to?

2. If you owe additional taxes, the best day to file is April 15. Again, why give the government you money any sooner than you absolutely have to?

3. If you are worried about an audit, the best day to file is — believe it or not — Oct. 15. That's right, you should go ahead and pay your estimated tax bill on the April 15th deadline, but you should file IRS Form 4868 requesting the automatic extension on actually filing your return. The reason is that the IRS selects returns for audit during the summer months and, by fall, the quota for that year's audits has largely been filled. Factor in scheduling problems and inattention by exhausted IRS personnel who have to review tax returns kicked out by the computer, and it becomes increasingly unlikely that your return will be picked. Warning: Be sure to pay exactly as much tax on April 15 as you think you're going to owe. (In fact, it's not a bad idea to go ahead and have your taxes finished by then, even though you're planning to get an extension.) If you pay less than 90% of what you actually owe, you'll be hit with a penalty and possible loss of your extension.

BETTER LATE THAN ON TIME?

There are at least 3 other good reasons for seeking an extension of the filing deadline for your federal tax returns:

1. You're involved in a complicated financial transaction and need more time to adequately evaluate the tax consequences.

2. You are missing necessary tax documents or vital information needed to complete your return.

3. You need more time to come up with the cash for your Keogh account

contribution. (These can be made up to the extended due date of your return — as late as Oct. 15.)

Extension Timetable: You can get an automatic 4-month extension by filing Form 4868 by April 15 and paying the balance of the tax you expect to owe. A second filing extension of 2 months is possible, but not automatic. The IRS demands a valid reason before granting an extension until Oct. 15.

Repeat Reminder: A filing extension is not a paying extension. You must enclose a check for the estimated tax due or the extension won't be valid. You'll also be hit with late-filing and late-payment penalties, plus interest on the taxes paid after the deadline.

10 EXCUSES THE IRS ALWAYS ACCEPTS

As just mentioned, you'll be hit with a penalty for filing a late return without an extension — unless you can come up with an excuse the IRS buys. Believe it or not, there are at least 10 excuses the IRS always accepts:

1. Your return was filed on time but sent to the wrong IRS office.

2. Your return reached the IRS late, but you sent it by certified mail so you can prove you got it to the post office on time.

3. You have advice in writing to prove that you relied on bad information from an IRS employee.

4. Your return was filed late because a fire, flood or other disaster hit your home or business, destroying your tax records.

5. The death of an immediate family member (or of the taxpayer himself) is always accepted. An incapacitating illness is also usually persuasive.

6. You were unavoidably called out of the country on critical business. (You can sometimes even get away with a delay if you were merely forced to be out of town and away from the site of your tax records.)

7. You couldn't get the proper tax forms or information from the IRS in time, even though you requested them well before the deadline.

8. You never had to file a particular kind of form before, and thus were ignorant of the law until it was too late to get the information needed.

9. You were unable to meet with an IRS representative regarding questions on your return, even though you tried — and can prove it.

10. A professional tax adviser told you a tax return was unnecessary.

Making Your Case: Don't wait until you get a penalty notice. Request the penalty be set aside in a letter to your local IRS Service Center. Explain why you filed late, pleading "reasonable cause" — a good phrase to use. Attach your letter to your late-filed return.

MEETING THE IRS DEPENDENCY REQUIREMENTS

What are the rules of dependency for tax purposes? Five tests must be met to qualify:

1. Relationship — Family relations (child, grandchild, stepchild, sibling, step-sibling, parents, grandparent, stepparent, niece, nephew, aunt, uncle, in-law) need not be a member of the taxpayer's household for the taxable year. Otherwise, a dependent person must belong to the taxpayer's household.

2. Citizenship — The dependent must be a U.S. citizen, or a resident of the U.S., Canada or Mexico for some part of the year.

3. Joint Return — The dependent must not file a joint return.

4. Gross Income — Dependent can't have more gross income than the amount of the personal exemption ($2,300 for 1992). Social Security benefits and other non-taxable income are not included as gross income for this purpose.

(There are exceptions to the gross income provisions that involve minor children.)

5. Support — Generally more than half the dependent's support must come from the taxpayer. Note: The custodial parent, in cases of divorce or separation, gets the dependency exemption unless he or she expressly waives it.

MAKING UP FOR POOR RECORD KEEPING

Your records are in disarray and you face an audit. What do you do? Head for Argentina? No. Do your best to recall your expenses. The IRS has been known to be tolerant of such reconstructed documentation. Note: reconstruction doesn't mean fabrication or falsifying documents; that is illegal. Here's how to proceed:

* Try to get copies of missing receipts. Failing that, use canceled checks that prove payments.

* Collect facts to back up your deductions, even though you can't document every dollar claimed.

* If necessary, get affidavits from third parties.

* Ask ahead of time which items the IRS auditor wants to examine.

* Prepare (and bring along) worksheets showing how you calculated all lump-sum deductions.

* For business expenses, write down details you recall — for instance, list person you entertained along with date, place and business purpose.

* Substantiate business travel, listing people met and their business connection. You might bring along relevant business correspondence.

C. Key Tax-Cutting Tips & Tools

GUIDELINES FOR DEALING WITH YOUR ACCOUNTANT

Don't make the mistake of dumping all your receipts on your tax accountant's desk and walking away. To maximize your deductions, you need to work with him or her — and understand the process. Here's a checklist:

1. Bring everything. Follow-up information, especially after your return has been prepared, will cost your accountant time — and you money.

2. Categorize expense information. Financial and tax-preparation software can be used for this. (One of the best packages we've found for this purpose is Kiplinger's "TaxCut." Available for IBM and compatible computers in both DOS and Windows versions, will automatically categorize expenses, working in conjunction with many accounting and money-management programs, and calculate your taxes, indicating which forms are need. It also has a "Help" function that provides tax tips and strategies. To order, specify the version desired and send $39.95, plus local sales taxes, to Kipling TaxCut, P.O. Box 912, Fairfield, CT 06430, or call 1-800-365-1546, Ext. 10, to order using your Visa, MasterCard or American Express card.)

3. Flag unusual deductions such as unreimbursed business travel, dependent care, job-hunting expenses.

4. Tell the accountant about any changes in your personal or financial status that would affect your tax situation.

5. Decide in advance your audit tolerance. Aggressive deductions also increase the likelihood of an IRS audit. A conservative filing will save you less but cut your audit risk.

6. Be prepared for an IRS audit anyway — and be aware that you're responsible, not your accountant. Keep all your tax preparation worksheets with your receipts so you can show how you calculated various expense figures.

Word to the Wise: Accountant-client communications aren't privileged like conversations between attorneys and their clients. An accountant can thus be required to testify against a client who has admitted he committed a crime. In other words, be careful what you tell your accountant — and, if you have anything to hide, consider hiring an attorney first and having him hire the accountant. That way the umbrella of privilege will cover the accountant.

THE BEST TAX SHELTER IN AMERICA TODAY

By far, the option that provides the most tax benefits in America is ownership of your own business. When you own a business, you can, among many other things:

* Deduct all business expenses.

* Deduct all interest on loans used for business purposes.

* Drive a tax-deductible company car.

* Live tax-free in company quarters under some circumstances.

* Deduct most travel and entertainment expenses.

* Deduct or depreciate all office equipment, furnishings, manufacturing machinery, computer equipment, software, etc.

* Set up pension plans that allow you to deduct large portions of your income on a pre-tax basis and deposit them in accounts that will earn tax-deferred returns until you begin to withdraw them.

What if you work for someone else and lack the knowledge, time or funds to start your own business? What's your best shelter then? No doubt about it, the answer is a 401(k) retirement account. With a 401(k) account, you can:

* Put a portion of your salary — up to 25% (though most employers limit contributions to between 11% and 15%), with an annual limit of $8,728 for 1992 — into a tax-deferred retirement account.

* Deduct the amount of your contribution from your income before federal, state, local or Social Security taxes are assessed.

* Choose to put the money in a variety of professionally managed investments, ranging from conservative, fixed-income instruments to aggressive

securities such as growth-stock mutual funds.

* Receive additional matching tax-free contributions (usually totaling about 50 cents on the dollar up to 6% or 7% of your salary) to the account from your employer.

* Avoid taxes on all earnings generated by the account until you begin to withdraw it (as early as age 59-1/2 and no later than age 70-1/2).

* Withdraw the money in a variety of ways in order to continue maximizing tax savings after retirement.

What's the second-best shelter for both business owners and employed individuals. Without question, it would have to be home ownership. When you own a home:

* Your mortgage interest is deductible.

* Your real estate taxes are deductible.

* You can defer taxes on an capital gains you make when you sell the home, so long as you are buying a costlier replacement (within 2 years of the original sale).

* Once you turn 55, you get a one-time exclusion from capital gains taxes of up to $125,000 in profits on the sale of your home (so long as you have lived in it for 3 of the past 5 years).

Despite recent tightening of tax laws, there are many other shelters and loopholes still available — but none can match the benefits of these 3!

A LEGAL WAY TO CUT YOUR TAX BILL 30% A YEAR

If you are self-employed, you can cut your annual tax bill significantly by making a contribution to a Keogh account or a Simplified Employee Pension (SEP) plan. These special retirement accounts allow you to contribute up to 20% of gross income or $30,000, whichever is less, to a special tax-deferred retirement account. Since the contribution is made in pre-tax dollars — i.e., money that hasn't

yet had federal, state or self-employment taxes withheld — you automatically reduce your federal tax bill by as much as 20%, regardless of your bracket. Throw in associated reductions in state taxes in high-tax states, as well as any reduction in the amount of self-employment tax (up to 9.76% of your AGI), and your contribution can responsible for an overall reduction in your annual tax bill of as much as 30%.

GET MAXIMUM TAX BENEFITS FROM YOUR CHARITABLE DONATIONS

There are many organizations in the United States that have tax-exempt status — and most people believe that donations to these groups are tax deductible. However, that's not the case. For example, donations to fraternal orders, which are tax-exempt groups, are not deductible on your tax return. If you have any doubt that your donation to an organization will be deductible, request a copy of the charity's financial statement or IRS Form 990. These should detail the deductibility of contributions to the organization in question. You can also request a copy of IRS Publication 78, "Cumulative List of Organizations," which is an annual listing of thousands of tax-exempt groups to which donations are deductible. To get a copy, call 1-800-829-3676.

SAVING TOO MUCH FOR RETIREMENT CAN BE COSTLY

Throughout "Money $ecret$," we have emphasized the importance of maximizing your retirement savings. However, it is possible to have too much of a good thing — and this is one area where that can happen. Once the assets in your IRAs, Keoghs, SEPs, or 401(k)s reach $1 million or more, you could be heading for other tax problems if you don't take some time out and re-evaluate your situation. While no set of rules applies to everyone, the example of a 53-year-old professional, as reported recently in The New York Times, could give you an idea of the potential problems that can result from saving TOO MUCH for retirement.

This man, who intended to retire at age 65 and wanted a comfortable life for himself and his wife, as well as a nice estate for his children, had built up a healthy $1.2 million in his retirement plan. The account's investments were returning an average of 9% a year — which meant the account would be worth roughly $3.5 million by the time the man turned 65. That sounds great, but there are problems. If the man died in the same year he turned 65, his heirs — other than his wife — would owe a 15% tax on excess accumulation, or $263,000. They would also owe a 55% estate tax, or $1.75 million. And, they would owe federal and state income taxes of more than $575,000. The net result: The family would get only about a quarter of the money that was in the plan — or $860,000.

In case you weren't aware of it, there is an obscure provision of the retirement savings laws that comes into play on large accounts, or when the account holder dies shortly after retirement. This is the excess-distribution penalty — a 15% levy that comes into play when annual withdrawals exceed about $150,000. Depending on the life expectancy tables in force, almost anyone with a retirement fund balance in excess of $1.2 million or so will have a hard time keeping annual withdrawals below the penalty limit. Add in the income taxes that will be due on the deferred contributions and their earnings, and you could wind up with some hefty tax bills in retirement. In fact, in the New York man's case, the projected bills were so large that he decided to start taking withdrawals at age 55 instead of age 65, paying the early withdrawal penalty for 4-1/2 years because it was lower than the excess distribution penalties he'd later incur. The withdrawn money — about $18,000 a year on an after-tax basis — went into trust accounts for his children, allowing them to escape the estate taxes and excess-accumulation penalties.

If you've saved too much for retirement, review your situation and make adjustments now — before you have to pay big tax consequences later.

WATCH OUT FOR TAXES ON ZERO-COUPON BONDS

Many people have chosen so-called zero-coupon bonds as vehicles for building education funds for their children or meeting other future needs, such as the purchase of a home. These bonds pay no annual interest, but rather are sold at deep discounts — sometimes as much as 95% — and then mature at full face value. Unfortunately, the federal government doesn't recognize the deferral feature on these bonds. As a result of recent tax law changes, holders of zero-coupon bonds are required to pay taxes on the "phantom income" generated by the bonds, even though they don't actually receive it until the zeroes mature. This means you will have to come up with as much as 31% of the increase in value of your bonds each year — and send it to Uncle Sam in the form of taxes. For this reason, many people are now limiting their use of zero-coupon bonds to IRAs or Keoghs, where the deferral feature of the retirement account shelters the "accreted" income on the bonds.

D. Getting Money Back From Uncle Sam

HOW TO COLLECT FROM SOCIAL SECURITY AT ANY AGE

You don't have to wait until you turn 65 (or even 62) to get some of your hard-earned dollars back from Uncle Sam in the form of Social Security payments. Millions of Americans — even children in some cases — legally collect Social Security benefits every year. How do they do it? That's what a new book by Discovery Publishers explains, spelling out in detail the various types of benefits for which you may qualify and providing step-by-step instructions on how to successfully apply for them. Among the topics covered:

* How to get a lump-sum payment of Social Security benefits.

* How you can collect Social Security and work at the same time.

* How to estimate your Social Security retirement income.

* What kind of medical benefits Social Security offers — and how you can qualify for them.

* Ways you can increase your benefit levels.

* How to get a refund if you've overpaid your Social Security taxes.

* How students ages 18 to 22 can qualify for benefits.

* How your marital status can affect your benefits (an anomaly in the law that has led many elderly couples to file for divorce in order to increase their retirement incomes).

* What other kinds of services are offered by the Social Security Administration.

The book costs just $12, with a full money-back guarantee, and you can order a copy by sending a check or money order to Discovery Publishers, 11160 Veirs Mill Road, L-15, Dept. 240-S, Wheaton, MD 20902.

112 GOVERNMENT PROGRAMS THAT COULD PAY YOU

Most people are fully aware of Social Security retirement and disability benefit programs — but did you know that there are more than 100 other federal programs that regularly make payments to Americans. In fact, according to a new book by California consultant R. Emil Neuman, 1 out of every 4 people in America collects some form of monthly payment from Uncle Sam — with the payouts totaling more than $250 billion a year. In addition to detailed information on applying for and collecting Social Security and other federal retirement benefits and federal disability payments, the book — titled "How To Collect Big Dollars From Uncle Sam" — also covers such topics as:

* How eligible couples can collect up to $1,100 a month to supplement family income.

* How to collect unemployment benefits, even if you quit or were fired for cause.

* How to get free government legal assistance.

* How to get a $250,000 government loan to buy a working farm or ranch.

* How to borrow up to $500,000 from Uncle Sam to start a new business.

* How to get a $15,000 loan for home improvements.

* How to collect more than $400 a month to help pay expenses for college, a trade school or on-the-job training.

* How to get free government medical coverage, including eyeglasses and dental care.

* How to qualify for government rent subsidies.

* What kind of free services the government offers — and how you can qualify for them.

The book costs just $12.95, plus $3 postage and handling, and can be ordered by sending a check or money order to R. Emil Neuman, 249 So. Highway 101, Dept. EC-01, Solana Beach, CA 92075. If not satisfied, you can return the book for a full refund within 30 days.

CHAPTER 16

TRAVELING IN STYLE

A. Reduced Fares & Special Rates

A LITTLE-KNOWN WAY TO TRAVEL FREE

If you like to travel, but your budget won't cooperate, you may be able to take advantage of a little-known method for earning free trips. Companies that set up tours and group-travel packages are always looking for people to coordinate travel arrangements and lead the tour groups. You'll have to deal with a few hassles, but you'll get to see everything the other group members do — and the tour company will pay all your expenses. There's a particularly high demand for bilingual individuals to lead both American tours overseas and foreign groups visiting the United States. If you're interested, simply check the Travel Section of your local newspaper to get the names of companies that put together tours — and give the manager a call.

GO BACK TO SCHOOL — AND SAVE ON TRAVEL

If you're over 60, you can get some great travel bargains — and brush up on your education — through an organization called Elderhostel. The non-profit group sponsors 1- and 2-week "learning vacations" for seniors at more than 1,200 universities and colleges around the world. You stay in dorms and eat cafeteria food, but the cost is under $300 a week for most U.S. campuses and under $500 for European destinations. You do have to pay transportation costs. For a free catalog explaining the program and describing the various destinations, write Elderhostel, 75 Federal St., Boston, MA 02110.

SAVE UP TO 50% ON ALL YOUR TRAVEL EXPENSES

When it comes to travel, timing can be everything. Any time you are planning a trip to a destination with seasonal rates, you can save big money by scheduling your visit just before or just after the busiest season. The attractions will still be the same and the weather will most likely be nearly as good, but airlines, hotels, tour companies and even some restaurants will offer discounts of as much as 50% because of the reduced demand. Bonus: You won't have to fight big crowds to do the things you want.

Ask for Discounts: Even if you don't travel off-season, you should ask for any discounts or reduced fares that hotels or airlines may be offering but not yet publicizing. Many travel-related businesses also offer special rates for children and senior citizens, but you'll have to ask to get them if they aren't currently being promoted.

TRAVEL FREE BY BECOMING A TRAVEL WRITER

Up until about 20 years ago, there was no better job in the newspaper or magazine business than that of travel writer. In an effort to get exposure for their hotels, attractions and vacation meccas, resort managers literally begged these writers to accept free flights, free accommodations, free meals and numerous other benefits just so they could additional media exposure — and, of course, the extra business generated by such exposure. Then, however, came Watergate — during which the managers of the major media chains decided they could hardly serve as the watchdogs of government if their own reporters and writers were accepting free trips, free theater tickets and other benefits from sources they were supposed to be objectively covering. As a result, journalists were largely

banned from accepting freebies — and publishers started paying the freight for their travel writers, theater critics, etc. However, as times got harder and budgets got tighter, the media companies were forced to institute cutbacks — and one of the easiest things to cut was travel solely for the purpose of reviewing resorts and favored destinations (as opposed to travel for "hard news" stories such as wars and disasters). This left a huge void in the field of travel and resort promotion, which is now being filled largely by freelance writers — who not only get many of the same freebies formerly accorded to newspaper and magazine reporters, but also get paid by the editors for the stories that result.

So, how do you get in on the action. Obviously, it helps if you can write — though you certainly don't need to be a professional. Travel editors are more interested in real-life experiences and alternative viewpoints than they are in clean, grammatically correct copy (after all, that's what editors are for). And, resort managers just want the exposure (they let the editors worry about the quality of writing). Thus, the best approach is to contact your local newspaper, ask for the travel editor and tell him you have plans to visit a particular country, region, resort or other location of interest (the more exotic the better, though you should keep in mind the travel tastes of the people who read the paper). Ask if he or she would be interested in seeing an article describing your experiences when you return. Editors are almost always to at least look at interesting articles, so it's likely the answer will be yes (without a commitment to publish, of course). You can then legitimately contact the promotional department, public relations officer or manager of the resort you plan to visit (or the tourist bureau of the city or country where it's located) and explain that you have a tentative assignment to do an article or series of articles about them, but that you could use some financial assistance with the expenses. Most tourist areas are used to such requests and have promotional budgets or trade arrangements with hotels and airlines that allow them to offer you free airfares or lodging in exchange for a favorable story. It won't work every time, but quite often it will — and the personal savings to you are well worth the attempt.

GET THE BEST RATE ON HOTEL RESERVATIONS

Even though many hotel chains have a national reservation number, you won't always get the best rate by calling it. Local hotels often adjust their rates to reflect changes in room demand or seasonal factors that don't apply on a nationwide basis. As a result, you can often get big savings on rooms by making your reservation directly with the hotel at which you plan to stay. Best Strategy: Call both the local hotel reservation desk and the chain's nationwide toll-free reservation number, then make your booking through the one that quotes the best rate.

SAVE 25% TO 35% ON HOTEL RATES JUST BY ASKING

It's also possible to save as much as 35% on your hotel expenses just by asking to be booked at the hotel's corporate rate rather than at the regular rate. This won't work at many resort areas, but it will in most major cities, where competition among hotels is stiff and the leading chains routinely offer discounts to business travelers. You will have to make arrangements in advance in order to receive the special rate, and some hotels won't give it to you unless you stay there a minimum number of nights each year. However, others will automatically give the corporate rate to anyone who writes for reservations on their company's letterhead stationery.

SAILING TO BIG SAVINGS ON CRUISES

With the economy still sluggish in the United States, Europe and Japan, many people have cut back sharply on luxury vacations and high-priced trips. As a result, many of the companies that offer such excursions are offering sizable discounts to both win back customers and fill empty space. And, the luxury cruise lines are no exception.

Cruise ships sailing the waters of the Caribbean, Mexican Riviera, Alaska, Mediterranean and the worlds other tropical or scenic seas now have more than 100,000 berths available — berths that need to be filled almost every week of the year. That means they need more than 5 million passengers annually — and are willing to provide big discounts to get them. In fact, if you call your travel agent right now and ask about sailing next month, you can probably get an automatic discount from published fares of at least 10% — and more likely 20%. Wait until right before sailing time and express your willingness to take "space available," and you can likely get 50% to 60% off.

Of course, most of us would rather have a little more notice and flexibility in picking our trips — and, fortunately, similar discounts are available on more advance bookings if you're willing to put in a little effort to pick out special promotions and stay away from peak time periods. You can also pick up big savings by pre-booking early voyages on new ships, which will still be working out kinks and getting their levels of service up to par. (Six new ships were scheduled to begin sailing in 1993, 2 are set for 1994 and 2 more for 1995.) In all cases, you can probably find these discounts yourself, but most travel agents will happily spend the time to ferret out the best deal for you, so why not use their services.

Sail for Free: You can also manage big savings by booking along with a group — such as bridge players, ballroom dancers, investment clubs, civic groups, etc. — or sail for FREE by putting together such a group yourself and taking the package to the cruise line. Discounts tend to be lower for cruises to the most popular destinations, so you can also increase savings by choosing more out-of-the-way places (ideal for those who care more about how they get there than where they're going).

Extra Savings Tip: Cruises are beehives of activity (though you can just sit and laze in the sun if you desire), so you won't be spending much time in your cabin except when you're sleeping. Given that, you can save as much as 50% off the cost of the trip by booking the lowest class of cabin rather than the most expensive. With the exception of the Queen Elizabeth II, cruise ships today make no class distinctions in terms of services, entertainment or food, so the only price variable involves the size and location of the cabin. Pick the cheapest cabin, and you'll get just as much service and fun as the high rollers at half the price.

Getting to the Ship: If the cruise package you select offers an airfare option for getting to and from your ship's sailing point, be sure and take it. The cruise lines pay subsidies to the airlines for these flights, meaning you can usually save 30% to 40% over the best price you'd get if you tried to arrange air transportation yourself. This is particularly true if you take a cruise that starts and ends at 2 different locations, as is the case with many Panama Canal and 1-week Mexican Riviera cruises.

A Little Adventure: If you have some extra time and want to try something different, why not sail aboard a freighter. Many of the newer freighters have space for 6 to 20 passengers and regularly book voyages for people who are more interested in kicking back on deck with a good book and lots of fresh sea air than in seeing a show or playing in a shuffleboard tournament. The food is usually quite good, though the selection will be more limited, and the accommodations are comparable to those on cruise ships. The costs usually run a little lower than published cruise line fares, but the freighter companies usually don't offer discounts as their profit comes from cargo rather than passengers and they don't care if they sail with empty cabins. Also, you will probably have to pay extra for your airfare. For more information, call Freighter World Cruises at 818-449-3106. The handle bookings for more than a dozen different shipping lines and also publish a newsletter called "Freighter Space Advisory," which comes out every 2 weeks and costs $27 a year.

B. Other Tips for Savings & Safety

PROTECT YOURSELF AGAINST HOTEL ROBBERIES

A favorite trick of hotel hold-up men is to phone a guest's room and, pretending to be the manager or desk clerk, advise that a maintenance person is heading up to check out a reported gas leak, water leak or other problem. When the guest opens the door in response to the expected knock, out comes a weapon — and out goes the guest's money and jewelry.

What to Do: Should you ever receive such a call, immediately dial the front desk or manager's office to confirm that the request is legitimate. If it's not, request that hotel security be sent to your floor.

Second Choice: Demand to see identification through the peephole if the room door has one, or request that the alleged maintenance person come back in the company of someone who has a hotel master key.

Key Safety Rule: Never open your hotel door in response to an unidentified knocker — even if you're expecting someone.

BEAT HIGH HOTEL LONG-DISTANCE CHARGES

Hotels are notorious for imposing excessive charges for long-distance calls made from in-room phones — and using your phone company calling card may not protect you. Many hotels add a charge to your bill every time you ask for a connection to a long-distance carrier, even if you use a calling card. However, you can beat this system by bunching your calls. When you finish one, don't hang up. Instead, wait for the person you've called to disconnect, and then press the pound button (#). You'll get a new dial tone, at which time you can dial the next number. Continue the process until you finish all your calls, and the hotel should bill you for only one long-distance connection.

SAVE ONE DAY'S CAR-RENTAL CHARGE

If you arrive in a city late in the day and are staying at a hotel near the airport, don't head straight for the car rental counter. Instead, take the free hotel shuttle or a cab to the hotel, spend the night and rent your car the next day (you can take the shuttle back to the airport), thus saving a day's rental charge.

TRAVELING IN DEDUCTIBLE STYLE

Your business travel doesn't have to be bargain basement. Some luxuries are justifiable (by you to your employer), and deductible (by your employer to the IRS). Here's a high-flying list:

1. Suites in fine hotels — if they are to be used for business meetings.

2. First-class airfare, to help you work (or sleep in comfort so you'll be ready for important business meetings or client calls.

3. A limo to and from the airport and to and from your hotel — especially if you're on a tight schedule or have important appointments.

SAVINGS TIP FOR TRAIN TRAVELERS

Most U.S. railway fares these days have a heavy front-end load, so be sure to book round-trip tickets. For example, a one-way Los Angeles-to-Las Vegas

Amtrak ticket costs $65 (rates subject to change), but a round-trip ticket is only $68. Also be sure to ask for excursion fares, which are designed for short-stay, round-trip travelers. A regular New York-to-Philadelphia-and-back ticket on the Metroliner recently cost $92, while a round-trip excursion fare was just $47.

PLANNING AHEAD FOR SAFER OVERSEAS TRAVEL

Foreign travel offers tremendous pleasure, giving you a much better view of the world in which you live. However, in these unstable times, with ethnic and religious conflicts around the globe and the ever-present threat of terrorist activity, overseas travel can pose some serious dangers. Fortunately, many of these dangers can be reduced with proper planning before you go, and some sensible precautions while you are traveling.

Things To Do Before You Go:

* Check the vaccinations you will need well in advance of your trip. Some may take more than one inoculation, with as much as a month between shots.

* Make sure your passport is up to date or, if you don't have one, get it — along with any needed visas — at least a month in advance. Also get some extra photos made for possible use on foreign driver's licenses, travel permits or for a new passport if yours is lost.

* If you've traveled using your existing passport, make sure the stamps inside won't cause you problems on your current trip. For example, if you've been to Israel, you should probably get a new passport before traveling to Arab countries.

* Set up a file at your home — with a copy at your office if you are traveling on business — containing key information about your trip. This should include your itinerary, complete with flight numbers and times; a Xerox of your airline ticket, passport and visas; a record of your blood type, other medical conditions or restrictions, eyeglass prescriptions and a copy of your vaccination certificates; a list of traveler's check numbers and an emergency communications plan (which we'll explain in a moment).

* Make sure all your personal and financial papers — from insurance policies to banking records to wills — are in order and that someone at home has access to them should you encounter problems abroad. This could include giving a power of attorney to your spouse or another person. You may also want to leave special instructions on what your family or business associates at home should say or do in case you become the victim of a kidnapping or hijacking, particularly with regard to talking to the press.

* Set up an emergency communications code and give a copy to someone

at your home or office. The code should use a short, easily memorized list of seemingly innocuous words that actually have predefined alternate meanings. For example, the word “fine” — used as in “I am fine” — could actually mean “I am sick or injured.” With such a code, you'll be able to describe your conditions even if your captors monitor or restrict your communications.

In-Flight Precautions:

* Select an aisle seat near the rear of the plane. Not only do you have a better chance of surviving a crash at the back of the plane, but the aisle seat will give you access to exits on both sides of the plane. This is particularly important if a crash should result in a fire that blocks exits on one side of the plane. Seat selection is also important in the event of a terrorist attack. Hijackers tend to focus their attention near the cockpit, so you are less likely to be the target of a direct threat if you are in the rear of the plane. (Note: In the event of a terrorist takeover, try to shift out of your aisle seat; this will further reduce your chances of direct contact.)

* Fire is the biggest danger on planes. As a result, you should always wear cotton or pure wool when traveling. Avoid synthetics like polyester or nylon, which melt when exposed to fire. You might also look into some of the new safety products on the market — items like the “Survivaid,” a small pouch containing a flame-proof hood with a filter for smoke and toxic fumes (available for $29.95 from Survival Products Inc., Box 100428, Fort Worth, TX 76185).

* Terrorists will usually try to single out Americans, most likely by demanding everyone's passport. They also tend to focus their attention on government officials, military personnel, business executives and Jewish Americans. If you fall into any of these categories — or if you merely want to give yourself added protection — try to stall by keeping your passport in your carry-on luggage in the overhead compartment. That way, if you are able to move from your seat, you won't have your passport with you.

* Avoid carrying a briefcase or anything else that would identify you as a business traveler. Corporate executives are often targeted simply because terrorists view them as symbols of the capitalist system. In addition, they are more likely to be selected as hostages because of the potential for ransom payments by large companies.

* If you are Jewish or have a Jewish sounding name, you might attempt to throw the terrorists off track by carrying a pocket edition of the King James version of the Bible, wearing a neck chain with a cross or carrying other Christian religious objects in your carry-on luggage.

* You might also consider carrying a fake passport and ID cards (available from International Documents Services in Houston, Texas, for around $150). If you are traveling on a diplomatic passport, you should also get a tourist passport

and turn that over if demanded.

* Even with these precautions, you may eventually have to give up your real passport or identify yourself as an American. If that happens, do your best to remain calm and avoid antagonizing the terrorists. Under no circumstances should you act belligerently or in a threatening manner as the terrorists will feel compelled to punish your behavior to re-establish their authority over the other passengers.

Proper Behavior in a Foreign Country:

* You encounter your first real risk almost immediately after arrival. Once you pass through customs, you must walk through the terminal, luggage in hand, in search of a taxi or bus to take you to your hotel. This makes you a perfect target for pickpockets or thieves working today's crowded airports. To protect yourself, carry your money and important papers in a safe pocket or zipped inside a pocket in your carry-on bag, with the bag's strap securely wrapped around your arm or over your shoulder.

* Once you arrive at your hotel, take the time to find out where the exits are on your floor in case of fire or other disaster. Be sure to locate both the exit to the roof as well as to the ground floor, just in case a fire should break out on floors below yours.

* After you are settled into your hotel, it is a good idea to register with the U.S. Embassy — particularly if you are visiting a country where there is a possibility of unrest. In most countries, this can be done by phone and the time it takes could prove well spent in the event you have a problem — from something simple like needing a lost or stolen passport replaced to something major like needing emergency medical assistance or a safe haven in the event of civil unrest or a natural disaster.

* Once you move out into the city — whether on business or pleasure — try to avoid attracting attention to yourself. Act like you know what you are doing and where you are going, dress like the natives dress and don't wear expensive jewelry or carry exotic camera equipment.

* If you are in a country where there is a threat of terrorist activity, vary your routines and your routes as much as possible and avoid publicity or association with others who may be terrorist targets. You should also avoid letting the staff at your hotel or the local office of your business know your exact schedule.

* Should you encounter rioting or a public demonstration, the safest action is to move away from the disturbance and get indoors. If you are in the street when shooting breaks out, lie down immediately and cover your head with your arms. Don't look up or get up until the shooting stops — then get away as quickly as

possible. If you are in your hotel when shooting starts, turn out the lights, close the curtains, put your mattress or bed against the window and get on the floor.

* Be aware of local laws and any unusual restrictions. In many countries, you are not allowed to photograph public buildings, bridges, military installations and other such facilities. Avoid anything to do with illegal drugs. If you do run into legal problems or get detained by local police, stay calm and be cooperative with officials. Ask to contact the U.S. Embassy, which is your right under international conventions, but be polite with your requests — not demanding.

* Don't be an "ugly American." Whether traveling for business or pleasure, show respect for your hosts. Be polite to shopkeepers, hotel staff and others you may encounter and show consideration of local customs and habits.

AN EASY WAY TO GET A BETTER EXCHANGE RATE

When you're in a foreign country, you'll probably want to use the local currency (businesses in many tourist destinations happily take U.S. dollars, but you tend to get better prices if you pay in native money). Unfortunately, many currency-exchange operations in popular tourist spots don't give very good rates on dollar conversions.

A Better Idea: Leave most of your dollars at home and use your ATM card to make withdrawals at overseas machines. Most ATM transactions in a foreign currency are converted to dollars at the "wholesale" exchange rate — i.e., the rate banks get on conversions of $1 million or more. As a result, you can often get as much as $10 more on a $200 withdrawal from a foreign bank's ATM than you'd get if you went inside and changed your money (or cashed a traveler's check) at the counter. (Note: If you're worried about finding an ATM in a foreign country, most American Express offices have them. Simply ask American Express for a list of its offices in the country you're planning to visit and you'll always know where to get cash.)

The Catch: Your U.S. PIN (personal identification number) may not work overseas. Check with your bank or credit card company before you go to find out — and have them issue you an international PIN if you need one.

AVOID FOREIGN DRIVING HASSLES

If you plan to drive while in a foreign country, you may need either an International Driving Permit (which is valid in more than 100 nations around the world), or an Inter-American Driving Permit (good in 20 different countries in

North and South America). These permits, which are issued for a 1-year term, can be obtained at any AAA office (even if you're not a member) and usually cost around $10. Photos are required, so be sure to take along 2 passport-type pictures when you go to AAA.

HOW TO CANCEL NON-REFUNDABLE AIR TICKETS

Everyone who travels by air is familiar with the phrase "some restrictions apply" and the concept of the "Super-Saver," non-refundable airline ticket. However, in spite of all the hoopla, it's possible to routinely cancel these tickets and still get a full refund. The key is to work through a cooperative travel agent. When you purchase a discounted airline ticket from an agent, he or she will make your reservation immediately. However, because travel agencies pay airlines only once a week, your money won't be forwarded for up to 7 days — making it possible for you to cancel the reservation and get your money back. Not all travel agents will help you in these situations, but most will if you are a good customer and they want to keep your business. (Note: Airlines will give your money back if you have to change your plans due to a medical emergency, death or other major problem.)

Money $ecret: If you can't qualify for a discounted airfare for an upcoming trip because you won't be staying over a weekend or fulfilling some other requirement such as traveling on a weekday, you may still be able to save money through a little trickery. Often, 2 round-trip "Super-Saver" fares will cost less than a single full-fare round-trip ticket. If that's the case, you can book your outgoing flight as a round trip returning at a later date that will qualify you for the discount. Then book another round trip from your destination city, leaving on the date you want to return from your current trip and returning at some future time (but before the return trip on your outbound round trip). By doing this, you'll save money — even if you use only half of each round-trip ticket. However, you'll also have another free round-trip ticket to the same location that you can use for pleasure or another business trip. (Obviously, you'll have to juggle your schedule so the dates of second trip match the ticket dates — but the free trip should more than make up for your trouble.

CHAPTER 17

WORKING MORE WISELY

A. Getting Ahead in Your Job

2 CAREERS & TOO MUCH STRESS

These days, couples must often make difficult choices in order to provide a comfortable healthy environment in which to raise their families. Nearly 70% of married couples must rely on two paychecks to make monthly mortgage payments on their homes, and, in comparison to spending an average of 19% of their earnings in 1970 on home ownership, families now spend an average of 27% of their incomes. To meet the demands of their mortgages, Americans must work longer hours (an average of six hours a week more than 20 years ago), often commuting greater distances for higher paying jobs, thereby reducing the amount of time spent with their families. When you add to that the stress factor of managing such tight schedules, the remaining family and parenting time available is reduced in both quality and quantity.

Meeting the Challenges: If a couple's choice is to move out of a fast-paced city environment in order to provide an easy, comfortable suburban or country home in which to raise children, they are confronted with the problem of whether to accept lower paying jobs in local communities (provided they can find them) or facing a long commute. They will also incur increased expenses in the cost of commuting (at 33 cents a mile) and the cost of additional child care. Some tips on managing:

1. Minimize commuting costs and time by working longer days so that you can decrease your work week to four days, for example, instead of five.

2. Set up a home office with computer and fax transmittal systems, which would allow one or both partners to work at home some of the time — and can also reduce child care costs.

3. Car pool whenever possible — either with office or work mates and friends, or with your spouse.

4. Often a spouse can adjust his or her work shift in ways that complement the other's work shift so that one parent is available to the children more of the time — again, reducing child care, and providing more parental nurturing for the children.

5. If your employment allows flex-hours, choose to begin and end your work day when traffic is lighter.

6. Analyze the expenses of sending school-age children to private schools which provide on-site after-school care versus public schools and paid after-school care that is often off the school campus. Think in terms of stress on the children, and of the extra services private schools often provide, in addition to smaller class sizes and higher quality education. Often you will find that the benefits of a private school are not as expensive as you might have thought — and will give you greater peace of mind as you work.

7. Network in the new community and keep an updated resume ready for opportunities of local employment when they do arise. If even one spouse is able to avoid a commute — even at a lower wage, the reduction of stress and ability to spend more time with the children may be worth the decrease in pay — not to mention the decreased cost of commuting.

8. Remember to negotiate with an employer if both spouses' jobs provide duplicated benefits, such as dental and health coverage. It is possible that one spouse's benefits can be converted to cash.

10 MISTAKES IN LOOKING FOR A NEW JOB

Everyone knows that finding a new job is no easy task, especially in today's difficult economic market. However, you can improve your odds of landing a new position if you steer clear of these 10 common mistakes:

1. Inadequate self-assessment. Ask, "What am I especially good at? What do I have to offer?"

2. Neglecting key facets of a good job search. Use personal networking, classified ads, employment search firms, research, a direct-mail campaign and

targeting specific companies. Of all these, personal networking is most effective, decisive in up to 70% of hires.

3. Failure to map out a search campaign.

4. Failure to keep careful records of what you do, whom you speak to. Information is crucial in a job search.

5. Succumbing to negative attitudes. Put out positive energy, and you'll connect with people.

6. Sending out resumes, writing letters — but neglecting telephone networking. Phone calls are the way things happen.

7. Failure to maintain your vitality and energy level. Job hunting is hard work. Without rest, exercise and good diet, you'll burn yourself out.

8. Inadequate or no preparation for interviews. Go to the library and research your target company.

9. Lack of good grooming and appearance. First impressions are often decisive.

10. Failure to follow up ... and follow up ... and follow up. Interaction makes jobs happen.

PLANNING AHEAD FOR A JOB CHANGE

If you are considering changing careers, it's wise to plan ahead to safeguard your finances during the transition to a new position. Before you leave your present job, pay off your debts, especially those high interest credit cards. Make a budget and stick to it. Remember, you'll have a lot of transition expenses, especially if you're moving to a new city, and your earnings may be reduced until you get fully integrated into your new employer's payroll cycle. You should also budget additional savings for medical expenses as most company policies don't cover new employees for at least 90 days — and some have 6-month waiting periods. Save money for the change by eating at home more often, delaying new clothing purchases and holding off on buying a new car or other luxury items. If you are leaving your job to become self-employed, you may want to start your business at home to keep costs down. Be sure to plan carefully for the transfer or rollover of all pension, profit-sharing and retirement account benefits, especially now that the government imposes a 20% withholding of taxes on lump-sum payouts made directly to employees. Important: Always try to leave your current position on the best possible terms. After all, you might just need the job back if your new career, business or employment doesn't work out.

THE BEST STRATEGIES WHEN ANSWERING AN AD

So, you've studied the ad and you think you're perfect for the job. Then don't delay — send your resume with a cover letter right away. Put them unfolded in a 9" x 12" envelope, and send it air express to ensure prompt and traceable delivery. If you are responding to a blind ad using a U.S. Post Office box, be sure to use Express Mail, not Federal Express or UPS. If you don't hear from the company after 2 weeks, send another resume. This time highlight with a colored marker those qualifications you feel are right for the job. Include a note stating that this is another copy of your resume, and that you feel you fit the job perfectly and would like an interview. Another approach is helpful in responding to blind ads. Take an educated guess what companies could have placed the ad and then

send a cover letter and your resume to the person at each company most likely to be the supervisor for the department with the open position. If you've heard nothing after 2 weeks, go ahead and respond to the blind ad with another letter and resume. You can't lose anything by trying this, but if you're lucky and guess the right company, you could wind up in a priority position for an interview — or maybe a job that's open, but wasn't advertised.

16 KEYS TO COMING OFF WELL IN JOB INTERVIEWS

The initial interviewer is probably not the person you'll wind up working for, but a favorable impression is still critical if you hope to make it to the second round. Here are 16 ways to put your best foot forward:

1. Go to a lot of interviews. Practice helps.

2. Interview yourself at home — before a mirror or with a tape recorder or video camera.

3. Be friendly — but not overly friendly. Polite and pleasant are best.

4. Don't judge the company on the preliminary interview.

5. Customize your resume to suit the job for which you're applying.

6. Steer the interview gently toward your areas of strength.

7. Make yourself physically comfortable during the interview.

8. To make sure you're on time, but don't be too early.

9. Worst interview days: Mondays and Fridays. If possible, don't be the first applicant interviewed.

10. Don't smoke. If the interviewer smokes and offers you a cigarette,

politely refuse.

11. The higher echelon the interviewer, the more you should learn something in advance about him or her.

12. If the interview is being frequently interrupted by phone calls, suggest you come back another day.

13. If the interviewer stops talking, don't ramble. Ask a question, like: "Is there something else you'd like to know about me?"

14. Toward the interview end, state that you'd like the job, you like the company and would like to work for him or her. It's also effective to exhibit confidence, for instance: "I know I can do the job."

15. Send a follow-up note to the interviewer, plus a thank-you note to the interviewer's secretary.

16. Afterward, analyze what went wrong — even if nothing apparently did. You'll improve your performance next time.

SETTLING ON A SALARY FOR YOUR NEW JOB

The hardest part in a successful job interview is usually salary negotiation. Here are 4 simple strategies:

1. Don't discuss salary in detail until you're close to getting an offer. If an interviewer insists, you can state your current salary and suggest it as a likely indication of what you're expecting in a new position.

2. The time to get down to serious negotiation comes when they've decided they want you and are preparing or have already made an offer.

3. Don't ask for more than the market will bear unless you can offer some good reasons why you're worth the extra money.

4. Be willing to compromise within reason (you don't want to take a pay cut unless you're facing unemployment otherwise), but try to get something extra in exchange, such as an added perk, extra insurance benefits or, at the very list, a guaranteed performance review and salary increase within a short period of time (say 6 months).

THE BEST DAY TO ASK FOR — AND GET — A RAISE

Believe it or not, the best time to start campaigning for a raise is the day you're first hired. Don't ask about money or try to lock in specific salary commitments, but do set up

goals and performance standards as the basis for future wage negotiations. Other things you need to know about your company to improve your chances of getting a sizable raise:

* The pattern of raises for your type of job.

* The extent to which pay scales are embedded in a budget process.

* How much latitude your boss has in granting raises.

* Business conditions in the company and industry.

When the time comes to actually ask for a raise, follow these additional strategies:

* Don't let your request be brushed aside. Make a date with your boss to talk money. If he puts it off, persist.

* If your supervisor holds back, isolate the major factor. ("No money in the budget this year.") Then nail down an agreement that your performance has been excellent. Finally, attack the main obstacle, pointing out the advantages of rewarding your performance.

* Don't threaten to quit. Even if you're a dynamo, the boss may take you up on your offer to get rid of a potential rival.

INSIDERS' SECRETS — HOW NOT TO GET FIRED

Every employee dreads hearing the words, "You're fired!" Here are some steps to help you avoid ever hearing that phrase:

* When you suspect you might be in danger of being fired, go directly to your boss and talk things over. Be direct.

* If there's a problem with your work, ask why they aren't pleased with your performance and what you can do to improve it to make them happy.

* Show your boss a self-made personnel file that summarizes your successes on the job. Include any commendations, favorable reviews or memos praising your work. Inform your boss that this is what you've done for the company so far, but you are willing and eager to do more.

* Offer to work overtime or even weekends if that's what it will take to get the job done.

* Ask your supervisor for any suggestions he might have about you or your

performance, and pledge to follow them.

Your boss should be impressed with both your candor and your desire to make improvements or increased efforts. However, if you discover that he is set on firing you, go to his supervisor and plead your case there.

WHEN IT'S TIME TO LOOK ELSEWHERE

When should you consider bailing out of your company? Here are 6 signs that it may be time to hit the road:

* Top management is headed for disaster.

* Your company has had sensational success — and faces an inevitable downtrend. It's always better to quit a winner.

* You're contributions toward the company's success aren't rewarded or acknowledged.

* Your company badly lags the competition.

* You've lost interest, run out of ideas, don't know what you're doing there.

* A relative of a top manager wants the same job you want next.

Before you leave, review your career plan and target your next rung on the ladder.

NON-COMPETITION CLAUSES — MOST ARE ILLEGAL

Even though many companies make you sign job-termination agreements that contain them, most "non-competition" clauses arising out of an employer/employee relationship are unenforceable — unless you receive specific compensation for agreeing to them. Courts have consistently ruled that a former employer can not legally deprive

you of your right to earn a livelihood at your established trade or profession. However, you can be sued for using proprietary information or methodology belong to your former employer to benefit a new boss or to set up your own business. Admittedly, this can be a fine legal distinction, so you should avoid signing any document that contains a non-compete clause unless the terms and exclusions are spelled out in detail — letting you clearly know what you can and cannot do — and are agreeable to you. If your employer insists on such a clause, you should ask for compensation in exchange for signing — or refuse to sign. Very few companies will take action against you unless and until they have strong evidence that you are making improper use of proprietary information you gained while employed by them.

Warning: Some employers try to trap you up front by including a non-competition clause in your initial employment agreement. However, when challenged, these have consistently been held too vague and non-specific to be enforceable. Non-compete clauses are legal — and, in fact, are quite common — in cases involving the sale of a business. Usually, a portion of the sales price in any business purchase is designated as payment for non-competition. However, if you are the seller, you should attempt to have as small a portion of the sale price as possible so designated. The reason? Monies paid for non-competition are taxable to you as ordinary income over the duration of the period covered by the agreement — not as capital gains on the sale of the business. The buyer, on the other hand, will likely want a large portion of the sales price allocated to the non-competition clause since he is allowed to deduct such payments as ordinary business expenses.

THE 10 MOST IN-DEMAND JOBS OF THE FUTURE

If you're considering a career change or planning on starting a new business — or if you're merely getting ready to head off for college — it's not a bad idea to do a quick review of projected job demand in the years to come. According to a recent survey of corporate officials and employment professionals, certain fields will be super hot in the coming decade — and others will be downright cold. A big factor, both groups agree, will be a growing emphasis in both industry and government on environmental clean-up and ecologically sound business practices — and that shows up clearly in the following list of 10 hottest job opportunities of the future:

1. Electronic engineering. As society's dependence on technology rises, so will the need for people who design and test new products — from advanced computer equipment to robots. According to the Bureau of Labor Statistics research, America will need 40% more electronic engineers by the year 2000 than are currently available. Starting salaries range from $30,000 to $35,000 and top-level professionals will pull down $75,000 to $90,000. Owners and managers of companies involved in the field will, of course, do even better than that.

2. Environmental engineering. This is a fairly new field, involving the integration of new technologies into everyday life. It covers everything from ergonomics (how furniture design impacts work performance) to development of pollution-free manufacturing processes. Salary ranges are about $5,000 a year less than for electronic engineers, but people who come up with innovative new ideas that win public or governmental acceptance can expect big earnings.

3. Industrial hygiene. Strict new environmental and occupational safety legislation, along with public demand for stricter enforcement of pollution and

waste-control laws, has created a huge corporate demand for people in this field, which deals with everything from noise abatement to the "sick building" syndrome. Despite extensive new training programs at many colleges and corporations, demand for qualified people will likely exceed supply until well after the year 2000. Entry-level salaries are around $28,000 to $33,000, while top-level corporate posts can pay up to $125,000 or $130,000 a year.

4. Loan workout specialists. These are financial professionals who are trained in the restructuring and rescheduling of delinquent loans or those in default. The growth in this field is a result of the savings and loan disaster of the '80s, as well as the many problems the banking, brokerage, insurance and pension industries are still facing. Jobs are available both with banks and other financial companies and with consulting firms that specialize in this area. Starting salaries range from $31,000 to $40,000, with growth to the $75,000 to $80,000 area.

5. Compliance officers. This is another high-growth area thanks to the burgeoning array of new federal regulations to which businesses are subjected every year. Charged with analyzing new laws, gauging their impact on a company and formulating strategies for adhering to them, compliance officers need both legal and business management training, as well as technical knowledge in some cases. Salaries range from $35,000 to $40,000 at the entry level and can top 6 figures for more experience pros.

6. Food distribution managers. The place to be in the food industry these days is where the elderly are. This year, sales by food service companies to nursing homes exceeding $2 billion, and that figure is expected to hit $2.5 billion by 1996 and $3.1 billion by 2001. How does all this food get there? That's what food distribution managers do, determining food production needs for various markets, including schools, nursing homes, hospitals, grocery chains, even the military. Usually, these people are employed by the food service companies, but actually work under contract at the site of the client business or facility. Multilingual capabilities are a plus. Starting salaries range from $22,000 to $25,000, with growth to the $40,000 to $45,000 range.

7. Forensic accountants. These people are financial detectives. They go over the books of bankrupt companies, analyze the paperwork underlying complicated financial schemes, sniff out insurance frauds, uncover improper securities trading, reassess overvalued assets and even figure out disputed family finances in divorce or inheritance cases — then prepare reports that lawyers can carry into courts in search of redress. Most are employed by accounting firms, but work under contract to lawyers. Entry-level pay starts at $30,000 to $35,000 and rises quickly to $125,000 a year and beyond.

8. Health designers. These professionals are charged with redesigning homes and office buildings to better meet the needs of those who use them. A major growth area due to the rapidly increasing population of elderly people,

most of whom would prefer to stay in their own homes if the buildings could be retrofitted to accommodate health and access problems. Other jobs are available with architectural firms specializing in nursing home and hospital design. Salary range is $25,000 to $30,000 to start; $75,000 and up later.

9. Systems analysts. All through the 1980s, companies of all types raced to computerize. Now, these same firms are desperately seeking people who can help them more efficiently use all the expensive equipment they've installed. Senior analysts work with management to figure out what jobs a system must accomplish, while junior analysts program the computers and help users when glitches occur. Entry-level salaries range from $25,000 to $30,000, with growth to $60,000 to $65,000 a year.

10. Computer security specialists. Once corporations get their expensive data systems on line, they expect them to provide the company with a competitive edge — an edge that could be lost if some other company managed to steal important data. These people devise strategies for protecting computers, the data they hold and the systems they run from failure, sabotage, espionage, hackers, viruses and a whole variety of other electronic ills. (If you're still not sure what they do, rent the movie "Sneakers" and let Robert Redford show you.) Most jobs are with consulting firms rather than in-house. Salaries range from $30,000 to $35,000 for starting technical types up to $80,000 or more for real computer geniuses.

B. Super Sources for Second Incomes

HOW TO TURN YOUR IDEA INTO BIG MONEY

Build a better mousetrap and the world will ... well, you know. Indeed, coming up with an idea for a new product, service, manufacturing process or anything else can often be the start of your personal road to riches. However, it's a long way from idea to positive cash flow. For starters, an idea can be good and still not be worth pursuing from a profit standpoint. To determine if your idea has monetary merit, check it against this list:

* Does the product or service really satisfy a recognizable need?

* Does it have a clear competitive advantage over similar products or services already on the market?

* Even if it does have an advantage, will it be going up against a brand-name product that's so ingrained you'll never be able to shift people away from it? (You may be able to make a far superior cola, but people will still automatically ask for a Coke or a Pepsi when they order.)

* Does it have a broad market appeal, or is it highly specialized? (Few product developers are interested in something for which there are only 10 customers worldwide.)

* Is it a one-shot deal, or can it be improved, upgraded or expanded upon to ensure a continued flow of business and new customers?

* Can it be produced and/or delivered at a cost that will allow pricing comparable to other available products and services? (Even a perfect mousetrap won't sell if it costs $2,000; it's more cost-efficient to get a cat and let a few of the little critters get away.)

* Is the concept simple to explain, or will excessive marketing costs be necessary to demonstrate the worth of the product or service?

If you can answer all — or most — of these questions positively, then you've got a shot at success, but it still won't be easy. Basically, you have 2 choices if you want to move ahead from here:

1. Develop and market the product yourself, or set up a store to begin offering the service. This can be the most rewarding method, but it can also be the most frustrating — and the failure ratio is high. First, you have to find the money to begin the development process, which usually means locating venture-capital types and convincing them of the merit of your idea (very few banks will loan money for product or concept development unless you already have a well-established company with a proven track record and other assets). You then have to build or locate a manufacturing facility, develop a distribution network, plan a marketing campaign, set up accounting procedures and deal with a thousand other things from licensing requirements to sales tax permits. You also have to worry about protecting the idea until it is fully marketable. (There have been a number of cases where an idea was stolen by someone who was able to get it into production before the person who came up with it could — leaving the originator in a lagging position from which it was impossible to recover. This is a particular danger with service ideas, which are extremely easy to copy — quite legally if only a minor change in the concept is included.) There are, of course, professionals who can help you with all these things, but they cost money — which is always in short supply in start-up or development situations.

2. By far the easier — and sometimes more lucrative method — is to simply sell your idea to someone who already has the infrastructure in place to turn it in to reality. They get all the headaches — and the bulk of the profits, of course —

but you still get a healthy royalty without having to do anything else. The best way to find a potential buyer for your idea is to use an agent — a consultant who specializes in product development and has contacts within a variety of companies and/or industries. Almost every major city has several of these, usually listed in the Yellow Pages under the headings "Business Consultants" or "Product Development." Be sure to find a reputable agent, one who will provide references and credentials, and who will sign a confidentiality contract before requiring you to provide precise details of your idea. Depending on the consultant's view of your potential for success, he may be willing to work on a contingency basis — or he may demand a fee based on his estimate of the actual time involved. Obviously, you can also attempt to contact the leading companies in the field encompassing your product or idea without the help of an agent, but your chances for success are much more remote now than they were 10 years ago. Many companies no longer accept unsolicited ideas from individuals under any circumstances — fearful that even looking at a spec sheet could subject them to a lawsuit if they happened to be working on something similar on their own. Others will talk to you only if you fully detail your idea (they don't want to waste time on marginal concepts), which you may not want to do. Thus, your best approach is probably to work through an agent.

It's not an easy process, but it is still possible to turn your ideas into big money — so start thinking today.

A 6-STEP PLAN FOR PROTECTING YOUR IDEAS

The easiest way to come up with a great new idea these days is often to steal someone else's. For that reason, you need to be extremely careful in trying to both patent and sell your idea or product. Here are 6 steps you can take to protect yourself:

1. Keep detailed notes covering every step of the development process or explaining the exact circumstances, including dates and times, under which you developed your idea. This will provide a complete record "from birth" to prove your creation of a product or concept should you have to go to court and challenge a potential rip-off.

2. If you have a new product, keep all sketches, drawings and preliminary models that you made during the development or design process — for the same reasons outlined in No. 1.

3. Keep a comprehensive phone log listing everyone you talked to about the product or idea, as well as a duplicate file containing copies of all letters sent to companies or other potential buyers.

4. Work with one potential product developer at a time. This may seem agonizingly slow and delay introduction of your new product or idea (and the

rewards you'll net from it), but the time involved and the money you forfeit will seem like nothing compared to the time and money you'll lose if you wind up in the middle of a legal battle between 2 competing developers, both of whom thought they had an exclusive arrangement with you.

5. Don't accept any verbal promises or make any verbal commitments. Insist that everything relating to a potential development deal be put in writing, and have your attorney (and accountant, if necessary) review the contracts before signing.

6. File for patent or trademark protection as soon as you can qualify. If need be, employ the services of a qualified professional in the field to find out exactly what you have to do, and when and how to do it. Beware: There are a lot of scam artists in the patent field — people who offer to handle all the details of your application process for a fee. Many of these people will simply collect your money and do nothing, while others will actually analyze your idea or product and then attempt to sell it to someone else without your knowledge. Deal only with reputable patent attorneys and consultants who can verify their credentials, have proven track records, belong to local professional organizations and are willing to provide references.

4 SPARE-TIME BUSINESSES THAT CAN NET YOU $500 A WEEK

Maybe you're not interested in coming up with the next Xerox copier — or even the next Pet Rock — but you would like to earn a few extra bucks by working in your spare time. Millions of people earn extra money this way, and you can too. Here are some ideas for ways to generate spare-time income without a lot of investment or extra training:

1. Buy and sell items from the Classified ads. Many people who have specialized knowledge in a given product area, such as furniture, antiques, cars, tools or appliances, make several hundred extra dollars every week by looking for underpriced items in the newspaper ads, buying them and then reselling them at a fair price — either through other ads, in small shops or out of their homes or garages. This requires some start-up capital and can involve a lot of driving and a little knowledge of marketing, but bargains abound in the Classified sections, and you can turn a quick profit if you have the knowledge to recognize good value and the patience to wait for a buyer willing to pay the right price for it.

2. Operate a personal dating service. Many busy people don't have the time to get out and meet people or actively cultivate social relationships these days. They also can't see paying $2,500 or more to some of the big-name computer or video-dating services. However, they will pay you $200 or $300 a year to pick out potential social companions for them and arrange introductions. If you belong to a number of organizations, work in a large company, live in a big

apartment complex or just know lots of people, you can easily serve as a matchmaker. Or, you can do the job more professionally, running ads in local newspapers offering your services. You'll have to do client interviews, maintain files and most likely produce data sheets on each of your clients, but you should still be able to make a nice profit — and provide a valuable service in the process.

3. Operate a social scheduling service. This is a natural outgrowth of the dating service idea, but it works for working married couples as well. Because they're so busy, many people who would love to go to theater performances, concerts, dances or other special events don't find out about them until it's too late to get tickets or make plans. For a nominal fee, you can interview people and then maintain file cards or computer records listing their entertainment interests, preferred days for social activities, price limitations and seating preferences. You can then monitor upcoming events in your community (it's easy to get theater schedules, concert schedules, etc., from the sponsors, as well as from area universities and chambers of commerce), call your client with the suggestions and, if they are interested, choose a date and purchase or reserve tickets for them (you can even boost your profit by charging a slight mark-up for your ticket-buying efforts). You can also enhance your service by planning the entire evening for clients once the main event is selected, perhaps making dinner reservations, arranging for flowers, etc.

4. Perhaps the easiest way to make money in your spare time is to turn your hobby into a business. Here are some examples:

* If you enjoy making crafts, sewing, doing embroidery, knitting, etc., sell your products at local flea markets, craft fairs or holiday boutiques. Many larger cities also have crafts guilds where you can have your wares displayed and sold on consignment.

* If fishing is your thing, why not take someone else along and charge them for your services as a guide or charter captain. You might also tie flies for trout fishermen and sell them, or make lures and have local sporting goods stores sell them on consignment. If you've got a typewriter or home computer, you could also produce a weekly or monthly tip sheet, detailing the best fishing spots, what type of fish are biting best and other information. You can either advertise for subscribers or have local stores or gas stations sell copies for a share of the profits.

* If you like working on your car — and are good at it — you may also

be able to work on other people's vehicles for a fee. Be careful, here, however, as many states regulate mechanics and having private work done on a vehicle can sometimes invalidate the manufacturer's warranty.

* If you like children, consider starting a babysitting or day-care service.

Again, however, you may run into licensing requirements and liability considerations, so don't just start operating without first doing a thorough investigation.

Added Hobby Money Tip: If you own lots of sports or recreational equipment, you can recover some of your cost and eventually make a little profit by renting out items you're not using. Check with your insurance agent first, though — just in case you might face a liability problem.

TURNING YOUR HOME COMPUTER INTO A BUSINESS

A home computer is a part-time business (or a full-time one, for that matter) just waiting to happen. Here are just a few of the ways you can make money with yours:

* A typing service. The bulk of the work done on computers involves word processing, which means things have to be typed. You can do everything from school reports to manuscripts, charging by the hour or by the page.

* Letter-writing service. Many people hate to write letters, so you can do it for them. Prepare a library of business letters, complaint letters, etc., and then customize them for your clients so all they have to do is sign their name.

* Resume service. People have a hard time presenting themselves objectively, but you can do it easily. Interview them, then design and print out the most effective resume for their needs. (There are lots of books to help you in this area. Just check the library.)

* Message service. A computer makes it easy to keep a log of phone numbers and messages for individuals who need more service than a simple answering machine can provide.

* Be a computer teacher. If you're a real whiz, you can teach your computer skills to others and charge for it. If you're a master at one or more of today's complicated computer software programs, you can also do specialized work that other computer users might not have time to learn.

* Research service. If your computer has a modem, you can tap into hundreds of data banks and bulletin boards around the country, doing research for school papers, business briefs, marketing reports, etc. Charge for both your time and your on-line and phone expenses.

* Desk-top publishing. Many people want fancier presentations than they can get from their word processing programs, but they don't want to go to the trouble of learning and using complex desk-top publishing or slide-preparation programs. You can do it for them.

* If all else fails, sit down at your keyboard and write the next "great American novel" — or anything else you think might sell, from cookbooks to children's stories.

C. Business Ownership = Big Benefits

ARE YOU CUT OUT TO BE AN ENTREPRENEUR?

As was mentioned in Chapter 15, Tax Tips & Traps, owning your own business is the best tax shelter available in American today — and can also be a source of huge rewards, in terms of both money and personal satisfaction. However, not everyone is cut out to be an entrepreneur. Here are 10 factors that business professionals and psychological experts say enhance your chances of success as a business owner. See how well you fit the profile:

1. One or both of your parents were or are self-employed.

2. You've been fired more than once in your career.

3. You operated small businesses of some sort or another — from paper routes and lemonade stands to actual manufacturing or retail operations — before you were 20.

4. Most of your career has been spent working at companies of less than 100 employees.

5. You're the oldest child.

6. You're married.

7. You have a bachelor's degree, but no advanced degrees.

8. Your relationship with the bread-winning parent was strained

9. You're excited by new financial plans and ideas.

10. You enjoy being with people.

If you see a pattern starting to emerge here — and it fits your life — maybe you should consider making the move into self-employment.

HOW TO USE YOUR PENSION FUNDS TO START A BUSINESS

If you're tired of working for someone else and would like to go out on your own, you may be able to use your accrued pension funds to finance your move. No, not by quitting, taking a lump-sum distribution, paying a huge tax bite and penalties and then using what's left for financing, but rather by doing some clever financial maneuvering that not only frees up your cash but avoids any tax consequences. Here's how it works, assuming you have $80,000 in accrued pension benefits and need $40,000 to start your business:

* Several months before you plan to quit your present job, go ahead and form a new corporation for the operation of your new business.

* Once the incorporation process is complete, have the corporation adopt a qualified profit-sharing plan, making sure that the new plan has a provision that allows loans to be made to participants equaling at least 50% of their vested interest in the plan.

* Quit your current job, explaining that you are going to work for this new corporation and instructing the benefits office at your now ex-employer's company to transfer your lump-sum pension distribution into the new firm's qualified pension plan.

* Under the terms of your new pension plan, have it loan you 50% of the vested amount in your account — or $40,000 — to be repaid over a period of 5 years at a rate of interest comparable to current market rates.

* Use the loan to actually begin business operations at your new corporation.

This technique preserves the tax-deferred status of your pension funds, saves you around $28,000 in taxes and penalties that you would have had to pay on a regular distribution and provides the needed capital for your new business without forcing you to go running hat in hand to lenders or other money sources. Obviously, however, there are numerous key details that must be attended to in order for everything to be legal and pass muster with the government, so be sure to enlist the aid of your attorney and accountant.

LITTLE-KNOWN MONEY SOURCES FOR NEW BUSINESSES

Say the word "loan" and most people automatically think bank. However, banks are extremely reluctant to make loans for new businesses — especially if it will be your first venture into the entrepreneurial world. Fortunately, as you've just seen in the section on using pension funds, there are a number of other places to get money to start a new business. Here are a few:

* Uncle Sam has at least 3 programs that grant loans to potential business owners. One of these requires location in a specific area or "enterprise zone," and another has minority involvement requirements, but the third is open to virtually anyone who can qualify. Contact your nearest Small Business Administration office for more details and application forms.

* The government, as well as many private foundations, also makes available grants (which don't have to be repaid) to people willing to start businesses that serve the public interest or fulfill the goals of legislative

programs. The SBA can also provide information on many of the government grants, and their are a number of books that list other private sources. You can also get a free information brochure by sending a stamped, self-addressed envelope to the Grant Information Service, P.O. Box 5100, Vero Beach, FL.

* Most states also have business development offices that provide both loans and/or grants to potential business founders. Check with your state's Economic Development Office, the State Treasurer's Office or the state Chamber of Commerce (all listed in your phone directory) for more information.

* If you can clearly show the potential of your business product or service idea, you may be able to attract venture-capital financing. Ads for venture capital are featured in the Business Sections of most larger daily newspapers, as well as magazines specializing in small-business operations.

* Consider a small private stock offering. A number of regional stock brokerage firms specialize in raising capital for small and start-up business ventures. A solid business plan and some heavy duty research will be required before you can go this route, but if you've got a good idea with a strong potential market, this could be a key funding source.

* Ask your potential clients for funding. If you've come up with an idea for a product or service that's badly needed by other companies in a particular industry or manufacturing sector, they may actually be willing to help finance your start-up costs, just to speed their own access to your potential solution to their problems.

* Pledge personal collateral to secure a regular bank loan, or use a home equity loan. The risk here is obviously high since you could lose your home or other property if the business goes bust. Still, it's an option — if you have sufficient collateral, that is.

* Ask your family or friends for a loan. We've put this last for a very good reason. Loans among friends or family members can be a great source of tension and conflict, so you shouldn't use them unless you've exhausted all other alternatives. However, if you have — and you still firmly believe in your idea for a new business — it may be worth the risk to get started.

BUYING A PROFITABLE BUSINESS WITH NO MONEY DOWN

If you can't raise the money to buy or start your own business from any of the sources we've listed, you still have one other option — buy a business with no money at all. No, don't laugh — it is possible. This concept was the entire basis for the leveraged buyout craze of the late '70s and early '80s. Here's how it works:

* A new corporation is formed with the stated purpose of buying an existing business.

* This corporation carefully reviews all existing assets of the business to be purchased and agrees to pledge those assets as collateral for a loan to help with the buyout. Assets with value include receivables (on which as much as 80% of face value can be borrowed, either from banks or from so-called "factors," who specialize in short-term business loans); inventory (good for 60% of listed value); and land, buildings and equipment (60% to 75%).

* In many cases, the money borrowed in these assets will actually exceed the purchase price and provide some extra working capital with which to operate the business. However, if it won't, the selling company may be willing to take what is known as a subordinated note for part of the purchase price — or a bank, venture-capital company or management group might kick in needed capital, based on the company's profitable history and its projected future earnings.

This smacks of high finance — and it is. However, deals of a similar nature can also be worked on many smaller businesses, including single stores — especially if the current owner really wants to get out. It also carries a fair degree of risk (as Michael Milken found out) since any downturn in the economy in general or the business in particular could make it impossible to meet obligations on the loans.

Note: This only works with successful, reasonably debt-free companies. If a business is already in trouble or deeply in debt, it's a good bet both that its assets are already pledged to other sources or that it won't have enough cash flow to make payments on new loans feasible.

FRANCHISING — THE EASY WAY TO BUSINESS OWNERSHIP

Franchising lets you own a business in a field you like without having to go it alone and take all the risks yourself. With a franchise, you have a built-in support system and a well-established infrastructure to help with problems, both large and small. And, though it might not appear that way when you drive down a main street in any U.S. city, there is a broad range of franchising opportunities beyond the world of fast food. Among some of the other franchised businesses currently available are:

* Consulting firms.

* Accounting and tax services.

* Computer sales and repair services.

* High-tech and electronics sales.

* Personnel development.

* Auto repair or quick-lube shops.

Perhaps the biggest benefit of moving into a franchised business is the low rate of failure. There are over 3,000 franchisors in the U.S., accounting for more than $615 billion in annual retail sales. If you want to research a franchise, you'll need to study a Uniform Franchise Offering Circular (UFOC) or a Federal Trade Commission disclosure document. The UFOC is required in more than a dozen states, but either document should give you all the information you need to make an intelligent decision about a franchise including: * The identity and type of business.

* A description of the corporation.

* The names of principals and directors.

* Full corporate financial disclosure, including any bankruptcy history.

* Details on fees, royalties and other payments.

* Investment requirements and obligations.

* Supply provisions (some franchisees are required to buy only goods or services supplied by the franchisor or an approved third party).

After looking over the documents, it's wise to speak to other franchisees — successful and unsuccessful — in your area. It's also a good idea to consult a franchising attorney. Once you've decided on a franchise, examine the upfront costs. These costs vary from franchise to franchise, but a typical agreement is for 10 years. These costs include equipment, building costs and employee training. Look at the continuing royalty fees — usually 3% to 9% of the gross revenue. There might also be a mandatory advertising fee — usually 2% to 4% of the gross. Finally, if your franchisor requires that you buy goods from him or a designated third party, compare those prices with other suppliers in the open market.

8 SECRETS TO BUYING A FRANCHISE

Opererating a franchise is a very exciting enterprise, but it also holds some risks. Here are some questions to help you determine if a franchise operation is a legitimate success — and also help you get the best deal when buying one:

1. Where does the parent company get the bulk of its income? If it is supported primarily by new franchise fees, does the company have a solid base and will it be around tomorrow? If it's not adequately capitalized, what happens if no other franchises sell but yours?

2. Is the company sound financially? This may sound like an obvious question, but it's sometimes hard to answer. If the franchising operation is a division of a large corporation with many subsidiaries and affiliates, it may be difficult to discover where assets and liabilities truly reside.

3. If the franchisor has undergone recent or multiple reorganizations, it's wise to find out why.

4. If there are state or government-imposed escrows of franchise fees — or administrative orders outstanding against the company — this could mean trouble with existing operations, and for you later on.

5. Look for hidden costs. Check the footnotes of the company's financial statement for any special items that may end up costing you money.

6. Has the franchise taken a good hard look at your business qualifications? A good franchisor will be very discriminating.

7. Does the company test market its advertising? How much of the annual fees go into local and national advertising and market research? And, as a franchisee, do you have a voice in where your advertising dollars are spent?

8. Finally, is the franchiser connected to your competitors, and what protection does the franchiser offer from those selling similar products?

Make sure you get satisfactory answers to all these questions, as well as any others that might apply to the particular franchise you are considering, before you sign any papers or put up any cash. A franchise can be a wonderful opportunity for entrepreneurial individuals — but it can also be a nightmare if the parent company starts to fall apart.

THE 4 BEST FRANCHISES TO LOOK AT NOW

If you decide a franchise is right for you, here are the 4 best areas to look into now, according to business projections for the 1990s:

1. Fast Food — It's no surprise that fast food outlets are still the most successful franchises in the country — and, according to the experts, there is still plenty of room to grow as the ever-more-hurried pace of American life leads more and more people to eat out and eat quickly.

2. International Markets — Many franchises that are household names here are just beginning to gain in popularity overseas. If the idea of owning a business in a foreign country appeals to you, experts say growth could be phenomenal in coming years. Take a look at Mexico and the burgeoning Eastern Europe markets. People in these 2 areas often share the same appetites as Americans (thanks to television), and many U.S. franchises are now in high demand there.

3. Emerging Technology — The personal computer industry has opened up many new franchise opportunities in such areas as desktop publishing, presentation graphics, computer design and other high-tech fields. The franchisor's infrastructure provides the support needed to make the personalized services offered by the franchisees profitable, which wouldn't have been possible a few years ago.

4. Computer Literacy — This is an outgrowth of No. 3. As more and more people move into the computer age, buying their own systems, there is an ever-increasing demand for quality instruction. And, a number of franchisors have stepped in to fill the gap, some covering a full range of markets and others specializing in key segments, such as small children or business owners. Most of these franchise operations also feature computer hardware, software and programming support, consultation and service.

WARNING: MARRIAGE MAY BE HAZARDOUS TO YOUR FINANCIAL WEALTH

As we've seen in several recent films and TV movies, divorce can degenerate into all-out war. Many spiteful spouses seek to divide and destroy family assets. If there's a business in the family, this can be especially destructive. And, unless you lay out some basic offensive strategy, not even a pre-nuptial agreement can guarantee that your business won't be among the casualties.

Whether you live in a community-property state or an equitable-distribution one, each spouse is entitled to a portion of the couple's joint assets — and, in most cases, the family business is the single largest asset. How much of the business rightfully belongs to who depends on many factors. Courts generally consider the role each partner played in the creation and preservation of the business, but a spouse may argue that his or her efforts provided the opportunity for the other to succeed. Even if the business was established before the marriage, a spouse can be considered to have contributed to its increased value. As a result of these arguments, your spouse may be entitled to a bigger share of the business than you might expect, putting a heavy strain on your cash flow. Or, even worse, if the business can't generate enough income to allow for a buyout, you could wind up having to sell it to satisfy a cash settlement.

A well-crafted shareholders' agreement can prove invaluable in preventing the destruction of a business. It should include a provision for buyouts that contains a detailed explanation of the process to be used in establishing the value of the business. You might also include a detailed payment schedule for settlement of any claims against the business as the result of a potential divorce. And, though a prenuptial agreement may not always hold up in court, here are a few additions that could strengthen your position if you do use one (which you should):

* Both parties should be represented by their own attorney.

* Sign the agreement before the wedding.

* Each party must fully disclose all assets and their value.

* Have a consistent policy that all who marry into the family agree to a pre-nuptial contract.

* Finally, have the family business attorney send a letter to the engaged couple suggesting a pre-nuptial agreement. This move prevents that awkward moment when one party has to bring up the issue to the other, almost always resulting in hurt feelings or outright resentment.

MINIMIZING TAXES WHEN YOU SELL YOUR BUSINESS

If your business is a big success, there will come a time when someone will want to buy it — or you will finally decide to retire and want to sell it. Either way, you want to be able to salvage as many of the fruits of your labors as possible from the sale — not send them off to Uncle Sam. Here are some tips on selling your business the smart way:

* Always make sure all the terms and conditions of the sale are spelled out in detail in a valid acquisition contract.

* Be sure the contract exactly specifies the nature of all the assets being sold. Tax consequences can be quite different for proceeds from the sale of different assets, such as machinery, inventory, accounts receivable and good will.

* Make sure the contract contains clauses that both protect the buyer from any unknown liabilities you transfer to him at the time of the sale, and protect you from any liabilities that may arise as a result of his operation (either successfully or unsuccessfully) of the business after the sale. You don't want to be accused of hiding problems, which could invalidate the sale, nor do you later want to be the target of any claims that might result from the new owner's mismanagement or poor business practices.

* Work closely with your accountant and financial advisors to set up the most advantageous payment terms. There are times when a lump-sum cashout will be best, but there are others when you may be better served by taking extended or deferred payments, shares of stock, an annuity — or even payments in kind (some other type of property or business interest).

* If the new owner plans to keep you on, either to manage the business or as a consultant, make sure the terms of that agreement are spelled out in a separate employment contract. Tax treatment is different for income generated by legitimate employment or consulting work than it is for compensation arising solely as a condition of the sale of the business. Warning: If you are doing legitimate work for the company — or, for that matter, merely collecting a "courtesy" salary as a result of the sale — be sure the employment contract contains a clause specifying that your position can be terminated only "for cause." You don't want to sell the company thinking you'll be drawing a guaranteed salary for the next 5 years only to find yourself fired at the whim of the new owner after 6 months.

* Make full use of legal and financial professionals. The sale of a business, particularly a large one with lots of tangible and intangible assets, can be one of the most complicated transactions you'll ever undertake, and it is fraught with tax consequences. The money you pay for quality professional help will be well spent in the long run.